The Celtic,

Glasgow Irish

and the

Great War

The Gathering Storms

ISBN 978-0-9541263-2-2

Illustrations and Photographic credits:

The author would like to thank the families of the individuals whose images appear in this publication. Acknowledgement is also due to a number of institutions, archives and museums that provided graphics:

Front and back cover:

National Army Museum, Celtic Graves Society.The O'Kane family,

Inside pages:

The Maley family, the Childers family, Glasgow Caledonian University Archives, (Gallacher Memorial Library). The National Library of Scotland, National Library of Ireland, National Army Museum, Mitchell Library, Glasgow City Archives, The Highlanders (Seaforth, Gordons and Camerons) Museum, Argyll and Sutherland Highlanders Museum, Glasgow Observer, Glasgow Daily Record, Glasgow Evening Times, Glasgow Herald, Dundee Courier, Freemans Journal, Lepracaun, Reynold's Newspaper, Reynolds Newspapers, Celtic Graves, Celtic Wiki, Marie Rowan, and Jamie Fox.

Prologue

The series of books, *The Celtic, Glasgow Irish and the Great War*, examines the social history, political atmosphere and wartime experiences of the Irish Roman Catholic community that had settled in Glasgow and central Scotland over the course of the nineteenth century. The books survey the community's support for and attitude to the British war effort over the course of the Great War seen through the prism of their greatest sporting achievement, the Celtic Football Club.

Book One	The Gathering Storms	
Book Two	The Storms Break	Season 1914/15
Book Three	The End of Innocence	Season 1915/16
Book Four	The Blood Sacrifice	Season 1916/17
Book Five	An Ocean of Blood	Season 1917/18
Book Six	The Never Ending Trials	Season 1918/19

The first book in the series, The Gathering Storms, sets the scene for the following books and paints a picture of the origins and life experiences of the Glasgow Irish community in their adopted homeland. Labelled "The Glasgow Irish" by the wider Glasgow community, from whom they had been effectively ostracised, the title was a colloquialism for an Irish Roman Catholic or their descendants and was a term of derision, hatred and contempt. By 1914, the Glasgow Irish community had coalesced into a cohesive and in many ways autonomous society, which mirrored very many aspect the wider Glasgow and Scottish community. The book sets into context the interactions between the Glasgow Irish and the wider Glasgow community, and their attitudes and political opinions as the clouds of war – both in Ireland and Europe – gathered overhead. The book also covers the formation and early history of the Celtic Football Club, provides pen pictures of a cross section of its founding fathers and explains the special relationship between the club and its Glasgow Irish supporters.

Each of the following five books is set within the context of the Celtic football team and its sporting performances over the five football seasons that were affected by the Great War. The major, political, social, military and footballing events as they impacted the Celtic and the Glasgow Irish community are detailed. Tens of thousands of the Glasgow Irish fought and thousands died not just for the freedom of Ireland and other small nations, but for the freedom of Glasgow and Scotland.

This is the story, too long ignored, of the Glasgow Irish community's massive contribution to the British war effort. Almost every modern Celtic supporter who can claim a historic connection to the Glasgow Irish community will almost certainly have had an ancestor or close family relation who, like millions of other young men, were sucked into the apocalypse that was the Great War.

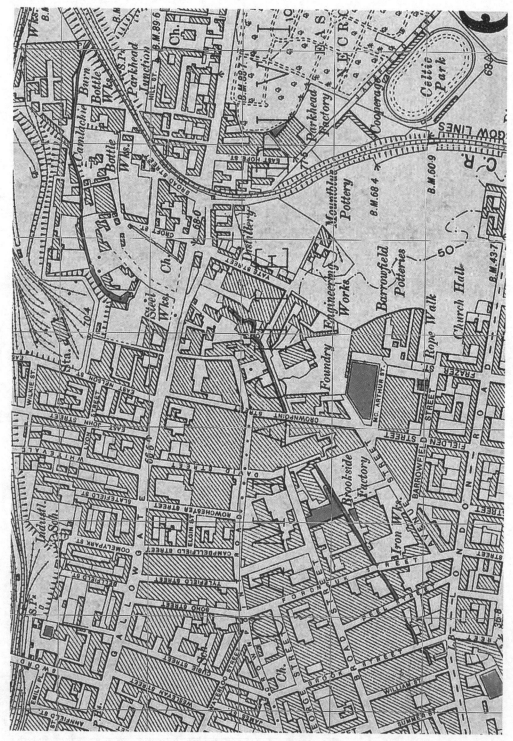

The Celtic Heartland 1894
@National Library of Scotland

Acknowledgements

I wish to express my gratitude to the descendants of the individuals mentioned in the book. I would also like to thank the staff at the various libraries, archives, regimental museums and records offices for their assistance during my research. In particular, the Mitchell Library, the National Archives, the National Archives of Ireland, the National Library of Scotland, the National Army Museum, the Glasgow Caledonian University Archives: The Gallacher Memorial Library, St Mary's University College and Glasgow City Council Archives and Museums.

I am grateful to the Glasgow Catholic Observer, the Glasgow Herald, Glasgow Evening Times and the Scottish Daily Record for permission to reproduce various graphics published in their period newspapers.

A special thanks goes to the authors of the many books, particularly Celtic books from which I have drawn much information and inspiration.

Thanks also to the members of the Celtic Graves Society, Kerrydale Street and to the Celtic Wiki for their dedicated and tenacious research and enthusiasm for all things Celtic. A particular thank you is due to Jamie Fox for his timely advice and encouragement.

I have made every reasonable effort to contact the copyright holders of material reproduced in this book. If any involuntary infringement of copyright has occurred, sincere apologies are offered and the owners of such copyright are requested to contact me.

All errors and omissions are, of course, entirely my own.

The author can be contacted through the website at: www.theglasgowirish.com

Ian McCallum

Glasgow

September 2013

Foreword

Celtic Football Club's speedy and spectacular rise to fame must surely have exceeded even the wildest expectations of its founders, who could not have envisaged their creation developing into the most visible and enduring symbol of that section of the Irish diaspora which has made such a significant contribution to life in Glasgow (and the West of Scotland, for that matter).

The author's fascinating chronicle of the growing pains of that community inevitably lays considerable emphasis on the aspirations for Home Rule in which several Celtic personalities played an active part through organisations such as the Irish National League as a movement grew which would have an impact on the lead - up to the Great War which convulsed these islands a century ago. Given the community's lingering sense of 'underdog' status, there was a certain degree of inevitability that its own hopes for the old country and the instinctive Irish sympathy for the fate of small nations would draw it into the conflict, despite its grievous overtones, as exemplified by the pall cast over the family by the loss on French soil of a son born to Tom Maley, a dashing and popular winger in Celtic's earliest days. For the likes of young Joseph Maley and the father of the late Sean Fallon (of whom a more committed and loyal servant of Celtic FC it would be impossible to conceive), the plight of 'plucky little Belgium' - as Stephen Sullivan's biography of Sean has revealed - was a cause that they could not ignore.

Ian McCallum's narrative brings into sharp focus the truly remarkable early decades of Celtic's history, culminating in the impact on the club of one of the most tragic and momentous events in world history.

Pat Woods

Contents

Illustrations

Dedication

This series of books is dedicated to the forgotten and ignored Irish Nationalists who saw a third option for Ireland, who fought imperialism and for the right of self-determination for small nations. To the Great War generation of the Glasgow Irish that answered the bugle call of their home city and by doing so helped win a place in the sun for their children and grandchildren. Finally, to people of all nations who see the act of remembrance as simply honouring the fallen and not a political statement.

Perhaps there is hope!

Dublin, 16 April 1966

Mr de Valera, President of the Republic of Ireland, who with 100 riflemen fought British troops in Dublin during the 1916 uprising, today embraced the man who accepted his surrender. Captain EJ Hitzen, aged eighty, now of Grimsby, was the guest of the Irish Government for the 50th anniversary commemorations. Members of Mr de Valera's battalion exchange cards at Easter and Christmas with Captain Hitzen and send him shamrock on St Patrick's Day. Today he had tea with Mr de Valera and Mr Lemass, the Prime Minister.

Dublin, 17 May 2011

HRH Queen Elizabeth II visited the Republic of Ireland, the first British monarch to do so for 100 years. Within three hours of her arrival she and the Irish President Mary McAleese both laid wreaths at the Garden of Remembrance in Dublin dedicated to those who had fallen in the struggle against British rule in Ireland. The following day wreaths were again laid, this time at the Irish National War Memorial at Islandbridge, Dublin, dedicated to the memory of the Irishmen who fought and died while serving in the British Army during the Great War.

The last word on the fate of the forgotten Irish Nationalist soldiers is best left to Stephyn Gwynn, himself one of the forgotten Irish soldiers of the Great War.

It may be O Comrade that Ireland
Casting a backward glance on the road she has travelled
Will turn and yearn in her heart for the valour she once rejected Ö.
Will cry to her own sick heart, my faithful, my children, my lovers who never hurt me.
You also are Ireland.

Stephyn Gwynn 1864–1950

THE GATHERING STORMS

IAN McCALLUM BEM

Introduction

"If, you know the history," as the Celtic song goes, you must also know and understand something of the narrative of the Irish diaspora on the Clyde. To understand the mindset of the Irish Catholic community living in and around Glasgow on the eve of the Great War, it is vital that one understands the strength of their Irish and Roman Catholic roots and their life experiences in their new Scottish homeland. Central to the story of the Catholic Irish in Glasgow is the volatile and all too often violent relationship between their ancestral homeland and England and later Ireland's place in the United Kingdom of Great Britain and Ireland.

As a result of the industrial revolution and the disastrous Irish potato famine of the mid-1840s, successive waves of Irish immigrants, mostly Roman Catholics, arrived in Scotland over the course of the nineteenth century. Sizable Irish Catholic communities were established in Dundee and in Edinburgh, but most remained closer to where they landed, in Glasgow, its satellite villages and in pockets scattered across west central Scotland. The Catholic Irish immigrants and their descendants settled in the most Protestant, anti-Catholic country in the whole of Europe. The Scots had over a period of 300 years been indoctrinated with the belief that Roman Catholics were adherents of an old, fatally corrupt superstition that had been driven out from Scotland. They had been taught that the Roman Catholics, particularly Irish Roman Catholics, were illiterate, beggarly, lawless, drunken, needy and treasonous. An alien race, to be shunned and avoided in case they contaminated and polluted! The desperate condition in which the majority of the Catholic Irish arrived in Glasgow simply reinforced their long-held perceptions.

There was in fact a great deal of accuracy in the Scots' perceptions of the first waves of the Catholic Irish: very many were exactly what their detractors complained of. They were *illiterate* because they had been denied access to education. They were *beggarly* because they had never been allowed to succeed. They were *lawless* because they had been denied access to an impartial legal system. They were *drunken*, having been driven to alcohol by the sheer hopelessness of their situation. They were *needy* because they had been pushed to the very edge of extinction through starvation. They were *treasonous* because in Ireland they had been treated as slaves by invaders, who regarded themselves as their colonial masters.

On their arrival in Glasgow and Scotland the Catholic Irish were forced to confront and endure the humiliations and indignities suffered by unwelcome, needy incomers. They were seen as ignorant, diseased, drunken, shiftless scroungers and a massive burden on the righteous, sober, hard-working and respectable Protestant ratepayers. They were labelled the "Glasgow Irish", a vulgarism for an Irish Roman Catholic or one of Irish descent, and the title was one of hatred, ridicule and contempt. To the people themselves it would in time become a badge of honour and distinction.

The Glasgow Irish as a result of their race and religion suffered decades of institutionalised racism, sectarianism and discrimination. They encountered an all-pervasive attitude that because of their race, and political and religious beliefs, they were lacking in loyalty and the qualities of responsible citizenship. This widely held perception resulted in the stigmatisation and marginalisation of the Catholic Irish community. As a result of racism, bigotry and discrimination in the workplace, the Glasgow Irish were confined to the lowest, poorest paid occupations and were driven by the resulting dire economic conditions into what were almost medieval slum housing areas and into a social and economic cocoon. This low-wage economy resulted in economic stagnation and they lived their entire lives in unimaginable squalor and abject poverty. Marginalised and set aside, they were forced to survive on the edges of the wider Glasgow community. The first generations of Glasgow Irish suffered persecution and alienation, seeing it as a "rite of passage". The people endured, praying that their trials and tribulations would not be in vain and that their children and grandchildren would someday reap the benefits and achieve the place in the sun denied to them.

It was recognised that social respectability was the key to acceptance by the wider Glasgow community and that acceptance would lead to improvements in their social and economic conditions. The Glasgow Irish were therefore encouraged to strive, like their Presbyterian neighbours, for the distinction of social respectability. Thanks largely to the improving organisational structures of the Roman Catholic Church, and the hard work and dedication of hundreds of priests and thousands of the laity, by the early 1880s, the negative perceptions of the Glasgow Irish held by the wider Scottish community were being challenged. Led by their priests and community leaders, a concerted effort to improve social attitudes saw very significant numbers of the Glasgow Irish turn away from the demon drink, then seen as the root of most social ills, to join the League of the Cross and the Catholic Young Men's Society, both temperance organisations. By the mid-1890s, the hopes and aspirations of the early Catholic Irish immigrants to see their community advance were beginning to be realised.

In the vanguard of the Glasgow Irish community's advance was the Celtic Football and Athletic Club. Established in November 1887, the club was created as a community asset and was largely a means to an end. The end in question was to achieve a material improvement in the social and economic conditions of the Roman Catholic community in Glasgow and, it should be noted, not just Irish Roman Catholics. The *raison d'être* of the distinctly Irish Catholic club was to feed and clothe desperately poor children in three of Glasgow's east end parishes and it was this spirit of community solidarity, so vital for survival in the last four decades of the nineteenth century, that was absorbed into the very soul of the club. A philosophy of inclusiveness and welcome was established almost from the start and would remain a fundamental feature of the club.

Association football has been described as the opium of the masses and this was certainly true of the Scottish and particularly the Glasgow working class. The average Glaswegian male was completely fitba daft. No community anywhere in Britain took to football like the

Glaswegians; the city was unique with six senior teams and three stadiums (Hampden, Celtic Park and Ibrox Park), which could hold in total more than a quarter of a million people. The overtly Irish and Catholic Celtic club's immediate and spectacular success in the world of Scottish football, which was at the time run by stuffy, middle-class Presbyterian gentlemen, highlighted and trumpeted the fact that the Glasgow Irish community could strive to succeed, they could achieve and they were much more than the old perceptions belied.

To the Glasgow Irish community, the club quickly became much more than simply a football team; the Celtic itself had become the physical embodiment of the Glasgow Irish identity, the very essence of their community, a highly successful symbol of the heights that could, given the opportunity, be scaled. It became an icon that the community was proud to be associated and identified with, and a tie that bound the community together. On conversion to a limited company in 1897, the community-owned asset passed into the hands of private business, but it no longer mattered who owned or controlled the club: the Glasgow Irish community had helped create it, build it and nurture it and now they unconditionally supported it. The club had become the single greatest ethnic and cultural focus of the community and had transcended the mere playing of sport. The option of whether the Glasgow Irish would or would not support the Celtic was removed from them at birth. Irrespective of whether you were a man or a woman, young or old, football follower or not, being born Glasgow Irish meant you were born to and always would, irrespective of where you happened to be in the world, support the Celtic and most importantly what it had come to represent: cultural togetherness, inclusiveness, openness, social awareness and compassion for those less fortunate. That the Celtic supporters themselves had much to do with the success of the club there was no doubt. From the moment of its inception, the officials and supporters of the Celtic club were inextricably linked culturally, socially and politically. By 1914, the Celtic Football and Athletic Company Limited was probably the wealthiest, most powerful club in Scotland and undoubtedly the most successful team in Great Britain. The Great War would usher in massive changes to society, but irrespective of the pressures and horrors of the war, one thing would remain exactly the same, the average Glasgow working class male would remain completely fitba daft.

The Glasgow Irish on the eve of war made up around seventeen per cent of the Glasgow population. The latest generation of the Glasgow Irish, better educated than ever before, were forcing their way into mainstream society and were at the forefront of the drive to challenge ancient injustices. The social advances brought their own problems and the Glasgow Irish were a community in transition, toiling with overlapping identities – ethnic, religious and political. Just how Scottish or British did third- or sometimes even fourth-generation Glasgow Irish feel and how much loyalty did the Scots-born Glasgow Irish feel they owed to their new homeland? Although the majority of the Glasgow Irish community had been in Glasgow for decades and had generations of children born and raised in the city, very many still regarded themselves as Irish and took a very great interest in the fate of the auld country. For decades their wholehearted political support was given to constitutional Irish nationalism in the guise of the Irish Parliamentary Party and its Home Rule movement. The most famous of the Glasgow Irish political organisations was the Home Government Branch of the Irish National League. For forty years the vast majority of the Glasgow Irish community's political leaders were members of the organisation and devoted to Irish Land Reform and Home Rule.

At a national level, British politics in the years leading up to the Great War was dominated by three subjects: industrial unrest, female suffrage and, above all, the conundrum that was Ireland. Over the two decades spanning the end of the nineteenth century and the beginning of the twentieth, major social and political advances had been made by constitutional Irish Nationalists. In Ireland, millions of acres of land had been returned to the native Irish, education was finally reaching the masses, local politics were increasingly being dominated by the native Irish and a confidant and wealthy, politically astute Catholic middle class had emerged. A new national awareness and spirit had also taken root and with Home Rule for Ireland seemingly only a matter of time, the Catholic Irish were as prosperous and politically strong as they had been for centuries. Much of what generations of Irish Nationalists had dreamed of appeared to be on the cusp of being realised.

The resurgence and advances of Irish Nationalism had resulted in an upsurge in Unionism, particularly Ulster Unionism, as a decidedly worried Protestant community sought to strengthen ties with England. By the eve of the Great War, a political impasse over Home Rule had taken Ireland to the verge of civil war. Unionists and Nationalists armed their followers and confronted each other over the barrels of guns, determined to impose their vision of Ireland on the other community, by force if necessary. The war would lead the British state to make great demands on its citizens: there were catastrophic casualties, economic hardships, food rationing and military conscription. Throughout mainland Britain these hardships were endured by a people united for the sake of national survival. In Ireland, they fell on a country riven with institutional racism and bigotry, bitterly divided between British Unionism and Irish Nationalism, and with more than a hint of militant trade unionism and revolutionary socialism thrown into the toxic mix. It is one of the paradoxes of the Great War that its outbreak, despite the carnage it unleashed in Europe, at least postponed a civil war in Ireland.

Outwith the bubble of the damnable Irish question, like the rest of society, the Glasgow Irish were living through a feverish, rapidly changing decade of massive social instability. Mass education and new political philosophies alongside exciting new technologies – wireless, X-rays, airplanes, motor cars, telephones, cinema – were all transforming almost every aspect of people's lives. The British people, including those on the island of Ireland and their Glasgow Irish cousins, reacted to the times by joining associations and mass movements – for social welfare, for workers' rights, for the rights of women, for the control of alcohol, for Irish Home Rule, against Irish Home Rule – all of which gave a sense of purpose and belonging. While Britain attempted to throw off the last vestiges of a feudal system that saw a small landed elite hold and use political power for the benefit of their own class, the capitalist and landowning elites fought to preserve their privileged positions, while the seething masses of the working class boiled with indignation at the massive differentials in wealth and lifestyles. Tens of millions of workdays were lost due to industrial action as the working class organised into trade unions since they were no longer prepared to accept the status quo.

In Europe, the decades spanning the nineteenth and twentieth centuries had seen the delicate balance of power that had keep the continent largely at peace since Waterloo, upset by the emergence of an economically and militarily dominant German state. Fear of German militarism saw its neighbours Russia and France tie themselves into a series of treaties and pacts, while Germany, fearful of a war on two fronts, allied itself to the failing Austro-Hungarian Empire and to a reluctant Italy. In the years preceding the outbreak of the Great War, a series of minor wars in the Balkans and diplomatic incidents elsewhere heightened international tensions. A massive expansion of the German Imperial fleet challenged Great Britain's mastery of the seas, forcing the British to ally themselves with two old adversaries, France and Russia. An international sense of foreboding, of a gathering storm, grew, with most diplomatic observers feeling that a war was inevitable – it was coming, it was just a matter of when. By the beginning of 1914, the major European nations stood in two opposing camps: Britain, France and Russia known as the *Triple Entente* on one side, and Germany, Austria-Hungary and Italy known as the *Triple Alliance* on the other. Any incident involving any of these countries would see a chain reaction, dragging all the nations, like prisoners manacled together at the ankles, into war.

Chapter One

Just Exactly Who are "The People"?

At the start of the eighteenth century, Glasgow was a sleepy backwater, a university town of around 13,000 god-fearing Presbyterian souls who could paddle cross the River Clyde at Glasgow Green without getting their knees wet. In fact, the town was so small that when threatened by the Highland Host during the 1715 Jacobite rebellion, the citizens were able to dig a defensive ditch completely around its boundary. However, all that was already in the process of monumental change. Glasgow's spectacular growth from sleepy university town to industrial colossus began with the 1707 political union between Scotland and England, as a result of which English commercial markets opened up to Glasgow entrepreneurs. When Daniel Defoe visited Glasgow in 1727, the changes were instantly recognisable even to the visitor and one-time English spy. He described the city thus:

> *Glasgow is a city of business and has the face of foreign as well as domestic trade; ney, I may say, 'tis the only city in Scotland, at this time, that apparently increases in both. The union has indeed, answered its end to them, for more than any other part of the kingdom, their trade being new formed by it; for as the union opened the door to the Scots into our American colonies, the Glasgow merchants presently embrace the opportunity.*

The Glasgow merchants almost monopolised the tobacco trade with the American colonies and brought a great deal of wealth into the city. When Defoe was in town he noted that Glasgow was sending fifty sailing ships every year to Virginia and New England. By the time of the American Revolution in 1777, the trade was worth a staggering £630,000 and the population of the city had more than trebled to 42,000 largely as a result of tobacco. It must be said, although to a much lesser degree, also to slavery. Vestiges of the importance of the tobacco trade can still be seen today in the street names of the city centre. Virginia, Glassford, Jamaica and Tobago streets all commemorate the importance of the tobacco trade or traders. The Glasgow tobacco lords made great fortunes, but the American Revolution of 1777 effectively destroyed this lucrative business almost overnight. The next stage of Glasgow's growth was based on sugar and on textiles, cotton in particular. Glasgow's imports for the year 1771 record 60,000 pounds of cotton wool imported from the West Indies. At first, the wool was spun into a rough fabric of linen and cotton, but in 1780 on a loom in the Anderson district of Glasgow, the first web of pure cotton was produced and the industry took off.

In 1790, the number of Scots emigrating to the Americas in the early phase of the Highland Clearances and the boom in Scottish, particularly Glasgow, manufacturing was such that it created a shortage of labour. Unskilled Irish Catholics had been coming to the west of Scotland for years, mostly for seasonal agricultural work, but they returned home at the end of the season. The early phase of the Scottish Industrial Revolution coincided with a revolution in Scottish agriculture, which saw the destruction of the old communal fermtoun farming system. This resulted in very many small farm leasers and their families being driven from the soil as open land was enclosed and the small farms consolidated into larger more productive units. The dispossessed farmers were forced to become landless labourers or were sucked into the new mills and factories of the rapidly industrialising towns, particularly across Lowland Scotland. The Irish agricultural labourers, willing to work for less, stepped into the agricultural labour gap this created and began to arrive in Scotland in ever increasing numbers, particularly around harvest time. It was said the Irish agricultural labourer could make £3 over the season, which they carried home to help see their families through the winter. The transitory Irish agricultural labourer quickly became an indispensable part of the Scottish rural economy. As a result of the expanding cotton weaving industry, Glasgow also became a popular place of resettlement for Irish Protestants, mostly Ulster Presbyterians, who shared a common ancestry and cultural heritage with Lowland Scots. Skilled in linen handloom weaving, many came to work in the fiercely independent cotton weaving communities in what were then villages round Glasgow, such as Bridgeton, Calton and Dalmarnock. By 1830, Bridgeton would be able to boast two Irish communities housed in two separate areas called "Dublin Land" and "Wee Belfast". The latter housed the Protestant Ulster weavers.

Around 1791 a consortium of Glasgow manufacturers invited some Scottish Highlanders who were planning to emigrate to America to come work in the city. These people, although Scottish, spoke only Gaelic and were regarded by the Lowland Scots as Irish in all but title. The Highlanders, who were all Roman Catholic, required and obtained assurances from the manufacturers that they would be free to practise their faith without hindrance in the staunchly Protestant city. At the time there were more anti-Catholic societies in Glasgow than there were actual Roman Catholics. The assurances were given and the manufacturers established a temporary chapel in a tennis court at Mitchell Street for the Highlanders. It was the first overt Roman Catholic chapel in the city since the Reformation. In 1792, the Highlanders were joined in Glasgow by another group of Highlanders en-route for Canada, mostly Gaelic-speaking McDonnells or McDonalds from Glengarry. Like the first group of Highlanders, the McDonnells, who settled to the east of the city at Bridgeton, were all Roman Catholics. By 1795, some 600 Catholics were celebrating mass in Glasgow and in 1797 a new chapel was established in Marshall's Lane in the Gallowgate. The chapel was opposite the new Barracks, placed there to be near the guardroom and under the protection of the military. Just ten years earlier a couple of hundred yards to the north, a number of weavers, including some Irish Protestants, while on strike over wages, burned and destroyed webs in the Drygate and Calton districts. The Provost of Glasgow called out the military and when the riot act was read, the strikers refused to disperse. The military opened fire and six men were shot dead near the Hangman's Brae (at the north end of Barrack Street, near modern day Tennant's brewery) and several more were wounded.

The Catholic Chapel, Marshall Lane 1898.

(Glasgow City Archives and Special Collections)

At the internment of the martyrs in the Calton, 6000 mourners turned out. In 1793, Britain had gone to war as part of a European coalition opposing revolutionary France and by 1794 the war had resulted in severe trade disruption and large-scale unemployment in Glasgow. Of course, the Catholic Highlanders, were among the first to lose their jobs. As Roman Catholics they were unable to access any form of Protestant Church charitable relief and were faced with a catastrophic situation. Confronted with destitution and starvation and led by their priest Fr McDonnell, the Glengarry Highlanders volunteered to enlist into a militia regiment being raised by their clan chieftain, Alexander McDonnell of Glengarry. The regiment would later be titled the Glengarry Fencibles. Despite enlisting to fight the French, the Glengarry Fencibles never saw a Frenchman: in 1795 they were sent first to guard Guernsey from invasion and in 1798, much to their horror, sent to Ireland during the United Irishman's Rebellion. The Glengarry regiment returned to Glasgow where it was disbanded in 1802. No better off than when they enlisted, Fr McDonnell, who had served with the regiment as its chaplain, finally led his Highlanders to Upper Canada. The departure of the Highlanders left the city's Catholic population in 1805 at around 450. The Protestant-led United Irishmen's rebellion against the British government in 1798, in which both Catholics and Presbyterian Protestants participated, cast a long shadow over their loyalty and in its aftermath neither Catholic nor Protestant Irish were welcome in Scotland. The new Catholic chapel at Marshall's Lane, and the native Glaswegian's attitude to both the Irish overall and Roman Catholics in particular living in the city at the time, is described in Glasgow, Past and Present, a series of reminisces first published about 1849:

> *It was a small unpretending edifice, built in 1797, and capable of containing 600 people. There the few "Papists," as they were popularly called, long assembled under one priest to celebrate those rites, which the Glasgow people in the olden time scarcely tolerated. I well remember seeing the Catholics on Sundays and festivals going stealthily along Gallowgate and suddenly darting off into the obscure "Marshall's Lane," as if to escape observation. Glasgow people were not overly fond either of Irish or Catholics and within my recollection it was quite a novelty to hear the brogue.*

Notwithstanding their unpopularity with the Glasgow citizenry, the Glasgow manufacturers continued to encourage the Irish and Highlanders into the city and by 1817, there were enough Catholic children to establish a Catholic Schools Society, supported, in the teeth of popular Protestant resentment, by the Protestant manufacturers. Despite the periodic industrial downturns, Glasgow's trade was soon booming again and on the back of a rapidly expanding manufacturing base the city's population exploded. In 1801 it stood at 83,000, at 110,000 in 1811, by 1821 it had surpassed 147,000 and ten years later passed the 200,000 mark. Just 100 years earlier the city's population was less than 20,000.

Between 1790 and 1850, over 300,000 Irish men, women and children arrived and settled in Scotland, the vast majority of whom were Roman Catholic. Although there was a continuous stream of Irish arriving over the period, they also came in three distinct influxes and for three distinct reasons. Firstly, the seasonal agricultural workers, who had been coming across the Irish Sea for many years, initially went back home at the end of the harvest, but as the Scottish industrial revolution took off more and more remained after the season finished, sucked into the manpower-hungry mills and factories. In 1801, Paisley was the third largest Scottish town after Glasgow and Edinburgh, with a population of 31,000. Between 1801 and 1821 it increased by over fifty per cent to 47,000 as shawl weaving, thread manufacture and cotton spinning became the staple industries. According to the 1821 Paisley census, in the burgh part of the town alone (excluding the Abbey parish) nearly sixty per cent of the population were immigrants (i.e. born outside Paisley) and almost mirroring the Glasgow numbers, about one-sixth of the incomers were Irish born. According to the marriage register of Paisley's St Mirin's Roman Catholic Church, which opened in 1808, the Catholic population of the town at the time was around 860. By 1816 there were over 1000 and by 1821 probably 2500. As in Glasgow, not all the Roman Catholics were Irish; some were Highlanders, especially girls from the Western Isles who came for seasonal work in the bleachfields and dye works. Of 100 marriages conducted at St Mirin's between 1808 and 1812, over sixty per cent of the celebrants were born in Donegal, Tyrone, Derry or Antrim.

As the pace of the industrial revolution increased, it heralded the appearance of the second group of Irish, the famous or infamous Irish navvy. Many thousands of Irishmen came over to build the great sinews of the industrial revolution: the canals, roads, railways, tunnels and bridges. Highly transitory, they moved around the country between large building projects, which could last years. They came simply to earn money and intended after a few years of hard graft and moving between construction projects, to go home with enough money to set themselves up. From around 1820, significant numbers of these early Irish were also being sucked into the burgeoning Scottish industry and were remaining in Scotland, having seen that the grass was indeed greener on the other side of the hill. Scotland offered much higher wages than could be earned in Ireland and the Irish who settled were motivated by the desire to improve their existence.

Most of the Irish were attracted by the boomtown wages on offer in Glasgow. According to the New Statistical Account for Glasgow, in 1831 of an estimated population of around 202,000, there were 26,500 Roman Catholics in the city, with many more in the surrounding parishes. These figures were later disputed and the number of Roman Catholics was put as low as 20,000. Around the mid-1820s, the Irish began to settle in and around Glasgow's satellite villages as they too began to expand alongside the city. In 1835 there were forty-five Irish Roman Catholic families living in Hamilton Parish. They heard mass once a month when the priest came up from Glasgow, while in nearby Paisley Parish there were over 3500 Roman Catholics mostly Irish. It was noted that the priest was actually responsible for another 3500 Catholics outwith Paisley Parish. This probably included the 1000 odd Catholics residing in adjacent Neilston where by 1826 they already made up fifteen per cent of the population. In 1790 there had been only one Roman Catholic in the whole of Neilston Parish. Interestingly, it was noted in the Neilston Statistical Account of 1835 that the Irish employed in manufacturing died on average 3.5 years earlier than their Scots counterparts employed in the same employment, at just 30.1 years of age. Scottish agricultural workers in the same parish died on average at age sixty. The Irish also began to arrive in large numbers in and around Coatbridge in response to both the developing coalfields and the introduction of the iron industry. The 1851 census of the town recorded that 35.8 per cent of the population were Irish born. Although there was no indication on the census of their religious affiliations, the largest proportion would have been Roman Catholic.

The vast majority of the Irish in Scotland came from the northern counties of Ulster. These Irish included a large proportion of poor Scots Irish Protestants, descendants of the plantation Scots of two centuries previous. Although statistical facts and figures of the period are often contradictory and confusing, some indication of the number of poor Irish Protestants in Glasgow during the early phase of immigration may be found in an 1818 report prepared for the Glasgow Kirk Session. The report covered eight Glasgow parishes and figures presented in a table of statistics. It shows that a total of 1182 persons applied for poor relief, of which 967 were Church of Scotland, 186 belonged to dissenting churches and twenty-nine were Roman Catholics. Of the total only 305 were born in Glasgow, 787 were born elsewhere in Scotland and ninety born in Ireland. Taking the figures at face value and assuming all twenty-nine Roman Catholics were Irish, it would suggest sixty-one of the ninety Irish applying for poor relief were Irish Protestants. The parish with most Irish applicants of both denominations (twelve Roman Catholics and twenty-two Protestants) was Blackfriars, one of the poorest districts, which took in the area around Glasgow Cross and the High Street.

By 1831, the population of Glasgow was such that housing and what little social amenities that did exist were simply overwhelmed. In 1736 only sixteen public wells provided water for a population of around 20,000. In 1800 the population was well in excess of 75,000 and there were still only thirty public wells. By 1831, 202,000 people lived and worked in Glasgow, 35,000 of whom were Irish born. Of the overall population of 202,000 an estimated 104,000 were Established Church, while Seeders, Dissenters, Episcopalians and Roman Catholics were estimated at 98,000. Only 20,000 to 26,000 of them were Irish Roman Catholics. Almost half of the overall population was aged less than twenty. The population of the city had grown so fast, by 1830 it was largely composed of incomers. It was later noted in evidence to a Select Committee on poverty, "The population of Glasgow may be divided into five parts, of which the native inhabitants would be one fifth, the Scottish Lowlanders two fifths, the Scottish Highlanders one fifth and the Irish one fifth." The first Irish immigrants of both traditions were therefore just another group of what was largely an urban population of incomers. By 1835, around 40,000 Irish Catholics were crammed into a few acres in and around the centre and eastern wards of the city. In just 300 square yards of the Bridgegate (*Briggait*) district, over 1140 Roman Catholics were crammed into the most insanitary conditions imaginable, and alongside them lived 2300 desperately poor Protestants, Scots and Irish. The poor Scots and Irish Protestants had been sucked into the city by the same economic pressures that brought in the Irish Catholics. In 1839, an appeal for funds was published in the Irish newspapers to help build a Catholic chapel in the east of the city. At that time the Catholic Church itself estimated the number of Catholics to be nearer 50,000. All these figures should be taken with a pinch of salt as vested interests both Catholic and Protestant gerrymandered the numbers for their own aims.

In a damning report into the state of the Glasgow poor, the health authorities described their living conditions as squalid beyond imagination. The poorest lived in late medieval and ramshackle buildings thrown up in haste to accommodate the migrant workers around Glasgow Cross. In the Trongate, Saltmarket, Gallowgate and High Street there were as many as a thousand people living in a single slum-ridden acre. Overcrowding was only part of the problem since dirt breeds disease. Like all towns of the period, Glasgow was no stranger to typhus and typhoid, but trade connections with the newly acquired Empire brought a new terrifying plague: *cholera*. The first cholera epidemic in 1832 killed 3000 in Glasgow and it was the poor who bore the brunt of the epidemic. Neil Arnott and James Kay reported on the *Prevalence of Certain Physical Causes of Fever* (1838):

In Glasgow, which I first visited, it was found that the great mass of the fever cases occurred in the low wynds and dirty narrow streets and courts, in which, because lodging was there cheapest, the poorest and most destitute naturally had their abodes. From one such locality, between Argyle Street and the river, 754 of about 5,000 cases of fever, which occurred in the previous year, were carried to the hospitals. We entered a dirty low passage like a house door, which led from the street through the first house to a square court immediately behind, which court, with the exception of a narrow path around it leading to another long passage through a second house, was occupied entirely as a dung receptacle."

From a beautiful late medieval city surrounded by cornfields, orchards and flower gardens only fifty years previously, Glasgow had in the course of a single generation evolved into one of the biggest slums not only in Scotland or Britain but also in Europe. The early 1830s saw the first railways being built largely by Irish navvies and Glasgow's heavy industry began to vie with textiles for the available manpower as inventions like the blast furnace and steam power took off. The first steam-propelled ship, the *Comet*, was built at Port Glasgow and began to ply between Greenock and Glasgow in January 1812. The first cross-channel steamboat crossed the Irish Sea between Glasgow and Belfast in 1818. By 1833, passengers could make the crossing from Belfast to Glasgow for just six pence. That year the fine new steamer *Antelope* began to ply the Belfast to Glasgow route as was proudly reported in the Glasgow Argus. The newspaper also noted that on her arrival at Greenock, she had upward of a thousand of the most wretched of *misgoverned* Ireland's poor on her decks. By 1839, a French visitor to Ireland, Gustave de Beaumont, was able to write:

In all countries, more or less, paupers may be discovered; but an entire nation of paupers is what was never seen until it was shown in Ireland. To explain the social condition of such a country, it would be only necessary to recount its miseries and its sufferings; the history of the poor is the history of Ireland.

Thirty years later, there were a dozen steamships trading between Glasgow and Ireland alone. In 1835, the first iron ship called the Plata was launched into the Clyde at the Broomielaw. The launch would herald the start of industrial shipbuilding on the Clyde. Coal was required in large quantities to feed the thousands of ovens and boilers, and the Irish found employment opportunities in the coalfields of Lanarkshire, Renfrewshire and the Lothians. The coal from Lanarkshire was transported into the city on barges plying the Monkland Canal. Connecting with the canal was the Garnkirk railway opened in 1831, which ran between Glasgow and Airdrie. The railway and the Monkland Canal were both constructed largely by Irish navvies.

The Scottish Lowlands led by Glasgow and the west was in the full blast of an industrial revolution that would enrich a few but impoverish and enslave many, many more. Although desperately needed by Scottish industry, the Irish, and to a lesser extent the Scottish Highlanders, were not welcomed by many who regarded themselves as indigenous Lowland Scots. Although the Irish in general suffered racism, it was the Irish Catholic who took most of the bigotry. The Lowland Scots found the Roman Catholic faith of the vast majority of the Irish and a significant portion of the Highlanders, highly offensive to their Presbyterian beliefs. In addition, they felt their own jobs were under threat from the incomers, who were often willing to work for less, but it was stated repeatedly that Scottish employers:

> Decidedly prefer the Irish as labourers, either to the English or the Scotch; they work with more heart and good will and are more civil and attentive. Highlanders could be got in sufficient numbers, but we do not like them so well; they are not so willing and obedient, nor so hardworking and industrious.

The Irish from Ulster proved to be especially well suited to handloom weaving as many had experience in the linen industry in Ireland. Employers found that they required little or no apprenticeship and picked up the tasks quickly. In terms of whether the Irish were there to replace native workers, testimony demonstrates that:

> We find them useful labourers and their services are of considerable importance to us; at present we could not do without them. In this part of the country, the Scotch do not show too much disposition for labouring work; they would rather go to trades. Even the hand-loom weavers, whose wages are so low, do not either themselves attempt to be labourers, or bring up their children to it.

The Scots who moved from rural or northern regions to the rapidly industrialising south did not offer what the employers required. "The Highlanders are largely a pastoral, a fishing, or an agricultural people and are not suited to the work of factories or to weaving; they are moreover, less ready and willing to work than the Irish and show themselves less facility in adapting themselves to new kinds of labour." There was competition for employment between the Irish and natives in some sectors of industry; in the iron industry and in coal mining in particular, the Irish were in direct competition with the native population. However, due to the economic growth, demand for labour in these industries more often than not exceeded supply. Despite these facts, the Irish gained a reputation for taking over the jobs of the natives. Some were accused of strike-breaking and some, undoubtedly the most desperate, did indeed resort to strike-breaking in the Lanarkshire coalfields. The native workers, who were just beginning to organise, saw this as forcing down wages for all.

There is some compelling evidence that Orangeism and bigotry particularly within the Lanarkshire coalfields and the Govan shipyards, both bastions of the order, actually impeded the development of trade unionism. Many of the skilled trades and crafts of the shipyards and heavy engineering firms, which then dominated the Glasgow industrial landscape, were Protestant closed shops. When religious bigotry saw the Glasgow Irish prevented from joining the fledgling trade unions, it left them with little choice when employers offered strikers' jobs, but at reduced wages. In fact, with the exception of the iron foundries and mines, the Irish and Scotch workers were seldom in competition for jobs, simply because for the most part the Irish were forced to take on the low paid, menial jobs that the native Scot would not take. The Glasgow satellite town of Coatbridge is a good example of where religious bigotry saw the exclusion of the Glasgow Irish from trade unions. By the early 1860s a large number of immigrant Irish, both Catholic and Protestant, had settled in and around the town that was dominated by the iron industry. There the Protestant Irish, many recruited from the Belfast shipyards, monopolised the skilled trades in the industry, while the Glasgow Irish were commonly assigned to the unskilled jobs, as labourers and furnacemen. As in the Glasgow shipyards, the volatile Ulster mix brought religious rivalry into the industry and retarded the development of trade unionism among the ironworkers of the area. Likewise, the skilled engineering jobs in Coatbridge were the preserve of the Scots and Irish Protestants. Towards the end of the century, the local branch of the Amalgamated Society of Engineers met in the local Orange hall, effectively barring any Catholic from joining. Reputedly, there was not a single Roman Catholic member of the society in the district until 1931. However, by the 1880s, the Glasgow Irish would not only be participating but would take leading roles in organised Scottish labour, particularly in the mining and weaving industries. Robert Chisholm Robertson, for example, was one of the pioneers of trade unionism among the Scottish miners and for several years was the secretary of the Forth and Clyde Miners' Association. He was among the first leaders of the Independent Labour Party. He was a practicing Catholic and a socialist, while remaining a passionate Irish Nationalist. As a prominent member of the Irish National League, he was often at loggerheads with the leaders of Irish Nationalism in Scotland over their refusal to muster the Glasgow Irish Catholic vote for the fledgling Labour party. He was only one of a small army of Irish immigrants who played a major role in the Scottish Labour movement, including of course a certain Edinburgh Irish socialist, James Connolly.

By 1841 it was officially estimated that there were around 44,000 Irish-born residents in Glasgow, or around sixteen per cent of the population. If you add those who could be considered to be of Irish extraction, the figure would be very much higher. The arrival in Glasgow of the third group or wave of Irish immigrants was by far, the most dramatic and obvious. It was spearheaded by the arrival of the first shipload of skeletal, starving poor of the Great Potato Famine (An Gorta Mor). Tens of thousands would follow them, washing up in the city between 1846 and 1850. Here was the highly visible manifestation of centuries of English and then British misrule in Ireland, compounded by the current government's laissez-faire attitude of non-intervention.

Over those terrible years, millions of men, women and children starved to death or were killed by disease or were driven from their homes by the desperation of starvation and abject poverty. John Mitchel, leader of the Young Ireland Movement, wrote the following in 1860:

> *I have called it an artificial famine: that is to say, it was a famine which*
> *desolated a rich and fertile island, that produced every year abundance*

and superabundance to sustain all her people and many more. The English, indeed, call the famine a "dispensation of Providence;" and ascribe it entirely to the blight on potatoes. But potatoes failed in like manner all over Europe; yet there was no famine save in Ireland. The British account of the matter, then, is first, a fraud – second, a blasphemy. The Almighty, indeed, sent the potato blight, but the English created the famine.

Charles Trevelyan

The central figure in the British government's response to the disaster unfolding in Ireland was Charles Trevelyan, Assistant Secretary to the Treasury between 1840–1859. This position put him in charge of the administration of the Government's Famine Relief efforts over the course of the Irish Famine. Trevelyan was a stiff, unbending, English official who firmly believed in *laissez faire* (essentially, market forces should be allowed to run their course), he thought the Government should not intervene, and warned the people would get into the habit of depending on state aid. In addition, he held racist and bigoted views of the native Irish, reflecting that commonly held by the English ruling class. He saw the Famine as a mechanism for reducing surplus population in Ireland. He also thought it was a judgement of God sent to teach the selfish, perverse and turbulent Irish a lesson. The sheer scale of the calamity became such even he was forced to respond, but his intervention was too little too late. His importation and distribution of Indian corn, although it was not known at the time, only exasperated the problem. The starving people given the corn expended more calories making it fit to eat, than they received from the corn when it was consumed. His response to the Famine gained for him a place of infamy in Irish history and a well-deserved reputation as a cold-hearted and uncompassionate administrator. All that said he was acting on behalf of and with the full support of his political masters. On 27 April 1848 he was given a knighthood for his services to Ireland.

Tens of thousands of Irish, particularly from the nine northern counties of Ulster, took the cheapest and quickest route out and made their way to Scotland. Many were assisted to leave Ireland, their two-penny fare paid by near bankrupt landowners and their factors desperate to get the starving tenants off their lands and expense accounts. In most other cases the cost of the fare represented the fleeing people's entire worldly wealth, some having to sell what little they possessed to raise the fare for themselves and their family. After a perilous nine-hour trip across the Irish Sea, the massively and, no doubt to some, comically overcrowded paddle steamers disgorged their pathetic human cargo at Greenock or Glasgow's Broomielaw Quay in the very centre of the city. Day after day, hundreds of semi-naked skeletons staggered from the boats, totally destitute, straight onto the city centre streets. Considerable numbers of them were so ill or enfeebled they were taken directly to temporary wards set up outside the Royal Infirmary. Hundreds went straight from the boats or hospital to a pauper's grave pit in Sighthill Cemetery. The sheer scale of the dispossessed arriving in Glasgow was staggering and, had it been a military invasion, the city would have been overrun. Indeed the Glasgow Herald on 11 June 1847 headlined an immigrant story with the banner "Irish Invasion". Hundreds of native Glaswegians gathered at the river Clyde to stare awestruck at the sight of a tragedy of truly biblical proportions unfolding before their eyes. Not all were moved by the pathetic sights; some were there to shout abuse and derision. During 1848, the average weekly inflow of Irish into Glasgow was estimated at over 1000, and the figure for January to April of that year was put at 42,860. Although the vast majority of the famine victims were Roman Catholic, it should be noted that there were also many Irish Protestants driven from Ireland over the same period.

On their arrival in Glasgow, the immigrants were largely on their own. The lucky ones had contacts in the city that might be in a position to help them settle in. For the very unlucky, it was some food, medical treatment if required and a return trip back to Ireland. Often they were immediately turned around and dispatched back to Glasgow again. Between August 1845 and July 1846 the Glasgow authorities removed around 2000 persons, mostly Irish, at a cost of £133 16s 9d. For the vast majority of the immigrants who had no contacts in the city, sustenance and survival was down to the generosity and sympathy of the decidedly worried Glasgow citizenry and gaining employment very quickly. It is to staunchly Presbyterian Glasgow's eternal credit that its citizens did for the most part deal compassionately with the humanitarian catastrophe with which they were suddenly confronted. They did feed, clothe and administer to the sick and they did allow the vast majority of immigrants to settle, and at considerable personal cost to the average Glaswegian. The citizens acquiesced despite the fact that they saw the vast majority of the immigrants as members of a despised race and religion. Unlike today when a city council is under a legal requirement to house the homeless, then there was no surplus social housing or basic needs funding. With no central government-funded safety nets, no voluntary organisations ready to step in to represent the interests of the destitute, Glasgow had no obligation to assume responsibility for the desperate situation it found itself presented with. For the most part, the charitable assistance came straight from the pockets of Glasgow's citizens.

The Poor Fund was British society's nineteenth century's version of social security, a slightly different version of which operated in each of the home nations. Originally set up in Scotland in the sixteenth and seventeenth centuries, it was intended for and designed to alleviate the plight of the few dozen deserving poor of each individual parish. It was maintained by a tax on the parish heritors (property owners), parish fees (births and marriages), collections at the church door on a Sunday, voluntary donations and bequests. The individual parishes of the Church of Scotland administered their own parish funds. There were various rules attached to applying for aid, most notably for the immigrant was the residency clause. A person had to have been living in the parish for three years before they were eligible for help. Although the Poor Law in Scotland was different from that in force in Ireland, much the same principles applied. Any expense born by the parishes into which the immigrants arrived should technically have been passed back to the immigrants' home parish. Unfortunately, during the famine years, the Irish poor fund system was for the most part bankrupted by the number of people applying for relief. By the start of the 1840s, the Church of Scotland was itself also in trouble. Factions had always broken away from the Established Church of Scotland, but in 1843 a split known as the *Disruption* cleaved the church in two. The split had a disastrous effect on the Church-administered Poor Fund as the breakaway Free Church took fifty per cent of the heritors and fifty per cent of the donations. Every penny was needed to provide incomes for their 500 ministers and to pay for a massive church building program of over 400 churches. The pressure on the old Poor Fund was so great, a commission was set up to look at how the laws relating to the relief of the poor could be modernised. The commission recommended a new system of Parochial Boards, which were introduced with the Poor Law Act of 1845. Funds were now to be raised by compulsory assessments on property owners and tenants. Still based on the parish, the Parochial Boards were responsible for their own poor, i.e., those born in the parish, those who had lived there for five years and those who came into the parish by marriage. Relief was still conditional; it was not for the unemployed. Those who could qualify included the sick, deserted married women, widows, foundlings and deserted children.

A report to the Board of Supervision drawn up to show the number of destitute Irish landed in Glasgow over the period January 1847 to November 1847, shows the scale of the problem facing the city authorities. The number of destitute Irish landed at Glasgow over the period was 49,993. The total expense incurred by Glasgow over the period on account of the influx was a colossal £21,303. The total included: £6000 for temporary relief, £8000 for erecting a new Poorhouse and Fever Hospital, £713 for infirmary charges, £200 for medicine and poignantly £576 for burials. These were colossal sums of money for the times, and it was monies largely raised by voluntary contributions. It is interesting to ponder the likely response of the Glasgow citizenry of today being presented with a similar catastrophic humanitarian situation. Although the destitute Irish washing up in Glasgow needed and for the most part received immediate aid, the majority of them passed through the city and moved to other parts of the country. The figures from the national censuses of 1841 and 1851 reveal that the numbers of Irish-born living in Glasgow only increased by 15,500, while the population of the city increased by 70,000. Most of the increase in the population came from the surrounding rural areas.

After the immediate famine crisis was past, there was a distinct hardening in Glaswegian and Scottish attitudes to the Irish Catholics living in their mist. Although each previous migration phase had seen the Irish treated with racism, bigotry, hostility and derision, they were initially too few in numbers, too widespread and too transitory to be seen as any great threat to the Scottish way of life. Additionally, the lack of any significant Roman Catholic Church infrastructure meant many of the pre-famine immigrants lost their faith. The scarcity of priests saw marriages between Catholic couples regularly conducted in Protestant church manses. The Protestant ministers were happy enough adding what they saw as converts to their flock at the expense of the Church of Rome. Scottish and Glasgow society at large had contented itself for the most part with poking fun at poor, stupid Paddy in jokes, songs and comic cartoons. The famine influx had seen the Irish arrive in such numbers, over such a short time span and in such desperate need that they were now being regarded as a very serious threat to Scottish society. In 1841, the National Census showed that 4.8 per cent of the Scottish population was born in Ireland. By 1851 that figure had increased to 7.2 per cent. The census figures for 1871 show, by percentage of population, the largest centres of Irish settlement as Dumbarton at 17.7, Greenock 16.6, Glasgow 14.3, Airdrie 14.2, Dundee 11.9, Paisley 9.8 and Hamilton 8.6. In Glasgow's satellite town of Coatbridge, the number of Irish born reached 33%.

The desperate condition in which the Irish arrived in the city simply reinforced the long-held perceptions of the Irish being ignorant, diseased, drunken, shiftless scroungers and now a massive burden on the hard-working Protestant ratepayers. Worst of all as far as staunchly Presbyterian Scotland was concerned, the vast majority were *Roman Catholic* adherents of an old, superstitious religion, which had been driven from the country 300 years previously. They were now seen as a very definite threat to Scottish culture, an entirely "alien race". In the 1850s anti-Catholic publications appeared, two of which, the *Bulwark* and *The Scottish Protestant,* were particularly poisonous. The latter went so far as to draw a link between famine victims and the menace of popery on the march: "If the hopes of Popery to regain her dominion of darkness in this kingdom of light are beginning to revive, it is because she is colonising our soil from another land, with hordes of her barbarised and enslaved victims, whom she proudly styles her subjects." The Roman Catholic Church also was becoming better established and much better organised; the Glasgow Irish therefore became much more visible and by definition easier to attack. The Irish became a target for most of Scotland and Glasgow's ills. In November 1848, the dreaded Asiatic cholera had reappeared in the city and by the time the outbreak had run its course in March 1849, 3777 citizens had died from the pestilence. It was noted that unlike the visitation of 1833 when the outbreak was confined mainly to the slums in the city centre, this time the plague reached the middle and upper class areas. The dirty, lazy, drunken Irish got the blame, with the authorities calling for the central government to address the very obvious problems in Ireland that drove the immigrants out in the first place. Another significant factor in the increase of sectarian and racist tensions in central Scotland was the growth of Orangeism.

We are the People!

It is worth pausing at this point to examine the origins and something of the history of the Ulster Scots community and of the Orange Order, widely regarded as a violently anti-Catholic, Protestant-supremacist organisation. The organisation was established in 1795 after a sectarian riot near Loughgall, Co Armagh. During the affray, over thirty people, mostly unarmed Roman Catholics, were killed. The riot, grandly termed the Battle of the Diamond, involved two vigilante groups. On the Catholic side were the "Defenders" and on the Anglican Protestant side the "Peep O' Day Boys". The Orange Order was so named to commemorate the victories of

Dutchman Prince William of Orange (King Billy) and more particularly his victory at the Battle of the Boyne in 1690. The organisation's self-professed aims were to uphold the Protestant faith and later to preserve the Union of Great Britain and Ireland (later Northern Ireland). Ironically, for the first forty odd years of its existence its membership was exclusively Anglican; the Presbyterian Ulster Scots, who would later become the bulwark of the organisation, were then seen as dissenters by the Established Anglican Church of Ireland and were not allowed to join the Order. The Orange Order had come into being in a period of great political unrest in Ireland, particularly in Ulster where the Presbyterian Ulster Scots had for the best part of eighty years suffered much the same indignities as their Catholic neighbours – crushed under the weight of the infamous Penal Laws. For eight decades tens of thousands of Ulster Scots had been forced to flee to the New World to escape the religious and political persecution in Ireland. The contemporary image of the Ulster Protestant is commonly that of the Presbyterian Orangeman, with all his exaggerated loyalty to Britain and the Crown. For the dispossessed Presbyterian Ulster Scots, the exact opposite was true; having lost everything in Ulster, very many arrived in America with an intense hatred towards all things British.

As a result of the total subjugation of the native Catholic Irish and the alienation of the Ulster Scots, the rule of the Protestant Ascendancy, known in Ireland simply as *the Ascendancy*, was perpetuated. Never was there such a parcel of rogues in a nation! For them, Ireland was there to be plundered and from their privileged positions as practical governors of the country they enriched themselves and their friends at the expense of the common people of Ireland. The only recourse for Irishmen was appeals to the British parliament, which more often than not fell on deaf ears, while the same parliament passed legislation that would advance its own commercial interests by crippling Irish shipping and effectively destroying Irish exports and commerce. The commercial protectionism and national self-interest ensured that Ireland was impoverished while England prospered. It was publicly mooted over the period that the legislation was part of a deliberate British policy to keep Ireland poor.

In response to the political unrest in Ireland, the British allowed a degree of devolution with the creation of Grattan's Parliament in 1792. This was dominated by English appointees and it was completely unrepresentative and massively corrupt, although it did enjoy a large degree of legislative independence. That same year a convention, composed mostly of Ulster Scots Presbyterians numbering around 100,000, met at Dungannon, Co Tyrone. One of the resolution proclaimed "that the claim of any body of men other than the King, Lords and Commons of Ireland, to make laws to bind the kingdom was unconstitutional, illegal and a grievance". Another declared support for their oppressed Roman Catholic fellows: "As Irishmen, as Christians and Protestants, we rejoice in the relaxation of the laws against our Roman Catholic fellow subjects." The latter motion was proposed and seconded by a ruling elder and Presbyterian minister. In response to the need for Irish parliamentary reform, in 1791 three Protestants, including two Presbyterian ministers, formed the Society of United Irishmen. Included in a number of resolutions adopted by the United Irishmen was that: "No reform is practicable, efficacious, or just, which shall not include Irishmen of every religious persuasion." The United Irishmen were led by Protestant Theobald Wolfe Tone, who advocated universal suffrage that would include Irish Roman Catholics. He wrote *Argument on behalf of the Catholics of Ireland,* a very remarkable hypothesis considering the age and religious and political environment. The radical views of the United Irishmen attracted government suppression and persecution and, inspired by the American and French Revolutions, the organisation itself was gradually transformed from advocating radical political change to a revolutionary movement.

In the midst of the civil unrest, the Orange Order was established with the remit to protect Protestant privilege in Ireland. The paramilitary organisation then set about a systematic campaign of terror in the surrounding Armagh countryside. Shortly afterwards the Governor of Armagh, Lord Gosford, gave his opinion of the new group to a meeting of magistrates: "It is no secret that a persecution is now raging in this country… the only crime is… profession of the Roman Catholic faith. Lawless banditti have constituted themselves judges." In the period of heightened tension in Ireland caused by the United Irishmen, the terrified Ascendancy government, using the age-old *divide and rule* stratagem, played the infamous *Orange card* for the first time. The Orange Order was deliberately used by the Anglican Irish government to encourage sectarian hatred and division between Ulster Scots Presbyterians and native Roman Catholics in Ulster, by inventing and spreading "fearful rumours of intended massacres of all the Protestant people by the Catholics." In what must be one of the first instances of the modern military being put into a difficult and distasteful position, the military commander in Ulster at the time noted: "As for the Orangemen, we have rather a difficult card to play... we must to a certain degree uphold them, for with all their licentiousness, on them we must rely for the preservation of our lives and properties should critical times occur."

Seeking French help to overthrow English or British rule, the United Irishmen's uprising was planned for 1796, but a *Protestant wind* smashed a French invasion fleet transporting 14,000 French soldiers to Ireland. Despite the setback, by the following year the United Irishmen's ranks had swollen to well over a quarter of a million Irishmen of all religious persuasions and the island was on the brink of revolution. In 1798, Wolfe Tone led the United Irishmen in the first major rebellion in Ireland since 1641. Ironically, and not for the last time, Irish Protestants would take a leading role in a Republican struggle for Irish independence. Although it was an Ireland-wide rebellion, it was patchy and sporadic and practically confined to the counties of Antrim, Down, and Wexford. In Co Antrim and Co Down some thousands of United Irishmen, mostly Presbyterian farmers armed with pikes and muskets, rose in rebellion. The United Irishmen's rebellion was a disaster with the rebels routed throughout the island. Wolfe Tone was captured during a half-hearted French invasion at Ballinamuck and later committed suicide while awaiting execution. The United Irishmen's rebellion of 1798 failed, but terrified at the prospect of another united Presbyterian/Catholic uprising, the Anglican Ascendancy redoubled its efforts to ensure antagonism between Presbyterians and Catholics was fostered. One of the major weapons in their policy of divide and rule was to give the Ulster Scots a few crumbs of relief, petty privileges which set them apart from their Catholic allies but which were valuable enough to make a difference in their lives, Another was the continued use of the Orange Order to foster fear and distrust.

The ideals of Orangeism appear to have been first imported into Scotland by returning Scottish militiamen deployed to Ireland from south Ayrshire during the 1798 rebellion. The Order spread quickly; by 1807 there were Orange lodges in Maybole, Tarbolton, Wigtown, Girvan, Stranraer and Argyll. By 1813 there was one in Glasgow and in 1821 the first ceremonial parade took place in the city. In 1822 and 1823 they paraded through the streets in their annual Orange Walk, but the Glasgow city magistrates were so concerned at the disorder and violence they attracted, that they banned them for the next fifty years. The Order's Scottish membership was topped up by Irish Protestant immigrants, driven to Scotland by the exact same economic pressures as their Catholic neighbours and by 1830 there were a total of seven lodges in Glasgow. The passing of the Catholic Emancipation Act in 1829 saw a surge in membership and by 1834 Glasgow Irish Protestants were the proud possessors of thirty-five Orange lodges. Just a year later the Orange Order admitted for the first time all non-Catholics. Despite the ban on their marches, Orangemen were free to meet publicly in an orderly fashion, but all too often the meetings ended in riots or violence. In the 1830s there were some very serious violent incidents outwith Glasgow; at Girvan, a number of people were reportedly killed during an Orange riot. To defend their town, the citizens actually charged and presented down the main street a four-pounder cannon to await the rioting Orangemen. At Airdrie in 1835, Glasgow Ribbonmen organised a counter march to an Orange parade. After the Glasgow men left, local Roman Catholics were victimised in their homes. Police reports from the Calton and Gorbals from 1836 both state that, "The Irish fight in the street and in the home. The rows of the Irish are chiefly among themselves, between the Catholics and Protestants, although sometimes the Scotch and Irish are mixed in the same brawl." Despite the massive influx of Irish Catholics into the very Protestant city, with the exception of the odd melee and isolated incidents over the 1840s and 1850s, there were remarkably few major tribal or sectarian clashes in Glasgow.

Over a weekend in August 1875, a very serious sectarian clash did occur at Partick, then a burgh in its own right and separate from Glasgow. A mob of several hundred Orangemen attacked Irish Home Rule supporters returning from a political rally in Glasgow. The Nationalists were ambushed at Partick Cross and over a weekend of rioting, the Lord Provost of Partick was forced to have the Riot Act read out. Thousands of pounds worth of damage was done and hundreds of people injured. In the subsequent enquiry the Orangemen got most of the blame though the Home Rulers, it was thought, contributed greatly to the continuance of the disturbance. The Glasgow Herald newspaper, appalled and disgusted at the behaviour and with more than a hint of racism wrote: "It is some consolation to note that the combatants on both sides were Irish, and while it was the Orangemen who bore the greater weight of the blame, if one side was wicked enough to give challenge, the other side was wickedly eager to accept it." The ubiquitous Scottish worthies, appalled at the riot disturbing the peace of the Presbyterian Sabbath, called for both Irish organisations and their processions to be banned. The following weekend, the adjacent Govan parish, fearful of a repeat of the riot in Partick, called for 200 shipyard workers to volunteer as special constables. It was stipulated that the volunteers must not be members of the Orange Order or Home Rule supporters.

Scottish Orangeism never became an attractive berth for respectable Scottish Protestants and the Order, certainly in Glasgow where it was strongest, appears to have been regarded as a distinctly Irish organisation and largely the preserve of the Protestant Irish. In 1881, fully seventy-two per cent of Orange lodge masters and secretaries were born in Ireland. Under the guise of an educational requirement stipulated within the constitution of the Order, members are encouraged to enrol their children into the organisation, thereby establishing a tradition of family membership. Very young children are still a common sight marching alongside adults in Orange Order parades. This tradition of father to son membership is reflected in a favourite hymn of the Order, "The Sash my Father Wore". However, no more than two per cent of adult male Protestants in west central Scotland have ever been members of the Order, with the ethnic Ulster association appearing to be less attractive to the native Scottish Presbyterian. While the classic institution of Orangeism is inherently anti-Catholic and bigoted, it is important to understand that not all Orangemen are bigoted and anti-Catholic: many simply see the Order as a fraternal organisation. Indeed, many Orange Order members have Roman Catholics within their own extended families. The modern Orange Order is also involved in extensive charity work throughout the world. The Protestant Irish were eventually fully absorbed into the native Scottish community, most had Scottish or English surnames and being co-religionists they largely disappeared as a separate and visible ethnic entity.

There are now only two remaining visual legacies of the early Protestant Irish immigrants in modern Scotland, the Orange Order and Rangers Football Club based at Ibrox Park, Glasgow. The Order still commands significant, largely working class, support in Scotland and as a generality, a good predictor of the number of people of Irish Protestant descent is the strength of the Orange Order in a particular part of the country. The descendants of the Protestant Irish can also be seen in significant numbers within the support of Rangers Football Club, many of whom are also members of the Orange Order. In response to the footballing success of the Celtic, an overtly Irish Catholic football team with Irish Nationalist sympathies, the football supporters within the Glasgow Irish Protestant *Orange and Unionist* tradition adopted Rangers Football Club as their own favourite. In reality, they could have chosen any of the other Glasgow teams since a considerable number of them lived and worked in Glasgow, with easy access particularly to Partick and to Queen's Park. Their support was given specifically to Rangers because at the time, they were the only west of Scotland team capable of mounting a prolonged challenge to the success of Celtic. The Protestant Glasgow Irish support for Rangers was therefore based on opposition to the Irish Catholic Celtic, rather than supporting a team purely on footballing skills or territorial allegiances, as would be the norm. Up to that point, there were no political or religious labels attached to Rangers Football Club and indeed a very friendly rivalry existed between the two Glasgow clubs. As late as May 1903, anti-Catholic feelings were obviously still absent from the Rangers Club itself since the management allowed a Rangers team to play Hibernian in a charity game to help raise funds for a Roman Catholic school building fund. The gate money from the 2–2 draw played out at Easter Road helped build the Star of the Sea School in Constitution Street, Leith.

In the decade prior to the Great War although there was already a distinct Irish Protestant flavour to Rangers Football Club, several Roman Catholics did regularly play for the Ibrox side. One such was Willie Kivlichan, a devout Roman Catholic doctor of medicine. Kivlichan played twenty-nine times for Rangers (he scored against Celtic) while a student attending Glasgow University. Willie was educated at St Joseph's College in Dumfries and was an overt practicing Catholic and a member of the Third Order of St Francis. Kivlichan later played for the Celtic and would become the team doctor, attending legendary Celtic goalkeeper John Thompson when he received his fatal injury at Ibrox. This all changed when an Orange/Unionist faction took over at the club around the time of the Great War. All that is not to say that everything was sweetness and light before then. During a match in September 1894, Rangers player's spat "Fenian", "papist" and "Irish" at the Celtic players during a game that was, even for the times, marked by the ferocity of the play. The admittedly biased sports reporter of the Glasgow Observer commented that he had never seen so many fouls committed by the one team (Rangers) and wondered what had brought about the change in what were previously friendly relations.

At the turn of the twentieth century, the issue of Irish Home Rule roused deep feelings and brought many Scottish-based Ulster Protestants onto the streets to protest. The Irish Catholic community of course led counter protests. In 1912 with the Home Rule for Ireland debate reaching a crescendo, Orangemen James Craig and Sir Edward Carson established the paramilitary Ulster Volunteer Force (UVF) in Ulster. At the same time the arrival in Govan of the Belfast shipbuilders, Harland and Wolff, and their notoriously sectarian employment policy, polarised and compounded political differences in Glasgow. Willie Maley, in his *Story of Celtic*, reports there being no serious trouble between Rangers and the Celtic prior to 1912. This suggests that the arrival of the Belfast shipbuilders had a significant effect on the relationship between the two football clubs. It was also the year Sir John Ure Primrose became president of Rangers FC. The former Glasgow Lord Provost was a long-term Rangers supporter and early photography enthusiast. He is credited or blamed with the introduction of Rangers' notorious anti-Catholic player policy; however, prior to taking over at Rangers he was happy enough to lecture, usually on photography, to numerous Catholic organisations including the Catholic Literary Society. His predecessor, James Henderson, had been well respected in the Catholic communities, but Ure Primrose assumed the chairmanship at Rangers at a politically divisive time. He broke away from the Liberal Party to join a Conservative/Unionist alliance and became a vocal west of Scotland anti-Home Rule advocate. He shared a Glasgow platform with Sir Edward Carson in October 1912 and his reputation among the Glasgow Irish nationalists suffered accordingly. Despite all that, when Ure Primrose's wife died in May 1913, the Glasgow Catholic Observer offered the former Lord Provost the sincere sympathy of the Glasgow Catholic community. Adding, "although not of our faith or politics he is a friend to the Catholic community".

Much of today's enmity between the supporters of Rangers (Protestant and British Unionist) and Celtic (Catholic and Irish Nationalist) is based on these ancient sectarian rivalries, while the Unionist/Nationalist politics of the recent Troubles in the north of Ireland has continued to pick at the scab. It is important to note that not all Rangers supporters are Protestant and Orange any more than all Celtic supporters are Catholic and Irish Nationalist. It should also be noted that away from the intensity of a Celtic versus Rangers game, very many of the opposing fans are great friends and workmates and with the boom in mixed marriages after the Great War very many are interrelated. Indeed, such has been the number of mixed marriages over the second half of the last century, few supporters of either team could claim not to have some family connection to either tradition or a foot in both camps. Rangers Football Club discontinued its shameful policy of excluding Roman Catholics in the late 1980s and during a game between the clubs in 2011, there were more Roman Catholics in the Rangers team than in the Celtic team. Many of the Celtic's greatest heroes were Protestant, including the immortal manager Jock Stein, though none have been overtly Orange. Having said that, early Celtic goalkeeper Tom Duff was verbally attacked by Hibernian fans at Easter Road for his Orange tendencies.

Alienation, Association and Faith

Irish immigration to Scotland and the rest of the world continued, even during what might be regarded as prosperous times in Ireland. In what became almost a rite of passage, the most able of an Irish family would leave home to travel to foreign lands, where once established they would send money back to help those who had remained behind. Unemployment, low wages, sectarianism, landlordism and lack of social mobility were the main *push factors* forcing them out of Ireland. Regular employment, higher wages and at least the possibility of some advancement were the main *pull factors* sucking the Irish into Scotland and into the central belt in particular. Those who came to Scotland and Glasgow found a network of relations, friends and acquaintances ready and willing to help to support them through the first difficult weeks and months as the newcomers found their feet. In 1871, four out of the ten largest Irish communities in the UK were in Scotland.

The alienation of the Glasgow Irish community brought about by constant exposure to racism, sectarianism and discrimination, allied to their own parochial outlook and the lack of any significant social interaction between the communities, resulted in the building and reinforcing of barriers that for decades prevented their assimilation into the wider Glasgow community. In addition, because of their strict adherence to their Catholic beliefs, young Glasgow Irish men and women tended, through the strict supervision of their priests, to associate and marry within their own community, thus preventing inter-religious marriages. The scale of this can be seen in Greenock, where it was found that in 1851, 80.6 per cent of Irish men and women had found marriage partners amongst their own kind. Forty years later the number was still almost as high at 72.4 per cent. Such a situation made it difficult for the Irish Catholic to assimilate into the mainstream of Scottish society. Even in those mixed marriages that did take place, it was the Irish Catholic identity that was transferred to the children. At the same time, the constant topping up of the community with fresh Irish immigrant blood preserved the ties between the Glasgow Irish and the auld country, as did the retelling of old tales and the singing of old songs. This led to a tendency for the Glasgow Irish to cling to their Irishness and to see themselves as Irish first and Scottish or British second, if at all. It should also be noted that the immigrant Irish themselves also contributed to the situation. While most Irish immigrants arrived in the city with few possessions, they were not without baggage. Unsurprisingly considering the political and social situation at home, immigrant Irishmen stepping off the boat at the Broomielaw already nurtured a well-developed sense of persecution and banishment and possessed a folk history that sentimentalised their exile and romanticised Ireland's struggle for self-determination and nationhood. The chips on the Irish exile's shoulder, allied to the systematic animosity they felt from their host nation, helped cement the alienation and encourage a siege mentality.

The Irish poor of both religious traditions continued to arrive in Glasgow in the decades after the terrible famine exodus, although in much reduced numbers. Many of those arriving were just as hungry and desperate as the victims of the Potato Famine. Always at the very edge of subsistence even in the best of times, it took very little to tip the Glasgow Irish or indeed any of Glasgow's poor into destitution, pauperism and into the poorhouse. Scottish attitudes to the Irish were complex and constantly shifting, ranging from complete indifference, to absolute hatred because of their religion, their charitable neediness and political violence, which was expressed both in Ireland and in mainland Britain in various ways and at different times. Caricatured in the print media and in music halls first as harmless or stupid, whiskey-drinking yokels, Irishmen increasingly came to be represented, especially after the rise of the Fenian movement in the 1860s, as apelike monsters, a threat to law and order, middle-class values and even the Empire itself. This later portrayal resonated through the educated British middle classes at the same time as Darwin's theory of evolution, and the violent Nationalist Irish were shown as subhuman, half men, half beasts. Encouraged by Church of Scotland ministers preaching the dangers of popery in their midst, the Catholic Irish were socially, if not physically, set apart from the wider Scottish and Glasgow communities. Unlike cities such as Liverpool, there were never any specific Irish ghettos established in Glasgow; however, economic necessity forced the Catholic Irish to concentrate in the poorer districts of the city around the High Street and Saltmarket and across the river in the Gorbals district. Later, in the wake of the city's housing improvements, the Irish were dispersed around the city with enclaves established in Anderston, Townhead, Calton, Cowcaddens and the Garngad. In each, they lived in slums alongside the poor Scottish Highlanders and equally poor Lowland Scots. Some districts like the Gorbals and the Garngad came to be regarded as little Irelands, but in reality the Irish were simply the largest and most vocal tribe in the area.

Ranked among the poorest Glaswegians were very many of the Protestant Irish. They had arrived in the city in considerable numbers over the same time periods, labouring under exactly the same economic pressures. In Ireland, and Ulster in particular, Protestants would have had very little contact with Roman Catholics, and now they found themselves living cheek by jowl with the hated papists. In the mid-1830s, the Irish of both religious persuasions were seen by the native Scots-Glaswegians as just troublesome Irish. In 1831, the police superintendent responsible for Calton district gave a breakdown of the nationalities of the inhabitants under his jurisdiction. There were 13,554 Scotch, 8890 Irish and 157 English. According to the 1861 National Census, Glasgow could boast 63,574 Irish-born citizens. As late as the 1880s, both Irish Catholics and Irish Protestants were still largely lumped together by the wider Scottish and Glaswegian population. Both could suffer similar degrees of racism from the indigenous Scots simply by being Irish. However, as second- and third-generation Glasgow Irish Protestants began to lose their broad Ulster Irish accents and became less visible, they were absorbed into the wider community, while the Irish Catholics, mainly through their adherence to an expanding and increasingly high profile Roman Catholic Church, continued to be ostracised and marginalised. By the mid-1880s, thirteen per cent of the city's population was Irish born, but bringing their children and grandchildren who still regarded themselves as Irish into the equation, the figure is dramatically increased. In 1881, twenty-three per cent of the people in Glasgow's parish poorhouse were born in Ireland. The admissions registers of Glasgow's notorious Barlinnie Prison over the same period show that just under one-fifth of the prisoners were Irish born; of these one-quarter were Protestant and three-quarters of the whole came from Ulster. For every Catholic prisoner born in Ireland, there were two Catholics born elsewhere.

The Roman Catholic community in and around Glasgow and later across much of central Scotland were labelled with the derogatory *Glasgow Irish* tag. Similarly, Scottish Catholics, mostly Highlanders and Islanders, were also tarred with the same brush and lumped in with their Irish cousins. Even as succeeding generations lost their Irish accents, it was still the case that their Irish surnames or the school they attended were used to identify them as a member of the Glasgow Irish community and by definition therefore a Roman Catholic. Very many changed their names: O'Malley became Maley, the 'O' was dropped from O'Reilly, O'Shaughnessy and O'Donnell. Irish surnames were deliberately Anglicised, Gallagher became Gallacher and Darragh was changed to Darroch in an attempt to blend in with the local community. The social alienation and discrimination took many forms and sectarianism was particularly prevalent in the workplace where many occupations were entirely closed to the Glasgow Irish because of their religion. Entrenched employment practices where the all-powerful foreman had the authority to hire and fire, saw the Glasgow Irish at the mercy of their religious affiliations and saw them permanently assigned to semi-skilled or labouring positions. The Glasgow Irish dominated in general labouring, basic level tailoring, dockyard, steelworks and gasworks labouring, mining, construction and casual work like shoe and boot repairs. A hierarchy of Freemasons and Orangemen in engineering, ironworking and shipbuilding ensured that Protestant brothers dominated in all the key skilled trades. By controlling access to apprenticeships, they maintained that domination and thereby secured the core skilled positions in all of the heavy industrial professions for future Protestant generations. Similar practices existed in white-collar occupations; prior to the Great War it was almost unheard of for a Roman

Catholic to have a position within Scottish banking. Even in domestic service, one of the lowest paid occupations, bigots advertised in newspapers for Protestant cooks and maids. In response to the social alienation, the Glasgow Irish developed a siege mentality and over the second half of the nineteenth century, largely under the direction of the expanding Scottish Roman Catholic Church, cocooned themselves in a self-sufficient social community, which operated alongside the Scottish and Glasgow communities.

Archbishop Eyre

It would be impossible to exaggerate the importance of the Roman Catholic Church in the everyday lives of the Glasgow Irish over this period. When Pope Leo XIII restored the Scottish hierarchy in 1878, he appointed Englishman, Charles Petre Eyre the first post-reformation Archbishop of Glasgow. Born in 1817, he was the son of an old Derbyshire noble family which had retained their Catholic beliefs throughout the English reformation. The appointment of a son of the nobility helped to defuse much of the opposition to the restoration of the Scottish hierarchy in Glasgow and helped smoothed the path for the subsequent expansion of Catholic Church infrastructure in the city. The appointment of an Englishman also helped to repair the rift between the feuding Scots and Irish factions within the Scottish Catholic Church. A massive school and church rebuilding programme was instigated and parish reorganisation undertaken. Under Archbishop Eyre, and later the Glasgow Irish's own John Maguire, who succeeded him in 1902, they created a Glasgow Irish society that mirrored that of mainstream society, particularly regarding education, social services and charity. Over 230 priests, very many of them Irish, administered to their flock, forming particularly close ties by tending the sick and identifying with the plight of the poor. To service a flock of some 380,000 Roman Catholics living in Glasgow and Lanarkshire, there were by 1914, ninety-one parishes in the archdiocese with 271 active priests. In 1872, the Established Church of Scotland surrendered responsibility for the education of its youth to the state. Roman Catholics, unable to contemplate the possibility of their children being exposed to Protestant influences, remained outside the state education system, building and maintaining their own schools. By 1914 there were more than 50,000 school children on the rolls of its schools, which employed over 1,200 teachers. Catholics like everyone else paid for education through the local rates, but with the exception of an annual central government grant, money to maintain the schools and to pay for its teachers was paid for directly from the pockets of Scottish Catholics. This militated against the Catholic system's ability to develop much beyond the elementary level and Catholic children were less well taught and less well housed than their Protestant contemporaries. Affordable, private High schools for the small Catholic middle class like Notre Dame High School for girls and St Aloysius for boys were available to those Glasgow Irish who could afford the fees. St Aloysius contributed greatly to the social mobility of the Irish community in Scotland over the course of the middle to late nineteenth century and very many of the Celtic club's founding fathers were educated there. The schools were run by Jesuits,

Marists and the secular clergy, and by a number of orders of nuns, who also ran the teachers' training college at Bearsden. It would be 1918 before the Scottish Education Act, guaranteeing a Catholic education, would see parity of education standards. Catholic organisations also managed a refuge for destitute children, orphanages, hospitals, old people's homes, a deaf-and-dumb institution, hostels for working girls and friendless women, a home for training domestics and two more for rescuing prostitutes. Two industrial schools, Slatefield and St Mary's, and a boys' reformatory at Parkhead took care of neglected or delinquent Catholic children. There was also a centre from which trained nurses went out to nurse the sick poor in their own homes, which like the other charities had its own social context with committees of patrons and lay helpers.

The Roman Catholic Church in Glasgow contributed massively to the spiritual and social well-being of hundreds of thousands of Irish and Scottish Roman Catholics, but for the most part, it, like the Glasgow Irish community itself, was marginalised in the national life of Scotland. Although very many priests and ministers were colleagues on forums such as school boards and many became close personal friends, the politics of the Established Church of Scotland simply could not recognise or involve to any great extent the Church of Rome. This was to such an extent that, with the odd unavoidable event or occasion, such as the death of the Pope, the works of the Roman Catholic Church were seldom reported in the mainstream Glasgow or Scottish press. Of course, considering the dogma of the Victorian Roman Catholic Church itself, it could hardly be described as ecumenical.

In addition to the national newspapers, the Roman Catholic community in Scotland had access to a number of publications aimed specifically at them. Most notably, the Glasgow Observer, which covered Glasgow and its environs, but was also sold nationwide. It's off shoot publication, the Catholic Herald, covered the Catholic communities in Aberdeen, Dundee, Edinburgh, Clydesdale and Lanarkshire. The Glasgow Observer was founded in 1885 by and for the Irish Catholic community in Scotland and among the men who drove the original project through was Celtic founding father Dr John Conway. Mr Charles Diamond, a Derry born Catholic newspaper baron, Irish Parliamentary Party and later Labour Party MP, took over the newspaper in 1887 and by 1894 had become its proprietor. Over the course of the next fifty years the Glasgow Observer would become the principle newspaper of the Catholic Irish in Scotland.

(Courtesy the Scottish Catholic Observer)

As the newspaper's banner suggests, the newspaper was very heavily influenced by the Roman Catholic Church. In addition to the usual outlets, the ethnic community newspaper was sold every Sunday at the back of Catholic chapels nationwide. Although it was sold throughout Scotland, the Glasgow Irish regarded it as their very own. Immensely influential and popular, the weekly broadsheet, published on a Saturday, was seen as representing the Irish Catholic community's interests and contributed greatly to community cohesiveness. The newspaper championed constitutional Irish

Nationalism and its campaigns for Irish Home Rule and land reform. Reflecting the anti-drink policy of the Catholic Church and its strictly teetotal owner, Charles Diamond, the newspaper was staunchly pro-temperance and regularly attacked the Home Government branch for its association with the drinks trade. The at times toxic relationship, would last for more than two decades, resulting in the Home Government branch launching the *Glasgow Star* in 1903 as a direct competitor. The Star absorbed the Glasgow Catholic Examiner and was considerably less parochial, at least to start with. The Star aspired to be the Nationalist and Democratic organ of the Glasgow Irish community and adopted a very distinct socialist slant.

Although, its designation as an Irish Nationalist and Catholic newspaper ensured it was parochial and partisan, the Glasgow Observer quickly developed into a vehicle that helped build bridges across community divides. Reflecting the goals and aspirations of the Glasgow Irish to be accepted by the wider community, it often highlighted and emphasised the respectable Glasgow Irish's civic loyalty and their assumption and acceptance of wider responsibility, particularly with regards to social and welfare matters. Initially, the newspaper was anti-socialist reflecting the Roman Catholic Church's belief that socialism in the fullest sense and Catholicism could not be compatible. However, as early as 1891, under the guidance of left-leaning Charles Diamond, the newspaper made a distinction between the anti-clerical socialism of continental Europe and the Labour movement in Scotland. The Glasgow Irish socialist John Wheatley worked on the Glasgow Observer for a time and used the newspaper as a political platform. By the outbreak of the Great War, the Glasgow Observer had already established itself as the key voice of the Glasgow Irish, highlighting and reflecting on subjects that were of most importance to its readers, but always with an Irish Nationalistic and Roman Catholic slant.

Mr Charles Quin

This is probably a good point at which to introduce the Glasgow Observer's sports and football coverage and its Celtic-minded sports commentator, the *Man in the Know*. Considering that the Celtic club had been formed as a social organisation, the Glasgow Observer took surprisingly little interest in the goings-on at the club for the first four or five years of its existence. The newspaper would periodically carry stories concerning the Celtic, including its AGMs, but with a few exceptions it seldom covered the football games in any great detail. Around the middle of 1893, a trainee journalist called Charlie Quin joined his brother David Mitchel Quin on the staff at the Glasgow Observer. Charlie would remain there as a journalist, sports commentator and news editor for over forty years. Charles Quin was born in 1867 in Pomeroy, Co Tyrone, but in the mid-1870s his family moved to Glasgow where they settled in the Gorbals district. After a period of service as a pupil teacher at St Francis' School in Glasgow, he attended St Mary's Teacher Training College in Hammersmith, London between 1888 and December 1889. Already a keen Celtic supporter, Charlie made his way to the Oval at Kensington to see the bhoys play Corinthians on 16 February 1889. After proclaimed the invincibility of the new Glasgow Irish side to his fellow pupil teachers, he was forced to eat some humble pie when the bhoys were over-run by the Englishmen and beaten by 3 goals to 1.

After qualifying from St Mary's in December 1889, Charlie moved back to Glasgow and quickly gained a position as a probationary schoolteacher at St John's school in the Gorbals. At the time of the national census in April 1891, he and his widowed mother were living in Glasgow's Gorbals district. With his older brother, David Mitchel Quin, already well established as a journalist at the Glasgow Observer, in 1893 Charlie decided to give up teaching to try his hand as a reporter. Charlie's arrival at the Glasgow Observer coincided with the explosion in the popularity of sport and of professional football in particular. Reflecting the growing interest among its readers, from 1894 more and more sporting and football stories were being carried in the Observer. The sports stories were usually short, stand-alone pieces or snippets tucked away in the "Glasgow Gleanings" column, which covered the general mishmash of life in the Glasgow Irish community.

Already known at the newspaper office as a passionate Celtic supporter, Charlie was given the job of covering the 1894 Scottish Cup final in which Celtic faced their old friends Rangers FC. The Celtic were beaten by Rangers by 3–1 and the Glasgow Observer carried a detailed and, for the period, a fairly long, report of the game itself. The match report was factual, fair and unbiased, but in what would become a hallmark of Charlie's reporting style when commenting on the Celtic, as a club supporter he usually managed to find some crumb of comfort or encouragement even in defeat. It was probably Charlie Quin's first serious foray into the world of sports journalism. After the start of the 1894/95 football season, Charlie Quin was asked to contribute to the Glasgow Observer's new, weekly sporting column, "Football and Sporting News". Writing under the nom de plume "The Celt", Charlie's first articles established a proprietary style of writing about the Celtic, where somewhat biased Celtic supporter's concern and interest in what he clearly regarded as his club was discernable in almost every article. In addition to reporting on the football games, Charlie would regularly comment on the politics and management of the club and when it was felt necessary, his column was regularly used to support, encourage, castigate or condemn the Celtic management. In his first article, published on 22 September 1894, the Celt highlighted a lack of charitable donations to the Poor Children's Dinner Tables; three weeks later he returned to the same subject when he hoped that when the club's debt was finally cleared, a big effort would be made to make up the shortfall in donations to the Children's Dinner Tables. The following week he was reporting that a number of charitable requests, including one from the Dinner Tables, had been refused by the Celtic business committee.

For the first few years of carrying sports stories, the Observer, uncertain of exactly how to present the various sporting subjects, tried several different approaches to its coverage. Its uncertainty was reflected in the constantly changing formats and headers tried out at different times: "Football and Sporting Notes", "Scottish Football", "Scottish Sporting Gossip", "Gossip about Sport" and "Sport" and the "Celt's Weekly Letter" were all tried before finally it settled on "Sports and Pastimes". By the beginning of 1897, the "Sports and Pastimes" banner had a subheading entitled "In Celtic Inner Circles" written by the *Man in the Know*. Charlie, probably through his close personal friendship with Thomas E Maley and his family dating from their teaching days, was indeed now in the Celtic inner circle, so much so he was the only non-player or non-committee member allowed to remain in the pavilion when three Celtic players went on strike on 28 November 1896. From that point on, when the newspaper carried stories about the Celtic, they were generally very detailed and at times intimate. Very often the first news of the Celtic was broken through Charlie Quin's *Man in the Know* column and his adjoining "Brevities" of very short related notes.

As the Glasgow Observer's sports column and Charlie's own career at the newspaper developed over the years, Charlie was the main, but not the only sports journalist, who contributed to the Observer's sports column. Very often the sports column, particularly during football's close season, would contain articles with no accreditation. In March 1903, the Home Government branch took over the ailing Glasgow Examiner and launched the Glasgow Star and Examiner. Charlie Quin contributed as the *Man in the Know* to a sports column entitled "Amongst Footballers." He and old Celtic stalwart Johnny Campbell would contribute to the column until August 1908. Charlie Quin's close friend Tom Maley would himself take over the Glasgow Observer's sports column after his *sine die* suspension from English football in 1906. The massively informative "Tom Maley's Notes" ran in both the Glasgow Observer and the Glasgow Star until 1911 when Tom's English football ban was lifted and he went south to manage Bradford Park Avenue. On Tom Maley's departure, Charlie took over the column again and the "In Celtic Inner Circles" by the *Man in the Know* reappeared. In 1914, Charles Diamond appointed Charlie's brother David Mitchel Quin the Managing Editor of the Glasgow Observer. By the outbreak of the Great War, the *Man in the Know* was a sports commentator of international renown, who's inside knowledge of Celtic FC and of football and sport generally was recognised worldwide. After a disastrous fire, which destroyed most of the Celtic's pre-1930 records, the *Man in the Know*'s in-depth and very often emotional articles are a major, though tainted by favouritism, research asset for those wishing to study the Celtic. The Glasgow Observer and the *Man in the Know* would cover the story of the Celtic FC for the next thirty odd years; even after Charlie's death in 1933, the column would continue. Through the distribution of the Glasgow Observer and the Glasgow Star, the triumphs and disappointments of the Celtic club would be carried throughout the Irish diaspora, contributing greatly to the worldwide fame of Celtic FC.

The final two decades of the nineteenth century saw Glasgow's industrial economy at its peak. The city's heavy industries – iron, steel, engineering and shipbuilding – were all doing well, largely, it must be said, on the backs of Glasgow Irish labourers. Glasgow industrialists had a key advantage over other parts of the country when it came to bidding for orders: they paid their unskilled and semi-skilled workforce significantly less than anywhere else, allowing them to undercut their competitors. At this time half of all the men employed in shipbuilding in Britain were working on the river Clyde. The Scottish economy had grown rapidly over the previous thirty years and the wealth of the nation had almost doubled. By the beginning of the 1890s, the Glasgow Irish community had managed to siphon off a little of the wealth, but despite a growing commercial and professional presence, the vast majority remained concentrated in the poorest housing and in casual, low-wage employment. The trickle-down effect of the wider prosperity allowed the Glasgow Irish community, within its own very much lower working class parameters, to thrive. The Glasgow Irish ran hundreds of successful small businesses, particularly for second-hand clothes, cobbling, boot-making, pawnbroking and the spirit trade, where Presbyterian morals allowed them to totally dominate the latter.

Over the second half of the nineteenth century, Scottish and British society developed an association culture, where everyone was a member of some club or organisation supporting some cause or other. The Glasgow Irish increasingly reflected the trend and encouraged by their religious and social leaders, they joined in droves the myriad of Catholic and political associations, societies, confraternities and sodalities which emerged. Women, although they were kept separate, were also becoming involved, joining organisations like the Temperance Society and later the Woman's League for Suffrage. The emerging Glasgow Irish bourgeoisie joined active political organisations like the Irish National League, St Andrew's Young Men's Society, Sinn Fein and the Catholic Socialist Society, where they assumed leadership roles. Many also joined quasi-religious social groups, like the church-led League of the Cross, an organisation that promoted total abstinence. Nearly every parish had its own workingmen's conference of the Society of St Vincent de Paul, which raised £6000 a year for local poor relief. The exclusively Catholic, Ancient Order of Hibernians (AOH) was the bigoted Catholic version of the Orange Order. Seen as the lineal successor of the Ribbonmen of the nineteenth century, in 1883 the Catholic Church issued an official condemnation of the organisation. Anyone identified as being a member could be refused the sacraments, although some priests turned a blind eye. By the turn of the twentieth century, the AOH had cultivated an image of respectability and had morphed into a popular working-class organisation and the Church ban was reversed in 1907. The AOH provided three basic functions: economic, political and social. Economically, it provided social insurance by being a friendly society, while socially, its very many branches ran clubs like flute bands and Irish dancing groups and events like concerts and outings. Women had their own organisations within the Order. Politically, it acted as another arm of the Nationalist Irish Parliamentary Party and in 1909 Joe Devlin Nationalist MP for West Belfast, became head of the Order. Devlin had been born into a working-class family from the Falls Road and moved into politics from journalism after working for a while for the Irish News. Edinburgh-born socialist and Irish Republican martyr James Connolly called them the "Ancient Order of Irish Hooligans". The Irish National Foresters, a politically minded friendly society, claimed over 22,000 members in western Scotland in 1907. There were still others: the Catholic Literary Society, the Catholic Young Men's Society, various dramatic societies and billiards, swimming and football clubs. The driving force behind very many of the organisations was, of course, the Catholic Church. It wanted the migrant Irish to claim their own stake in the wider community by showing that the Catholic community, as a whole, could be responsible and respectable citizens. This could best be achieved by active participation in organisations and associations that contributed to the wider civic society, leading to the Glasgow Irish being accepted as equals in Scottish society.

The British Class System

In order to fully understand the mindset of both the Glasgow Irish and the British people generally in the period prior to the Great War, it is very important to understand something of the structure of the society in which they lived. In the nineteenth and early twentieth centuries, *race hierarchy* and *social class* had become an integral and absolutely fundamental part of British social and political thinking. In a period of rampant nationalism, particularly throughout Europe, a notion of Anglo-Saxon superiority led the English and Germans in particular to believe that they were the superior race among inferior races. Even within Britain itself, there was a very definite pecking order. At the top of the racial pile and regarded as the most *advanced* race was the Anglo-Saxon English, followed by the hybrid Lowland Scots, who were a mix of Anglo-Saxon and Celtic. The Celtic nations were seen as inferior to both, with the

Scottish Highlanders coming before the Irish Celts or Gaels and the rural Irish (Catholic) Gaels at the very bottom – they were regarded as the least developed. Cartoons in the press and magazines of the times often portrayed the Irish as ape-like or as having crude facial features. In the 1860s, the debate among scientists about the relationship between humans and animals prompted British racists to make frequent comparisons between Irish people, black people and apes. The Cambridge historian Charles Kingsley wrote to his wife from Ireland in 1860: "I am haunted by the human chimpanzees I saw along that hundred miles of horrible country... to see white chimpanzees is dreadful; if they were black one would not see it so much, but their skins, except where tanned by exposure, are as white as ours." The Scottish Referee famously carried racist cartoons, depicting a Gaelic Celtic player as some sort of dumb ape-like creature, alongside a caricature of a noble Anglo-Saxon Rangers player. In the same sports paper, published in mid September 1889, the Celtic versus Queen's Park Scottish Cup first round tie was promoted as a Celt versus Saxon clash. The racist cartoons that regularly appeared in the press and popular magazines such as Punch, reinforced the stereotypical view among the general English/British populous that the Irish were by nature lazy, feckless and drunken. Within this race hierarchy, the structure of British society was firmly based on the class system.

The social class – upper, middle or lower – into which a person was born defined much of the remainder of their lives and permeated almost every facet of that person's life. Although definitions of class varied, for the most part each class was based on wealth, education and occupation. Class drove the British, like no other nation in the world. Even today people can still be divided into social classes, upper class, middle class and working or lower class. The class to which you belonged was dictated by how much money, influence and position you held. In addition, at the very top of the British class system was the Royal family and the great aristocratic families. These were the descendants of the old courtiers, who provided the social circle that surrounded the sovereign and were for the most part people born into the old medieval landed families. At the end of the nineteenth century, they and their minor relations or the gentry as they were known, still owned vast tracts of land in family estates. The differentials in wealth were colossal, in 1874 the Duke of Sutherland could drew an income from property of over £56,000; while the Duke of Buccleugh who owned a very large slice of Dumfries-shire could boast an annual income of almost £100,000. The top 1% of society enjoyed a personal income 200 times greater than that of the lowest 30%. In comparison a highly skilled artisan might earn around £78 per annum.

The upper classes, which comprised mostly the wealthiest families, formed the highest tier of society and saw themselves as a social elite. They were people who for the most part inherited wealth and whose families had been wealthy for a number of generations. They could be members of minor landed families or members of very wealthy families whose money came from industry, finance or business. Generally, they were so wealthy they were not required to work since they had private incomes from investments and business. They wielded enormous power and influence both financially and politically. Members drawn from this elite social group occupied all the top positions in the British government, judiciary, business, finance, clergy and the military. Virtually, all political and financial power in Britain therefore rested in the hands of this self-serving, self-perpetuating social matrix. It was from this social group that all other classes drew their codes of conduct and whom they endeavoured to emulate. Because of their power and position, very few examples of their scandals ever became public knowledge. This upper tier of society, alongside the established churches of the home nations – the Anglican Church of England, the Presbyterian Church of Scotland and the Anglican Church of Ireland – were seen as the great pillars of British society, and were commonly termed the British Establishment.

Class tiers existed within the middle and lower classes, with the upper and lower middle classes and the upper and lower working classes. A family considered to be upper middle class in 1900 would have had an average annual income of £750 to £1500. The man of the house was likely to be a merchant banker, judge, senior solicitor, senior physician or a major manufacturer. His household would likely include three to seven live-in servants. A middle-class family would have on average an annual income of around £150 to £500. The man of their house would typically be an office manager, factory manager, small business owner or a head teacher. They might have had a single servant or more likely a woman who came in on a daily basis to clean. A lower- or working-class household would have an income of less, most very much less, than £150 per annum. An artisan or very skilled tradesman might be regarded upper lower class, while a semi-skilled worker such as a carter or semi-skilled labourer in a shipyard would be regarded as just working or lower class.

Even the lowest of the classes was subdivided – into the "respectable" and "unrespectable" working classes. A respectable lower working class man might be an unskilled labourer, regularly in employment, perhaps working with a tradesman. An unrespectable lower working class person would be someone who was usually unemployed and regularly on the *parish*, depending on charity to survive. The family might be dysfunctional, with the breadwinner regularly drunk and in prison, perhaps with their children in care. The unrespectable lower working class were vilified, stigmatised and regarded as parasites by all classes except their own. Today the unrespectable lower working class would be called the "underclass"; a typical member would be someone who is long-term unemployed, living in an inner city housing estate, perhaps a drug addict and totally dependent on state benefits. In times of austerity many of these people are again being seen as unrespectable, and vilified and stigmatised as scroungers.

At the turn of the twentieth century, around twenty-five per cent of the British people were living in poverty. For the most part they could be found in all the major cities of what was at the time the wealthiest nation on earth. At least fifteen per cent were living in abject poverty, at a subsistence level where they had just enough money to feed, clothe and provide accommodation for themselves. An underclass, which made up another ten per cent, could not afford even these basics and could not feed themselves or their children adequately. This underclass depended to a greater or lesser extent on charity (the parish) and often resorted to crime in order to survive. The main cause of poverty was low wages. While the main breadwinner remained fit and in employment, the family could scrape by, but it would only take the main breadwinner to become ill or to lose their job to plunge the family into abject poverty and into the ranks of the underclass. When such a financial disaster struck, a family had few resources to which they could turn for immediate relief. The local pawnshop was usually the first port of call. The first pawnshop opened in Glasgow in 1813 and by 1830 there were thirty. The Glasgow Irish came to dominate the trade simply by the sheer number of the Glasgow Irish forced to turn to them. The ubiquitous three golden balls became an integral part of working class life well into the 1960s. After everything of value had been pawned, the only recourse open to a family in distress was to turn to the extended family. It was the strength of family ties that kept many of the Glasgow Irish from having to resort to the parish.

For the working class, poverty tended to go in cycles. They were born into poverty, in their early working lives they were relatively affluent, then they themselves got married and with young children to support were plunged back into poverty. When their children grew to working age, the family's finances improved again. Finally, when old age arrived it was back into poverty and probably the poorhouse, followed by a pauper's grave pit. In the case of the Glasgow Irish, the pauper's pits were at Dalbeth or St Kentigern's Cemeteries. In 1906, a Liberal government was elected, which introduced free school meals paid for through the rates, old age pensions and formed wages councils, which set minimum wage levels for the very lowest paid workers. In 1910, the first Labour Exchanges where jobs were advertised were set up, and the following year an act established a national insurance scheme for workers in industries prone to frequent lay off. The scheme included short-term unemployment and sickness benefits, which gave those affected some breathing space before have they had to resort to the parish. Prior to the Great War, periods of unemployment tended to be short term and industry specific; however, between 1910 and 1914 despite the industrial unrest, the country had low unemployment rates.

Most of society's socials ills from crime, drunkenness, poverty and promiscuity were largely attributed to failings in man's character. It was therefore seen as being incumbent on an individual to strive to improve himself and his family and to achieve the highest possible personal standards. By doing so he earned the highly desirable badge, irrespective of class, of social respectability. As a result of the Victorian ethic of self-improvement, people at all levels of society aspired to climb in class, while the loss of class was something to be ashamed of and something to be kept secret or hidden. Even at the lowest level of society, the loss of class from respectable to unrespectable was something to be avoided at all costs and people went to enormous lengths to keep up the pretence of class, which personal circumstances dictated they could no longer maintain.

Badges of class and respectability took on various outward signs; for the upper class it was their clipped English accent or it might be travelling first class on the railway or membership of a private club. The middle classes would regard employing at least one full time servant as fitting of their class, while the man of the house would go to a white-collar job wearing a suit, tie and a bowler hat. At the other end of the social spectrum, the badges of the lower classes for men would be wearing hobnailed boots, jacket and cloth cap to work. A working class person would never dream of occupying a first- or second-class carriage on the railways, but would be expected to use the third-class carriage.

Married women of all classes were disenfranchised and remained at home where the house and children were her responsibility. Upper- and upper middle-class wives managed their houses and children through nannies and as many servants the household could afford. Lower-class women, condemned to a life of drudgery and hard toil, looked after their own numerous children and made sure their own windows were clean, the brass-work shined and their front doorstep was whitened. Failure to meet the standards set by her neighbours would result in the loss of face and social standing within her class. A badge of respectability for women was their headdress: upper- and middle-class women would not be seen outdoors without a hat. Respectable lower-class women too could aspire to a hat even if only worn on Sundays or special occasions, but would wear a scarf or turban otherwise. A woman of the lowest working class would not wear any headdress, but might pull their shawl up to cover their heads especially if they were talking to someone they might regard as their social better or when going to Mass. In Glasgow, as a token of derision, such women would be called a *hairy*, a term still in common usage today.

For education, the middle classes endeavoured to send their children to the best schools and the upper middle class would send their children to private boarding schools alongside the children of the upper class. The school that a child attended was very often more important than any academic achievements and nepotism was simply a way of life. A nod from a powerful upper-class backer was enough to open just about any door. From their expensive private schools, upper- and upper middle-class children would aspire to go to university, with Oxford and Cambridge (Oxbridge) the natural choice of the upper class and an aspiration for the middle classes. The people who occupied the very highest and most powerful positions in Britain were almost exclusively Oxbridge graduates, particularly the politicians and the judiciary. Since only the upper and a select few of the middle class could hope to attend Oxbridge, this ensured most of the power and therefore wealth remained with the same ruling elite, most of whom were related by blood or marriage. Lower-class children were educated at state schools and for the most part were taught the basic three Rs and few aspired to further education. Most lower-class children were forced by economic necessity to leave school as soon as officially possible (at fourteen) in order to contribute to the family finances. Exceptionally gifted working-class children depended on receiving a scholarship to progress their education after reaching school leaving age. Scottish Catholic children were educated in their own schools, which remained outside the state system until after the Great War. The quality of their education, in a system that depended on an often financially hard-pressed Catholic community for funding, was variable to say the least. Many of the teachers were gifted Catholic children who became unqualified pupil teachers. The first Catholic Teacher Training College in Scotland was opened at Bearsden, near Glasgow, in 1894.

Each person was expected to know the class to which they belonged and therefore to know their place in society. Upper-and middle-class people were brought up to believe the lower classes were dirty and inferior, although they were prepared to employ them as servants. There were over two million servants in Britain at this time.

It was possible to move between the classes but it became increasingly difficult the higher a person climbed. People were for the most part expected to socialise and to marry into their own class. Common expressions referring to class still in common use today are, *he or she married below or above him or herself and he or she are getting above themselves*. Even after a person climbed in class through talent and hard work, it was often the case that they were never totally accepted by their new class and would never be able to shake off entirely the badges of their previous lower class. The middle class was notoriously jealous of its position within society and often lower-class people who managed to join the middle class were treated with derision and contempt and were better treated by the upper class.

British society and the class system were underpinned by a hierarchical deference to one's social betters. Each class was for the most part highly deferential to the class above and consequently people of whatever class regarded those below them in class as inferior. An example of this was the tradesman's entrance into upper- and some middle-class people's homes where visitors below the class of the owners were required to use a back or side door. The front door of the house was reserved for use by people of the same or a higher class. Another example was the custom of doffing one's cap or for a woman to curtsy to a social superior. The system of class hierarchy in the workplace can be best seen in the staff of a large upper-class household where they ranged in position from the lowly kitchen or scullery maid to the butler, each with their designated place within the household and at the staff dinner table. People of all classes regarded it as perfectly natural to assume that an individual, who occupied a higher class, was simply better than someone in a lower class. It naturally followed that they knew better and their opinions and decisions should be deferred to in most matters.

A Brave New Century

At the start of the new century, the social and cultural ties of the Glasgow Irish to the auld country remained immensely strong. However, significant inroads had and were being made into the wider Scottish community. As Scottish and Glaswegian influences increasingly affected the Glasgow Irish, there was an inevitable degree of ethnic fade. Therefore the children of the Irish immigrants born in Scotland were increasingly establishing emotional and cultural bonds in their own homeland. It was the second and third generations of Glasgow Irish, who, despite the bigotry, racism and poverty, were becoming involved in local politics and taking part in the likes of school boards, standing in parish board elections and participating in various cross-community projects. In 1884, the Representation of the People Acts had doubled the British electorate from 2.5 million to five million men including a half million Irish Catholic voters, but the right to vote continued to be conditional on wealth and property and handicaps were introduced to ensure only the respectable working class qualified. Now sixty per cent of all adult Scottish males could vote including some working-class men, but those on the voter rolls were the city ratepayers, therefore the poorest were still disenfranchised. Since the Glasgow Irish were overrepresented in the poorest paid, unskilled occupations, as a community they were politically underrepresented. In 1911, the enfranchisement rates for three of Glasgow's municipal wards that contained large concentrations of Glasgow Irish were: Cowcaddens 36.8 per cent, Calton 38.9 per cent and the Gorbals 46.6 per cent. The Glasgow Irish accounted for around seventeen per cent of the population of the city, but they still only had around eight per cent of the vote.

Although by the first decade of the twentieth century, the Glasgow Irish were very definitely being drawn into mainstream Glasgow society, they remained firmly lodged at the very bottom of the social ladder. The major reasons for the lack of social mobility were the old favourites, racism and bigotry, although the independent but seriously underfunded Catholic education system was another contributing factor. The Glasgow Irish for the most part could only find work in the unskilled sectors of the job market. Representing around sixteen per cent of the total Glasgow workforce, they were overrepresented as labourers at 32.0 per cent, dockworkers

21.8 per cent, gas workers 27.9 per cent, ironworkers 24.4 per cent and in the liquor trade at 33.5 per cent. In semi-skilled occupations, such as carters, lorry-men and van-men, they accounted for only 7.9 per cent. In the building trade as builders, masons and bricklayers the figure was 8.2 per cent, while as labourers working for these tradesmen they were 47.7 per cent. As would be expected the Glasgow Irish were grossly underrepresented in the professions with only 3.4, 1.7 and 0.2 per cent, respectively, employed in education, medicine and law. The racial discrimination and religious bigotry suffered by the vast majority of the Glasgow Irish ensured they were firmly entrenched on the lowest tier of the British class system. It took very little to tip them from respectable to unrespectable, which helped cement the negative stereotyping from which they already suffered. All that said, the general perception among the Glasgow Irish of the time was that progress was being made and that the Irish were no longer confined *exclusively* to the *low jobs* as was once the case. Glasgow employers were finding that the Irish were capable and reliable and business acumen and self-interest overrode racism and bigotry. Even the Glasgow Observer was moved to comment that in fairness most Glasgow employers were very impartial as to whom they employ. The newspaper regularly carried small biographies of the latest Roman Catholic who qualified as a solicitor or doctor or who had been appointed into a promoted position in the civil service or industry.

Although there was undoubtedly a very distinct "we ourselves" aura about the Glasgow Irish, the notion should not be taken too far. The British people, including those on the island of Ireland and their Glasgow Irish cousins, reacted to their times by joining associations and mass movements – for social welfare, for workers' rights, for the rights of women, for the control of alcohol, for Irish Home Rule, against Irish Home – all of which gave a sense of purpose and belonging in rapidly changing times. By the turn of the twentieth century, there was extensive interaction between the wider Glaswegian populace and the Glasgow Irish, particularly in the workplace, through the various associations and in welfare campaigns like the pro-temperance total abstinence movement. The Celtic's first patron, Archbishop Eyre, spearheaded the Glasgow Catholics' drive towards respectable living and good citizenship through temperance, founding a branch of the League of the Cross in each parish. It was badly needed: between 1871 and 1874, over 126,000 people were arrested for being drunk and incapable. The Irish, of course, had a well-earned reputation for drunkenness, matched only by the Scots themselves. Bridges were also built in local political organisations and trade unions, which crossed traditional religious boundaries. The Rifle Volunteers was another organisation where men of differing religions and none met and worked together, and socialised during and after their duties. Thousands of Glasgow Irish men were members of the part-time military force and in the case of the Garngad district, also known as *Little Ireland*, the local unit was the 8th Bn The Cameronians (Scottish Rifles), based just a hundred metres away in Cathedral Street. The part-time battalion was known as simply the 8th Scottish Rifles and recruited its men mainly from the Garngad, Townhead, Springburn, Calton and Maryhill areas of the city. Such was the make-up of the battalion, it took on a decidedly Glasgow Irish flavour. Neither the Rifle Volunteers nor their successors the Territorial Force (TF) created in 1908 enjoyed a great reputation for their soldierly qualities and they were held in very low esteem by the military authorities, while the general population ridiculed its members as the *Saturday Night Sojers*. However, men of all religious persuasions did train and mix socially while at training camps and some of the regimental loyalty and camaraderie of the regular army did rub off on the part timers.

Most importantly, the absence in Glasgow of complete residential segregation meant some social interaction between communities was inevitable. In fact, poor Irish Catholics and their equally poor Protestant neighbours living cheek by jowl in the slums may have felt they had more in common with each other, than with the middle classes of both religions and ethnicities living in Glasgow's new red sandstone tenements with their wally closes or in the garden villas in the suburbs. This residential mixing created a shared sense of grievance among slum dwellers, whether Catholic or Protestant, and did much to reduce tensions. While the average Protestant and Catholic may not have been drinking buddies or socialised together to any great extent, it is difficult to totally ignore neighbours for long when they share the common experiences of poverty and want. The shared experiences and common humanity undoubtedly brought neighbours of both religions, particularly the women, together in mutual support. It is hard not to feed a neighbour's hungry child alongside your own when you know that you may need that neighbour to feed your own child the following week. In addition, a peaceful life up a mixed religion Glasgow tenement close demanded some basic social pleasantries, although, the more rowdy parties around 12 July or St Patrick's Day would most certainly have caused some periods of *we're no talkin tae thy Orange or Fenian bastards*. By the outbreak of the Great War, the generations of the Glasgow Irish who felt the deepest personal connection to Ireland and who were the most passionate about her causes had largely passed. Despite their passing, many of their Glasgow Irish descendants maintained close family links to the auld country and remained intensely interested in Ireland's well-being. However, despite the close ties, an inevitable degree of ethnic slippage saw the latest generations of Glasgow Irish form a very definite attachment and commitment to Glasgow and Scotland. The resulting dual Scots-Irish identity was one in which most of the Glasgow Irish were completely comfortable and it showed in their increasing participation in the wider community. It is also highlighted in their awareness of and identity to their own social class.

After a struggle of over thirty years, by the summer of 1914 it appeared that the implementation of John Redmond's Home Rule Bill for Ireland was a foregone conclusion. With the holy grail of constitutional Irish Nationalism seemingly achieved, the Glasgow Irish had already begun to turn their full political attention to their own social and economic problems. The social position of the vast majority of the community meant that they were naturally drawn to the socialist policies of the Labour movement and encouraged by the likes of John Wheatley, Willie Gallacher and Patrick Dollan, the Glasgow Irish began increasingly to turn their political attention away from Ireland. Britain was going through the birth pains of a developing democracy, attempting to throw off the last vestiges of a feudal system that saw a small landed elite hold and use political power for the benefit of their own class. As the capitalist and landowning elites fought to preserve their privileged positions, the seething masses of the working class boiled with indignation at the massive differentials in wealth and lifestyles.

By the time of the 1911 national census, 45.6 per cent of the population of Scotland lived in the central belt's industrial areas, while Glasgow was a world metropolis, a renowned industrial colossus, which dominated the world in engineering and shipbuilding and the term *Clyde built* was a byword for engineering excellence. The city had gained wealth and prosperity as a direct result of the union of Parliaments and profits from tobacco, sugar and cotton, then coal mining, textile, iron and the railway industries. By the mid-1870s, the Clyde had replaced the Thames as the centre of British shipbuilding and by 1885 ten Scots firms produced twenty per cent of Britain's steel output. Railway locomotives built by the North British Locomotive Company based in Springburn were sold all over the world and accounted for half of Britain's total production. Overall the Scottish engineering industry employed 78,000 workers. The shipbuilding, railway and heavy engineering industries in Glasgow and the west of Scotland created a new social force, the *industrial working class*. By 1892, two-thirds of all trade unionists in Scotland worked in Glasgow. The city itself was at the centre of an industrial Clydeside conurbation that stretched almost continuously for over fifty miles. Despite the seeming invincibility of British industry, many sectors were in fact in decline and with its reliance on heavy industry, whose markets were largely overseas, the resulting fluctuations in demand produced regular downturns and unemployment. Politically, the city was traditionally a Liberal stronghold but at the turn of the twentieth century the Conservatives and Unionists assumed control of the city council. The Scottish Labour movement had at last begun to gain some traction; the first working-class representatives were elected to the town council in the 1890s and the city got its first Labour MP in 1906. The build-up of armaments in the decade preceding the Great War papered over the cracks in this increasingly outdated economic structure and the underlying social problems were forgotten.

The city and its suburbs were a seething mass of over a million souls, 700,000 of whom were crammed into Glasgow's three central square miles, the densest concentration of people in the whole of Europe. Scotland, like the rest of Britain, was a country marked by deep inequalities in the distribution of wealth. Millions of its people of all religious and political persuasions were condemned to restricted and unfulfilled lives, caught up in a never-ending cycle of toil, poverty and want. The city's lower or working class, was an irreverent ethnic melting pot of Scots Highlanders and Lowlanders, Irish and Glasgow Irish, Jews, Italians, Poles even a few English, a vibrant mix of the godly and ungodly, the former usually only on a Sunday. They lived cheek by jowl, irrespective of race or religious persuasion, in the ubiquitous soot-blackened grey stone tenements laid out in a horseshoe to the north, south and east of the city, very many still in appalling slum conditions. It was a dirty, unhealthy, hard-working and equally hard drinking (there were 1200 pubs in the city in 1912) city of predominately hard-grafting, increasingly militant manual workers, all striving to succeed or at least to survive without having to resort to the parish.

Chapter Two

The Beautiful Idea

The Early Celtic Club

It is widely recognised that the most obvious example of the emergence of the Glasgow Irish into mainstream Glasgow society was their participation in sporting clubs, particularly football clubs. Sport, until the mid-nineteenth century, was the preserve of the upper and middle classes, since they were the only people with the free time and the spare cash to indulge. The upper- and middle-class sportsmen favoured rugby, cricket, lawn tennis and field sports such as hunting and shooting sometimes with horses and dogs. While the upper class took to these pastimes naturally, the middle classes would often struggle to aspire in an effort to emulate their social superiors. The aforementioned is a generality and some of the lower classes may also have participated in any of the sports mentioned. Until the last couple of decades of the nineteenth century, for the most part the working class had little spare time, energy or cash to play any sports. When the working week was shortened and a few pennies became spare, the working classes took to football and the game was soon their passion. By the end of the nineteenth century, the sport of association football had become a previously unseen phenomenon. It was so popular it was termed the "opium for the masses". In the mid-1880s with the working week cut from sixty to fifty-four hours, millions of football-mad men and boys flocked to watch or play in matches held on the newly freed from work Saturday afternoon.

In Scotland, the game of football was controlled by the Scottish Football Association (SFA), which was founded in a temperance hotel in Glasgow in March 1873. The driving force behind the formation was the middle-class sporting gentlemen of Queen's Park Football Club, but other clubs that joined the fledgling association were Clydesdale, Vale of Leven, Dumbreck, Kilmarnock and the Third Lanarkshire Rifle Volunteers. The clubs came together in response to the booming popularity of the game in Scotland and the need to create a controlling body. The most obvious solution was to form an association along the same lines as the Football Association (FA) in England. The early remit of the football associations was that they acted as legislative bodies to oversee the rules of the game, ran their own challenge cup competitions and organised international matches. The association's overriding aim was the promotion of the game of football according to the association rules, and the SFA had practically little to do with individual club fixtures. For the first seventeen years the game in Scotland remained strictly an amateur sport, controlled solely by the SFA and led by middle-class sporting gentlemen. Towards the end of the 1880s the game began to change, transforming from an amateur pastime, into a very lucrative arm of a rapidly expanding mass entertainment industry. As large sums of money became more available in the game, the integrity of the sport and of the amateur sporting gentleman came under pressure. So much so, that in 1887 it was proposed at a general meeting of the SFA that the religious and political affiliations of referees be made public. At this time matches between teams were hit-and-miss affairs, usually organised by their club secretaries. Challenge games, or friendlies as they were known, and local cup competitions dominated the sparse fixture lists, but since there was no central body to organise games, clubs could go weeks without any opponents to play. The premier football competition in Scotland was the Scottish Football Association Cup. Played for annually, the trophy was commonly known as the Scottish Cup. As early as 1873, a consortium of Glasgow merchants put up a trophy with the proceeds of the knockout tournament going to charity. The trophy became known as the Glasgow Merchants Charity Cup and would hold a particular place in the affections of the Celtic club and its supporters. The Glasgow Football Association had been founded in 1883 and they too put up a trophy, which was known as the Glasgow Cup. Both tournaments were open to clubs based in and around Glasgow and both became for a time much sought after prizes, second only to the Scottish Cup itself.

In response to public demand for more football games, the need for a structured, regular programme of football matches became obvious. Representatives of the leading Scottish football clubs meet in the Commercial Hotel, Glassford St, in Glasgow on 20 March 1890 to discuss the question of organising league matches. The result of the meeting was the formation of the Scottish Football League, which was inaugurated at the end of April 1890. Although an autonomous body and totally separate from the SFA, the members of the Scottish League were still required to be members of the Association and recognise the primacy of the SFA. The Scottish Football Challenge Cup remained the premier competition, while club players chosen to represent their country in international matches were required to play, irrespective of the pressures of league football. The first league fixtures were played in August that year and after a shaky start, the league took off, proving to be a great and enduring success. Three years later, following England's lead, professionalism was introduced into the Scottish game and at the same time the league split into two divisions. The birth of the professional game came in response to a general demand for recreation. The British working classes had found themselves with a free Saturday afternoon after the working week was cut to fifty-four hours and with a few extra pennies in their pockets to spend on something other than food, clothes and rent. By the turn of the twentieth century, association football had come to be regarded by the middle and upper classes as very much a *working-class* pastime as they watched millions of working-class men flock to support their chosen teams every Saturday afternoon during the football season. For most working-class young men, football was a dream factory where for ninety minutes they left the drudgery of their existences behind at the turnstiles to fantasise of someday emulating their footballing heroes, themselves working-class lads who had escaped the pits or the mills to enjoy the big wages and adulation of a professional footballer.

At all levels of the game, teams were entering competitions and playing numerous friendlies among themselves. Through the sport, teams and their supporters interacted with each other both on and off the pitch. Match results and the performance of individual players and teams gave working-class men a common interest and brought them together, particularly in the workplace, to discuss the games and results. Unlike other sports, which required a special ground or equipment, football at the grass-roots level could be played in the street or backcourts with just a ball or tin can and a couple of jackets for goalposts. The kids were mad for the game and canny headmasters encouraged regular attendance by buying footballs and giving them out as prizes. A ball was a major investment for a school: a leather ball cost around six shillings with a top quality hand-sewn one in the region of ten shillings. Just about every community and organisation produced football teams, which played at every level of the game from a kick-about in the street, to games for school boys, juniors, amateurs and by the mid-1890s professionals. Schools, public houses, factories, mills and military units produced their own teams. Hundreds of football teams were formed in a flush of enthusiasm only to disappear as the keenness for the team faded. By the late 1880s, it is reckoned that one in four males in central Scotland was a member of a football club. The Glasgow Irish fielded well over a dozen teams just at the schoolboy, juvenile and junior levels and most of the teams reflected their Irish origins in their chosen names: Townhead Emerald, Whifflet Shamrock from Coatbridge, Croy Celtic, Govan Hibs, Kirkintilloch Harps, Kilsyth Emmet, Wishaw Hibernian, Govan and Cambuslang Hibernian, to name but a few. In addition to junior teams, the Irish who settled on the east coast of Scotland produced two senior teams, Hibernian in Edinburgh and Dundee Harps, later known as Dundee United. Until 1893 and the introduction of professionalism, the teams playing at the top level of the game in Scotland were amateurs; players and officials were not paid salaries but players were paid expenses and for time off work if injured during a game. In the early days of the game, football was very much a contact sport with shoulder charging and waist-high tackling the norm. Such was the regularity of serious injuries that the General Accident and Employers Liability Assurance Company offered an insurance policy for footballers killed within three years of sustaining an attributable injury while playing football.

More often than not the Scots Irish football clubs were founded or supported financially by the priests of their local Roman Catholic parishes. As far as the Roman Catholic Church was concerned, football and other sporting clubs served a number of purposes. They provided a pastime that absorbed the youthful energies and enthusiasms of young men; they kept them under the priest's watchful eye at a time when proselytisation was a major concern and they allowed the priest to maintain some influence over his flock while they were increasingly coming into contact with outside, Protestant influences. In addition, membership of sporting clubs helped young men develop their bodies at a time when the health of the British working class in general was shockingly bad. Over forty per cent of young men applying to join the army could not pass the basic medical examination. The Hibernian Football Club, founded in 1875 by the Irish Catholic community in Edinburgh under the guidance of Irish cleric, Canon Edward Hannan, was the most successful of the early Catholic clubs. Membership of the club was originally open only to practising Roman Catholics and was so overtly Irish and so closely associated with the Irish Home Rule movement during the early 1880s, that when the club first applied to join the Scottish Football Association they were denied membership because they were not Scottish enough. However, as early as 1888, the Hibernians were protesting that the club was open to members and players of all denominations and could cite a couple of examples of Protestant players who had turned out for the club.

A key date in the history of the Glasgow Irish community is 12 February 1887. On that day the Hibernian team of Roman Catholics won what was Scottish football's blue ribbon prize, the Scottish Football Association Cup. Hibernian's Scottish Cup success electrified the Irish throughout Scotland including, of course, the Glasgow Irish. Messages of congratulations poured into Hibernian, among them one from the St Mary's Young Men's Society signed by its chairman James Curtis and another from the Home Government Branch of the Irish National League signed by Mr Hugh Murphy. Immediately after Hibernian's Scottish Cup victory at Hampden Park, the club's Glasgow Irish supporters organised a post-match celebration at St Mary's Hall situated in the massively deprived Calton district of Glasgow. At St Mary's the Hibernians' celebration dinner was chaired by local hero, Glasgow Irishman Dr John Conway MD, and the convivial atmosphere, encouraged some guid owld Oirish craic. Someone, reputedly the Hibernian's club secretary John McFadden, suggested that Glasgow should have its own version of Hibernian. Listening intently in the audience were two Marist Brothers Walfrid and Dorotheus, headmasters of Sacred Heart and St Mary's Schools, John Glass, James McKay, John O'Hara, William McKillop, James Quillan and Patrick Welsh all principal Catholic laymen of the East End. At the end of the month, the Hibernian team and staff were invited back through to Glasgow where they were the guests of John Ferguson, Hugh Murphy and the Home Government branch of the Irish National League. In recognition of the club's Scottish Cup victory, the players were each presented with a gold medal by the branch members. Among those present on the night and who would have a future connection to the Celtic club were: Tom Maley, Jerry Reynolds, James Quillan, John H McLaughlin, John O'Hara, Joe McGroary, James McKay and Pat Gaffney.

The Hibernian had on a number of previous occasions played charity games in the city for the benefit of their Glasgow Irish cousins. In another generous gesture they agreed to play Renton FC for the East End Catholic Charity Cup after the current football season finished. True to their word, on 28 May, the Hibernians, or Hibs as they were also known, played Renton at Barrowfield, the ground of Clyde FC. The match was played in front of 12,000 spectators and on behalf of the Poor Children's Dinner Tables run by the Conferences of the St Vincent de Paul Society of St Mary's and Sacred Heart parishes. The game ended in a hard fought 1–1 draw but the replay contested at the beginning of August, saw Renton slaughtered the Hibs by 6–0. Future Celtic hero Neillie McCallum scored five of Renton's goals. The event organisers included Brother Walfrid, Joseph A Foy, a Bridgeton publican and John Glass a local foreman glazier. Brother Walfrid noted with great wonderment and increasing interest the number of people who would actually pay money to watch a game of football. After winding up the accounts of the game, the kernel of an idea formed in the fertile mind of the Irish born headmaster. Previous charity games including one just finished had been played on the grounds of established football clubs that had given the use of their parks gratis. Brother Walfrid's idea was that if possible, a suitable field should be procured as a recreation ground for the school children, and at the same time be the venue of charity matches played from time to time in aid of the St Vincent de Paul Society. A committee was duly formed to bring the recreation field project to fruition.

As the weeks passed Brother Walfrid joined the dots in his own mind and began to come up with a much bigger plan, he discussed his idea with his close friend Dundee-born Brother Dorotheus. The idea was, of course, a football team, but this team would be different: it would be formed by gathering together the best Roman Catholic players in the west of Scotland, its remit would be to play games explicitly in aid of Catholic charities. Any monies raised by the team would, after expenses, be specifically but not exclusively given over to the St Vincent de Paul Society's Poor Children's Dinner Tables. The dinner scheme provided one hot meal per day at the nominal cost of a penny to deprived and hungry children. The scheme was desperately needed and was already well established in the church missions in St Mary's and St Michael's and in Brother Walfrid's own Sacred Heart and had proved to be massively successful. The scale of child neglect in the wealthy Victorian city was staggering. Thousands of children were taken into care every year and placed into orphanages, industrial schools, day schools, training ships or placed under the care of the School Board. The urgency and scale of the problem in the east-end is further highlighted by the fact that in the month of December 1887, the Poor Children's Dinner Table missions fed 53,147 meals to hungry Glesga weans, not all of whom were Roman Catholic.

Given the aim of the football team, it was important that it be an immediate success on the field and a team that would attract the interest and support of the Roman Catholic community throughout Glasgow. To that end, the new football team would endeavour to emulate the Hibernian's success by casting its net wide when recruiting players and would not depend solely on local players and local support. The key to success was to form a football team using established, well known players, who would be capable of attracting large crowds of paying spectators immediately, therefore only the best available players, playing attractive, entertaining football would suffice. Having convinced each other that the idea had some merit, the two Marists threw themselves wholeheartedly into the project. They realised that the potential rewards, both financial and social, of a Glasgow Irish football team being successfully established and going on to emulate anything like the success of the Hibernian was potentially enormous.

The brothers kicked the idea around the parish and beyond for a few weeks, endeavouring to gauge and muster support for their project. Selling the idea was something of an uphill struggle; the sight of the clergy trying to put together funds and muster support for a football team was not an unusual one. In the past the community had donated time, effort and money, but all previous attempts at sustaining and maintaining teams had failed, including Walfrid's own Eastern Rovers team, usually through lack of organisation and on going commitment. The problem was trying to convince the sceptics that this team would be more than a just another one of a score of such teams doomed to failure. They received some added impetus for their scheme from a heated debate then on going in the newspapers regarding the distribution of funds from the Glasgow Merchants Charity Cup football competition of 1887. In June, a Mr James MacCardle complained in an open letter to the press that despite a purely Catholic football club (Hibernian) being the means of drawing more than one fourth of all the proceeds of the charity matches (£1200), plus the fact that one half of the gate money at the Hibernian versus Renton game was received from Catholic spectators, not a single penny from the competition was given to Catholic charities. He asked whether it was thoughtlessness or bigotry.

Brother Walfrid adopted something of a pragmatic approach to the problem of mustering community support for his project. He cast his net outwith the confines of a single parish in which such a scheme would usually find itself restricted to and employing his famous powers of persuasion, he convinced the massively influential Glasgow Irish politician Hugh Murphy, then second only to John Ferguson himself, at the Home Government branch of the Irish National League to lend his support. The men then persuaded two well-known Catholic personalities, Dr John Conway, a local medical practitioner, and Joseph Shaughnessy, a high-profile, Glasgow Irish solicitor from nearby Rutherglen, to throw their considerable weight behind the project. John Glass who worked alongside Brother Walfrid on the Hibernian/Renton committee back in May was a very close friend and political ally of Hugh Murphy and needed little persuasion to come on board. Also persuaded to get involved were a number of politically and socially aware parishioners, some of who were former pupils of Walfrid. The two Marist brothers also showed they were willing to *sup with the devil* by extracting the promise of financial support from a number of the local bar owners and spirit merchants. This move would have raised some eyebrows, since personal health and respectability, promoted largely through the Church-sponsored temperance movement, and the disreputable drinks trade were not easy bedfellows. However, this strategy of getting the wider Glasgow Irish community involved would be the key to the success of the venture. Over the autumn, representatives of St Mary's, St Andrew's and St Alphonsus and the St Vincent de Paul Society held a number of large and boisterous meetings in St Mary's Hall where all aspects of the proposal were discussed, including the name of the club. As the weeks passed, the scheme began to come together and by the late autumn it had morphed from a recreation ground, to a football team to a football and athletics club. The football and athletic club concept, it was decided, would cover more Catholic touchstones, involve more young men and would be more of a community asset.

Finally, on Sunday, 6 November 1887 after Mass, a meeting was held in St Mary's League of the Cross hall situated at the rear of 67 East Rose Street to finally decide whether to form a club or not. Once described as *a mean little hall*, it was reached by passing from East Rose Street, through an alleyway called *Irish Wynd*. In the event, they decided a club would be formed, and on that date the Celtic Football and Athletic Club was born.

A committee was elected and a club constitution agreed. The club would be a democratic, membership-based organisation with each member having a single vote. The club members would vote for a committee at an annual meeting and that committee would run the club for

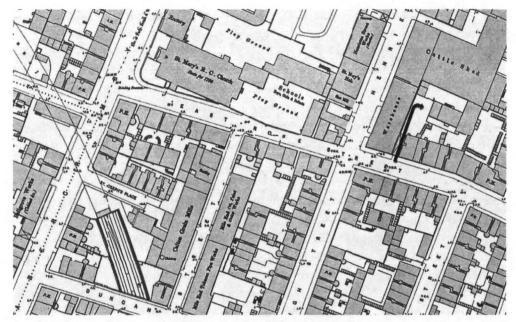

Birthplace of Celtic at 67 East Rose Street

the next year. It was further agreed that any profits from the football games played by the team would help maintain the Poor Children's Dinner Tables. Once the decision to launch the football and athletic club was taken, the committee composed of representatives of each of the three parishes was tasked with taking the project forward. Within a week progress had been made; subscriptions were sought, promises of support were called in. The recreation ground already identified and leased for five years by the committee back in October was chosen as the location for the first Celtic Park. The rent had been set at £20 pa but before the lease could be signed it was raised to £50. The park at the junction of Dalmarnock Street and Janefield Street, adjacent to the Eastern Necropolis, had already been used as a football ground by the then defunct Oxford (Glasgow) FC.

By the beginning of 1888, after a number of disagreements between the parish representatives, the club committee had solidified with the representatives of St Mary's appearing to have taken effective control of the project, although a small cabal of St Andrew's representatives remained on board. Once the office bearers had settled into their tasks, subcommittees responsible for the park, team, finance and matches were formed. In addition to Brothers Walfrid and Dorotheus, who occupied honorary positions on the various subcommittees, the following individuals emerged as office bearers: Dr John Conway, who chaired the celebration dinner for Hibernian, was appointed honorary president; foreman glazier, John Glass, was appointed president; James Quillan, a successful east end businessman owning several cooperages, was appointed vice-president; John O'Hara, a cobbler and trade union activist, was appointed club secretary and the post of treasurer was given to twenty-eight-year-old Hugh Darroch, a local pawnbroker.

The main characters who made up a boisterous committee were John H McLaughlin, a university-educated, leather manufacturer's clerk; James McKay, a local hairdresser; Patrick Welsh, master tailor and former Fenian activist; crusading solicitor Joseph Shaughnessy; Daniel Molloy, an ironmonger's traveller; Joseph F McGroary, a recently qualified solicitor and associate of Joe Shaughnessy; John C. McDonald, a steam engine fitter and athletics supporter from Springburn and Michael Cairns, yet another law agent and close friend of Dr Conway. Representing St Andrew's parish on the committee were: Joseph M Nelis, a local pawnbroker and parochial board member; John A MacCreadie, the eldest son of a famous Glasgow Irishman; Dominick MacCreadie, the owner of the Old Empire Bar in the Saltmarket. These men were all brought together for the charitable cause, but they were not strangers to each other; some had been schoolmates, most were now community leaders and had worked together in political and or religious groups. Indeed John Conway, John H McLaughlin, Joseph Shaughnessy and Joseph F McGroary were all old St Aloysius College boys, while John Conway, John MacCreadie, Joe Nelis, Joseph McGroary and Michael Cairns were all former pupils at St Mungo's Academy. In addition to being members of St Andrew's parish, Nelis, and MacCreadie were members or former members of the Caledonian Catholic Association. In fact, most of the main characters involved in founding the club and the early years of its development formed a complex matrix of inter-related family, social, professional and political connections.

While the park subcommittee under convenor Mr John Brien, a local Catholic builder, set about addressing the problem of converting a recreation ground into a top flight football stadium, another subcommittee, led by John Glass, set about creating the first football team. However, there was a caveat: the new team would have no time to develop or evolve; it was required to be an immediate success. This stipulation led to the Celtic committee's infamous and distinctly shady recruiting and more importantly retaining practices, operated in the main by John Glass and John O'Hara. Their actions were facilitated by the supposed amateur status of the Scottish game and the highly dubious system of the paid amateur it encouraged. With all that in mind, in late November or early December, Brother Walfrid, John Glass and Pat Welsh took a trip out to the Lanarkshire village of Cathcart, where they hoped to persuade Catholic schoolmaster Tom Maley to get involved in the project. Tom was already an established footballer having turned out for the military team the Third Lanarkshire Rifle Volunteers, Partick Thistle and the Hibernians and was something of a local personality in the game. Tom Maley had been on the platform back in February when the Hibernians had been presented with their medals by the Home Government branch and it was his personal contacts within the game as much as his footballing prowess the visitors were interested in. The Celtic deputation wanted Tom to compile a hit list of top, west of Scotland players who would be willing to turn out for the new club. The Maley family were Glasgow Irish and already well known in the district, where the father, Sergeant Thomas Maley, a retired regular army sergeant, was now employed as a drill instructor with the Rifle Volunteers. Although the deputation really wanted to talk to Tom, he was out courting when they arrived, but his younger brother Willie was at home. Willie was really more into athletics than football but he also had turned out for the Third Lanark side and for his local village football team. In the event, both brothers were persuaded to join the project and it was a defining moment for the Celtic club. Both men would become hugely influential figures in the history of the Celtic, Tom as a player, office bearer and committeeman, and Willie as a player, match secretary, future manager and club legend. Tom Maley would many years later describe, sitting night after night in the old League of the Cross hall under the chairmanship of Dr Conway, going through lists of names attempting to build the team. During which time JH McLaughlin sat at an old, badly tuned piano trying to keep them entertained. If John Glass started to sing, that was the sign that it was time to go home.

Association football in Scotland was then officially amateur, with players only to be paid reasonable expenses and for time off work. As amateurs, none of the players were attached by legal contracts to specific clubs; however, in the days of gentlemanly conduct, a man's word was his bond and a gentleman's agreement or promise carried a good deal of weight, but only up to a point. To turn out for a club in a cup competition was enough to tie a player to that club for the remaining games of that year's cup competition, but other than in that cup, players were free to play for whichever team they chose. Although players were officially amateurs, there was an undercurrent of professionalism and working-class players were becoming increasingly aware that they could get paid, albeit by sleight of hand, for their skills and that a good living could be had from the game. With the game in England already allowing professionalism, the major English clubs regularly conducted forays into the Scottish game, enticing Scots players south with promises of wages the working classes could only dream of.

At the end of December 1887, Brothers Walfrid and Dorotheus decided the club needed some heavyweight support, both to advertise the project and to rally the wider Glasgow Catholic community to the cause. They got both the nod of approval and a blessing from Englishman, Archbishop Charles Eyre of Glasgow, who agreed to be the club patron. The Archbishop also contributed a twenty-shilling subscription fee.

In January 1888, the following statement was released:

> **CELTIC FOOTBALL AND ATHLETIC CLUB** *Celtic Park, Parkhead (Corner of Dalmarnock and Janefield Streets)*
>
> *Patrons His Grace the Archbishop of Glasgow and the Clergy of St Mary's, Sacred Heart and St Michael's Missions, and the principal Catholic laymen of the East End.*
>
> The above Club was formed in November 1887, by a number of Catholics of the East End of the City. The main object is to supply the East End conferences of the St Vincent de Paul Society with funds for the maintenance of the 'Dinner Tables' of our needy children in the Missions of St Mary's, Sacred Heart and St Michael's. Many cases of sheer poverty are left unaided through lack of means. It is therefore with this principal object that we have set afloat the 'Celtic' and we invite you as one of our

ever-ready friends to assist in putting our new Park in proper working order for the coming football season.

We have already several of the leading Catholic football players of the West of Scotland on our membership list. They have most thoughtfully offered to assist in the good work.

We are fully aware that the "elite" of football players belong to this city and suburbs, and we know that from there we can select a team which will be able to do credit to the Catholics of the West of Scotland as the Hibernians have been doing in the East.

Again there is also the desire to have a large recreation ground where our Catholic young men will be able to enjoy various sports which will build them up physically, and we feel sure we will have many supporters with us in this laudable object.

Any subscriptions may be handed to any of the clergy of the three Missions or to the President Mr John Glass, 60 Marlborough Street, Glasgow. Dr John Conway, 14 Abercromby Street, Glasgow, or to Mr J. O'Hara, 77 East Rose Street, Glasgow, or to any member of the committee, and the same will be gratefully acknowledged in course.

In response to the appeal from the Archbishop of Glasgow, the Catholic community of the East End rallied to their religious leader's call. A unique bond formed between the club and supporters as the Glasgow Irish community became deeply involved with and emotionally connected to the Celtic project right from the start. With funds tight, the people contributed a few desperately needed pennies into the plate at Mass or put in a few hours hard graft at the building site for the new park, encouraged no doubt from the pulpits of the parishes that would benefit from the venture were it to succeed. So the supporters dutifully provided their muscle and sweat, and toiled to create the Celtic club's first football ground. Many turned out after having laboured all day in physically demanding jobs or gave up their few precious hours of free time on a Saturday afternoon or on Sunday after Mass. Others, the very many unemployed or under-employed, had much more energy and time on their hands to help. In the days before earth-moving machinery, they dug with pick and shovel, carried the spoil in wheelbarrows, flattened and rolled the pitch, built the terrace banking with the excess spoil and erected fences. They even built a main stand that could accommodate a thousand spectators, beneath which was changing rooms for players and officials. Finally, they erected the goalposts and ran a flag, white with a green crossbar, up the flagpole. They then stood back to admire their handiwork and it was indeed something to behold and something the Glasgow Irish could be very proud of. After a Herculean effort, they had created from a piece of almost waste ground, a first-class football park in just five cold, wet winter months.

Brother Walfrid's Weans

(Glasgow City Museums)

By the beginning of May 1888, the new ground at Parkhead was ready for its first match and on 8 May the Hibernian travelled through to Glasgow to fulfil a promise Canon Hannan had made to Brother Walfrid, that the Hibernian would formally open Celtic Park. The game was against Cowlairs, a team from Glasgow's Springburn district and based largely on the massive railway works of the same name. On a chilly Tuesday evening, a crowd of 5000 spectators, including Brothers Walfrid and Dorotheus, watched Dr Conway and Joseph Shaughnessy lead the teams onto the park. The doctor then placed the ball on the centre spot for the first time amid the cheers of the spectators. The match ended in a 0–0 draw but it was a highly entertaining one for all that. The depleted coffers of the new Glasgow Irish club benefitted greatly from gate receipts from which the Hibernian agreed to waive their own expenses. Although the game ended in a scoreless draw, everyone was pleased with the spectacle and well impressed with the stadium; everyone that is except the owner of the ground on which the stadium was built, Roxburghshire farmer, Mr Alexander Waddell. He'd let the ground to the club as a recreation park for school children, and the odd game of football, now there was a lumping great football stadium on his land. He let the club know that he was very unhappy with the alterations, and he was considering court action. Joseph Shaughnessy, representing the Celtic committee, let him know that the club would raise a counter writ and the matter was quickly dropped, but ominously not forgotten.

After the game the officials and players attended a social function in the Royal Hotel on Glasgow's George Square. Although there are some obvious absentees like John Glass and Brothers Walfrid and Dorotheus, the list of Celtic officials supporting Dr Conway, who presided at the function, is probably the clearest indication of the personalities involved in the Celtic project at the time. They included Messrs Shaughnessy, JF McGroary, McGallagley, J McKay, Chas Campbell, WF O'Brien, Jas Quillan, H Darroch, O'Hara, TE Maley, W Maley, Pat Glass, W McKillop, Curtis, Welsh, D Blayney, H Blayney, D Molloy, McLaughlin, Green, Gaffney, Gines, McDonald, Dolan, Vaughan, McHugh, M Rogers, J Rogers, Kilpatrick, Shannon, Curtis, McFadyen, Connell and Doyle. The Celtic committee were still trying to put together their team and unfortunately for the Hibernian club, a number of their players were on the target list. Amidst the celebratory atmosphere at the Royal Hotel that afternoon, the Hibernian hierarchy either had a premonition or had picked up vibes or rumours regarding the Celtic's interest in their players. In reply to Dr Conway's toast to the Hibernian, an uneasy John McFadden declared: "It would be a sad day for the Irish in Scotland when residents in one city would act in an unfriendly way towards those in an other." Tom Maley, sitting among his former Hibernian teammates, toasted "The Celtic!" Unknown to Hibernian, Tom Maley and John Glass had previously spoken to players James McLaren, John Coleman, Mick Dunbar, Pat Gallagher, Willie Groves and Mick McKeown, all of whom were sitting in the audience having just christened the new Celtic Park by playing for Hibernian. They would all be playing in Celtic colours at the start of the new football season come August, having succumbed to John Glass's gift of the gab and the weight of his wallet. Renton FC, another of Scotland's top teams, was also raided and their captain and Scotland internationalist James Kelly and star striker Neil McCallum were also secured for the Celtic.

For the most part, the power brokers at Celtic got around the amateur status by skimming gate receipts and buying their star players licences for public houses from which they obtained an income unrelated to football. An amazing array of Celtic players suddenly developed a previously unheld business interest in the wine and spirit trade. It should be carefully noted that the vast majority of the senior Scottish clubs engaged to a greater or lesser degree in the same shady practices, including Hibernian themselves, who were at the time of the Celtic raid, in the process of trying to entice Scottish internationalist James Kelly away from Renton. Celtic's early success was undoubtedly down to illegal payments and inducements to players. The only difference between the Celtic and other clubs was the number of players, the sums involved and the intensity of the effort. The raid by Celtic would have disastrous consequences for the Hibernian, who saw the heart torn out of their team. That John McFadden later allegedly absconded to America with all their funds did not help and the club effectively went out of operation for three years.

That the final spark that ignited the idea of a Celtic football club came at a social event should come as no surprise. Sporting conviviality was an essential part of male-dominated Victorian sport in general and the game of football in particular. So much so, the sporting publication the Scottish Referee from its inception in 1888 including a column called *The Social*

Circle, where the various club smokers, concerts, soirees, after game suppers and club parties were highlighted. In fact, in some ways the social reputation of a club was as important as its sporting prowess or success and more than one club went to the wall after over spending on their social budget. Most sporting clubs had their own offshoots of musical, choral, dramatic, cycling; snooker and golf groups and Celtic would be no different. Indeed, at the time it was considered that one of the main functions of any good sporting organisation was its ability to encourage sociability where manners and gentile behaviour could be encouraged or if necessary taught. After game teas and suppers, where players and officials socialised, were the norm and after major games like cup finals, the socials were elaborate affairs with after dinner speeches, toasts and replies, all conducted in a very formal setting. This social side of the game helped people from different social and political backgrounds mix with the classic example being John H McLaughlin, future Celtic vice-president and chairman, who regularly played the organ at Rangers FC events, while the Rangers Musical Society reciprocated in kind. The St Patrick's Day soiree of the Catholic Literary Society of 1891 saw Rangers musicians on the bill and accompanying John H McLaughlin in the "Wearing O' The Green" and "Comrades in Arms". For the ordinary Celtic supporters after the game, it was probably back to the social club, Hibernian hall or pub where the merits of the respective players and teams were discussed. Although first thoughts of football supporters and pubs may be ones of drunkenness and rowdyism, a very significant amount of literature in the form of poetry and song emanated from such establishments. The connection between football, sociability and public houses can also be seen in the close association between football players and public houses. Many players, particularly Catholic players, saw the ownership of a public house as a means of social mobility and a vehicle that allowed them to prolong their fame and popularity after their playing days were over. While several players made the transition from player to full-time publican very successfully, for others it led to their ruin. The practice was often commented on. As early as 1890 the Scottish Sport newspaper commented, "The Celtic club dispenses with the lily hand of charity succour to the sick and proportion to the poor; on the other hand it watches indifferently, if it does not encourage, its young men throwing themselves recklessly into a business of which every tendency is towards moral ruin." The paradox that was abstinence and temperance and the liquor trade in which so many officials and players at Celtic would later become involved would prove to be uncomfortable bedfellows.

On Monday 28 May, a Celtic team played their first game against the Glasgow Rangers reserves, also known as the *Swifts*. Before the game the club officials agreed that it would be regarded as *unofficial* and would not be counted towards the total statistics at the end of the season. Prior to the start of the football league, the only way teams could measure themselves against each other over the course of the season was to total up victories, draws and losses over all games played. The first Celtic team was, in fact, a select side of players that had been brought together specifically for the occasion. The guest players' clubs may or may not have been aware that the Celtic committee was targeting a number of their players. The players Celtic was targeting were largely based in the west of Scotland and a new first-class team based in

Glasgow would in itself be an attractive proposition for them. Those guest players interested in joining the new set-up, but still undecided, took the Swifts game as an opportunity to see exactly what would be on offer at Parkhead. As far as the Celtic committee was concerned, the game would both bring in some much needed cash and allowed the committee to see the potential new Celts in action. At the top of the Celtic's hit list was the famous James Kelly, the Renton FC star, who was playing for the current Scottish Cup holders and newly crowned World Champions. A week earlier, Renton, based in the Dunbartonshire village of the same name and led by Kelly, had beaten the mighty West Bromwich Albion, the English FA Cup holders to claim the astounding title. James Kelly was born in the village to Irish parents and was the football superstar of his day. If the Celtic could persuade the Scotland internationalist to join them, it would send out a very powerful message of intent and encourage others to take notice of the new outfit. Other Celtic targets in the select team were: Neillie McCallum, born in Dumbarton of Irish parents, another Renton player whose goals had helped them win the Scottish Cup; Mick Dunbar, born in Cathcart and living in Busby, Renfrewshire, and turning out for the Hibernian; James McLaughlin, born in the north of Glasgow at Springburn, mostly associated with local team Cowlairs, but who had just spent a season at Hibernian; and John Madden, born in Whiteinch and at the time working as a riveter in the shipyards. He was a key player and a great favourite at Dumbarton FC. It was John Madden who led the line for the Celtic that first game against the Rangers Swifts. On that fateful day in May 1888, the pride of the Glasgow Irish, Celtic, turned out for the first time resplendent in their new colours of white shirts with a green collar and a Celtic cross in red and green on the left breast. The shirts were a donation from Penman Bros., a large drapers and clothiers shop situated at Bridgeton Cross as their contribution to a local good cause. The team on the day was; Mick Dolan (Drumpellier), Edward Pearson (Carfin Shamrock), James McLaughlin (Govan Whitefield), Willie Maley (Cathcart), James Kelly (Renton), Phil Murray (Cambuslang Hibs), Neil McCallum (Renton), Tom Maley (Cathcart), John Madden (Dumbarton), Mick Dunbar (Hibernian) and Charlie Gorevin (Govan Whitefield).

Over 2000 spectators watched the match, which ended in a 5–2 victory for the Celtic. Neillie McCallum scored Celtic's first ever goal with a header in from a corner kick. James Kelly got a second and Tom Maley got the Celtic's first ever hat-trick, his last goal laid on by Neillie McCallum. The Rangers had reputedly only played a few of their regular first team; it was the first and last time they would ever underestimate the Celtic. At six pence a head, a gate of 2000 was a good crowd; however, a large proportion was women and priests who were admitted for free. Still, it was a good result and a very encouraging start, but most encouraging was the fact that James Kelly agreed to throw his lot in with the Celtic. Such was Kelly's personal reputation he was immediately handed the club captaincy and almost certainly a very large and quiet illegal financial inducement. With James Kelly on board, most of the Hibernian players made their move and joined the Celtic, as did Neillie McCallum and Mick Dolan. John Madden remained undecided, first he said yes, then was dissuaded by Dumbarton, but finally joined the Celtic the following season. Many years later Willie Maley emphasised the importance of capturing James Kelly when he commented, "no Kelly, no Keltic". As expected the social aspect of the game was observed when immediately after the match the players, officials and selected club members of both Celtic and the Rangers Swifts retired to St Mary's Hall where they treated themselves to a slap-up supper and a concert.

The new football team played a series of challenge games over what would normally be regarded as the close season for football as they tried to put together a side for the opening of the 1888/89 football season in August. At this point in time there was no Scottish League set-up and fixtures were a series of matches organised by the club match secretaries themselves and often free weekends when teams had no opponents to play were advertised in the sporting press. It was important for the Celtic club to play as many games as possible in order to establish credibility for the team and a reputation of reliability for the club prior to the commencement of the new football season. On 21 August 1888, the Celtic Football and Athletic Club was just one of a number of clubs that successfully applied to join the Scottish Football Association.

Season 1888/90

The Celtic entered into their first full football season with a new but very experienced team, comprising much of the inspirational cup-winning Hibernian team. In mid-October, the Celtic went through to Easter Road, home of the now financially failing Hibernians, to play a friendly game. As might be expected, the Celtic got a very frosty reception from the Hibernian supporters. In fact, the atmosphere became so poisonous a decidedly nervous referee finished the game early and at the whistle the crowd came onto the park to have more than a quiet chat with the players they considered deserters. On 6 October, having received a bye in the first round, Celtic met Shettleston at Parkhead in a second round tie of the Glasgow FA Cup. The result was a resounding victory for the Celts by eleven goals to two. In the third round of the then very highly regarded Glasgow FA Cup, played on 27 October 1888, the Celtic met their good friends Rangers in what, according to Tom Maley, was the first "official" meeting of the clubs. The game was played on a windy, drizzly Saturday at old Ibrox Park and the large crowd of around 4000 were exposed to a bitter south-westerly. The Celtic team on the day was Dunning, Gallagher, McKeown, McLaren, Kelly and W Maley, McCallum, M Dunbar, Groves, Coleman and TE Maley. The Celtic kicked off into a stiff breeze, but there was little advantage to either side such was the strength of the gusting wind. The Celtic made most of the early pressure but after twenty minutes it was Rangers, who, against the run of play, broke away to score, much to the delight of their supporters. It was the last time they cheered that day as much to their disgust the Celtic led at half time by 2–1 and went on to crush the favourites by 6–1 with three of the Celtic goals coming in five, second half minutes. The scorers for the Celts on the day were Groves, Dunbar (2), Coleman, Tom Maley and Kelly. The Celtic went on to reach the semi-final of the Glasgow Cup, where, in a game

The 1888/89 Celtic Team

First Celtic team picture. Officials (back row) left to right, J. Anderson (trainer) J. Quillan, D. Molloy, J. Glass, J. MacDonald; centre and right J. O'Hara and W. McKillop. Players, left to right (middle row) W. Groves, T. Maley, P. Gallacher, W. Dunning, W. Maley, M. Dunbar; (front row) J. Coleman, J. McLaren, J. Kelly, N. McCallum, M. McKeown.

marred by crowd trouble, Queen's Park, widely regarded at the time as the top Scottish club, beat the bhoys 2–0.

By the end of 1888 and what had been a very busy year, the committeemen of the new Glasgow Irish club had every right to be pleased with themselves. The Celtic project was up and running and thus far had gone well, very well indeed, better probably than any of them had a right to expect. The club had amazingly played thirty-six games since the end of May, finishing with a charity friendly on the last day of the old year 1888. They had won twenty-nine, drawn two and lost five, a remarkable performance by any standards. Unbelievably, by Christmas time the Celtic had even reached the semi-final of the Scottish Cup, just one more win away from the final of the holy grail of Scottish football. Over the festive season, the committeemen and team were the toast of the east end and were invited to all the functions held by the various Irish organisations in the area. On 12 January 1889, the Celts beat Dumbarton 4–1 in the semi-final of the Scottish Cup to reach the final in the first year of the club's existence. The Celtic would face Third Lanark in the final on 2 February at old Hampden Park in Cathkin. In what became known as the Snow Final, the game was played in blizzard conditions but prior to kick-off both teams agreed to play the game as a friendly. In the event the bhoys were well beaten by 3–0 but the game had already been declared void due to the atrocious conditions under foot. The replayed final was, after a protest by Third Lanark, played a week later in fine conditions in front of 15,000 spectators. On the day the Celts were the best team on the park, this despite the fact that they were forced to play the majority of the game with ten men after Johnny Coleman went off injured. The Celts spurned a number of chances to win the game, particularly in the second half, while the Volunteers took their opportunities when they presented themselves. The Volunteers eventually ran out the winners by 2–1, taking the Scottish Cup for the first time in their history.

Despite the bitter disappointment of losing a cup final that they could and should have won, it was a major achievement for the club to make the final in the first place. By the end of the football season in May 1889, the Celtic was declared an undreamt of triumph both on and off the park. In season 1888/89, the Celts played fifty-six, won forty-two, drew three and lost eleven. They scored 197 goals and conceded eighty-five. The team was generating unheard of sums of money for Catholic charities and Brother Walfrid and the committee were delighted with its progress over the first season. The success was such that in addition to playing games worth around £150 to the specific charities concerned, the Celtic presented various Catholic charities with a total of £421, a very sizable sum at the time. Furthermore, each of the parish's Poor Children's Dinner Tables received a weekly allowance of £5.

A glance through the club's first balance sheet shows a number of interesting charitable donations, including £5 for the Catholic chapel in Glasgow's infamous *Bar-L*, properly known as Barlinnie Prison, and two donations, one of £45 and another of £18, were made to the cash-strapped Hibernians. Although the club's main focus was to provide funds for Catholic charities or Irish causes, the club also contributed funds to the wider community. On 1 November 1889, the new façade of the Templeton carpet factory building at Greenhead Street, Bridgeton, collapsed in high winds. The façade fell onto weaving sheds where 140 women and girls were working. Twenty-nine women were killed and scores more injured. A disaster fund was set up to which the Celtic club contributed £20. The club also sent £10 to the Penicuik Disaster Fund when sixty-three men and boys were killed in a fire at the Mauricewood Pit. In the late spring of 1889, reports of a serious outbreak of yellow fever in the Brazilian city of Rio de Janeiro moved the Celtic committee to take the team to Coatbridge where they played Albion Rovers for the dependants of the victims. An early indication of the club's political leanings can also be seen in the £10 sent to support the handloom weavers of Bridgeton and another £10 sent to the Fr McFadden defence fund. Fr James McFadden was the diminutive parish priest of Gweedore, Co Donegal. He ruled his flock with an iron hand, while at the same time he protected their interests by committing totally to the Irish Land League's Plan of Campaign. The local authorities ordered the arrest of Fr McFadden after Sunday Mass on 3 February 1889 and in the resulting fracas, a police inspector was killed by a crowd of parishioners determined to protect their priest. Fr McFadden and twenty-four others were arrested and tried for murder. He was bound over to keep the peace, but a number of his parishioners received jail sentences. These were very serious amounts of money being generated by the football club and the men behind the Celtic project must have thought they had won a lottery. A general labourer earned around fifteen shilling (75p) a week, therefore £10 was almost fourteen weeks wages for a labourer.

Contention, Argument and the Glasgow Hibernian

While the first impressions of the foundation and early years of the Celtic club may appear a triumphal march of aspirational, like-minded Irishmen, nothing could be further from the truth. Within weeks of its creation, the Celtic club was in grave danger of being torn asunder after a serious disagreement among the parish representatives assembled to put the project together. Like Irishmen the world over, the Glasgow Irish revelled in contention and argument and almost immediately factional disagreements caused most of the representatives of St Andrew's and St Aloysius to fall away leaving the project largely in the hands of the representatives of St Mary's Parish. By the middle of the Celtic's first football season, 1888/89, yet another split had formed. The club's vice-president, Mr James Quillan, whose supporters were known as Quillanites, led the dissatisfied faction. They were threatening a breakaway and by the late spring of 1889 the dispute was coming to a head. With the loss of the Celtic club's records in a stadium fire in 1929, the exact reasons for the dissatisfaction are unclear; however, even at the time interested parties, like the sporting press, found it difficult to pin down exactly what the dispute was about. Almost from the formation of the Celtic club it had attracted criticism for some of its methods and actions as the committeemen threw themselves with gusto into the shady world of the paid amateur sportsman. The Scottish Referee in May 1889 reported:

> We cannot refrain from putting on record our opinion that the scandals which have been too frequently raised about the club and out of which some people are making capital, tend to show up its management in very bad light. While we are not inclined to believe all that has been said, we are of the opinion that in the great mass of damaging gossip which had been put in circulation there is bound to be some truth.

Unable to get solid facts, the sporting press speculated on the reasons for the dissatisfaction at Celtic: not all the players and committee members were total abstainers, some players had been placed at considerable expense into public houses, no club statements were being produced, the committee were stingy with their donations to charity, excessive expenses were drawn by players and committeemen, and club officials were overspending on entertainments at social events and on providing players and officials with overly expensive after match teas. In mid-February 1889, the Celtic team travelled to London to play the famous Corinthians. The payment of expenses to the players for the trip appeared to be over generous, allowing them to have a very jolly old time in the capital, so much so it raised charges of professionalism in the press. In truth, it was probably a combination of all of the above and more. The actions of John Glass and his subcommittee in raiding the Hibernian team were considered as overstepping the mark, even in the shady world of the paid amateur. The sporting press were, of course, well aware of the bribery and corruption among most of the football clubs and supposed amateur players. They even joked that when John Glass asked John Madden, then trying out for Sheffield Wednesday, what it would take to get him to play for the Celtic, the ex-shipyard worker supposedly asked for a shipyard. He never got the yard, but whatever he got from John Glass was substantial enough for him to come back to Glasgow. However, the Celtic's Hibernian raid was widely seen as stabbing good friends in the back and it had offended the honour of the gentlemen of the sporting press. The Scottish Referee newspaper commented:

> It is not generally known that the object which, the promoters of the Celtic FC had in view when they organised the club was charity. This is a laudable fact and one worthy of all credence. In regard to this a few may be rather sceptical, after the manner in which the new combination was brought together.

Despite donating £60 to the failing Hibernian club, the Celtic's reputation suffered accordingly and the Celtic was never allowed to forget the damage done to Hibernian.

The very impressive revenues raised by the Celtic's games for charitable causes also came under scrutiny by the press. They felt since the Celtic loudly and often trumpeted the fact that proceeds of their games would go to charity, many spectators would go along specifically because of the charitable causes and that therefore they were entitled to know how much money was raised and how much of it actually reached the charities. The Celtic management felt it was none of their business and felt the press attacks were reflections of a wider animosity directed at the Glasgow Irish club because of its success. So started a very uneasy relationship between the Scottish press and the Celtic club, which persists to this very day. The rumours, slanders and conflict within the Celtic club had therefore been going on for some months and would come to a head at the club's AGM due to be held in mid-June. The Quillanites met in a Bridgeton hall at the beginning of June and let it be known that they were in discussion with Hibernian to relocate to Glasgow or if that failed, to establish a new football club in the east end of Glasgow. The significant sum of £500 had already been raised and the site of a new park identified. The move was intended to pressurise the Celtic club into concessions, particularly the removal of club president John Glass. After a meeting with the Celtic leadership it was agreed that their project would be put on hold until after the club's AGM to be held in a fortnight or so. To further muddy the water, a statement was later issued to the press denying that any meetings had ever taken place.

The Celtic's annual general meeting was held on 18 June 1889 in the Mechanics' Hall, Canning Street, in the Calton. The conference was held behind closed doors with the press specifically excluded and exactly what was debated is unknown. James Quillan attempted to have the players excluded from the meeting, questioning their right to participate. Tom Maley vindicated the players' position in an impassioned speech and on the nod of Brother Walfrid the players were allowed to remain. It can be surmised that the Quillanites raised issues: the treatment of the Hibernian club, now in very severe financial trouble, and what they saw as the misappropriation of charitable funds with the likes of James Kelly, Willie Groves, Paddy Gallagher and Mick Dunbar all being bought public house or whisky shop licences as an inducement to play for the club. These were not inconsiderable sums; James Kelly's licence reputedly cost £650. They may have highlighted what they regarded as over generous expenses paid to the players and committeemen, such as those paid on the team's recent London trip. As far as James Quillan and his supporters were concerned, the committeemen and players were routinely receiving payment for what they were supposed to be doing for nothing, thereby lessening the money available for the charities. All these incidents and more had been previously picked up and printed in the press to the detriment of the reputation of the club and its office bearers, including the Roman Catholic clergy who were so closely associated with the Celtic. No doubt James Quillan would have ended his pitch to the Celtic membership by announcing that they were in discussions with Edinburgh Hibernians about moving through to Glasgow and that a considerable sum had already been amassed to begin the building of a playing field. A site less than a mile from the Celtic park had already been identified and designers and contractors were standing by awaiting instructions. The chosen location of the new ground at Rutherglen Road was obviously with a view to split the Glasgow Irish support on which the success or failure of the Celtic club depended. James Quillan wanted the removal of John Glass and if he were not replaced, he and his supporters would move to establish the new football club.

It is unclear exactly what counter arguments John Glass and his subcommittee put but it is known that a number of the most prominent players, no doubt including James Kelly, Willie Groves, Paddy Gallagher and Mick Dunbar, threatened to leave the club if John Glass were replaced. Quillan had obviously anticipated such a move hence the attempt to exclude the players from the meeting. When the meeting was over, it emerged that the coup had failed with the Quillanites failing to muster enough of the membership to oust John Glass, who had success on his side. James Quillan, of course, could not continue as vice-president and resigned although he retained his club membership. He was replaced as honorary vice-president by Belfastman Francis McErlean, a local pawnbroker and soon to be father-in-law of Celtic's captain James Kelly, who was also on the committee representing the players. It was later reported in the press that: "Peace has broken out at the Celtic Club with the defeat of the Quillanites", but outwith those at the meeting no one was quite sure what had gone on. Tom Maley later made light of the entire episode. It should also be noted that if Brother Walfrid, who was at the meeting, was unhappy with the way the club was being run, he made no public statement to the fact. The office bearers and committee that would see the Celtic through season 1889/90 were: Dr Conway, honorary president; John Glass, president; Francis McErlean, vice-president; Hugh Darroch, honorary treasurer; John O'Hara, secretary; William Maley, match secretary and James Curtis, match secretary (reserves). The committee included: James Kelly, the current team captain, Joe Nelis, Joe Shaughnessy, Michael Cairns, John H McLaughlin, William McKillop, Tom Maley, Daniel

Molloy, John McDonald and Joe McGroary. A new name, David Meikleham, appears among the Celtic personalities around this time. Scots Catholic Meikleham was born in Rothesay and would play a very major roll in the life of the club over the next seven years. His name is listed on the 1889/90 Celtic club fixture card as a committeeman. With the Quillanite threat seen off, John Glass felt confident enough in his position to immediately start negotiations with John Madden to entice him away from Dumbarton FC.

Not content in defeat, the Quillanites went back to Edinburgh where the Hibernian club was on the brink of collapse. There they tried to persuade the Hibernian's management to move the club through to Glasgow where a new stadium would be built for them. Despite their dire situation the Hibernians decided to tough it out and remain in the east. After their attempt to persuade Hibernian to flit from Edinburgh failed, the Quillanites decided to form their own team. Inevitably and with a disconcerting lack of imagination, they called it Glasgow Hibernian. How involved James Quillan himself got in the Glasgow Hibernian is unclear; however, he did back the project with a line of credit worth at least £10, but then appeared to distance himself from the club. On 23 September, it was reported in the Scottish Referee that the objectives of the new outfit would be: the public distribution of aid to charitable institutions, to widen the resources of recreation for the working classes and to popularise the game generally. All in, around fifty names were added to the Glasgow Hibernian's Club members list. This alternative Glasgow Irish club was a serious threat to Celtic, one which if successfully established, would split the Glasgow Irish support and threaten the viability of the entire Celtic project. The Glasgow Hibernian committee rented a plot of land on Rutherglen Road just a mile from Celtic Park where they had a football ground laid out. Their park, designed and built by the same people who built Hampden Park, included a running track surrounded by palings. To show their serious intent they even hired Paddy Cannon a well-known Glasgow Irish athlete as their professional trainer.

By August 1889, the Glasgow Hibernian team was beginning to take shape having enticed a number of players targeted by Celtic to Rutherglen, including James Coleman, who, having previously pledged himself to Celtic, gave John Glass and his committee a taste of their own medicine when he defected. The Glasgow Hibs would also tie up the likes of Willie Dunning, John Tobin, James McLaughlin, Michael Murray, John Cunningham, John O'Conner and even the irrepressible and future Celtic favourite Jerry Reynolds. The football ground was just about ready for the 1889/90 season and the Glasgow Hibernian played their first game on 7 September 1889, a Scottish Cup first round home tie, where they were defeated 3–1 by Partick Thistle. The defeats just kept coming with Queen's Park bundling them out of the Glasgow Cup in the first round a fortnight later at what was now being called Hibernian Park. The latest defeat led the Scottish Referee to note: "The Irishmen's interest in our cups is being gradually narrowed down. The Glasgow Hibs are out of both the Glasgow and Scotch Cups, while the Celts are out of the Scotch." A week or so earlier Queen's Park had knocked the Celtic out of the Scottish Cup, after a replay. To be knocked out of two major cup competitions so early was a very serious blow to the fortunes of the Glasgow Hibernian, blows from which they would never recover.

Unfortunately for the club members and supporters the project was, like previous attempts to form a Glasgow Hibernian, doomed to fail. The new outfit staggered through their first season with a little help from a tournament organised by themselves from which they drew thirty per cent of the gates. Their trainer, Stirlingshire-born Paddy Cannon, a champion distance runner, put up one of his trophies as the prize. The details of the competition were published on 10 February 1890 and the committee endeavoured to get some of the English clubs to participate but none were interested. The competition went ahead with a few Scottish clubs and without the participation of the Celtic or Rangers. Dumbarton would win the competition by beating Partick Thistle 6–1 in the final. In a period when games were organised almost on a weekly basis, as soon as rumours surfaced that a club was in financial trouble it became increasingly difficult to get opponents willing to take the chance of not being paid their visiting expenses. In April, the pavilion at Hibernian Park was broken into for a second time, but on this occasion the perpetrators had more than theft in mind when they wantonly destroyed the team's strips and boots. The sporting press wondered: "What has the Glasgow Hibernian done to deserve such misfortune?" As the writing on the wall became more apparent, the first eleven players increasingly drifted away to other clubs as they recognised the inevitability that the project would fail. By the end of May 1890 the Scottish Referee was reporting, "Glasgow Hibernian players were chary to turn-out and that goalkeeper former Celt, Willie Dunning, couldn't be found." That was probably because Willie was already en route to England and fame and fortune with Bootle and later Aston Villa. Most people in the know were surprised that the club reappeared for the 1890/91 season, but just a few weeks later it folded with the members liable for the debts accrued. A Mr Thomas McDougall, wood merchant of Rutherglen Road, raised an action in the Glasgow Sheriff Court against club members for the outstanding amount owed him. Mr McDougall also happened to be the secretary of the failed Glasgow Hibernian. Immediately, all those members associated with the club denied any connection. No membership list or club rules could be found, therefore membership was difficult to prove. Only a certain Mr James Quillan of Janefield Street could be tied to the project.

With the failure of the Glasgow Hibernians the support of the Glasgow Irish went exclusively and wholeheartedly to the Celtic Club. Ironically, just four years later in August 1894, a correspondent in the Glasgow Catholic Observer would write:

> The idea in the minds of those who began the Celtic club was to do good to Catholic charities. That is now all over. The thing is a mere business in the hands of publicans and others. Catholic charities get nothing out of the thousands of pounds passing through the treasurer's hands. Can we not get a club that will carry out the original idea of Brother Walfrid? The income of the Celtic club is drawn largely from our own people.

Season 1889/90

For the Celtic club, season 1889/90 was another of continued progress both off and on the field, despite their early exit from the premier competition, the Scottish Cup knocked out by Queen's Park. The Celts were also knocked out of the Charity Cup, losing 2–0 to the Third Lanark Rifle Volunteers and lost the final of the Glasgow Cup 3–2 to Queen's Park. The fixture list for the season was largely made up of friendly or challenge games but all that was soon to change. The club's new-found celebrity and large support ensured it was in great demand as opponents. Already the Glasgow Irish side had established themselves as one of the leading clubs in the country. They gained a reputation for playing fast, attractive, attacking football – *scientific* football as it was then called. That style of play became the Celtic brand, an ethos that remains with the club to the present day. In addition to attracting their own Glasgow Irish, their style of play was also winning them supporters far outwith the Glasgow Irish community. The Dundee Courier reported on 11 November 1890: "The Celtic football team has one worshiper, an Aberdeen resident, who attends every match of the club wherever played." It was a very impressive show of loyalty, considering travelling conditions of the period. A search was conducted to find the fanatic but he was never identified. The dark side of football support also reared its ugly head that month. In what must be one of the first examples of its kind, a man called Devlin was killed in Queensferry, near Edinburgh. The tragedy occurred after a discussion over the relative merits of Celtic players Willie Groves and James Kelly turned to violence. Season 1889/90 would be the last of hit-and-miss friendlies and cup games as the clubs began to get themselves better organised.

In mid-March 1890, the club secretary of Renton FC sent a circular to fourteen of the major Scottish clubs requesting them to send two representatives to a meeting that would discuss setting up a Scottish Football League. In the event only twelve, Abercorn, Cambuslang, Celtic, Cowlairs, Dumbarton, Heart of Midlothian, Rangers, Renton, St Bernard, St Mirren, Third Lanark and Vale of Leven, attended. The two absentees were Clyde and Queen's Park. The idea behind the new league set-up was to bring some order and certainty into what were often chaotic match fixture dates and arrangements. The new Scottish Football League was inaugurated on 30 April 1890 and began with just eleven teams taking part, St Bernard falling by the wayside. The stuffy, middle class gentlemen at the SFA and their close allies and standard bearers of amateurism Queen's Park, then still a major force in the Scottish game, were less than impressed or supportive of the fledgling organisation. The SFA and the other regional associations correctly saw the new set-up as a threat to their authority and a stepping-stone to professionalism. Celtic's John H McLaughlin, as one of the prime movers of the league, was drafted onto the management committee and as league secretary began the delicate recognition negotiations with the SFA. As secretary, one of John McLaughlin's first proposals was that the league should adopt the procedures of a closed shop. League games were to take precedent over all other matches except Scottish Cup and county cup ties. Members would be forbidden

James Kelly

to play friendly matches against non-League clubs in towns where a league match had been arranged for that day. With only eleven and later ten clubs signing up to the Scottish League, this could be problematical since clubs still had to arrange friendly matches to fill up their fixture list. The Scottish sporting press, especially the highly influential Scottish Sport, was also highly suspicious of the Scottish League, "Our first and last objection to them [the League] is that they exist. The entire rules stink of finance, moneymaking and money grabbing." The new league set-up would certainly bring with it a much more serious, competitive edge to the games. Even the players would quickly notice the new competitive edginess and lack of sociability, bemoaning the loss of their after match teas. In season 1889/90, the Celtic played forty-seven, won twenty-seven, drew nine and lost eleven. They scored 129 goals and conceded sixty-four.

Season 1890/91

Season 1890/91 began on 16 August 1890 with the first of the new Scottish League matches. The Celtic's first game was at home to Renton and a sizable crowd of 10,000 turned up at Parkhead, only to see the bhoys drubbed 4–1. The game would later be declared void after Renton was expelled from the league. The following two games would prove to be even more of a disaster. The Celts won both matches, but when it was discovered that they had played an unregistered player, goalkeeper James Bell of Hurlford, two points per game were deducted as per the rules. At the end of the first league season, Rangers and Dumbarton were declared joint winners on twenty-nine points with Celtic finishing in third place on twenty-one. The loss of the deducted points made no difference to the Celtic's final league position. Some small consolation was the fact that Celtic beat Rangers 2–1 in the second last league game of the season, a victory that prevented Rangers winning the first league championship outright.

After their inauspicious start and despite John H McLaughlin's enthusiasm for the project, by the end of the first league season many at Celtic Park were not sure about the new league arrangements. Although filling match dates over Celtic's first two years had at times proved to be a struggle, the subsequent success of Celtic meant this was no longer the case. As free agents, the Celtic could arrange to play the most attractive opponents, who would bring in large crowds, while being tied into playing minor opposition in the Scottish League would prove much less attractive to the paying public. However, McLaughlin's closed shop proposals meant that to be outside the League could prove to be very expensive. The Celtic quickly fell foul of the League's new closed shop rules after arranging very lucrative home and away matches with Queen's Park, then still a major draw at the gate. As the standard bearers of amateurism, Queen's Park had refused to have anything to do with the League and had been effectively ostracised. The League ordered Celtic to cancel the games, much to the fury of both the committee and the Celtic supporters. One supporter took the trouble to write to the Scottish Sport newspaper asking who ran the Celtic club, the members or the Scottish League?

On 20 December 1890, Dumbarton controversially knocked the Celtic out of the Scottish Cup at the quarter-final stage. The pitch at Dumbarton's Boghead ground was more akin to a quagmire and initially both teams protested to the referee but with 10,000 spectators looking on, both agreed the match would take place, but would be regarded as a friendly. After winning 3–0 Dumbarton withdrew their protest and insisted the game was the official cup quarter-final tie. Celtic protested to the SFA but their protest was overruled on the casting vote of the chairman. On 14 February 1891 the Celtic won their first major trophy, taking at the second attempt the Glasgow Cup by beating Third Lanark 4–0 at Hampden Park. The cup final was reached by beating Battlefield, Northern, Clyde and Partick Thistle. The winning team was Bell, Reynolds and McKeown; Gallacher, Kelly and W Maley. Madden and Boyle, Dowds, Campbell and Dunbar. Willie Maley was judged to be the *Man of the Match*.

The sports correspondent, Our Own Celt writing for the Scottish Sport journal, described the after match social and the reaction to the win in the east end:

> *The team drove to the Alexandria Hotel in Bath Street, where a tea and social was held. They were followed by a large group of supporters with cards in their hats with the well-known and oft repeated expressions, "Hurry up, Celts", "Good old Celts", etc., etc. Naturally the Celts were on the best of terms with themselves, whilst the Third, like true sportsmen, showed no chagrin, but appeared equally as lively as their conquerors. Congratulations were offered in speeches by the Glasgow Association president and replied to on behalf of Celtic by John Glass. I made my way among the crowd, heard all sorts of criticisms and opinion and then marched eastward. Passing Mick Dunbar's establishment in the Gallowgate, I stepped in to make known the news-nothing else I assure you, though they do say Dunbar keeps a "fair blend". But the news had had been there before me. Taking the other extreme (in the matter of drink), I entered the St Mary's Hall. Billiards, etc. were at a standstill. One who had been at the game was giving a graphic account of the day. Many of the older men there knew nothing whatsoever of short passes, dribbles, shots, etc., all they knew, all they wanted to know was that their pets had won, and didn't they carry their heads high when the reciter of the narrative concluded by saying – "And, bejesus, that's how the best team that ever played football won the cup." I wound my weary way homewards and although sleep closed my eyes, my ears were ringing throughout the night with "Goal!", "Celts!", "Cup!".*

Celtic Squad and Officials April 1891

Civilian clothes (left to right) Paddy Gallagher. Mick Dunbar, Joe Anderson, Jimmy Boyle, John O'Hara, James Kelly, Tom Maley.
Players. Left to right. Back row. Jerry Reynolds, James Bell and Michael McKeown.
Middle row. Frank Dolan, James McGhee and Willie Maley.
Front row. John Madden, John Coleman, Peter Dowds, Sandy McMahon and John Campbell.

The Glasgow Cup and badges were presented at an official function in Moir's restaurant in West Nile Street on 24 February. John Glass accepting the trophy on behalf of the victorious team. After the function, Willie McKillop was made custodian of the cup and to celebrate the victory, he threw a party at his home in Monteith Row. As befitting his reputation as one of the finest restaurateurs in Glasgow, a sumptuous spread was laid out for his guests. A large number of Celtic personalities attended, including Hugh Murphy, Francis Henry, John McLaughlin, Mick Dunbar, Tom and Willie Maley, Paddy Gallagher, Davie Meikleham and of course the McKillop brothers. Tom Maley years later recalled the event with great fondness, lamenting the loss of so many of the personalities in the interim. The cup-winning team was Bell, Reynolds, McKeown, Maley, Kelly, Gallacher, Madden, Boyle, Dowds, Dunbar and Campbell.

The Scottish League and the SFA again locked horns towards the end of the first league season when a dispute arose over League teams playing in the Glasgow Merchants Charity Cup competition. The power struggle between the Scottish League and the SFA, who ran the competition on behalf of the merchants, was a clash of old and new bulls with the charities innocent third parties. The dispute was over games involving non-League teams, match dates and League influence on the SFA's Charities Cup committee. The League competition had begun in August and ran well into May, interfering with other well-established cup arrangements. The result of the dispute and subsequent deadlock was that the League members were not allowed to participate in that year's charity competition. The withdrawal of Celtic, Rangers and Third Lanark had a devastating effect on the Charity Cup's takings. Over the previous three seasons the competition had raised £1200, £1050 and £1700, respectively, whereas for season 1890/91 the total raised was just £150. When it came to distributing the funds to the charities, all received very much-reduced sums. The Evening News made a barbed remark regarding the one guinea given to three Catholic institutions: "The Little Sisters of the Poor, the Whitevale Refuge and the St Vincent de Paul Society, may thank their lucky stars they were included in this year's charity list, as the team of their complexion [Celtic] did not participate in the contest." The Glasgow Catholic Observer picked up the gauntlet: "The claim by Catholic charities to a share in the fund is based on the complexion of all the spectators who paid at the gate and not the complexion of the teams who play." The catastrophic drop in the charitable funds was a public relations disaster for the already far from popular Scottish League and it was quickly realised that a PR rescue mission was needed.

The Glasgow clubs that would have normally been involved in the Charity Cup competition, Celtic, Rangers and Third Lanark, sent representatives to meet with officials of the League to discuss the disaster. In a reflection of how serious Celtic took the situation, the club sent their big guns, John Glass, Joe Shaughnessy, Tom Maley and Willie McKillop, with John H McLaughlin already at the League, it was an impressive delegation from Parkhead. It was decided the losses to the charities must be made good and a Scottish League charity competition was hastily organised with Dumbarton asked to participate to make up the numbers up to four. Each of the clubs subscribed £10 towards the cost of badges in order that the gross drawings would go to charity. Celtic's Tom Maley and a certain Baillie Ure Primrose of Rangers, of whom we shall hear more later, were both seconded onto the Scottish League's temporary charities committee. The competition would be run over the last week in May, with the final to be held on 10 June. In the competition, Celtic first beat Third Lanark after a replay, but lost the final 3–1 to Dumbarton in what was their last game of the season. The League's charity competition raised over £800, but when added to the sums raised by the Charity Cup, the total still fell short of the sum raised the previous year by the charity competition. The press noted and applauded the money raised and recognised the considerable efforts of the league committee, but deplored the duplication of effort and encouraged conciliation between the warring factions. Ominously for the SFA, the Scottish League announced that the temporary charity subcommittee would remain in place. The Charity Cup dispute and the subsequent loss of revenue, of course, struck at the heart of the Celtic's very existence and the interference of the League in the Queen's Park arrangements no doubt raised eyebrows at Celtic Park, but for now the Celtic committee bit their tongues and went along with the new force in the Scottish game, but some were still far from convinced.

So ended the 1890/91 football season, the Celtic's third in Scottish football. The club record over the period makes for impressive reading. In season 1888/89, the Celts played fifty-six, won forty-two, drew three and lost eleven. They scored 197 goals and conceded eighty-five. In season 1889/90, they played forty-seven, won twenty-seven, drew nine and lost eleven. They scored 129 goals and conceded sixty-four. In season 1890/91, they played forty-nine, won thirty-four, drew seven and lost eight. They scored 148 goals and conceded sixty-two. The football record was trumpeted on the front cover of the club's official booklet issued in August 1891. The booklet also stated that: "In playing ability the Celtic stands second to none," and, "It is satisfactory to note that everything augurs well for the continuance this season of its past good form."

Chapter Three

Glasgow Irish Politics

From the moment of its inception, the officials and supporters of the Celtic club were inextricably linked culturally, socially and politically. As early as January 1889 the Scottish Referee sports paper was commenting that the Celtic club had the greatest number of friends (supporters) of any in the country. It also noted rather dismissively that few had any knowledge of the game and that their support was based largely on the fact that the club was Irish and Catholic. The Celtic club was by definition, Irish and Roman Catholic and the team players over the first couple of seasons were by necessity all Roman Catholic and the future leadership of the club would remain so. However, a non-sectarian attitude was quickly adopted and an atmosphere of inclusiveness and welcome introduced. Although it would be August 1891 before the first non-Catholic player goalkeeper Tom Duff was brought into the side, the Celtic had coveted Tom as early as September 1888 indicating a policy of non-sectarianism almost from the outset. The policy of signing players irrespective of their race or creed would become and would remain a fundamental feature of the club. While the club retained the Irish tag, the policy of signing players outwith the faith, removed the purely Roman Catholic tag. Of course, the club's Irish Catholic supporters remained completely identified with the club.

While the Glasgow Irish community built the club, including its first stadium with the sweat of their brows, the ethos and reputation of the club were largely fashioned by the high profile office bearers and committeemen. The Celtic club came into being at a time when it was common for organisations outwith the world of politics to hold and express political views. It was inevitable, therefore, that with the leaders of the club also holding memberships in the myriad Catholic and Irish Nationalist associations, societies and confraternities, some of the polities and beliefs of those organisations would seep into the football club. The Celtic club founded, built and now supported by the desperately poor Glasgow Irish community became immersed in the politics of social welfare and Irish nationalism and land reform both in Ireland and in the Scottish Highlands and islands.

The football club's ethnic origins, and the political and religious beliefs of its committeemen and the vast majority of its supporters, ensured it was regarded with suspicion by some sections of the Scottish political establishment. This was particularly true when it came to the politics of Ireland and particularly the subject of Home Rule. In 1896 it was widely reported that the Celtic club had sent its own delegation to the Irish Parliamentary Party's National Race Convention in Dublin. There they joined another dozen Glasgow nationalists also closely connected to the club. However, although fully committed to the causes of Irish Nationalism, the Irish immigrant community and its leaders were at the same time dedicated to the advancement of their own community in Glasgow and Scotland. In their view, their wholehearted and highly publicised support of constitutional nationalism in the guise of the Home Rule movement allowed them to advance both causes. By foregoing the physical force republican policies of the Fenians and the Irish Republican Brotherhood, the Glasgow Irish were demonstrating to their host society that they deserved its respect and that their contribution to the constitutional debate deserved recognition. Hopefully, their efforts would be rewarded by assimilation into the wider community leading to increased status and advancement. Since the history of the Celtic focuses on its more romantic, charitable heritage, what is often forgotten is the political heritage of the club, particularly over the first twenty years of its existence. It was a time when the office bearers at the Celtic club were actively engaged in current political debates and were unafraid to express their opinions publicly. Most of the personalities of the Celtic club demonstrated their political allegiance by their membership and indeed their leadership of the Home Government branch of the Irish National League (INL). This was an organisation that more than any other influenced the political opinions and beliefs of the Glasgow Irish of the period. The role it played in establishing the ethos of the Celtic club is overlooked or unknown by most modern Celtic supporters.

John Ferguson

The core values of the Home Government branch (HGB) based in Glasgow and led by many of the founding fathers of the Celtic were built into the very fabric of club. As on so many other occasions, a Protestant would be a major influence in the story of the Celtic. In this case, it was John Ferguson, a man born and raised in Belfast, the industrial heartland of Ulster Protestantism. Already an experienced political activist, after moving to Glasgow around 1859 he committed himself to mobilising the immigrant Irish in Scotland behind Home Rule and land reform issues. The Glasgow Home Rule Association was formally inaugurated in December 1871 and was affiliated to the Home Government Association based in Dublin and established in 1870 by Isaac Butt. The term "Home Government" was used before the words "Home Rule" became more popular.

The Glasgow Irish Nationalists stuck with the old name for their branch, highlighting the fact that its origin was contemporary with the very start of the Irish National movement. Later the branch developed into the Home Government branch of the INL and later the United Irish League (UIL), both organisations inextricably linked to the Irish Parliamentary Party (IPP). Both were committed to the two causes dearest to the Glasgow Irish, Home Rule for Ireland and radical land reform. John Ferguson was involved at every important point in the Home Rule movement's development over the next thirty years. Appalled at the sectarian hatred and violence in his native Belfast, which he would later call "a violent and feeble-thinking city", he came to realise that a workable Home Rule policy had to be formulated that catered to the fears of the Irish Unionists and that without them on board little would be achieved peaceably. He actively sought alliances with and supported the Highland crofters in their fight against landlordism in the mid-1880s. He brought Michael Davitt, the ex-Fenian prisoner and campaigner against landlordism, to Glasgow and he electrified audiences with his attacks on the structure of land ownership in Scotland as well as Ireland. Michael Davitt would later call Ferguson the "voice of the Glasgow Irish". John Ferguson also laid the foundations of an Irish radical alliance with the emerging socialist labour movement in Scotland. Proof of this commitment was apparent in the support for Keir Hardie's celebrated stand in the 1888 Mid-Lanark by-election and for the new Scottish Labour Party (SLP), which was formed in its wake. John Ferguson became, with some ideological and political reservations, an honorary vice-president of the fledgling SLP, which was a loose coalition of trade unionists, socialists, assorted radicals, land reformers, Irish nationalists and disaffected Liberals. Together the alliance was termed the 'forces of democracy'. The SLP would associate itself with an all-British labour movement and morph into the Independent Labour Party (ILP) in 1893. Elected to the east end ward of Calton in 1893, largely on the back of Irish votes, Ferguson became the effective leader of the democratic forces on the Town Council. His influence was such the early ILP candidates saw themselves as his disciples. The alliance can still be seen today in the overwhelming support and electoral success of the Labour Party in Glasgow, particularly in the city's east end.

At times Ferguson flirted with the shadowy Irish Republican Brotherhood (IRB), but he was never part of it. Although a committed Nationalist he rejected total separatism and argued for an essentially imperial model of national development with a fully self-governing Ireland. He envisioned an Ireland prospering from its membership of the British Empire, which would go some way to atone for past wrongs it had done to the Irish nation. The Home Government branch came to dominate Irish politics completely in Scotland and its weekly meetings were known as the parliament of the Glasgow Irish. It raised considerable sums of money for the IPP and brought all the major nationalist politicians of the time to Glasgow. Parnell, Davitt and John Redmond came and they were very happy to do so, recognising the importance of Glasgow Irish support.

The depth of involvement and commitment to Irish Home Rule by the Glasgow Irish is clearly highlighted during the Irish Race Convention of September 1896. The Irish Parliamentary Party called for a national convention to be held in Dublin for representatives of the Irish race throughout the world who were supporters of the Irish Home Rule movement. The subsequent assembly held from 1 to 3 September was attended by over 2000 individuals from throughout the world including the USA, Canada, Australia as well as Europe and was one of the biggest gatherings of its kind. Scotland was one of the best represented countries at the convention with delegates from Greenock, Hamilton, Dundee, Broxburn, Dumbarton and especially Glasgow, which sent delegates from a half dozen city branches of the Irish National League, the main UK-based organisation promoting Irish Home Rule at that time. Closely associated with the Home Government branch, the Celtic sent its own delegation with committeemen John Glass, Willie Maley and James McKay representing the football club. Only two men from Glasgow spoke at the convention, John Ferguson said:

I come from a land once hostile but now united in friendship for Ireland. I come from a country where we had to fight for our political rights and political existence as Irishmen a fiercer fight than any you have had perhaps in this or any country in the world. We have had Irishmen shot on the platform while maintaining our green flag above. We have had bullets through our windows to tell us of the hostile feeling of the Scottish people. That day has passed away and we roused the spirit of Celtic kinship amongst the Scottish people and to-day Scotland stands solid for Home Rule.

He ended with a verse of the "Wearing o' the Green". The second speaker was Glasgow Irishman Hugh Murphy, who was a founding father and a member of the original Celtic club committee. At a time when Irish Nationalism was still reeling from the Parnell divorce scandal, which split the movement, Hugh Murphy's speech included a plea for Irish political unity in the post-Parnell era.

John Ferguson *was* the Home Government branch and over the years he had been termed "the Celt of the Celts", "the land reform pioneer", "a great social reformer", "an Irishman first and always", "a soldier and servant of human liberty", and a "seer". What is certain was his profound influence on the men involved in the founding and early development of the Celtic club. John Glass, Joe Shaughnessy, John O'Hara, Willie and Tom Maley, James McKay, James Kelly, Hugh and Arthur Murphy, the McKillop brothers, Joseph McGroary, James Quillan, Thomas White, Thomas and Patrick Colgan were all disciples and the list could go on. All shared his, at times, paradoxical beliefs in a mix of socialism and capitalism, imperialism and Nationalism. It is interesting to note that John Ferguson, who was known to lecture at Celtic Brake Club meetings, was asked to formally open the Grant Stand at Celtic Park in October 1899, highlighting his continued influence on the Celtic leadership into the twentieth century. John Ferguson's Home Government branch was non-sectarian, socially aware, inclusive, outward looking and proudly Irish. How could the founding fathers so influenced, have created and guided a club other than one with the same principles? Three men are particularly associated with the Celtic club and the struggle for Irish Home Rule, land and social reform both in Ireland and in Scotland: Irish patriot Michael Davitt and Glasgow Irish brothers Hugh and Arthur Murphy.

The Irish social reformer Michael Davitt, born in Straide, Co Mayo, was probably the most famous Irish Nationalist political figure associated with the Celtic Football Club. Just a year after the Celtic club's formation, in what was a major publicity coup, the famous or infamous Irish patriot, land reformer and convicted Fenian gunrunner agreed to become the honorary patron of the football club. Although nothing more than a figurehead, his appointment cemented the Celtic's reputation of leaning towards the rebellious side of Irish Nationalism. At the time Davitt was a highly controversial figure in British politics, having formed the Irish Land Movement and been imprisoned for Fenian activities. His own family had been evicted from their home in 1850 when they migrated to Lancashire, England. As a seven year old, Michael was sent to work in a cotton mill and three years later he lost his right arm in an industrial accident. A self-taught socialist, he took evening classes in Irish history, joined the Fenians in 1865 and five years later was sentenced to fifteen years imprisonment for gunrunning. Released after serving seven years in Dartmoor prison, in 1879 he founded the Irish Land League; its objective was land reform with fair rents, security of tenure and freedom to inherit. The socialist from the industrial heart of England saw no difference in the struggle between industrial labourers and   their bosses and between tenant farmers and their landlords. Allied to Charles Stewart Parnell, who had campaigned for his release from prison, he was elected as the Irish Party MP for Co Meath in 1882. Davitt and the Irish Land League won a major victory during the Rent Wars, resulting eventually in tenants gaining the right to buy their land. The Glasgow Irish held a particular fondness for Michael Davitt with very many being the victims of rent-raking landlords themselves.

Michael Davitt

(United Ireland Magazine)

Although regarded as the leading figure in the Irish land reform campaign, Michael Davitt was also deeply involved and supportive of the Scottish crofters who were suffering the same injustices from their rent-racking Highland landlords as their Irish cousins. At the time that the new Celtic club project was being considered, Davitt conducted a tour of the Scottish Highlands to give moral and practical support to the Highland Land League, which was based largely on his Irish version. The tour by the Irish patriot and the plight of the Highland crofters were widely and sympathetically reported in the national press. While he attended a Highland Land League meeting in Skye, a resolution was moved and carried "that his visit was a happy augury of the union and co-operation of the Gaels of Scotland and Ireland in working together for those reforms so needful for the welfare of both. It is difficult not to consider the distinct possibility that Davitt and his Highland tour were the inspiration for the name of the Celtic Football Club, drawing as it does on the joint Celtic heritage of the Irish and Scottish Gaels. Like the rest of Great Britain, Glasgow had its fair share of IRB incidents and the Tradeston gasworks, Buchanan Street railway station, the Ruchill canal bridge and Dawsholm gasometers had all been attacked. Despite the Celtic club's overt Irishness and unashamed Nationalist sympathies, ex-Fenian Davitt's appointment as honorary patron undoubtedly raised eyebrows in some quarters.

For the most part, the leaders of the Celtic club were children of the Irish diaspora. Raised from infancy on stories of hunger and evictions, their commitment to Michael Davitt and his National Land League was total. For a decade, Davitt, from his position of honour with the football club, drew considerable financial support, particularly for evicted tenants from the Celtic club, its office bearers and from its Glasgow Irish supporters. On Saturday 19 March 1892, the Celtic club patron was invited to lay the first sod, a divot of Donegal shamrocks, in the centre spot of the only half-completed Celtic stadium. After the planting and lunch with the Celtic committee, he and John Ferguson joined the spectators to watch Celtic play out a 0–0 draw with Clyde. Later at a dinner to celebrate the Celtic's capture of the Glasgow Cup, Davitt was presented with a medal by John Glass to mark the occasion. The next day Michael Davitt, accompanied by Dr Joseph Scanlan, a local east end medic and lifelong Celtic supporter, addressed a meeting of the Home Government branch of the Irish National League in Glasgow. During the meeting he pleaded with the many representatives of the Celtic club present to redirect some of the money they had set aside for charities to be used to support evicted Irish tenants. While pleading for financial support from the Celtic, Davitt continually used the hard "K" when mentioning the team by name. Despite the laughter from the floor, he persisted to use Keltic throughout his speech. Several Glasgow newspapers carried the story of the divot planting ceremony and a supporter was moved to have published the following verse:

> *On alien soil like yourself I am here;*
> *I'll take root and flourish never fear,*
> *And though I'll be crossed and sore and oft by the foes,*
> *You'll find me as hardy as Thistle or Rose.*
> *If model is needed on your own pitch you will have it,*
> *Let your play honour me and my friend Michael Davitt.*

Shortly afterwards, a selfish supporter or more likely an aggrieved Scotsman incensed at Irish soil being transplanted onto Scotch, removed the divot in the dead of night. Whoever was the culprit, the curse cast was exactly the same:

> *The curse of Cromwell blast the hand that stole the sod that Michael cut;*
> *May all his praties turn to sand – the crawling, thieving scut.*
> *That precious site of Irish soil with verdant shamrocks overgrown,*
> *Was a token of a more glorious soil fitting far than fretted stone? Again I*
> *say, may heaven blight that envious, soulless knave;*
> *May all his sunshine be like night and the sod rest heavy on his grave.*

Michael Davitt would be back at Parkhead again at the beginning of August 1894. Again, the Celtic club pulled out the stops for their patron with £60, the proceeds of a game against Queen's Park, donated to the Irish Parliamentary Party fund. After the game, which ended in a 1–1 draw, Davitt met John Ferguson at his home in Lenzie. The following night he addressed a large meeting of the Home Government branch in Glasgow. Alongside John Ferguson, some of the Celtic committee were on the platform including John Glass, the two McKillop brothers and Hugh and Arthur Murphy. Such was the commitment of the leading members of the Celtic club to Davitt and the IPP that, despite it being a time of internal disputes over the club's constitution and of falling contributions to charities, there were consistently large donations made to Davitt, both on behalf of the club itself and individually from its officials. They were particularly generous in their support of Davitt's evicted tenants, a topic that was intensely personal to most of the diaspora. A £30 donation to the National Fund and £60 to the IPP was added to by the committeemen, who made their own personal donations; £5 each from the

McKillop brothers, Joe Shaughnessy gave £2, while John H McLaughlin, John O'Hara, James Kelly, Michael Dunbar and John Glass all threw in a pound.

Irish-born Arthur Murphy was a lifelong campaigner for the rights of the Glasgow Irish and his political influence among the Celtic leadership and the wider Glasgow Irish community over a period of fifty years was immense. He was born into a family of fervent Irish nationalists and one of the most esteemed families of the St Mary's congregation in the east end of Glasgow. His father, cabinetmaker James Murphy, was a native of Newtownbutler in Co Fermanagh. He came to Scotland in the mid-1860s, first settling his young family in Duntocher. By the time of James Murphy's death in 1912, the family had spent over forty years in Scotland and their names were household words among the Irish Nationalist community. When James Murphy died, two Celtic club directors, James Kelly and Mick Dunbar, represented the Celtic club and were among a who's who of Irish Nationalism attending the funeral. Like him, his two sons, Hugh and Arthur, and nephew George Murphy were devoted Irish Nationalists and prominent members of the Home Government branch. Although Arthur Murphy is probably better known to most Celtic supporters through the fact that his photograph appears in Willie Maley's Celtic book, his older brother Hugh Murphy was a founding father, sat on the original Celtic committee and was a colossal figure among the Glasgow Irish nationalists, indeed second only to John Ferguson himself.

Hugh Murphy

In 1920, the *Man in the Know* was asked by letter to name the Celtic's founding fathers. He replied that in addition to Brother Walfrid and John Glass, who launched the ship, and Dr Conway, Joe Shaughnessy, John McLaughlin and Stephen Henry who got on-board at the launch, it was actually Brother Walfrid and Hugh Murphy who were the keel-layers of the ship. These were the two promoters who gathered in the original band of helpers and the club was subsequently launched. Considering his pre-eminent position among the Glasgow Irish, it is no surprise that when Brother Walfrid decided to start the club he turned for help first to the hugely influential, Hugh Murphy. Deeply immersed in national and local politics, and therefore unable to take a long term leading role in the club, Hugh Murphy turned to his able lieutenant at the HGB, John Glass. That Hugh Murphy suggested John Glass was the man to take the Celtic project forward will come as no surprise considering Murphy and Glass were once described as bosom friends and companions. Indeed between the Celtic and the Home Government branch the pair were scarcely ever apart. Later described as a "keen supporter of the Celtic Club since its inception", Hugh Murphy was said to have opinions on players and play that was worth listening to.

In addition to his impeccable Irish Nationalist credentials as a long-term leader of the (HGB), and president of the Glasgow branch of the Irish Amnesty Association, Hugh Murphy alongside John Fergusson was an early supporter of the Scottish Labour movement. The HGB as the oldest and largest nationalist organisation in Scotland had been supportive of Labour candidates since the mid 1880s. In 1895, Hugh Murphy, now president of the HGB, openly supported Labour candidates in the general election. At a time when the Irish vote was still conditionally promised by the IPP to the Liberals, Hugh Murphy's support for Labour went even further than that of John Ferguson, much to the displeasure of the Glasgow Catholic Observer who saw support for labour as undermining the Home Rule campaign. Only a few months after the elections Hugh Murphy was working assiduously for the ILP candidates at the municipal elections. Hugh Murphy's socialist leaning were manifest when in support of a Labour candidate in Camlachie he argued:

> Over the past ten years we have seen candidates calling themselves temperance candidates or publican candidates, but they found that all in the Town Council, Liberal, Tory, Publican or Temperance united to put down the working man. These men only used the workman as a ladder to get into power and then kicked them away.

The collaboration between the Irish nationalists and ILP can be seen in the 1896 municipal elections when several Labour-Nationalist candidates stood for election. Among them Hugh Murphy, nominated by the Workers Election Committee and the INL to fight the east end ward of Whitevale. He failed to win the seat by just 130 votes. In August 1903, Hugh Murphy took ill suddenly after attending Sunday Mass at St Mary's and died within a few days at his home in the Gallowgate. Typically, he was en route to an Irish Nationalist rally in Airdrie when he fell ill. His death at the time was reported as being a "serious loss to the Irish Nationalists" and to have caused widespread sorrow among them.

At his funeral, his pallbearers reflected his great passions, politics and the Celtic. They included Arthur Murphy, William McKillop, Michael Davitt, John Ferguson, Michael Dunbar and his closest friend John Glass. Later his death was called "so sad a loss to the Home Rule movement". Such was the esteem in which he was held, shortly after his death a fund was set up to erect a memorial to the leader of the Glasgow Irish. Donations flooded in and was noted at the time that even the Protestant Lord Provost of Glasgow and seventy-seven bailies of the town contributed a pound or two. The Celtic club contributed a substantial £20 to the memorial fund and was, of course, well represented at both the funeral and subsequent memorial unveiling. The memorial very fittingly took the form of a red granite Celtic cross on which an Irish harp and shamrocks were sculptured. John Ferguson unveiled the memorial at a ceremony in St Peter's cemetery, Dalbeth attended by most of the leadership of Irish Nationalism including Joe Devlin MP.

Arthur Murphy, like his father, was a cabinetmaker by profession. He followed in his brother Hugh's footsteps by taking an interest in the Celtic club, becoming a committeeman in 1891 and remaining on the committee until 1897. He opposed the 1893 limited liability motion submitted by Joe Shaughnessy, stating the club was originally organised for the purpose of distributing charity to the deserving poor of the city, but if they placed the affairs of the club in the hands

Arthur Murphy

of a few moneyed speculators the amount of money that would be spent on charity would be very small indeed. He remained a fierce opponent of the limited liability scheme until it was introduced in 1897. Like his brother, Arthur Murphy was steeped in the politics of the Glasgow Irish and was closely associated with the Home Government branch of the Irish National League. In August 1888 at a meeting of the Home Government branch, a young Arthur Murphy moved a motion supporting the New Ross, Co Wexford, tenants faced with eviction and was among the Celtic founding fathers who opposed the British imperialist expansion in South Africa.

The second decade of the twentieth century saw the Glasgow Irish becoming increasingly involved in local politics, with their own social and welfare problems taking a more prominent part in their political ambitions. On the death of his brother in 1903, Arthur picked up his socialist banner. Once referred to as the Irish Kier Hardie, in early 1910, Arthur Murphy, now engaged in the wine and spirit trade, was president of the historic HGB when it was closed down, its membership rent asunder, split over support for Labour rather than Liberal/IPP political candidates. Celtic director Tom White, then acting as an election agent for a Labour candidate was offered the HGB chair but refused. Concerned at the development and with Home Rule seemingly within touching distance, John Redmond and Joe Devlin visited Glasgow in 1911 aiming to reinvigorate the Irish Nationalist movement. Arthur Murphy responded to Redmond's plea and reopened the Home Government branch. John Redmond MP was subsequently made honorary president of the HGB. For over thirty years, Arthur Murphy had been a committed supporter of the Irish Parliamentary Party and their non- violent version of Irish Nationalism but by mid-1914, with Home Rule for Ireland looking certain, Arthur Murphy again led the Glasgow Irish community away from Liberalism towards socialism. He became increasingly involved in the Scottish labour movement and encouraged the Glasgow Irish to focus their political ambitions on improving their own dire social and welfare problems. Over the course of the Great War, Arthur Murphy and the HGB would fully support the pro-British position of the Irish Parliamentary Party and John Redmond. In turn, the HGB would actively encourage the Glasgow Irish to support the British war effort. His service to the Celtic was recognised with the inclusion of his photograph, one of the few that featured in the book, produced by the club and written by Willie Maley to celebrate the Celtic's golden jubilee in 1938. Arthur Murphy JP died at his Rutherglen home in April 1941, aged seventy-nine.

At the same time as the formation of the Celtic Club was being announced in January 1888, the finishing touches were being put on Glasgow's magnificent new City Chambers. The imposing grandiose pile was built in the very centre of the city at George Square and was an impressive symbol of Victorian Glasgow's political strength, industrial might, historical wealth and imperial arrogance. The Lord Provost, Sir John Ure Primrose, a Master Freemason and Rangers Football Club official, had laid the foundation stone four years earlier. The City Chambers building cost an almost unimaginable sum for the time of £552,028. Including furnishings, the whole project cost £578,232. In 1889, a ten-day public viewing attracted 400,000 people and if the visitors thought the exterior of the building was impressive, it paled in comparison to the interior. The extensive use of Carrera marble, granite, stained glass, polished exotic woods, alabaster plasterwork, handmade glazed Italian tiles and mosaics provides a display of brazen opulence, which is truly awesome. Subliminally, the magnificent building faces west, towards the wealthier districts of the city. Its plain, work-a-day rear is the first view of the building when approaching from the impoverished east end.

While the city fathers were trumpeting the city's success and wealth, mortality rates among the poor children of Glasgow were among the worst in the western world. Housing conditions in the city were, even by the low standards of the period, disgraceful. Diseases such as measles, whooping cough and scarlet fever, all associated with poverty and overcrowding, were the main causes of death among children. The dire housing and living conditions experienced by the vast majority of the Glasgow Irish community meant they instinctively leaned towards the new political ideology of socialism. Indeed, very many of the community leaders among the Glasgow Irish were espousing and living socialist policies and principles without having the specific political label attached. Therefore, despite the early opposition of their priests, the Glasgow Irish were naturally supportive of the embryonic socialist organisations and were well represented among the leadership of the early Independent Labour Party (ILP) and other early socialist organisations. Very many of the early socialists came to politics by way of their Irish Nationalism. While Arthur and Hugh Murphy were undoubtedly the most politically active and socialist leaning of Celtic's founding fathers, the mention here of three men with Glasgow Irish roots, specifically socialist ideologies and a passion for the Celtic Football Club, will highlight the point.

John Wheatley

(Glasgow City Archives)

The name of John Wheatley and his contribution to the early Scottish labour movement is well known and greatly respected within Scottish political circles, particularly Glasgow socialist circles. What is less well known are his longstanding links to the Celtic founding fathers and Irish Nationalism and the part he played in the reconciliation of Catholicism and socialism. Born in Bonmahon, Co Waterford, but raised in Braehead near Baillieston, Lanarkshire, Wheatley was greatly influenced by the teaching and support of his parish priest, Fr Peter Terken. Largely self-educated, he read widely, including Francesco Nitti's book *Catholic Socialism.*

A devout Catholic and Irish Nationalist he was firstly a member of the Michael Davitt branch of the Irish National League, a branch of which his father was a founding member. He was later a member of the Patrick Sarsfield branch of the United Irish League and of the Daniel O'Connell branch of the Irish National Foresters the later founded by Celtic's John Glass, both based at Shettleston. He became president of the former in 1898 and the latter in 1901.

In 1906, John Wheatley converted to socialism, and founded and was the first chairman of the Catholic Socialist Society. The society was an attempt to reconcile Catholicism and socialism, therefore membership was confined to practising Catholics. However, it was not deliberately sectarian and its meetings were open to all. He meet with some fierce opposition from local priests and on one occasion a large, threatening crowd of parishioners gathered outside his Shettleston home. Despite his conversion to socialism he remained a devout Catholic and a fervent Irish Nationalist. The following year he joined the ILP started a printing business and began publishing political pamphlets. Wheatley wrote a large number of these including: *How the Miners are Robbed* (1907), *The Catholic Workingman* (1909), *Miners, Mines and Misery* (1909), *Eight-Pound Cottages for Glasgow Citizens* (1913), *Municipal Banking* (1920) and the *New Rent Act* (1920). He was already a sitting councillor for Shettleston in Lanark County Council when in 1912 he was elected for the new ward of Shettleston and Tollcross, beginning the dominance of the ILP in the east end of the city. Opposed to Britain's involvement in the Great War, he was one of the leaders of the Glasgow rent strike opposing the eviction of families whose breadwinner was in the armed forces. He was later elected to the House of Commons as MP for Shettleston. A lifelong supporter of the Celtic, he had various links with the club's founders, especially director Thomas White, who took over the running of the Glasgow Eastern Standard newspaper, which Wheatley had started.

William Gallacher

Willie Gallacher was the son of an Irish father and Scots mother and was born in Paisley in 1881. After losing his father aged just seven, which Willie blamed on the effects of drink, by his mid-teens he was a passionate member of the temperance movement and would remain a lifelong teetotaller. On leaving school aged twelve, he worked as a delivery boy, but left after a dispute with his employer. By age fourteen he had gained an apprenticeship as a brass finisher in an engineering works. Aged twenty-four he joined the ILP, but in 1906 switched to the Marxist inclined Social Democratic Federation, which soon became the British Socialist Party. In March 1911, John Redmond was the keynote speaker at a St Patrick's Day lecture in Glasgow. As a massively popular figure among the Glasgow Irish, over a thousand Irish nationalists packed into the hall to hear him speak, including Celtic's Tom Maley and his wife Elizabeth. Willie Gallacher was also among the crowd and he later recalled the occasion as one of the most moving of his life. "The Boys of Wexford was sung by a thousand Irishmen packed into the hall. Jesus! But the Irish blood in me leapt as I listened to them! Redmond tore into the subject of Home Rule like a man inspired." Willie Gallacher then spent some time in America before returning to Glasgow, inspired by the Industrial Workers of the World and their beliefs in syndicalist ideals. He found work in the Albion Motor Works at Scotstoun, where he became a shop steward with the Amalgamated Engineering Union.

The ILP supported Irish Home Rule and in 1913 supported the Dublin transport workers during the *Great Dublin Lock-Out*, raising over £3000 to support the strikers' families. On the outbreak of the Great War, Willie Gallacher became a major anti-war campaigner and led a strike in 1915 for a penny an hour increase for engineering and shipyard workers. He became the president of the Clyde Workers Committee during the conflict and was jailed for six months for criticising the war. Towards the end of the war he became involved in the fight to improve the conditions of the Irish tattie howkers, seasonal workers whose working conditions defied description. The campaign brought Peadar O'Donnell, the Irish republican and socialist activist into contact with Gallacher. Inspired by the Glasgow Irish socialist, O'Donnell went back to Dublin where he became an organiser for the Irish Transport and General Workers Union. Willie among others was arrested and jailed after the *Battle of George Square* in 1919 when the British government put tanks onto Glasgow streets and with Scottish battalions confined to their barracks, flooded the city with English troops. In 1920, he went to Moscow where he met Lenin. He would later help found the British Communist Party, becoming the Member of Parliament for West Fife as a communist in 1935. He died in Paisley on 12 August 1965.

Patrick Dollan

Yet another early Glasgow Irish socialist was Patrick Joseph Dollan, who was born in the mining village of Baillieston, Lanarkshire. The earliest influence in his life was his Irish Nationalist, Dublin-born grandmother who was one of the few people in the village who could read. He first learned of the struggles for Irish home rule and social justice at her knee, he held the candle while she read out loud the newspapers reports. He was educated locally at St Bridget's School but aged just ten, he was forced to leave to find work. By the age of fifteen he had joined his Irish father in the Baillieston pits. Despite working long, hard hours in the pit, he enrolled for evening classes in the Wellshot Academy in Shettleston, where he discovered he had a talent for writing. In early 1900 he became involved with the Miner's Union and came under the influence of John Wheatley and the socialist doctrine of the ILP. He wrote and had published a number of essays, usually on mining topics, as a result of which he began to gravitate towards journalism. Recognising his talent, John Wheatley determined that his young socialist protégé should become a full-time journalist and in 1911 he joined the left-wing weekly newspaper Forward. The following year he married active socialist and suffragette Agnes Moir (*the daughter of a staunch Orangeman*). He entered local politics when he was elected to Glasgow Corporation as the councillor for the Govan ward in 1913. Committed to grassroots community politics, he would remain a councillor until 1946. During the Great War, he and his wife regularly appeared on peace platforms and both he his wife were among the leaders of the Clyde Rent War in 1915. In 1917, Patrick Dollan would serve 112 days of hard labour in London's Wormwood Scrubs Prison for his outspoken opposition to conscription and refusal to find work of national importance. He would later become Glasgow's first Roman Catholic Lord Provost, receiving a knighthood in the 1950s. In later years he would make much of his childhood, to demonstrate how far working-class Roman Catholics from an Irish immigrant background could succeed in public life.

For the Glasgow Irish community, national politics in the two decades which straddled the old and new centuries were dominated by two topics: *Irish Home Rule* and *land reform*, both in Ireland and in Scotland. While the vast majority of the Glasgow Irish wholeheartedly supported Home Rule for Ireland, only a small minority of the whole were politically active, although a sizeable number could be marshalled for specific events. Those of the Glasgow Irish who were politically active largely came from the burgeoning upper working class and the middle class – shopkeepers, publicans, tradesmen, teachers and other professionals who had the time and energy left at the end of their working day. Rallied by the Glasgow Observer newspaper, the Irish vote conditionally went to the Liberal Party who promised to deliver both objectives. Over the same period, their involvement in local politics was fairly minimal, with much of their effort going on Catholic representation on school and parochial boards. However, with the appearance of the likes of Patrick O'Hare, the first Roman Catholic councillor, the Glasgow Irish were finding their voice in Glasgow Council's chambers. Pat O'Hare was a native of Monaghan who arrived in Glasgow as a young man in 1872. After working for three years as a labourer in the Blochairn Ironworks, he moved into the spirit trade as a barman. Over the course of the next

Patrick O'Hare

fifteen years he had progressed to the ownership of two bars in the Calton. A leading light in the Land League movement in Townhead and the Garngad, Pat O'Hare was the instigator and first president of the Townhead Land League branch. With the emergence of the Independent Labour Party (ILP) in the 1890s, the socialists attempted to involve the Glasgow Irish in local politics on their agendas. The ILP emphasised the class struggle and pushed for class solidarity on an agenda of better housing, wages and working conditions for all the working class. They hoped these objectives would cross religious and national divides and unite the working class, largely, it must be said, in the face of some fierce opposition from the Catholic Church. Between 1897 and 1906, Pat O'Hare of the ILP would be re-elected to the council twice in the Springburn electoral ward, an area with a very strong Ulster Protestant/Orange presence.

By the last decade of the nineteenth century the Glasgow middle classes had for the most part moved out of the city centre. The respectable upper working classes packed up too and moved to the new red sandstone tenements of Hyndland, Shawlands, Dennistoun and Anniesland leaving the city centre, the Gorbals and the east end to the Catholic and Protestant poor. Although the east end, including the old villages of Bridgeton, Mile-End and Shettleston had large Protestant communities, the general area including the Calton came to be regarded by the Glasgow population at large as an Irish Catholic ghetto and synonymous with lawlessness, idleness, drunkenness, squalor and social deprivation. Around the same time the expanding Glasgow Irish middle classes also moved into the suburbs, although socially they remained largely within their own Glasgow Irish communities. They were the nouveau riche of the Glasgow Irish, being entrepreneurs, professionals and businessmen, with a small but rapidly increasing number involved in law and medicine. The Glasgow Irish had come to dominate what was seen at the time as the highly disreputable liquor trade, this at a time when the temperance movement, including the Catholic League of the Cross, was at the height of its popularity. In keeping with the Victorian version of paterfamilias as displayed in the wider British society, the new Glasgow Irish middle class retained an active leadership role in their communities and it was from this section of the community that the Celtic club's founding fathers were drawn.

Chapter Four

The Founding Fathers

The definition of a "Founding Father" is open to interpretation and debate. Who should or should not be considered to be a founding father? Is there a cut off date for club membership, perhaps the first year? Is it about a personal contribution to the running or formation of the club, should only those members who served on the various committees be considered, or perhaps those who subscribed desperately needed funds to get the club off the ground. Possibly only the half dozen of the most famous members should be considered founding fathers. What then of the ordinarily club members that we only hear from at the twice-yearly general meetings, but who most certainly had a major influence on the ethos and direction of the club? What of the non-club members like the hundreds of ordinary Glasgow Irish who turned up after labouring all day to help build the first Celtic Park? Without a football park there would have been no club. The pen pictures which follows is not a definitive list of the individuals who might or might not be regarded as founding fathers, It is simply an attempt to shed some light on the characters and personalities of a cross section of club members who influenced the ethos and development of the club over the first decade or so of its existence.

The individuals involved in getting the Celtic Football and Athletic Club project off the ground were all Roman Catholic, all Irish or of Irish descent, and were all highly respectable and successful in their own fields of medicine, law and education or were men who had succeeded in business. For the most part they were already community leaders and well known to each other through their work in church, community or political associations, societies, confraternities, etc. Brothers Walfrid and Dorotheus chose them specifically because of their respectability and known leadership qualities, vital attributes if the Celtic project was to succeed in a Scottish football association run by stuffy, Presbyterian, middle-class amateur sportsmen. Almost to a man the individuals chosen were in some way associated with the temperance movement, particularly the Catholic League of the Cross and the Catholic Young Men's Society. Although several publicans or wine merchants were on the original subscriber list of 1887, none of the original office bearers were directly involved in what was regarded at the time as the highly disreputable liquor trade, although committeemen William McKillop had trade links as a restaurateur and Frank McErlean had wine and spirit interests in Belfast. Having assumed the classic Victorian paterfamilias role of community leaders, the political and social beliefs of the founding fathers largely created the renowned Irish Nationalist, charitable ethos at the Celtic club and greatly influenced the thinking and attitude of the club's supporters. Something of the character and beliefs of the founding fathers and their influence at the club, teased from the historical record, can be best be highlighted by short pen pictures of the men themselves.

Brother Walfrid

Brother Walfrid

The most famous of the founding fathers is the now legendry Brother Walfrid, born Andrew Kerins at Ballymote, Co Sligo, in May 1840. Aged fifteen, like so many others before him, he took the coal boat from Sligo, landing on the dockside at Glasgow's Broomielaw. His early life is something of a mystery; however, in 1864, Andrew took holy orders, joining the Marist Brothers (the Society of Mary), a relatively unknown teaching order. He was then given the name Walfrid to signify a rebirth into a new religious life. Brother Walfrid then moved at some point to France to begin his religious training, returning to Glasgow around 1869. In the National Census of 1871, he is listed as a teacher living in the Marist parochial house at 71 Charlotte Street.

It was thought that Walfrid had taught only at St Mary's in the Calton before being appointed headmaster of the newly opened Sacred Heart School at Bridgeton in 1874. However, compelling evidence has recently emerged indicating that he also taught at St Mungo's Academy. In January 1893, thirty-eight-year-old John McAdam, at the time the founder and editor of the Donegal Vindicator newspaper, published an article in the Glasgow Observer recalling his school days at St Mungo's Academy. The former Academy boy talked of Brother Walfrid and with great affection described him as being lovable, but quick tempered. He also recalled fellow scholars John MacCreadie, Joe Nelis, John Conway, Michael Cairns and Joseph McGroary. All those mentioned were later drafted in to help get the Celtic club off the ground by Walfrid. By the time of the 1871 National Census, John McAdam had left St Mungo's Academy and as a sixteen year old, was employed as a pawnbroker's assistant in Glasgow. This would suggest that Brother Walfrid taught at St Mungo's prior to leaving Glasgow for France. Later in his essay, McAdam expresses a wish that he could relive his happy school days, but he thought the dream would only work if Brother Walfrid could be induced to come cautiously up behind him in the way he remembered so well, and with an accompanying cuff on the ear, say: "Hold your pen straight." Unlike today where corporal punishment is considered unacceptable and is outlawed in schools, then a teacher cuffing a pupil on the ear would have been regarded as a very minor reprimand and entirely the norm. This was an era when very many school, including Roman Catholic schools employed former soldiers as disciplinarians. John McAdam's essay clearly shows that Brother Walfrid was enormously respected and held in great and long-lasting affection by his pupils.

Like the Calton, Bridgeton was an extremely deprived industrial area in what the city fathers of the time liked to think of as the Empire's second city. Every working day Brother Walfrid would have witnessed the plight of the poor of the east end, but as a schoolteacher, it was the hungry, beggarly children who tugged at his heart the hardest. He was also well aware that the local Protestant churches ran soup kitchens in the area and hungry children do not care which version of grace they say before they eat. Therefore, a soup kitchen for Catholic children would both feed hungry children and help keep his flock away from the wolves.

Brother Dorotheus

Brother Walfrid was supported in the idea by his good friend Brother Dorotheus, the headmaster of St Mary's School in the Calton. One of the forgotten men of the Celtic history, Dorotheus, born Henry Currie in Dundee, encouraged Walfrid in his various charitable schemes after he was given his own new school to manage in Bridgeton. When Walfrid, with the assistance of the St Vincent de Paul Society started the Poor Children's Dinner Tables in 1884, Dorotheus took up the idea and was soon providing dinners for over a 1,000 children per week in the Calton. He also had seen the potential of football as a vehicle for raising funds and had as early as 1886 been involved in organising charity football games between amateur teams with all proceeds going to the Dinner Tables.

These experiences, combined with the Scottish Cup success of Hibernian, persuaded the two men of the potential benefits of starting up a football club of their own. With the children in mind, they decided the primary objective of the proposed football club, if it ever took off, would be to raise money to help feed poor children in three east end Catholic parishes. The additional benefits of the venture would be to motivate young Catholic men to remain true to their faith and to take an interest in sport and fitness. It was also hoped that the club would help keep them away from the demon drink.

Although nothing specific is known of Brother Walfrid's politics, some indication can be gained from studying his chosen friends and associates. For example, when he decided to involve the laity in his Celtic project, he turned first to Hugh Murphy, a leading light in the Home Government branch of the Irish National League, for assistance. At the beginning of January 1889, Walfrid, who was by now the Brother Superior at the Marist house in Charlotte Street, and a party from the new Celtic club were guests at the first annual dinner of the O'Connell Branch of the Irish National Foresters' Benefit Society. The Irish National Foresters (INF) was an Irish friendly society, which supported Irish Nationalism. Embedded in its constitution was a call for a government for Ireland by the Irish people in accordance with Irish ideas and Irish aspirations. The event was held in the Pinkerton Halls in Bridgeton and among the Celtic party were Dr Conway, John Glass (founding member of the branch), JH McLaughlin, Dan Molloy and Neil McCallum, scorer of the Celtic's first ever goal. That night, McCallum also scored at the singing, accompanied by Dan Molloy on the fiddle and John McLaughlin on the piano. The toast of the evening was the INF, proposed by Dr Conway, and the night was brought to a conclusion with the singing of "God save Ireland". The vast majority of the organisations with which Walfrid was associated or involved, leaned, to a greater or lesser degree, towards the Irish cultural revivalist movement, which was, by definition, Nationalist in its sentiments.

Some indication of his leanings may also be gleaned from the popular supposition that he chose and pointedly argued for the new football club to be named "Celtic", the name being a link between the ancient peoples of Ireland and Scotland. The premise is that he argued for the Celtic name with most club members favouring the rather unimaginative Glasgow Hibernian. Although the heart and soul of the club were very definitely and obviously Irish, there were some Scots Catholic influences on the first very large and boisterous three-parish committees. The representatives of St Andrew's Parish would undoubtedly have comprised a number of Scots Catholics, not only was the parish the mother Church of the Scots Catholics in Glasgow, but it was the base of the Caledonian Catholic Association, an organisation whose remit included fostering relations between Scotch and Irish Catholics. Scots Catholics were, of course, the first Catholics to re-establish themselves in the city at the beginning of the nineteenth century and until the mass influxes of the Irish and their priests, the Church was very distinctly Scots. As early as 1830, the Glasgow hierarchy faced criticism from their Irish parishioners, who accused them of ignoring their interests in favour of the Scots Catholics. By the 1850s there was very real hostility in the Catholic Church in Scotland to the large numbers of Irish priests coming into the Church to service the phenomenal increase in Irish Catholics, as the Irish now far outnumbered the Scots in their own Church. The Caledonian Catholic Association, with the full backing of the Church, was tasked specifically with promoting the Scottish side of the Church and with bringing together Scotch and Irish Roman Catholics. Another powerful voice at the embryonic Celtic club was that of solicitor Joe Shaughnessy, who although of Irish stock had strong family links with the Scottish Highlands. His wife's family were Lochaber crofters and shepherds, who at the time were involved in the Highland Rent Wars. Before moving to Rutherglen, the Shaughnessy family were members of St Andrew's Parish. A number of other early Celtic committeemen, second- and third-generation Irish-Scots, were also members of the Caledonian Catholic Association, including Joe Nelis and Stephen J Henry.

As an academic, Walfrid would have been interested in the cultural and political developments then taking place in both Ireland and Scotland. At the time both countries were going through something of a cultural renaissance, rediscovering or reinventing their nationalism and joint Celtic heritage. In fact, Scotland, like Ireland, was agitating for increased independence from London through the Scottish Home Rule movement. This coincided with popular revivals of cultures and languages worldwide, a natural consequence of growing empires destroying native cultures. In the 1880s, the cultural rights of colonies were at the forefront of political debate all over the world. This was particularly true in Ireland, from which sprang a renewed interest in all things Gaelic. The renewed interest in nationalism, both in Ireland and Scotland, led to the rediscovery of a joint cultural heritage between the Celtic nations, particularly the immensely close social and family ties that once existed between the Irish and the Scottish Highlanders and islanders. The Scottish Highlanders and islanders, of course, experienced many of the same hardships as their Irish cousins, since their clan culture had been systematically destroyed during the eighteenth century.

Over the course of the 1880s, Scottish crofters had been in the midst of the Highland Land Wars. Thousands of crofters were in revolt and the police and the military were deployed to keep order. In mid-1887, when the name of the club would no doubt have been under consideration, the national newspapers had been for months carrying stories of rent-racking landlords, evicted Highland crofters, riots, mass imprisonment and forced emigration. All these events were profoundly felt by the Irish, who were experiencing much the same travails themselves. Michael Davitt, the Irish patriot and soon to be honorary club patron, was deeply involved in land reform. Although he was primarily concerned with Irish land reform, he soon expanded his remit to include the rights of crofters in the Scottish Highlands and islands. The Highland Land League was inspired by and modelled on Michael Davitt's Irish Land League. In late 1886, the government introduced the *Crofters Holding Act*, the main provisions of which were based on the *Land Act for Ireland*. When Michael Davitt visited the Scottish Highlands and islands, a report of the visit was carried in the Glasgow Irish's own newspaper, the Glasgow Observer: "Davitt in Highlands – the Tribune of the Celtic Race". In mid-May 1887 the Glasgow Observer carried the headline "Celt meets Celt" and described his visit to the west coast Highlanders as cousin meeting cousin. Adding, "This meeting will send a thrill of joy through the hearts of the scattered children of the Celt. One in blood and tradition, in music, custom and language, the Irish and his Highland brother are also one in suffering." At the end of April 1887, under the auspices of John Ferguson and the Home Government branch, what was described as a *Monster Meeting* was held in Glasgow and over 4000 Glasgow Nationalists turned up to support the Crofter's Aid Association. Another 2000 were locked out, unable to get into the hall. Among the worthies on the platform with future Celtic connections were Hugh Murphy and honorary club vice-president James Quillan. As far as the Home Government Branch was concerned, there were potentially thousands of Catholic Highland voters to be won over to Celtic political causes.

The supposition therefore that Brother Walfrid chose the name of the club to highlight the ancient link between the Celtic peoples of Ireland and Scotland may not be completely outlandish. He may have been responding to events that were both current and very personal, and the name of the new football club was a very public gesture of support for the Celtic Highlanders then under severe pressure. It was also not the first time that Walfrid had chosen a Scots-Irish name, having previously formed a junior football team, which he called *Columb*. The burial place of the Irish prince and Celtic church missionary on the west coast at Iona was a very popular pilgrimage for the Glasgow Irish. Having said all that, in reality, the reason why Brother Walfrid chose the name Celtic is unknown and any suppositions are mere speculation; the secret went to the grave with him.

Until his dying day Walfrid insisted the name be pronounced with the hard K as in Keltic, and not the soft S used for the club today. There has always been some debate over the pronunciation of the name. In fact, both versions are grammatically correct. The hard K only gained general popularity in the late nineteenth century through its use by academics. Therefore as an academic, Brother Walfrid would naturally, just like his contemporaries, use the hard K. It should also be borne in mind that all over the world where the Irish and Scots diaspora settled, immigrants were at that time founding their own Celtic clubs, most having nothing to do with football. There were already a number of Celtic football clubs, including a Glasgow Hibernian football team and indeed a Celtic Thistle football club based in Glasgow. There was also a very large and well-established Celtic Society with its own offshoot sports and social clubs all bearing the name Celtic in the city. All used the hard K; therefore the use by the Glasgow Irish of the soft S may simply have been an attempt to be a bit different. In 1909, Tom Maley writing in his notes for the Glasgow Observer thought that the S pronunciation was simply the supporters' mispronunciation of the name, which stuck. If Tom Maley didn't know for certain how the pronunciation came about then we will never know, but Seltic it is and Seltic it always will be. Very often the club is called the Glasgow Celtic; this is incorrect and 'Glasgow' has never figured in its title. Probably the first example of the error was in December 1887 when the Scottish Referee sports paper announced:

> We learn that the efforts which have lately been made to organise in Glasgow a first-class Catholic football club, have been successfully consummated by the formation of the "Glasgow Celtic Football and Athletic Club", under influential auspices. They have secured a six-acre ground in the East End, which they mean to put to fine order. We wish the "Celts" all success.

Brother Walfrid, we are told, also envisaged the new football club as a vehicle for bringing the socially isolated Glasgow Irish and the wider Glasgow communities together through sport. Like the suggestion that the Celtic was designed to help bring the Scots Highlanders and Irish together, there has never been any documentary evidence produced to substantiate this claim; however, the Roman Catholic Church was at the time spearheading a drive for social respectability and social integration for the Glasgow Irish. The club could therefore be considered as a vehicle for this and simply another facet of the Church's overall strategy.

Finally, we are told that Walfrid hoped that a successful Celtic club would bring some much needed pride and confidence to a close-knit but very hard-pressed Glasgow Irish community. In the event, the success of the Celtic not only brought pride to the Glasgow Irish community, but according to club member Mr Thomas Flood at the AGM of 1892, brought pride to the entire Irish race in Great Britain. At a time of rampant and institutionalised racism, the Irish as a race were seen as being inferior to the Anglo-Saxons. While all these progressive social ambitions were to be welcomed, for Brother Walfrid working at the coalface of child poverty, first and foremost in his mind was the problem of feeding hundreds of hungry children on a daily basis.

The Celtic Football and Athletic Club, as imagined by Brothers Walfrid and Dorotheus, was of course established and became an instant and undreamt of success. Previously unimagined sums of money were soon being raised and distributed to the Children's Dinner Tables and eventually to other charities and good causes. Brother Walfrid was involved with the Celtic until he was transferred by his order to a new position in London in August 1892. His departure from Glasgow coincided with the expansion of the game of football and in turn the rise of the modernising, power brokers at the club, who wished to put the club onto a more business-like footing by converting it into a limited liability company. Walfrid's departure also coincided with a significant debt burden being taken on by the club to finance the building of a new Celtic Park and a corresponding fall in the charitable donations distributed by the club. In what was perhaps an attempt by the traditionalist members, who opposed the direction in which the club was being led, to influence the general membership, a message from Brother Walfrid, then in London, was sent to the club in time for 1893 AGM. In his message, Walfrid assured the club members of his continued deep and sincere interest in the club to which his heart still clings. In the event, the threat of limited liability was seen off at this time but the power brokers would not be denied. The club was converted into a limited liability company just four years later.

Brother Walfrid apparently maintained an interest in the club until his death in Dumfries in April 1915, but his opinion of the path that the club took after his departure from Glasgow is unrecorded. Walfrid had a final meeting with his old comrades when he joined up with a Celtic party, including Tom and Willie Maley, chairman James Kelly and director Mick Dunbar, who were returning from a European tour in June 1911. He joined the Celtic party at Folkestone and travelled with them by train to London. Tom Maley, then a sports columnist with the Glasgow Observer, recorded the occasion and Brother Walfrid's affectionate comments regarding the club: "Well, well, time has brought changes; outside ourselves there are few left of the of the old brigade. I know nothing of the present lot [of players], but they are under the old colours and are quartered in the dear old quarters, and that suffices." Take from that what you will!

John Glass

John Glass

Second only to Brother Walfrid in the pantheon of Celtic deities is John Glass. A glazier to trade, in his The Story of the Celtic book written in 1938, legendary club manager Willie Maley would credit him as being the driving force behind the club's establishment and early success. Born in March 1851 at the Broomielaw, in what was the very centre of Glasgow's worst slums, his Irish parents, James and Ann Glass, arrived in the city from Donegal with the starving masses during the Great Famine. Sometime after his birth the Glass family moved across the river Clyde and into the epicentre of Irish Gaeldom in Glasgow, the Gorbals. Raised in the district he re-crossed the Clyde with his family settling in Bridgeton before his first marriage in 1868. In November 1884, recently widowed John Glass married Bridget McGreavy at St Mary's Chapel in Abercromby Street. At the time of the Celtic club's formation, John and his family were living at 60 Marlborough Street, on the Calton/Mile-End border, while he was employed as a foreman glazier with the Glass family's Wood and Glazing business. As first-generation Glasgow Irish, John was a passionate Irish Nationalist and was the treasurer of the Home Government branch (HGB) of the Irish National League (INL), which was dedicated to achieving Home Rule for Ireland. He was a great friend and supporter of Glasgow Irish leader and HGB chairman, Hugh Murphy. He was a founding member of the O'Connell Branch of the Irish National Foresters' Benefit Society, a friendly society based in Bridgeton, and was also the vice-president of the Camlachie Liberal Association. The British Liberal Party supported Home Rule for Ireland, though not all Liberals toed the party line. John Glass was reputedly blessed with the gift of the gab and actively tried to persuade Glasgow Irish voters to join Liberal Associations in order to influence the choice of local party candidates. The idea was to ensure candidates were true Home Rulers. At the same time he was just as committed to the advancement of his own Glasgow Irish community and was involved with the embryonic socialist movement through a personal association with local trade unions and through his support of the INL and its successor, the UIL, as they gave their backing to Labour candidates at local council elections. He was also on the committee of his local Catholic Union, an organisation committed to having Catholics elected onto school boards.

A man of explosive energies, John Glass was obviously a complete workaholic. His home at Marlborough Street was adjacent to East Rose Street, where in St Mary's League of the Cross hall at 67 East Rose Street he chaired the first meeting to discuss the formation of the football club. Already a well-known parish leader in the Calton, he was brought into the Celtic project by his best friend Hugh Murphy. He was already well known to Brother Walfrid having helped organise the Hibernian/Renton charity game in May 1887. John brought his drive, organisational skills, business acumen and building trade contacts to the table. He may also have had some input into the choice of the name of the new club. As an astute businessman, he would have realised that from a business angle 'Celtic' would be more likely to resonate with the thousands of Scottish Catholic Highlanders living in the area in a way that a specifically Irish, Glasgow Hibernian or Glasgow Shamrock would not. He was the club fixer, the man with the can-do, will-do attitude. If something needed organised or arranged or a problem needed resolved, he was the man to see. From the moment he chaired the first meeting, his enormous energy, drive and enthusiasm were directed into the new enterprise and the success of Celtic Football and Athletic Club became his life's work. Over the course of eighteen years he never missed a committee meeting and it was said of him that the Celtic was his chief delight. Willie Maley went so far as to credit John Glass with the club's very existence.

As early as 1889, the club's existence appeared reasonably secure, but what was in question was how it would evolve and the direction it was being led by its president John Glass. With the support of the club membership, he managed to survive two attempts at dethroning him, first by James Quillan at the 1889 AGM and by Dr Conway at the 1891 AGM. Depending on your point of view, John Glass was either a far-sighted visionary, who led the Celtic club through a period of massive expansion in Scottish football to a position of pre-eminence, or a cynical, manipulative schemer, an opportunist, who exploited a charitable ideal for personal gain and self-aggrandisement. Over the course of ten years he guided the amateur club from what was a parochial, charity-driven community asset controlled by its membership, to a leading professional football club, a very successful company with limited liability status in the hands of a few shareholders.

That John Glass led the club away from its charitable origins is without doubt, the only questions are ones of motive and the likely consequences for the club and for charity were the club to have remained true to its founding principles. Although no longer the sole aim or purpose of the club, charitable principles undoubtedly remained at the club after it became a public limited company and the Celtic contributed greatly to various good causes, but were they enough to counterbalance the charitable contributions that a much less powerful and most certainly amateur Celtic club may have been able to generate? We will never know the answer to the latter question, but that he and a few others personally gained from their association with the club is without doubt. Whatever the view, his contribution to the club was massive, an indication of which was demonstrated in 1897 when John Glass was voted an honorarium of £100 cash and 100 free shares in the new limited company. Within a year of the formation of the limited company, John Glass held 400 shares making him a major shareholders in the company. His brother, Peter Patrick Glass, described at the time as a builder living in Shawlands, acquired 200 shares at the initial issue and within the year had increased his holding to 401. John Glass remained on the board of directors until his death in very middle-class Saltcoats in 1906, far removed from the slums of the Broomielaw, Gorbals and the Calton. His body was brought back to what was described as his usual address at 597 Gallowgate to be buried at Dalbeth cemetery. It was said at the time, that he never recovered from the sudden death of his best friend and companion Hugh Murphy. Irrespective of his motives concerning the club, were it not for John Glass, the Celtic Football and Athletic Club in the form we know it today would most certainly not exist. After his death, most of John Glass's shares went to his prodigy and replacement on the Celtic board, Thomas White.

John Conway MD MRCS

The importance of John Conway MD MRCS in the formation and establishment of the Celtic Football Club is largely unknown to modern day Celtic supporters. He was the son of a Glasgow Irish pawnbroker, John Conway, who was described as one of the most spirited Catholics of his day and was the first Roman Catholic to sit on a parochial board in Glasgow. Dr John Conway was a very remarkable young man; born in 1864, he was educated at St Mungo's Academy and went on to St Aloysius College. From there he gained entry to Glasgow University, where he was one of the few Glasgow Irish Catholics to graduate as a doctor of medicine prior to the turn of the twentieth century. On graduation, he studied in London, where nine months later he was admitted to the Royal College of Surgeons. Despite his education and medical achievements, he spurned the opportunity to climb the social ladder and moved back to Glasgow and into the east end where he practised medicine among the poor. In June 1884, at St Alphonsus Chapel, he married 26-year-old Mary Burns, the daughter of Daniel Burns, a general dealer. The best

Dr John Conway

man at the wedding was William J Henry, brother of Stephen J Henry, soon to be one of the Celtic's founding fathers. The newly weds set up home in Morris Place, adjacent to Monteith Row and over looking Glasgow Green, but his practice was in Abercromby Street in the Calton. Working from there, he became acquainted with Brother Walfrid then headmaster of the Sacred Heart School at nearby Bridgeton. As a local doctor, no doubt John Conway would have been connected to the school or church in an official capacity, perhaps as a medical advisor. In addition to his medical work, John Conway was also renowned for his charitable acts and bequests. He was deeply involved with numerous Catholic charities and social organisations including the O'Connell Branch of the Irish National Foresters, his local St Alphonsus' Catholic Benefit Society, St Vincent de Paul, the Catholic Union, and the Whitevale Children's Refuge, where he was the appointed physician. Archbishop Eyre opened the rebuilt Whitevale or Catholic Children's Refuge in September 1890. The refuge was run by the Society of St Vincent de Paul and could cater for up to eighty children. The fact that he was only twenty-nine years of age at the time says something of the calibre of the man. He was also one of the principal promoters of the immensely influential Catholic Glasgow Observer newspaper, which was first published by the Glasgow Publishing Company in 1886. John Conway remained a director of the company until the rag was taken over by Charles Diamond in 1893.

No doubt at the urging of Brother Walfrid, who would have stressed the positive medical, social and charitable value of such a sport-oriented venture, John Conway agreed to become involved in the Celtic project and was appointed the football club's first honorary president. As a Glasgow Irish physician practising among his own people, it would be difficult to overstate the position of respect and affection he would have held within the Glasgow Irish community. Few of his patients would have been able to afford much in the way of fees and no doubt many sums were waved or a token accepted in their stead. In an age when ordinary working-class people deferred to those they considered their betters, the value of John Conway's positive, pro-active support for the new sporting venture would have been enormous. His influence and highly visible and vocal support would have greatly encouraged those in positions to offer practical help to look favourably on the enterprise. In addition, with respect to the staunchly pro-temperance atmosphere of the times, he brought some much-needed respectability to an organisation that would increasingly become embroiled in the disreputable drinks trade. Publicans and wine merchants would later dominate the Celtic's committee and would number some 23.3 per cent of the club's early shareholders. A Glasgow wag once called the future Celtic board six spirit merchants and one (John) glass. Despite the close association with the drinks trade, paradoxically the Celtic club also developed strong associations with the Catholic Young Men's Society and the League of the Cross, both staunchly pro-temperance organisations.

John Conway took his role as the club figurehead extremely seriously and was totally committed to the project, leading and representing the Celtic club at major social events. He spoke at a soirée of Celtic club members and friends in the Waterloo Rooms on St Patrick's Day in 1890, when he highlighted the progress of the club including having spent over £1500 on the field, with every penny paid off. He proudly announced that the Celtic club had already that year donated to charity a sum of £300 to £400. As the club, along with the game of football in Scotland, began to develop, a majority of the committee, led by John Glass, wished to take the Celtic down a more business-orientated route and to pay club officials an official salary. John Conway firmly believed the club should remain true to its founding principles, which envisaged all profits going to charitable causes. Wages and fees paid to club servants would naturally diminish the money available for the charities. The disagreement came to a head after it was discovered that two club officials had been paid without the prior consent of the members. What further rankled was the fact that John Glass wished to pay club secretary and current team player Willie Maley a wage even after the sums earmarked for charities had declined from the previous year. He had a point: that year 1890/91 from a total income of over £4400 only £445 had been given to charities, with the Poor Children's Dinner Tables receiving £220. The differences ensured that the AGM of 1891 was a lively affair.

Making a principled stand based on his own deep personal commitment to charity, John Conway lost the argument over paid officials and effectively lost the power struggle over the soul of the club. He was voted out of his position of honorary president in favour of Joe Nelis and at the same meeting failed in his bid to oust John Glass as club president. Dr Conway had paid the price of crossing John Glass and his supporters, many of whom were doing very well financially out of the Celtic club. It would appear the disagreements and subsequent split left bad blood between the doctor and his former friends at the Celtic. After being voted off the committee, the doctor appears to have cut all ties with the club and took nothing more to do with the project. He did however continue to work with John Glass and James Quillan at the O'Connell branch of the Irish National Foresters where all three men were trustees as late as November 1893. Dr John Conway was, in fact, the second high profile victim of the struggle for the soul of the club, it having already claimed the scalp of James Quillan, the club's first honorary vice-president, two years previously. Like during the Quillanite rebellion, Brother Walfrid appears to have remained neutral or unconcerned on the matter. It is difficult to imagine that if he was worried at the direction the club was being taking, he would not have used his enormous influence to change matters. The struggle for the soul of the club finally ended in 1897 when the community asset that was the Celtic club was converted into a public limited company, owned by its new shareholders. John Conway had been a very high profile honorary president, whose contribution was vital both in the creation of the club and to its survival over its first years when its future was most at risk. Dr Conway did not live to see the idealistic Celtic project turned into a business, dying suddenly in 1894. At the time of his death, despite his contribution to the Celtic, the club made neither note nor comment of his passing. The Glasgow Observer delivered its own plaudit to the good doctor when it published, "That it was greatly owing to his exertions that the Celtic Football Club was started and in acknowledgement of his efforts in that direction the members appointed him honorary president for three years." Dr Conway was buried at Dalbeth cemetery.

Joseph Shaughnessy

Joseph Shaughnessy

Another founding father who greatly influenced the direction and fortunes of the early club was Joseph Shaughnessy. Born in the east end of the city at Bridgeton he was the son of a Glasgow Irish spirit dealer, who moved to Rutherglen shortly after his birth. He was educated by the Marists at St Mungo's Academy and by the Jesuits at St Aloysius College. Finally, he studied law at Glasgow University qualifying in 1877 when he opened his own practice in Hope Street, Glasgow. Seven years before, as a twenty-one-year-old law apprentice he had married twenty-four-year-old Mary McDonald, a Scottish Catholic born at Fort Augustus. The couple were married in Mary's home in Glenmorrison but set up their own home in Rutherglen. By 1887, Joe Shaughnessy was a well-established and respected member of the Glasgow legal profession. He had been involved in a number of very high profile cases including the trial of the ten Irish Republican Brotherhood (IRB) men accused of bombing the gasometers at Glasgow's Tradeston district in January 1883. In December 1883, after being found guilty, five of the men were sentenced to penal servitude for life, the other five to seven years' penal servitude. Socially aware, Joe Shaughnessy was a crusading lawyer deeply involved with the welfare and civil rights of the local mining communities around his home in Rutherglen. He represented a number of the miners jailed after the Blantyre Riots in April 1887 and he would later be appointed agent for the Scottish National Miners Federation. He became an acknowledged authority on workers' rights and employment law and helped draft several pieces of important employer liability legislation. As a result of his representation of local miners, he was elected onto the Rutherglen Burgh Council, where he retained his seat for eighteen years. Brought into the Celtic project from the very start, his legal advice would have been vital in getting the project off the ground. His standing within the club is highlighted by his election to succeed Dr John Conway as honorary president at the club's AGM in 1891. His contribution to the club was not confined to legalities; by 1893 he was one of the club's major guarantors and is listed among the leaseholders of the new Celtic Park. It was Joe Shaughnessy who came up with the idea of experimenting with floodlighting; the innovation would not only allow football games to be played at night, but the stadium could also be hired out to third parties for use in the winter evenings. He and his eldest son John Shaughnessy took a keen interest in the Celtic Cycling Club and John could be found at the Celtic Sports umpiring the cycle events. Having put up considerable amounts of his own money to finance the club, it was he who first mooted the suggestion that the club be converted into a limited liability company at the 1893 AGM. His position regarding the matter is therefore completely clear:

At the present time every man was in favour of one man one vote and in matters football he could not see why they could not have a similar arrangement. It was said that lawyers endeavoured to make money out of everything, but he had no such intentions his only object being to benefit the club.

He worked towards that outcome until it was finally achieved. In February 1897, when the limited liability debate had finally come to a head, as one of the main guarantors of the club debt he let it be known that he would resign his position and sever all association with the club if the limited liability proposal was not passed. After the club was converted into a limited liability company, despite being one of the largest shareholders, he never took a seat on the new Celtic board, but it was on his motion, seconded by James Curtis, that Willie Maley was appointed team secretary of the newly formed limited liability company.

Some indication as to his political leaning may be seen by his appointment as secretary of the Rutherglen Liberals, his representation of the miners and the Fenian bombers and by his proposal of Michael Davitt, a former jailed Fenian and socialist land reformer, as honorary patron of the Celtic at the club's first AGM in 1889. Joseph Shaughnessy was a leading member of the Home Government branch of the Irish National League (INL). Although other INL branches concentrated almost exclusively on Irish political reform and land reform, Glasgow's Home Government branch took Michael Davitt and his land rights campaign, both in Ireland and in the Scottish Highlands, to their heart, despite Davitt often being at loggerheads with the leadership of the Irish Parliamentary Party. The Home Government branch's chairman, John Ferguson, recognised that common experiences and injustices over land rights united the native Irish and their Highland Celtic cousins. He ensured that the considerable political weight of the Home Government branch was thrown behind the Highlanders' cause. It is safe to say that Joe Shaughnessy was among the leading branch members driving the policy.

Although very definitely of Irish stock, Joseph Shaughnessy also had Scottish Celtic connections, through his wife Mary McDonald. Born in Fort Augustus near Glengarry, her family were shepherds and crofters in an area that had been a stronghold of Scottish Roman Catholicism since the Reformation. The collapse of the Scottish fishing industry in the 1880s and the continued drive for what were regarded as "improvements" saw crofters' rents racked and many Scottish Highlanders and islanders forced off their crofts. As in Ireland, rent-racking led to rent strikes and land-grabbing and provoked retaliatory measures in the form of evictions by the landlords. Like their Irish cousins, thousands of impoverished crofters, unable to afford the rents, were forced into immigration or migration, resulting in the Crofters' Wars of the mid-1880s. With his joint Irish and Scottish Highland connections it is surely no coincidence that it was Joe Shaughnessy who proposed Irish land reformer Michael Davitt as honorary club patron. Despite Michael Davitt's apparent turn away from the wilder side of Irish politics, his appointment as Celtic club patron would undoubtedly have raised eyebrows.

Joe Shaughnessy was also a devout Roman Catholic and over the course of a lifetime was deeply involved in the Rutherglen St Vincent de Paul Conference. He remained a faithful supporter of the Celtic until his sudden death in 1906. Such was the respect he engendered in Rutherglen and the surrounding district, all the shops in the town closed during his funeral and the flag on the town hall was flown at half-mast. His eldest son, John Shaughnessy, also a solicitor, would be voted onto the Celtic board in 1911.

John O'Hara

John O'Hara

An immensely influential but somewhat overlooked founding father was John O'Hara born at Graysteel in Faughanvale Parish, Co Derry, around 1843. As a child, he and his family arrived in Scotland during the famine years and settled in Bannockburn, near Stirling. By the mid-1860s, John O'Hara was living in Glasgow's east end where he was employed locally as a shoemaker. He became involved in the embryonic trade union movement within the shoemaking industry and by the early 1870s had taken on the role of branch organiser with the Boot and Shoe Operatives Union. After an internal union dispute between artisans who produced handmade shoes and boots, and the more downmarket riveters and finishers, in 1873 O'Hara helped form the breakaway, National Union of Boot and Shoe Riveters and Finishers (NUBSRF). The new union soon had 4000 members in thirty-five branches. John O'Hara represented the Glasgow branch at the first conference of the National Union of Boot and Shoe Operatives at Northampton in 1874. By 1875, the union was able to establish a funeral fund and offer sick pay of ten shillings a week. By 1887, its membership had grown to just under 10,000. John O'Hara's home was at 77 East Rose Street, just a few closes down from St Mary's League of the Cross hall. He was among the welcoming committee for the cup-winning Hibernian team to the east end. Given his background and living so close to the League of the Cross hall, it was probably inevitable that he would be drawn into the Celtic project from the very beginning. As a committeeman, he was nominated as a collector of club subscriptions when they were required in January 1888. With extensive organisational skills and experience through his work with the trade unions, he then took on the role as the first club secretary.

At a time when all the supposedly amateur football clubs were engaged in all kinds of financial shenanigans to get hold of or to keep star players, John O'Hara as club secretary, alongside John Glass, took the lead in securing and managing the Celtic players. He got involved with an unknown player (probably Mick McKeown) in a fight over money in which John was struck. He then got into hot water with the SFA regarding the methods employed in the acquisition of a number of players. It is more than likely that he was deeply involved in the illegal *tapping up* (poaching other club's players) of Celtic legend Dan Doyle, enticing him away from Everton in August 1891. At the time Dan Doyle had supposedly agreed to play for the Liverpool club Everton, and had accepted wages up front. On 10 August just before kick-off at a Cowlairs versus Celtic match, a reporter for the Scottish Sport described the following incident:

> On entering the Cowlairs enclosure, a jubilant Mr O'Hara button-holed me and with a mischievous twinkle in his eye quietly whispered, I'm sorry you're too late for the names of the teams but perhaps you can distinguish the men for yourself. There was something in his manner I did not quite understand but glancing over his shoulder, I was astonished to see the Everton cracks, Doyle and Brady.

Dan Doyle would remain at Celtic for the remainder of his career, becoming a club legend. John O'Hara would hold the post for three years, finally resigning at the AGM of 1891. At the time he was described as a much-abused official having taken most of the flak from the Quillanites during their rebellion. At the end of his final report as club secretary, he gave the meeting some idea of the unenviable nature of the post, declining to continue for any money. He was succeeded as club secretary shortly afterwards by John H McLaughlin. After becoming involved with the Celtic project, John O'Hara moved into the wine and liquor trade and over the course of the next ten years or so prospered, becoming by anyone's standards very wealthy. He took over the licence of a pub at 140 London Road, he had his own blend of Scotch whisky called the *Royal Shield* and later acquired the licence of the Clyde Vaults at Nuneaton Street and Norfolk Street. Although he retained a base in Glasgow, he moved his family's main home from the east end, to the gentile middle-class retreat of Rothesay on the Isle of Bute where he purchased an estate. Despite his many business interests he remained closely associated with Celtic, first on the committee then on the board of directors from 1897 holding 100 then 300 shares. He represented the club on both the Glasgow and Scottish Football Association boards. As a devout Catholic, he acted as the secretary for the St Mary's branch of the Catholic Union for over twenty years. He died suddenly in 1905 while still on the Celtic board, having been closely involved with the club from its inception and giving eighteen years of faithful service. On his death most of John O'Hara's shares apparently went to John Glass.

James McKay

James McKay was a member of the original Celtic committee and was club treasurer between 1892 and 1897, having assisted the previous treasurers Hugh Darroch, John H McLaughlin and Tom Maley. By the early 1830s, the McKay family with their widowed Irish mother at its head had settled in the Calton district. James McKay's father was born there in 1832 and would later own a hairdressers and tobacconist shop in the Gallowgate. In 1853, James McKay himself was born in the Calton and would follow his father into the hairdressing and tobacconist business. Described as quiet, unassuming and diligent, in addition to the vitally important role he played in the formation of the club, James McKay should be remembered for

James McKay

his leading role in the creation of the Celtic stadium. A stadium that very quickly became the top sporting venue in Scotland and which itself contributed largely to the success of the football team and the club. Appointed master of works, he supervised the laying out of the ground in 1892. Over £4000 would be spent on the project that included a new pavilion, but some money was saved when the stands from the old park were removed and erected on the new ground. The work was carried out while the city was going through a minor trade downturn and the club employed thirty local men at the new ground. By August that year, James McKay was selling season tickets for the new Celtic stadium for seven shillings and six pence, both for the stand and the ground. Almost immediately the new ground, in comparison to the first, was described as "Paradise". James McKay appears to have taken a personal interest in the new ground and was officially appointed oversman, instigating and supervising the series of improvements carried on at the ground over the next five years and he is credited with suggesting the later installation of the double track that would prove so profitable for the club in the years to come. That said, he did not always get things right first time. In September 1897, the new Celtic directors complained to the railway authorities about 200 spectators regularly using the embankment at the north-west corner of the ground to watch the Celtic games for free. Such was the regard in which James McKay was held by the club members and despite the on-going debate over the lack of charitable donations, at the AGM of 1894, they voted him an honorarium of £100. As club secretary he was one of the official Celtic party that attended the National Convention in Dublin in 1896 and the following year in April he sat on the provisional board when the club converted to a limited company. After the installation of the new board at the 1897 AGM, James McKay was no longer a power broker at the club, although he remained a fervent Celtic supporter and club member. He was at the epicentre of the Brake Club dispute over cut-price season tickets. The new Celtic directors refused to honour a ticket deal brokered in McKay's barber's shop between himself as club treasurer and Brake Club representatives. Throughout the furore, he remained strangely quiet on the entire matter. James McKay died in August 1924 at his home in Abercromby Street.

Thomas Edward Maley

The two Maley brothers, Thomas and William, came on board the Celtic project in December 1887. William, or Willie Maley as he was better known, would become in the truest sense of the word a legend at Celtic Park and his massive contribution will be examined in great detail in a later chapter. His older brother, Thomas Edward Maley, would gain an especial place in the affections of the early Celtic club's supporters and it was he that Brother Walfrid, John Glass and Pat Welsh went to see one night in November or December 1887 when the Celtic project was still in its infancy. Tom Maley, then still a trainee schoolteacher, was out courting his future

Thomas E Maley

wife Elizabeth, also a schoolteacher, when the triumvirate arrived at Sergeant Maley's door in Cathcart. After persuading Willie Maley, who was at the time really more into athletics, to bring his errant brother to have a look at the new east end club, the rest as they say was history. Fundamental to the early success of the new venture was the ability to attract top-class footballers to the team. Already very well known in footballing and athletic circles, it was Tom's personal contacts with the top players that helped bring the likes of James Kelly, Neil McCallum and John Madden to the new club. The two Maley brothers were in the first Celtic team, which played Rangers reserves in May 1888 and Tom would go on to play for the Celts until December 1890.

Tom Maley attended St Mary's Roman Catholic teacher training college in Hammersmith, London between 1885 and 1886, gaining his teaching certificate in April 1889. He was following in the footsteps of his older brother Charles Maley who attended the college between 1881 and 1882. Charles would later enter the priesthood as father Charles O'Malley. As schoolteachers, both Tom and his wife Elizabeth were committed educationalists and painfully aware of the desperate conditions in which many of the students found themselves. This became even more apparent in 1890 when Tom was appointed superintendent of the Slatefield Industrial School, situated just a stone's throw from Celtic Park. The institution catered for wayward and orphaned Roman Catholic boys who were among the very poorest of Glasgow society. It is no large leap of the imagination to assume the specifically charitable objectives of the Celtic club, aimed at securing funds for poor children, was a major deciding factor as to why Tom would get involved in the Celtic project in the first place. Other than its charitable aims, the proposed new football team was at the time just another Irish football team among many. It was probably destined to follow the same road to oblivion as so many previous such schemes and unlikely to have gained Tom Maley's support. With Tom in such close contact with the club and its power brokers, it is unsurprising that his Slatefield School also formed an association with the club. The Slatefield Boys Band often played at Parkhead both before the game and at half-time. An early club song played by the boys as the teams came onto the park was "Let Erin Remember". The support went two ways and Celtic Park was often the venue for the inter-industrial schools athletics meeting between Slatefield and St Mary's.

Totally committed to the charitable aims of the club, as early as 1891 Tom Maley sided with Dr Conway and the traditionalists, who believed that club officials should not be paid from the funds and all sums raised by the club should go to charitable causes. The modernisers included John Glass, John H McLaughlin, Joe Shaughnessy, John O'Hara and his brother Willie Maley. The power struggle for the soul and direction of the Celtic would last for over six years. Throughout the period Tom Maley vigorously and eloquently argued the case for sums to be made available for charities. At the 1891 AGM, no doubt as an olive branch to the Conway supporters, he was elected club treasurer. He delivered the annual financial report in June 1992, submitting an annual income of over £4460 and expenditure of £4448, leaving a balance of just over £20. Of the expenditure, £140 went to the Poor Children's Dinner Table, £50 went to the Evicted Tenants Fund and £10 was in aid of a memorial to the late Fr Cunningham of Cambuslang, an early fervent Celtic supporter. In 1893, Tom Maley was elected vice-president of the club. As an ordinary member at the 1895 AGM, Tom Maley drew attention to the fact that in the balance sheet no donation to the Poor Children's Dinner Table appeared. He passionately characterised this as a gross injustice and betrayal of the club's founding principles. He reminded his audience that the club had been formed to support the east end charities, yet out of a princely annual income of over £7000 not a penny went to the Dinner Tables. In fact, the last donation to the Dinner Tables was made at the AGM of 1892 when Tom Maley was club treasurer. The internal struggle would eventually result in a victory for the modernisers and in April 1897 the club was converted from a community-based, committee-led vehicle for raising charitable funds, to a profits-orientated public limited company with a board of directors and shareholders looking for a return on their investments. Tom Maley was voted onto the provisional board as a traditionalist representative, trusted to safeguard the members' interests while the mechanics of the transfer took place. Both he and Michael Hughes, another opponent of the limited liability scheme, were voted off the board at the first company AGM in June 1897.

Despite losing the war for the soul of the Celtic, Tom Maley remained a staunch supporter of the club, deciding to continue fighting the case for good causes from within the new company. His place in the affections of the Celtic supporters was not secured, therefore, through his footballing prowess or his politics, but through his unceasing and lifelong support for the charitable principles on which the club was founded. Tom and Elizabeth Maley were leading lights in the St Mary's branch of the Catholic temperance organisation the League of the Cross. The members, who practised total abstinence, held regular social functions usually to raise money for charitable causes. Tom and Elizabeth, no doubt with the children in tow, often contributed to the entertainment: Elizabeth sang while her husband operated a Lime-Light magic lantern show. The various parish League of the Cross organisations were also the focal points for early Celtic supporters clubs, which were called *Brake Clubs*. The Brake Club attached to St Mary's League of the Cross voted Tom Maley their honorary president and his portrait adorned their club banner. He had the pleasure of unfurling the banner at a concert in the Henrietta Street Hall. Described as gentlemanly, proper, polite and approachable, he was an acknowledged authority on the game. He was on occasion selected as one of the seven worthies tasked by the SFA to choose the Scotland international team.

Tom Maley's reputation within the game was such that in 1902 he was persuaded to give up his career as an educationalist to take up full-time football management. Tom would lead English first division side Manchester City to major successes but after a scandal involving illegal payments to Manchester City players in June 1906, Tom Maley and the club chairman were both banned from English football. The bonuses scandal effectively made him unemployable in English football and the family returned to Scotland. Thomas went back into education, gaining a headship at St Mary's School in Cleland, near Motherwell, in August. That summer of 1906 was a traumatic time for the Celtic-supporting Glasgow Irish. Over the course of twelve weeks or so, four colossal figures – John Glass, Joe Shaughnessy, John Fergusson and Michael Davitt – all died. At the beginning of September, Tom began to write the massively informative and very popular *Tom Maley's Football Notes* for the Glasgow Catholic Observer and Glasgow Star and Examiner newspapers. His remit was to deal critically with football matters generally, but with Celtic in particular. Through Tom Maley's notes, it is clear that he maintained a very intimate relationship with the Celtic club and its directors. Much of our insight and understanding of the early days of the Celtic club is due in no small part to his writings over the period. By 1908 the family were on the move again, with Tom taking over as headmaster at St Columba's School in Maryhill, Glasgow. On their return to the city, the family moved into a red sandstone tenement at 68 Wilton Street, situated in Glasgow's swanky west-end suburb of Kelvinside, but just a short walk to his school. By August 1911, Tom Maley, with the English ban lifted, was back in football and managing Bradford Park Avenue. One of the first things he did when he took over the side was to change their football strip to the Celtic colours of green and white hoops. In 1914 his club achieved promotion to the English first division.

Politically, like his brother Willie, Tom Maley was a Liberal, committed and supportive of their programme of social reform, but he was also a passionate constitutional Irish Nationalist. When John Redmond visited Glasgow in March 1911, Tom and Elizabeth were in the crowd listening to his passionate speech on Irish Home Rule. However, he was also a confirmed imperialist and like the rest of the Maley family, believed deeply that the British Empire, now rapidly transforming into an economic trading block or Commonwealth, could be a force for good. He had a deep and abiding respect for the British Army and guided many of his industrial school pupils into the ranks, seeing military service as an avenue for self-improvement. During the Great War, three of Tom's sons would see active service. Joe Maley, his second son, would make the ultimate sacrifice in 1915, serving with the Glasgow Highlanders. Despite his detachment from the club, he never relinquished his passion and interest in the Celtic and would remain deeply involved with the club in various capacities for the rest of his life. When he died in 1934, a Celtic shirt was placed on top of his coffin when it was lowered into the grave in St Kentigern's Cemetery in Glasgow.

John H McLaughlin

Undoubtedly, the least politically active founding father was John H McLaughlin. He appears to have had no great interest in politics – church, local or national. He was, however, massively interested and active in the boardroom politics of the Scottish football authorities. His family originally came from Donegal and his brother James McLaughlin was a Roman Catholic clergyman at Ampleforth Abbey. John H McLaughlin was educated at St Aloysius and the Jesuit-run Stoneyhurst College, before studying law at Glasgow University. In 1882, he was employed as a law clerk when he married local girl Elizabeth Shannon, the daughter of Charles

John H McLaughlin

Shannon, a recently deceased Irish pawnbroker. Three months later his first child was born at his mother-in-law's home at 381 Duke Street, Glasgow. By the time of the birth, James had given up any hopes of a career in law and gained employment as a mercantile clerk at a firm of leather manufactures based in Bridgeton. By 1887, John was living with his young family at Comelypark Street in the Calton and still employed as a mercantile clerk or cashier. The majority of John's spare time appears to have been taken up by his interest in music. As an accomplished organist and pianist, John was in great demand to play at Mass not only in his own St Mary's chapel but also at the many social functions that were so much a part of Victorian life. He regularly played the piano with the Rangers FC Glee Club and in return the Rangers Musical Association would accompany him elsewhere. With no previous association or knowledge of the game of football, it was probably his skills as a cashier, which saw him become involved with the Celtic project. In June 1889 he was listed as the joint treasurer with Hugh Darroch and in 1890 he became the youngest of the Celtic office bearers when appointed to the post of club treasurer. At the AGM of 1891 he replaced John O'Hara as club secretary, beating John McFadyen in a close vote. He would go on to hold the post for the next two years before being elected vice-president in June 1893.

Despite having very little sporting experience he was, as an administrator and legislator, indispensable to the development of both the Celtic club and the professional game of football in Scotland. Almost from its inception, the Celtic's large Glasgow Irish fan base and its immediate and continued success on the field, guaranteed the club a powerful voice among the football clubs and the Celtic's representatives were immediately and deeply immersed in the boardroom politics of Scottish football. John H McLaughlin was one of the two Celtic representatives who attended a meeting of the leading Scottish football clubs in the Commercial Hotel, Glassford St, in Glasgow on 20 March 1890. The meeting was called to discuss the question of organising league matches. On behalf of the Celtic club he cast an enthusiastic vote for the proposed league set-up. He then played the leading role in the subsequent organisation of the new Scottish Football League and went on to occupy various key positions within the League, including as its first secretary. The League was inaugurated at the end of April 1890 and the first fixtures were played in August that year. After a shaky start, the League took off and proved to be a great and enduring success. Most of the credit must go to John McLaughlin who nursed the fledgling organisation through its first difficult years.

In 1893, John McLaughlin became yet another of the committeemen to move into the liquor trade when he and his family moved to Hamilton where he took over as licensee of a public house. There he became a member of St Mary's parish and joined the Irish National Foresters. That same year, after a prolonged campaign led by John McLaughlin as the Celtic representative to the SFA, the nonsense of the paid amateur was swept away. Professionalism was finally adopted against stiff opposition within the amateur middle-class orientated organisation. Opposition was particularly strong among the smaller clubs, who had little reason to change from their amateur status. McLaughlin was quoted as saying: "You might as well attempt to stop the flow of Niagara with a kitchen chair as to stem the tide of professionalism." It was largely through the determination and drive of John H McLaughlin that professional football was introduced into Scotland. Willie Maley said: "With the legitimisation of professionalism, influenced by convincing arguments of JH McLaughlin, football seemed in a fair way to becoming a more honest and better organised sport." The introduction of professionalism saw the changes to the game accelerate and John H McLaughlin was honorary secretary and then vice-president of the Celtic club at a time of enormous transition in Scottish football, a transition that directly affected the Celtic and one that would magnify the existing internal division at the Celtic club.

Arguably, John H McLaughlin legislated Celtic onto a course that would allow the club to realise its full potential and without his drive and determination, Celtic as we now know it would not have existed, if it existed at all. After prolonged and at times heated debate over the direction of the club, the Celtic club was converted into a limited liability company in April 1897. John H McLaughlin with John Glass and Joe Shaughnessy had led the argument in favour of the move, but it was McLaughlin who took most of the flak from its opponents. The debate had gotten so venomous in 1896, that John McLaughlin sued a club member, Frank Havlin, for slander asking the court for a punitive £100 in damages. The McLaughlin versus Havlin court case highlights the fact that the division at the club also ran along class lines. Since the power brokers at the club came mostly from the moneyed classes, they and their motives were regarded with suspicion by the working-class members, who felt they were being driven from the club. In the event the sheriff threw out McLaughlin's libel case saying it should never have been raised in the first place. The move to a limited liability company also enraged the Roman Catholic Church, which saw the club as a vehicle specifically formed by the church to provide funds for charities. In its view the Celtic club had been hijacked and turned into a private business for the benefit of a few individuals. On transition to a limited company, John H McLaughlin became the first Celtic chairman holding initially 150 and later 300 shares. He would remain in the chair for the next twelve years.

Already unpopular with the Catholic Church, which blamed him for the loss of Celtic's charitable contributions, and with the traditionalists, who lost control of the community club, he also managed to fall foul of the Glasgow Irish Nationalists. At the end of 1899, while Celtic chairman and president of the SFA, he enthusiastically supported a 100-guinea donation from the SFA to a patriotic fund for the families of British soldiers then fighting in South Africa. At the time, there were thousands of working-class Celtic supporters fighting in South Africa with the British forces, including at least two former Celtic players, brothers James and John Devlin. From St Aloysius Parish alone, seventy-nine members of the Confraternity of Our Lady of Genazzano served during the conflict. McLaughlin's inexperience as a politician became apparent when he went further, denouncing the Irish Nationalist opposition to the British government's policy in South Africa, which had led to the Anglo-Boer War, as being the prerogative of "demented Irish politicians". The demented politicians included the now legendary Nationalist Michael Davitt, who resigned his parliamentary seat.

Not for the first or last time would the question of British imperialism split the Glasgow Irish Nationalists, including those supporters of the UIL, IPP and the ILP, including those at Parkhead. In fact, the British imperialist adventure in South Africa also greatly disturbed the wider British public, splitting public opinion. Despite the British government's divisive expansionist policies towards the Boer republics, the British military, which suffered very serious losses in action, largely remained above the political furore. Later the Army General Staff would be subject to severe criticism for their badly mismanaged Concentration Camp tactics, but the British public largely disassociated the military from the Government. The ordinary soldiers themselves received widespread praise for their bravery and moral and financial support for the bereaved, the wounded and their families. At the beginning of March 1900, a boisterous anti-war meeting was held in Candleriggs, Glasgow, chaired by John Ferguson with Kier Hardie, Lloyd George, Arthur Murphy and other prominent political figures on the platform. John Ferguson opened the meeting with the following statement:

> If anyone thought that they would hear a word said against the courage
> of British soldiers fighting in South Africa they would be mistaken. They
> deplored the deaths of the Gordon Highlanders and hated to hear of the
> Inniskillings being destroyed, but they also deplored the deaths of the
> gallant Boer farmers defending their country.

In June, while the Glasgow Observer carried a series of articles written by Michael Davitt entitled "The Boer Story of the War" it was also reporting that William McKillop had decorated his premises with Union Jacks to celebrate the relief of Mafeking and carrying sympathetic stories of Glasgow Irish soldiers serving with great bravery in South Africa. Therefore, although the likes of John Glass, James Kelly, Arthur Murphy and John McKillop were all publicly anti-war, John McLaughlin was not completely politically isolated at Parkhead in his support for British soldiers. Indeed, both John McKillop and Bishop Eyre had already contributed a significant ten guineas each to the same British Patriotic Fund as the SFA. In addition to the support given to the British military by William McKillop, the Maley brothers and by the Shaughnessy family, the pro-British imperialist sentiments of two of Celtic's founding fathers, Timothy Joe Walls and John A MacCreadie, also became very publicly apparent when they became embroiled in a slander case. The writ was raised by Belfast compositor Robert McPeake against the Scottish Daily Record newspaper. The newspaper alleged that McPeake had fought with Major Sean McBride's Irish Brigade in South Africa against the British, while McPeake denied the fact and sued. John MacCreadie, as a witness for the Daily Record, gave evidence to the court that while in Glasgow McPeake had admitted to him that he had fought with the Irish Brigade supporting the Boers. He made the statement in the presence of Timothy Joe Walls, who had himself recently spent some time in South Africa and whose brother Randolph was then serving with a British Yeomanry regiment on active service. John MacCreadie stated that on hearing McPeake's admission, an outraged Tim Walls told him that he should be shot. Joe Walls was abroad at the time of the trial. The court later found in favour of the Daily Record. Typically, the political differences at Celtic were not allowed to interfere with business and at the end of June 1900 the Patriotic Games, staged in support of the army fighting in South Africa, was held at Parkhead. The programme comprised almost entirely military competitors supported by numerous military bands and was a massive success.

Despite calls for John H McLaughlin's removal from his position at Celtic, he remained chairman until his death in August 1909. This incident apparently sealed John H McLaughlin's fate in the affections of the Irish Nationalist Celtic supporters and in comparison to the fulsome obituaries dedicated to his Celtic contemporaries, John H McLaughlin's was meagre and almost grudging. Tom Maley was one of the few who gave credit where it was undoubtedly due, when he stated that the establishment of the Scottish League and the legislation of professionalism in Scottish football were monuments to his labour. He was buried in Dalbeth Cemetery and both the Celtic club and Scottish football generally was well represented at the funeral; however, the leading Glasgow Irish Nationalists, such as Arthur Murphy, were conspicuous by their absence. While some understanding can be afforded to John McLaughlin's actions regarding the future of the club and his support for the British imperialist adventure that was the Boer Wars, it is difficult to justify his actions in suing Francis Havlin. The sum of £100 may have seemed a reasonable sum to McLaughlin, but it would equate to well over two years wages for gasworks labourer Havlin and would most certainly have seen him financially destroyed. Now largely overlooked or ignored as opposed to forgotten, John H McLaughlin's contribution to Scottish football and to the Celtic Club was immense and, politics aside, he deserves a much more prominent place in the history of the Celtic club.

William and John McKillop

The McKillop brothers, William and John, were among the original members of the Celtic club. Their parents, Daniel and Matilda McKillop, originally from Co Antrim, arrived in Scotland between 1853 and 1856 when they settled in Dalry, Ayrshire. There the family of three boys and six girls grew up in coal miner's cottages at Dalry and later at Catrine. In the national census of 1871, John McKillop, born in Co Antrim, is listed as a labourer in an ironworks, aged seventeen, while thirteen-year-old William, born in Dalry, is listed as a cotton picker in a factory. By early 1881, the entire family had moved to the Hutchesontown/Gorbals district of Glasgow, where oldest brother, John McKillop, was employed in a spirits shop, while William McKillop worked in a local cotton mill. The McKillop brothers' foray into the provisions business was a great success and the brothers soon branched into the licensing and catering trade, which led to the opening of the immensely popular Grosvenor Restaurant. Despite being Irish, the brothers won the catering contract for the Glasgow Exhibitions of 1901 and 1911, becoming in the process among the most famous businessmen in Glasgow. Further plaudits came their way

William McKillop

when their firm was chosen as the city chamber's official caterers for the visits of King Edward in 1903 and the Prince of Wales in 1909.

Both McKillop brothers were involved in the Celtic project right from the start; however, William immersed himself in the business of the Celtic club and was one of the original committeemen. Elected Celtic club vice-president at the AGM of 1891, William McKillop ousted the office holder Francis McErlean from the chair after two years' occupancy. He hosted a celebratory supper for the Glasgow Cup winners in March 1891, when John Glass presented him with the Celtic's first major trophy. He was elected honorary president of the club between 1893 and 1897. While John McKillop looked after the business, William immersed himself in Glasgow Irish politics and as honorary president of the Celtic club, he received fulsome praise from Michael Davitt for his ceaseless efforts in raising money for the Irish Parliamentary Party Fund. As a leaseholder and guarantor of Celtic Park, he was a committed supporter of the limited liability proposal. At the AGM of 1895, during a heated exchange over charitable donations versus club debt, he is credited with replying to a request for donations to charity as "clap-trap". After a long association with the Home Government branch of the INL, in 1900, William McKillop was asked by newly elected party leader, John Redmond, to stand for the Irish Parliamentary Party as a candidate for North Sligo and despite his support for the British military then fighting in South Africa he was duly elected to the House of Commons as an Irish Nationalist MP. There is also some compelling evidence to suggestion that William McKillop was commissioned into the 2nd Volunteer battalion Royal Scots Fusiliers in 1897. A military commission and some time served with the army was almost a prerequisite to a life in national politics. In 1906 he swopped seats and was elected MP for South Armagh. In support of the Armagh Gaelic Athletic Association, he presented the famous McKillop Cup. In 1908, he married Rose Dalton, sister-in-law of Willie Redmond. Yet another Irish Nationalist MP, Willie Redmond was the brother of John Redmond, leader of the Irish Parliamentary Party. After a lifetime of service to the causes of Irish Nationalism, William McKillop died in 1909 after a short illness. His funeral took place in Glasgow when over a hundred carriages made up the cortege as it made its way to Dalbeth RC Cemetery in the east end of the city.

John McKillop was also one of the original members of the club and was voted onto the first Celtic board after its conversion into a limited liability company in April 1897, personally holding 200 Celtic shares. By 1900, the three McKillop brothers, John, William and youngest sibling James, jointly owned 1000 Celtic shares. Although not as politically active as his brother, preferring instead to concentrate on running the family business, which in turn allowed his younger brother to devote his time to politics, John was a fervent Irish Nationalist supporter and contributed regularly and generously to various Nationalist good causes, including Michael Davitt's evicted tenant funds and the IPP. While supporting the IPP's opposition to British imperial expansion in South Africa, in 1899 he contributed a very significant ten guineas to

John McKillop

the British Patriotic War Fund to support the families of British soldiers killed and wounded in the Boer Wars. In 1909, the Celtic club hosted Irish Nationalist Party MP Joe Devlin during his visit to Glasgow. Joe was a fervent Belfast Celtic supporter and while in the city decided he would like to attend the Celtic versus Clyde game to be played that Saturday. After the 2–0 victory for the bhoys, director John McKillop escorted "Wee Joe" into the dressing room where he met the players and offered his congratulations. John McKillop remained an enthusiastic and committed director and supporter of the Celtic supporter until his death in December 1914. The McKillops' shares in the Celtic Club passed to the youngest of the McKillop brothers, James, and then to his son John. Named after his uncle, John McKillop, would serve alongside Tom Maley's son Josie in the Glasgow Highlanders during the Great War and would be commissioned in 1916, wounded in action in 1918 and awarded the Military Cross for his services. He survived the carnage of the Great War, to become a Celtic director in the mid-1920s, but died in uniform serving as a pilot officer with the RAF in 1942. The McKillop family retained an interest in the football club until the mid-1950s.

The Forgotten Fathers

In addition to the regular, high profile office bearers, there were another dozen and a half Glasgow Irishmen whose contribution as committeemen to the success of the early club was fundamental to the realisation of Walfrid's project. For the most part they are known simply as names on the early committee or member lists, but their contribution deserves much more recognition. The Celtic club committeemen were much more involved in the practical day-to-day running of the club than might at first be assumed or realised. In addition to the usual club meetings these men were involved as members of numerous subcommittees, in scouting and signing players, representing the club at various sporting and social functions, procurement, selling tickets, manning turnstiles, running the line in the days before official linesmen and manning key positions at the numerous sports events held at Parkhead, particularly the Celtic Sports Day. The committeemen were permanently on call and ready to step into any breach. Among those for which information can be teased from the historical record are the following: Davie Meikleham, Hugh Darroch, James Curtis, James Quillan, Stephen J Henry, Joseph F McGroary, Michael Cairns, Timothy J Walls, John A MacCreadie, Joseph M Nelis, Michael Hughes, Francis McErlean, John MacDonald, James Cairns, Frank Havlin, Dr Joe Scanlan, James Moore, Daniel Molloy and Pat Welsh.

David Meikleham

David Meikleham

David Meikleham, born in Rothesay in 1852, was one of the few Scots Catholics deeply involved in the Celtic project from its early days. By 1861 his family had moved from Bute to Glasgow and were living at Broad Street on the border between Calton and Mile End. In 1871, nineteen-year-old David was still living with his parents but now at Hunter Street, near the old army barracks on the Gallowgate. His father, William, had opened a shoe repair shop there and Davie worked in it as a shoemaker. Married in 1873, by 1881, David, his wife Robina and their four children were living just off Glasgow's High Street in Shuttle Street. Having set out on his own account, Davie was doing very well for himself, employing six men and a girl in his own shoemaking factory. At the time the Celtic was being established, Davie Meikleham would have been regarded as one of the new Glasgow Irish bourgeoisies and exactly the type of respectable Roman Catholic who would be encouraged to become involved. Better still he was a Scotch Roman Catholic at a time when the west of Scotland Catholic Church hierarchy was engaged in a serious push to involve Scotch Catholics in a church increasingly dominated by the Irish. As a leading parishioner of St Andrew's he was the secretary of the Caledonian Catholic Association, an organisation whose remit included fostering relations between Scotch and Irish Catholics. By 1886, thirty-nine-year-old David Meikleham had moved his family back into the Calton or Mile End at William Street now Templeton Street and was a parishioner of St Alphonsus. There he became a member of the Catholic Union and in February 1887 he was elected to represent the parish on the Central Committee of the Union. Prior to getting involved in the Celtic project, he was a member of the middle-class Queen's Park Football Club and appears to have been a very early supporter of the sport. His name first appears as a committeeman on the Celtic match fixture card for season 1889/90.

When the Celtic decided to move to a new stadium in 1891, the original arrangement was that the land would be leased for a period of ten years. By necessity the club took on a large burden of debt to finance the new stadium. Davie Meikleham was one of the four guarantors and leaseholders for the debt and as such was a permanent member of the very powerful business sub-committee. As a Scots Catholic he was one of the most influential men at Celtic and would remain so until the club was converted to a limited liability company and soon afterwards bought the freehold of the park.

In an atmosphere of paid amateurism in Scotland and professionalism in England, the shenanigans surrounding the acquisition and retention of players had by the 1892/93 season reached the stage of farce. Club committeemen were almost kidnapping players, hiding them in hotels or driving them from safe house to safe house in an attempt to keep hold of them. Celtic caused uproar by poaching Dan Doyle the season previously from Everton and then grabbed

Jimmy Blessington from Leith Athletic, hiding him in Glasgow. Meanwhile, prior to the start of the 1892/93 season two Celtic stars, Sandy McMahon and Neillie McCallum, had been grabbed by Nottingham Forest and taken south. John Glass, James Curtis, Davie Meikleham and a brother of Sandy McMahon set off in pursuit determined to get them back. Nottingham Forest moved McMahon about constantly and had him physically guarded by their committeemen. By sheer chance, Davie Meikleham spotted him in the street and bustled him into a taxi. After a mad dash to a provincial railway station pursued by the Nottingham Forest committee, the Celtic party made it back to Glasgow via Manchester. Thanks to Davie Meikleham's sharp eyes, Sandy "Duke" McMahon would appear over 217 times for the Celtic and would become one of the club's first great legends.

In mid-February 1893, Davie ran foul of John O'Hara's old boot and shoe operatives union when he became involved in an industrial dispute with the men at his factory. When the men went on strike, Davie took his outstanding work to fellow Celtic committeeman, Tom Maley, then the superintendent at the Slatefield Industrial School. One of the trades taught to the boys at the industrial school was shoemaking and Tom agreed to help Davie out of a hole. The move obviously undermined the strikers and the union reported the matter to the Glasgow Trades Council, who in turn wrote to the Secretary of State over the matter. As reported in the Glasgow Herald on Thursday 23 February, the Secretary of State informed Tom Maley that the industrial school should not take work from an employer in dispute with its men. It was a bad few days for Davie, Tom and the Celtic; the following Saturday 25 February, Celtic beat Queen's Park 1–0 in what should have been the final of the Scottish Cup, but the match was declared void owing to the atrocious condition of the park and the game was declared a friendly. The Celtic would later lose the replay 2–1. At the annual Celtic Sports meetings, Davie could be found alongside the majority of the committee, who acted as stewards. In keeping with the wider athletics side of the club, he and Joe Shaughnessy took a great interest in the popular Celtic Cycle Club. In 1895, Celtic beat Davie's old favourites Queen's Park 6–3 in the final of the Glasgow Cup. It was mentioned in the post-match commentary that with Celtic already the holders of the trophy, Davie was the custodian of the cup on behalf of the club. An old club legend was that he kept the cup under his bed for safekeeping. At the AGM of 1895, Davie was nominated to be vice-president of the club, but lost out to John H McLaughlin, Tom Maley having refused the position.

On the day of the players' strike in November 1896, Davie Meikleham was sent post haste from Parkhead to Cathkin Park where the Celtic reserves were playing Queen's Park Strollers. His instructions were to return with Tom Dunbar and he was back with Tom for the start of the second half. Not bad timing considering the trip was done by hansom cab. Luckily, Davie never had to depend on using his own horse, since the nag and its carriage had been stolen a month or so earlier. Like so many of the early committeemen, Davie Meikleham's contribution to the management of the club ceased on its conversion to a limited company but he later enjoyed a long association with the football club. In 1900 his slipper-making business ran into trouble and Davie was declared bankrupt. Immediately afterwards he moved into the still new telephone industry and was until his retirement a telephone sales manager with the Post Office. He like, Joe Nelis, had a long life, finally succumbing aged eighty-seven in May 1938, the year of the Celtic's fiftieth anniversary.

Hugh Darroch

Hugh Darroch

By November 1888, Hugh Darroch had held the office of treasurer at the Celtic club for the best part of a year. Born on the London Road to Irish parents, Hugh lost his labourer father at an early age. A pawnbroker by profession, he took over his mother's second-hand clothes shop and turned it into one of the most successful in the city. The shop was located in Bain Street, off the Gallowgate. He was an active member of the Catholic community and enthusiastically supported St Mary's Conference of the Society of St Vincent de Paul. He was also an early member of the Catholic Literary Society. The Christmas holiday period of 1888 was a busy time for Hugh, not only was he deeply involved with the increasingly successful Celtic football club, but also on Boxing Day he married widow Mary Walls. Dr Joseph Scanlan, a prominent club member, was his best man and would later marry Mary's younger sister, Sarah Walls. Shortly after their marriage, Hugh and his young family moved into the once very swanky Monteith Row, overlooking Glasgow Green. This address was once one of the most sought after in Glasgow, but by the late 1800s, most of the middle-class residents had moved to the west of the city leaving the row to the aspiring, respectable working classes, very many of them Irish. Also living along the row was Celtic committeeman William McKillop and Mr Francis Henry, a leading Glasgow Catholic and an original subscriber to the Celtic club. He was the older brother of committeeman Stephen J Henry. Hugh Darroch carried out the duties of club treasurer for the first two years.

In 1891 he became seriously ill with a malignant cancer on his neck and was attended by Dr John Conway. During his illness he appears to have shared the duties of treasurer with both John H McLaughlin and James McKay. Tragically, Hugh succumbed to his illness in September 1891 at his home in Monteith Row. He left Mary, widowed for the second time, with a baby son named after his father. Despite his short time at the club, Hugh Darroch's contribution was such that he was referred to as a "Father" of the club and was said to have "infused all his youthful energies and enthusiasms into the affairs and business of the club with such splendid results". It was also said that the Celtic had lost a zealous and devoted supporter. On the Saturday following, the Celtic players wore black armbands during their football match, possibility for the very first time. On the day of the funeral the flags at Parkhead were flown at half-mast as his cortege passed the stadium en route to Dalbeth Cemetery. Every club official and most of the players were present at the internment.

James Curtis

James Curtis

The family of James Curtis arrived in Glasgow from Ireland in the early 1850s when journeyman tailor William Curtis and his young wife Ann settled in the Calton at Sister Street. The family remained in the Calton for the next twenty odd years mostly in Abercromby Street before moving to Comelypark Place off the Gallowgate in the mid-1880s. A member of St Mary's Parish, by the mid-1880s James Curtis had qualified as a schoolteacher and was employed at St Mary's school under its Marist headmaster, Brother Dorotheus. In April 1887, James was the chairman of St Mary's Young Men's Society (YMS). Based in St Mary's church hall, the YMS was an organisation that encouraged an interest in Irish culture and heritage including poetry, dancing, history and the lives of illustrious Irishmen. As a member of the school staff, James Curtis was at the Hibernian FC celebratory dinner in February 1887 in St Mary's school hall. He was so impressed with the Scottish Cup victory he sent the Hibernians a telegram of congratulation on behalf of St Mary's YMS. With Brother Dorotheus, one of the originators of the idea, it was natural enough for him to become involved in the Celtic project from the outset. On the formation of the football team, James took on responsibility for the Celtic reserve team as its match secretary. He is listed on the 1889/90 season fixture list as such when his address was given as Bernard Street, Bridgeton, just a few hundred yards from the first Celtic Park and literally on the doorstep of the second. Like the Celtic first team, the second eleven under James Curtis was very successful and in the 1890/91 season the Celtic reserves won the senior reserve competition, the Scottish 2nd XI Cup, by beating St Mirren Strollers 13–1. It would be forty-four years before a Celtic reserve team repeated the achievement. In August 1892 and prior to the introduction of professionalism into Scottish football, James Curtis was in the Celtic posse sent to Nottingham to bring back McMahon after the Celtic star had been persuaded by Neillie McCallum to go for the big money in England. In May 1893, James Curtis was the Celtic representative on the Second Eleven Football Association board.

At the 1894 AGM held in the Mechanics Hall, James Curtis, then club secretary, delivered the club's annual report. He declared the season just ended one of the most successful in the history of the club and that the team stood second to none. The annual sports games were the most brilliant ever seen in Scotland and their park, now complete, thoroughly deserved its title of "Paradise". Some indication as to his thoughts on the subject of limited liability can be glimpsed when he ended his report by stating: "The club was started on behalf of charity and when the liabilities are cleared away, there would not be an association or club in Scotland who will come to the assistance of the needy with such good will." On 2 November 1895, he handed over responsibility for the reserves to former player and good friend of the Maley brothers, Johnny Coleman. Coleman was a cycling fanatic at the height of the cycling boom and opened his own bicycle shop in Dennistoun. Cycling played a very big past in the financial success of the Celtic over the two decades straddling the turn of the century. At the end of December 1895, after a suggestion by Rangers, the Scottish Reserve League was formed with five teams participating. The Celtic team built by James Curtis finished joint first with Heart of Midlothian, having played eight, won seven and drawn one. In recognition of his service to the club, he was voted a sum of £25 at the 1896 AGM.

He married on 12 July 1899 in St Mungo's and named his first son after his old headmaster, Brother Dorotheus. During his time with the Celtic reserves James Curtis contributed greatly to the success of the Celtic and brought the likes of Dowds, McArthur and Divers through to the first team. James Curtis retired from St Mary's School in 1921 due to ill health and shortly afterwards followed his family to Canada where they had emigrated some years earlier. In the mid 1920s James and some of his family moved to Melbourne, Australia where he died in 1933.

James Quillan

James Quillan

Glasgow-born James Quillan was the eldest son of Irish labourer Peter Quillan. In April 1874, eighteen-year-old James married his eighteen-year-old neighbour Roseanne Moore in St Andrew's Chapel on Great Clyde Street. His bride was the daughter of Irishman John Moore, a master confectioner by profession. Young James was something of an entrepreneur with a quick, shrewd business mind. He first occupied a premise in the High Street where he bought and sold oak casks. On his marriage certificate, James described himself as a barrel dealer. Within a few years of his marriage his business took off. In 1874 he was selling barrels, by 1881 he had qualified as a master cooper and owned a number of cooperages in Glasgow with international trade links. His interests continued to expand to include a large premise known as the Caledonian Cooperage at Janefield Street, just a few hundred yards from the original Celtic ground at Parkhead. His business success brought him to the attention of the Glasgow Irish community leaders and political activists and by 1887 he was a leading member of both St Mary's Parish and the Home Government branch of the Irish National League. He is described as "affable and social, always ready with purse or voice in support of the old cause" and "at the forefront of the Irish battle at a time when it was not fashionable to be so". He was reputedly in St Mary's Hall when the victorious Hibernian team were feted and was part of the Home Government branch party that presented the Hibernian team with their gold medals three weeks later. James Quillan was on board the Celtic project right from the start, subscribing a substantial twenty shillings and was subsequently elected the club's first vice-president. As such he was in the pavilion when Hibernian and Cowlairs opened the old Celtic Park and was at the soirée after the game in the Royal Hotel on George Square.

While still the Celtic club vice-president, James Quillan was also the leader of the malcontents who broke away after the 1889 AGM, to form the rival Glasgow Hibernian Football Club. Although the exact reasons for the breakaway are still open to debate, it would appear that he and his supporters were the first to contend that the club was being led away from its original charitable aims. In the subsequent power struggle, he and his supporters were unsuccessful in their attempt to remove John Glass. James Quillan was voted off the committee, but he remained an active member of the Celtic club. After the failed coup, and the formation of the Glasgow Hibernians James Quillan appears to have tried to distance himself publicly from the new Glasgow Irish side, which was an obvious rival for the loyalty of the Glasgow Irish football supporters. However, he seems to have been the power behind the throne, driving the project forward and backing the Glasgow Hibernian with a line of credit of at least £10. Given the parochial nature of the Glasgow Irish society it is unlikely that his involvement in the Glasgow Hibernians remained much of a secret for long, however, his involvement with the Glasgow Hibernians only publically came to light after the collapse of the football club in 1891. The former Celtic vice-president was the only individual that the Glasgow Sheriff dealing with a writ taken out against the club, could positively identify with the failed club, there being no membership or subscriber lists to be found. In April 1891, the court found James Quillan to be the driving force behind the Glasgow Hibernian club and the Sheriff commented that Quillan "appeared to be anxious that the new club be started but preferred his involvement and position with the club be kept quiet", which was hardly surprising considering was still involved with the Celtic club at the time. Despite the strained circumstances, he remained a member of the Celtic club, but he never again held office or gained a position on the committee. He did try for re-election onto the committee at the AGM of 1896, but fell well short when he only managed to get twenty-three votes. At that same meeting, he moved the acceptance of Willie Maley's annual report, his motion seconded by Joseph F McGroary. He was also one of the leading lights and promoters of the Hibernian Swimming Club based at the Gorbals baths, and for many years the club members competed for the Quillan Cup.

James Quillan's personal and business life went into a downward spiral in the last years of the old century. He first lost his wife in July 1897, remarried a year later and then became involved in a slander case against his former brother-in-law and fellow Celtic club member, Peter Winn. James Quillan lost the case and was forced to pay costs amounting to a very considerable £300. In early 1901, his business failed as he was forced to sell off assets to pay the court costs. In August 1901, the strain took its toll and he suffered a heart attack and died at his home in Parkhead. Like so many of the founding fathers of the club he was buried in Dalbeth cemetery.

Stephen John Henry

Stephen John Henry first appears on the committee lists for season 1891/92 and remained a member until season 1895/96. His family arrived in Glasgow from Maghera, Co Derry, prior to

Stephen John Henry

the famine and his father, Francis Henry, was an apprentice calico printer living in the Gorbals in 1841. By 1851, having qualified as a journeyman, Francis and his family moved to the Saltmarket where Stephen John Henry was born. By 1874, with his father deceased, Stephen was living in Monteith Row with his brother Francis and employed as an auctioneer. Stephen J Henry married Roseanne Quigley, whose father, Edward, was a Glasgow pawnbroker. By the time the Celtic club was being formed Stephen had moved into the pawnbroking business and was living in the new Dennistoun district at Roselea Drive, just a stone's throw from the Celtic stadium at Parkhead. The Henry family were leading Catholics in the east end where his elder brother, Francis Henry JP, an auctioneer by profession, was also the president of the Society of St Vincent de Paul and a member of the Glasgow Catholic School Board. Both brothers were members of the Caledonian Association. Stephen himself was described as "one of the most public spirited of our Catholic citizens" and among other community projects he was deeply involved in the welfare of the parishioners of St Mary's, where as a member of the Catholic Union he helped form a community savings bank and local unemployment bureau. One of the original members of the club, at the 1891 AGM Stephen Henry unsuccessfully ran against Francis Nelis for the office of honorary president after the resignation of Dr Conway. At the half-yearly Celtic club meeting in December 1891, Stephen Henry seconded a motion by a Mr Flood congratulating the team and supporters on a successful first six months commenting that:

> They had in the splendid report submitted by their Secretary, Mr McLaughlin, a proof of the ability of Irishmen to manage any concern in which they took an interest. They had in their team and club membership men who were fit to compete favourably with those of any similar institution in the country, and in the cup ties and other engagements which the club had before them he had no fear but that the interest of the club, the fair fame of their nationality, and the exposition of genuine football would be the first consideration of those players who had in the past represented the club with such splendid success.

The motion was carried unanimously. During the 1893 AGM he supported Joe Shaughnessy's limited liability motion believing that all club members should be responsible for the club debt stating:

> At the present time the trustees and committee had a heavy burden on their shoulders and they wished every member of the club to have an equal responsibility. The fact that a man was elected on the committee should be no reason why he should accept personal responsibility more than an ordinary member and by that means, instead of being handicapped as they

*were at present, they would be able to give considerably more to charity
than they had been doing for some time.*

Politically, like most of the founding fathers, Stephen Henry was a member of the Home Government branch and in March 1893, he and Hugh Murphy were actively engaged in the attempt to get Independent Labour Party candidate Kier Hardy elected in the Mid Lanark by-election.

By the time of the AGM of 1894, his enthusiasm for the office bearers had worn off somewhat. He felt the composition of the Celtic committee had stagnated with the same middle-class office bearers being re-elected time after time. Concerned that the Celtic committee consistently failed to reflect a reasonable cross section of the club membership, he attempted to broaden the make-up of the power brokers at Celtic when he proposed that the business committee be elected from the general body of the membership. He insisted that the club be governed on more democratic grounds and compared the present subcommittee to the hereditary House of Lords. He felt that since the business subcommittee had the whole management of the club in their hands they should consequently be responsible to the membership. His motion was opposed by JH McLaughlin and others who ridiculed the proposal, stating that every committee had the right to elect their own subcommittees. John McLaughlin thought he was bringing football down to the level of politics. After further discussion, Stephen Henry's proposal was defeated and the power at the club remained in the hands of the middle-class members who could afford to devote their entire time to the management of the club.

Notoriously guarded and secretive, the Celtic office bearers and committee had a strained relationship with the often hostile Scottish press and generally kept them at arm's length. In an attempt to introduce some transparency into the business of the club, at the 1895 AGM, Stephen Henry proposed that the press be allowed to attend. His proposal was seconded and it was agreed to admit the press. At the 1895 half-yearly meeting held in December, over 100 club members packed into the pavilion at Celtic Park. James McKay, the club treasurer, declared that despite a massive increase in revenues, Celtic's debt still stood at £1400. Although the membership had already vetoed any move towards a limited company, later in the meeting Willie Maley proposed that a special committee be formed to consider the question of limited liability and the best way to reduce the club's debts. Although totally committed to the charitable aims of the club and opposed to the floatation generally, Stephen Henry appears to have taken a pragmatic approach to the question of limited liability and the management of the club and he seconded Maley's proposal. After an exhaustive discussion lasting over two hours, a sizable majority again threw out the proposal. Stephen Henry would later serve on the subcommittee that drew up the articles of association, which saw the club converted into a limited liability company in April 1897. Like most of the committeemen outwith the main office bearers, who for the most part became directors of the new company, he largely disappears from the club history after its conversion into the limited company.

As the century turned, Stephen J Henry was affluent enough to be running two homes. He and the younger children remained at Roselea Drive in Dennistoun, while his wife and the older children lived in Millport on the west coast. In 1903 he took over his brother's auctioneers rooms in Glasgow's Trongate. By 1910, with most of his children grown and flown the nest, he and his wife had retired to the Ayrshire coast, first to Millport and by 1918 they had moved to Troon. Now a Justice of the Peace, he retained a house in Glasgow at 8 Kelvinside Gardens, while some of the children worked or studied in Glasgow. Three of his sons went to Glasgow University to study medicine; his second eldest son, Francis J Henry, qualified as a bachelor of medicine in 1901 and Stephen in 1908. The three served as Catholic officers during the Great War. Francis and Stephen were doctors with the Army Medical Corps, Francis winning a Military Cross in 1916. His youngest son, John Aloysius Henry, gave up his medical studies to enlist into the Royal Flying Corps in 1917. He would be killed in aerial combat while piloting an RAF airplane in August 1918. He had only arrived in France three weeks previously.

Joseph F McGroary

Joseph F McGroary

Joseph Francis McGroary was born in Glasgow's Milton district in 1865, the son of Bernard and Mary McGroary. The family were originally from Mountcharles, Donegal, and like so many of the Glasgow Irish they maintained close ties with the family left behind. Bernard McGroary prospered after arriving in Glasgow. First as a butter and egg merchant and later he owned a coal business. He could afford to send Joseph to St Aloysius College, a school reserved largely for the sons of the middle class Glasgow Irish. At St Aloysius he was a contemporary of John H McLaughlin and Dominic MacCreadie jnr. As a fifteen year old, Joseph entered the law offices of Joe Shaughnessy where he began his law apprenticeship employed as a clerk. Between 1883–1885, he studied law at Glasgow University qualifying as a Writer in May 1887, when he served out his traineeship with Joe Shaughnessy's firm. His involvement with the Celtic project probably came about as a result of his association with Joe Shaughnessy, when he found himself serving alongside his boss on the first Celtic committee. As a Celtic committeeman, he was among the dignitaries in the pavilion the evening the original Celtic Park was formally opened on 8 May 1888 and his name appears among the personalities who attended the after game function in the Royal Hotel on George Square. His name appears as a committee member on the first Celtic fixtures card for season 1889-90. On 12 August 1888, twenty-six year old Joe McGroary returned to Donegal where married in his home village of Mountcharles. Joe McGroary then brought his young bride Catherine; back to Glasgow setting up home in St George's Road. The day before the wedding Celtic had spanked Airdrieonians by 6–0 in their first foray into Lanarkshire.

Joseph McGroary was re-elected onto the committee for season 1890–91 but lost his place at the 1891 AGM. Whether on or off the Celtic committee, Joe McGroary always took an active part in what were at times, boisterous debates at the AGMs and half-yearly meetings. He vehemently opposed the limited liability proposal from the floor when his old boss Joe Shaughnessy first raised the subject at the 1893 AGM. He pointed out that the club had made great progress every year. They had had a bigger balance in years gone by, but there was no doubt that they had been progressing rapidly and having read over a number of the past balance sheets of the club, he went on to prove that there was no necessity for the proposed change, especially as the club was flourishing. He regained a place on the general committee at the AGM of 1895 with forty-five votes. Once back in the saddle he threw himself into the role, representing the club at numerous functions including the United Celtic Brake Club's annual meeting. At the half-yearly meeting in December, he was involved in a spat with John H McLaughlin over the sums expended on the stadium. He again lost his place on the committee at the 1896 AGM after a three-way tie for the last place. He remained against the idea of limited liability and in February 1897 he was a member of the subcommittee formed to look at setting up the scheme that would turn the club into a limited liability company. Deeply involved in local and national politics he was a member of the central committee of the Glasgow Catholic Union, an organisation that endeavoured to get Roman Catholics onto school and parochial boards. He also stood for the Barony Parish's sixth ward in the Council elections of 1895. The following year he was one of the Thomas Davis branch representatives at the Irish Race Conference in Dublin. Later that year he found himself being sued in court by a former employee who implicated him in an illegal betting operation dating back to 1895. In 1898 he emigrated to America, leaving under something of a cloud having allegedly been involved in an illegal betting scam. He remained in New York until 1935 when he returned to Mountcharles, Donegal. He died there in 1937 and is buried at nearby village of Frosses.

Michael Cairns

Yet another founding father involved in the law was Michael Cairns. Born in Glasgow in 1857, he was the son of an Irish master tailor. He appears to have lost his parents while still relatively young and went to live with relatives in Renfrewshire. He was educated at St Mungo's under Brother Walfrid and went on to qualify as a solicitor from Glasgow University under the Law Agents Act of 1873. He served his apprenticeship to the legal profession in the offices of Messrs Murdoch & Stewart, Glasgow. On leaving their office he became an assistant to AR Ferguson, writer, in Neilston, Renfrewshire, where he was agent for the Clydesdale Bank. He was also agent for the Neilston Branch of the West Renfrewshire Liberal Association. While based in Neilston he was a member of St Thomas' Parish where took an active part in its affairs. In January 1888, he presided over an evening of Irish entertainment set in the school hall where Fr Charles O'Malley and Tom Maley were among the performers. In early 1889 he began business on his own account in Glasgow and his wide circle of friends enabled him to

Michael Cairns

form a growing and prosperous business. His advice was always sound, and therefore respected, and he had every prospect before him of enjoying a successful professional career. He first appears on the Celtic committee in 1889 and he took a very prominent part in the management of the club, being described as an ardent lover of football. Soon after his arrival back in the city, he became involved in local politics and stood as a candidate for the Tenth Ward in the municipal elections of that year. A member of the Catholic Literary Society, during a break in their St Patrick's Day social meeting, he proposed in an eloquent speech the toast of "Ireland a nation". It was later noted that a most enjoyable feature of the evening was the artistic programme provided by the Rangers FC Musical Association. Described as genial and kindly of disposition, among his best friends was Dr John Conway. Like so many of the founding fathers he was destined to die young, succumbing at his home in Apsley Place, Glasgow, aged just thirty-five in 1892. His good friend Dr Conway not only attended him during his illness, but also would allow him to be buried in the Conway family plot at Dalbeth Cemetery.

Timothy Joseph Walls

Timothy Joseph Walls

Timothy Joseph Walls was born in Glasgow of Irish parents originally from Sligo. His father, Thomas, was a master bootmaker, who would eventually own a couple of shop in the east end of Glasgow. He introduced his entire family to the trade and when Timothy Walls was voted onto the Celtic committee in 1891, he too was a bootmaker. Described as honest and hardworking, he was a very popular character within the club. With a reputation for candour, his straight talking sometimes got the better of his discretion; this made him unpopular with some of the power brokers at the club. Tim Walls appears to have been against the limited liability plan and on occasion challenged the office bearers over what he saw as misuse of funds, particularly regarding committee hospitality. In January 1894 the committee proposed to offer Willie Maley £150 per annum as a salary for the position of team manager on a five-year contract. Tim Walls alongside John H McLaughlin opposed the payment of a set wage to Willie Maley. The debate dragged on for two months before the matter was settled.

Tim Walls again caused some excitement at the half-yearly meeting of December 1894 when he and James Curtis squared up over gate takings. In May 1895, Timothy Walls took himself off to South Africa and was given one of the largest send-offs ever afforded a Celtic club member. Over 150 gentlemen from across sport and business turned up at the Mikado restaurant in Jamaica Street, Glasgow, for the bash. In addition to the office bearers, the guest list comprised just about all the active members of the club. Described at the time of his departure as a big loss to the Celtic committee, he was an unrivalled worker, who never got the kudos or credit he deserved for his work. Some thought that was because he was in the habit of saying what he thought straight out, which was, even then, at times politically incorrect. Conspicuous by his absence was Willie Maley, although his brother Tom did attend. By June 1896, Tim was back in Glasgow and giving his impression of the "Dark Continent" to the Glasgow Examiner newspaper and attending the Irish National Amnesty Association's meeting in the National Hall in the south side of the city. The organisation agitated for the release of Irish political prisoners from English jails. Although he was a bootmaker to trade, like so many others associated with the Celtic club he took to the liquor business and by 1900 both he and his younger brother, Randolph, were publicans. Timothy held a licence for the Weavers Arms, later the Calton bar, in London Road, while Randolph held a licence for a bar in Queen Street.

Randolph Augustine Walls was a member of the Volunteer Yeomanry and stepped forward when the call went out for volunteers to serve in South Africa. In response to disastrous losses among the regular forces, it was decided that units of mounted infantry were required to counter the Boer's flying columns and the result was the Imperial Yeomanry. Volunteers from the Queen's Own Glasgow and Lower Ward of Lanarkshire Yeomanry formed the 116-strong 18th Company of the 6th Battalion Imperial Yeomanry. The volunteers were mostly middle-class men, who could afford to provide their own horse and uniforms, which was one of the conditions of service. The remaining three companies that made up the 6th Battalion were composed entirely of volunteers from other Scottish Yeomanry units. The 6th Battalion got a rousing send-off from thousands of relatives and friends as they left for South Africa from the Clyde on 23 February 1900. Timothy Walls took over his brother's public house while he was in South Africa.

Some insight into his politics can be glimpsed during the McPeake slander case. John A MacCreadie described to the court Tim Walls' attitude to McPeake and the Irish Nationalists who fought with the Irish Brigade in South Africa. In a demonstration of his customary candour, Tim told McPeake that he should be shot. His attitude might be seen as something of a paradox, since he was also a member of the Irish National Amnesty Association. Tim Walls appears later to have taken to the seas as a ship's steward and during the McPeake trial he was on board a ship heading for New Zealand. In 1907 he spent some time in America landing up in New York, but by 1911 he was back in Glasgow and, like so many of the founding fathers, died at the relatively early age of fifty, in July 1912. His obituary in the Glasgow Observer described him a Celt of Celts and he will be long remembered by the old generation. He was buried in a family plot in Dunoon.

John Aloysius MacCreadie

John A MacCreadie

The family of John Aloysius MacCreadie were originally from Donegal, the patriarch, Dominick MacCreadie having arrived in Scotland in the midst of the famine of 1847. After working around the country for several years as a navvy, he eventually settled in Glasgow where he set himself up as a rag merchant. By the early 1870s he had moved into the wine and spirit business and by the mid-1880s he owned the Old Empire Bar in Glasgow's Saltmarket. The district was, prior to the renovation of the area in the 1890s, one of the city's worst slum areas. Old Dominick became one of the best-known Irishman in Glasgow and his bar was the first stop for many an Irish youth newly arrived off the Irish boat at the Broomielaw. The family lived for many years in Steel Street, just off the Saltmarket and one hundred yards from the Old Empire Bar. John Aloysius MacCreadie was born in the Gallowgate in 1856, the eldest son of the family. He was educated first at St Andrew's School, then by Brother Walfrid at St Mungo's and later attended St Aloysius Collage, as did several of his younger brothers. In 1887 he married Catherine Hegerty of Dundalk, the sister of the mayor of Louth.

Around the time of the formation of the Celtic club, the MacCreadie family branched out into the metal, machinery and boilers business and John A MacCreadie was described in the 1891 National Census as a machinery merchant. At the time, thirty-two-year-old John MacCreadie was living with his young family in the east end at London Road. As representatives of St Andrew's Parish, the MacCreadie family were involved in the Celtic project from the start. After the falling out of the parish representatives, according to Willie Maley in his *The Story of the Celtic book*, the MacCreadie family stuck with the project. John MacCreadie appears to have been a footballer in his youth and came into the Celtic project with something of a reputation as such. He was the only one of the early members who had any knowledge of the game until the arrival of the Maley brothers. John MacCreadie was an enthusiastic member of the Celtic club and served on the committee for several years. During the 1892 AGM, he took the middle ground in the debate over paid officials, decrying the office bearers for appointing paid officials without putting it to the members, but he recognised the fact that a paid official was necessary to manage the club finances. A pragmatist, he served on the subcommittee that drew up the articles of association for the club's conversion to a limited liability company in April 1897.

The MacCreadie family were all members of numerous Irish organisations and supported all their various causes. John MacCreadie was the first president of the Donegal Reunion Society and a founding member of the St Aloysius Association alongside Joe Shaughnessy, Joe Nelis and Dr John Conway. He was also a leading member of the Catholic Literary Society and was a star turn at their frequent soirées. At the St Patrick's Day bash of 1891, he was accompanied by the Rangers Musical Association and John H McLaughlin in a rendition of "Wearing of the

Green" and was also renowned for a spirited rendition of "God Save Ireland". John MacCreadie took the leading role in instigating and organising the annual Smyllum Orphanage sports day. The charity sports became an established event and the day trip to the institution was one of the highlights in St Andrew's Parish year.

Like the majority of the founding fathers, John MacCreadie was a member of the Home Government branch of the Irish National League and a fervent supporter of constitutional Irish Nationalism. Around the turn of the century, he went into the wine and spirit business, although in his case it was a return to a very familiar profession, taking the tenancy of a public house at 75 Greendyke Street, near the headquarters of the Glasgow Highlanders. Having suffered for some years from a heart complaint, just before Christmas 1907, John caught a chill and took to his bed. The chill developed into a serious illness and unable to cope with the strain his heart failed and he died on 2 January at his home on London Street. His wife Catherine then took over the licence on behalf of her seventeen-year-old son, also called John Aloysius. John Aloysius MacCreadie was described as one of the most prominent and well-respected Catholics in the city. Most of the leading members of the Glasgow Irish community, including a large representation from the Celtic club and William McKillop MP, attended his funeral at Dalbeth Cemetery. His son, John, volunteered to serve with the 6th Bn Highland Light Infantry TF during the Great War and saw action with his battalion in Salonika. Both old Dominick MacCreadie and his son and namesake, Dominick MacCreadie junior, were also original and lifelong members of the club; however, unlike John Aloysius, they never served on any of the committees.

Joseph Michael Nelis

Joseph Michael Nelis

Another largely forgotten, but massively influential Celtic founding father, was Joseph Michael Nelis. A Glasgow-born pawnbroker, his parents arrived in Glasgow with the first wave of economic migrants in the early nineteenth century. His Irish-born father, John Nelis, was a provisions merchant well established in the Bridgegate as early as the 1830s. A St Mungo's Academy pupil he was taught by Brother Walfrid and later went to St Aloysius Collage. After leaving school, Joe Nelis followed his father into the provisions business trading as butter and egg merchants, no doubt Irish butter and eggs, which were massively popular at the time. He entered into the – pawnbroking business in 1874 when he married Sidney Collins. Her father was Irishman Patrick Collins, who owned a pawnshop in Rutherglen. Drawn into local politics, Joe Nelis was one of the very early members of the Glasgow Catholic Union, appearing on the platform as early as 1885 when he was a member of the Barony Parochial Board. In 1887, Joe Shaughnessy, Joe Nelis and Dr John Conway were founding members of the St Aloysius Association.

The family were living in Bridgeton at Newhall Terrace, now Greenhead Street overlooking Glasgow Green, when he was drawn into the Celtic project. Considering his parochial board background in 1887 he was on the Bridgeton Board as a manager of the poor – he would have been attracted to the Celtic club because of its charitable aims. He first appears as a committeeman in 1890 and replaced Dr Conway as honorary club president in 1891. Like the rest of the committee, he was involved in all aspects of the club, appearing as a steward during the Celtic Sports meetings and representing the club at various functions. In 1892, he accepted the Glasgow Charity Cup on behalf of the club from the Lord Provost at the city chambers. In his acceptance speech, he proudly emphasised the club's commitment to charity, stating that since its inception the Celtic had maintained, at its sole expense, free Children's Dinner Tables in Parkhead, Calton and Bridgeton and, in addition, over the previous three years the club had donated £1200 to various good causes. After Dr Conway was deposed in 1891, his supporters rallied to Joe Nelis, who became the focus of the traditionalist faction. He was among the men who put their money where their mouths were, and was one of the leaseholders or guarantors for the new Celtic Park when the land was first rented from Lord Newlands in 1891. In his capacity as honorary president he was present at the turf laying ceremony at the new Celtic Park when Irish patriot Michael Davitt laid the famous Donegal sod. He asked for three cheers for Davitt before the party moved to old Celtic Park to watch a game.

He vehemently opposed Joe Shaughnessy's first limited liability motion at the 1893 AGM, when he moved that the club remain as at present, in the hands of the members. He argued that:

> *Since the club had progressed every year that was sufficient to prove that as a club it could be made a pronounced success. A limited company would possibly mean profit to a few persons, but it would mean utter ruin to the club, which they should not forget was established for charity.*

When summing up he stated that he was willing to put up £500 of his own money, if it helped to secure the club in its present form. After the club's conversion to a limited liability company in 1897, like so many of the men drawn to the Celtic by its charitable aims, Joe Nelis disappears from the management of the club. He retired from the pawnbroking business in 1897 to move into the liquor trade, no doubt inspired by the success of the publicans involved with the Celtic. By the turn of the century he appears to have decided to try his hand in the wine and spirit business in Alexandria, but his wife died in 1900 in Helensburgh, and by April the following year he is listed as being a publican living in the north of Glasgow at Minard Road, Partick. Discounting Willie Maley, Joe Nelis was the longest-serving club member of the founding committeemen, getting a mention in Willie Maley's Celtic book written in 1938. He finally succumbed to the inevitable in 1943 and is buried in Dalbeth cemetery.

Michael Hughes

Michael Hughes

Among the most vociferous opponents of the limited liability scheme was Michael Hughes. Born in Glasgow's city centre slums in February 1855, Michael was the son of Irish labourer Partick Hughes and his wife Mary O'Rourke. By the age of eighteen, Michael was a journeyman japanner and married to seventeen-year-old Bridget Reilly, the daughter of a Glasgow Irish blacksmith. The young couple later set up home at Barrack Street, just off the Gallowgate. Once described as an *out and out abstainer*, by 1896 he had been associated with the St Alphonsus League of the Cross for eight years and had for three years in succession between 1892 and 1895 held the office of president. He apparently came late to Irish politics, but by 1896 he was the president of the Fr Maginn Branch of the Irish National League, where old Fenian Pat Welsh was his vice-president. Probably encouraged by Pat Welsh, he attended the Irish National Amnesty Association meeting held in Glasgow in January 1897. Described as a hard-headed, earnest, practical man of business, who, when he spoke, did so with caution and deliberation. An early Celtic club member, his name never appears on the committee lists, but alongside Frank Havlin he was a spokesman for the working-class element at the club. He and Frank Havlin proposed and seconded motions at the December 1895 club meeting to prevent the formation of a committee to look into the possibility of limited liability. After the vote to convert the Celtic into a limited liability company, he and Tom Maley were voted onto the provisional board of directors in March 1897. They were elected to represent the interests of the traditionalist club members, while the club went through the mechanics of the conversion including the issuing of shares. Like Tom Maley, he was voted off the board at the AGM of June 1897 by the new power brokers at the club. His name only appears in the history of the Celtic for a short period but his contribution was significant enough to warrant a mention in Willie Maley's speech given during the 1938 Jubilee Dinner.

Francis McErlean

Irishman Francis McErlean was born in Co Antrim around 1845. He married in Glasgow in 1869 when he described himself as a Belfast-based spirit merchant. His new wife, Bridget, was the daughter of Charles Gallagher, an east end pawnbroker. Immediately after the marriage, the new couple returned to Ireland where between 1872 and 1882 three daughters were born to them. By the mid-1880s, the family had moved back to Glasgow where Francis took over a pawnbroker's shop in the east end. On 5 March 1888, McErlean's pawnshop in Great Eastern Road suffered a serious fire and insured loses of between £500 and £600 were sustained. It is likely that Francis was in at the very start of the Celtic project and was influential enough to be regarded as one of its leading members. After the Quillanite rebellion in June 1889, Francis McErlean replaced James Quillan as honorary vice-president. In June 1890, he was appointed treasurer of the Fr Beyaert presentation fund committee. Joining him on the committee was future Celtic committeeman, Frank Havlin. The Catholics of St Michael's, Parkhead, were getting together to present Fr Beyaert with a going-away gift after it was announced that he was to transfer to Kirkintilloch. The Parkhead clergyman was among the first supporters of the Celtic club and his name appears on the first subscription list alongside his generous twenty shillings.

In January 1891, Francis McErlean's eldest daughter, Bridget, married the Celtic captain and Scottish internationalist, James Kelly. The young couple were married by Fr Beyeart in St Michael's RC chapel then located in Salamanca Street. In April 1891, the McErlean family, which included new son-in-law James Kelly, were living at Burgher Street, just off Parkhead Cross and a few hundred yards from the original Celtic Park. At that year's club AGM, William McKillop ousted Frank from his position as vice-president, meanwhile at the same meeting his new son-in-law was voted onto the committee. Like all the Celtic committeemen, Francis McErlean went the extra mile for the club and sold tickets for various club events from his pawnbroker's shop. As a Belfastman himself, Francis accompanied the bhoys on their Easter 1896 tour of the north of Ireland. During the trip he pointed out Paddy Farrell of Belfast Distillery to Willie Maley, who brought him onto the books in August. Voted onto the committee again at the AGM of 1896, he appeared as an official at that year's sports meeting. After the club's conversion to a limited liability company, Francis McErlean declined the opportunity to buy additional shares in the new enterprise and it would appear that the McErlean family returned to Ireland at the start of the twentieth century. He died at Portglenone, Co Londonderry, in February 1906.

John Charles MacDonald

John C MacDonald

Five-year-old John Charles MacDonald arrived in Glasgow with his Irish parents, Bernard and Catherine MacDonald, around 1860. After first living in a boarding house in the High Street, the family moved around the corner to another Irish boarding house in McPherson Street, next door a coffee-grinding factory. The family remained in what was one of Glasgow's worst slum areas for the next few years, where Bernard had found work as a railway labourer. By the time John MacDonald left school aged fourteen, he had joined his father labouring in the railway yards. In what was a very significant achievement for a young Catholic boy of the period, he picked up an engineering apprenticeship. By 1881, the family had moved a mile or so north to the heavily industrialised St Rollox Parish in Springburn. Bernard MacDonald continued to be employed as a railway labourer working in the giant St

Rollox locomotive complex, while in the National Census of 1881, John MacDonald is listed as being unmarried, living with his parents and described as a mechanical engineer. Ten years later he was described on the census return as being employed as a steam engine fitter. John C MacDonald was among the first members of the Celtic club and Willie Maley in his book, having dropped the C, described John MacDonald of Springburn as a "follower of Powderhall professional foot-running" and one of only two committeemen with any sporting knowledge whatsoever. How the Springburn connection came about is unclear, since the vast majority of the founding fathers lived in and around the east end. There is some evidence that John Charles MacDonald's uncle, another John MacDonald, also from Springburn, was a close associate of Dr John Conway.

John C MacDonald was in the crowd watching the Hibernian and Cowlairs play out a 0–0 draw when they opened the new Celtic Park and later attended the reception held in the Royal Hotel in George Square. While the committee were trying to put the original Celtic team together, it was John C MacDonald and John O'Hara who first approached James Kelly about defecting to Celtic. The pair failed, but the silver tongue of John Glass and his open wallet did the trick. John MacDonald is listed, again without the "Charles", on the first Celtic fixture card for season 1889/90 as a committeeman. As an athletics supporter, alongside Willie Maley he was a regular at the Celtic sports meetings, where he would act as an umpire. He and his uncle John MacDonald were founding members of the Glasgow and West of Scotland Catholic Literary Society alongside fellow Celtic committeemen Stephen J Henry, Hugh Darroch and John F McGroary. After serving on the Celtic committee for several years, by the mid-1890s, John C MacDonald's employment took him away from Glasgow. After working in Manchester and Leeds, by 1901 he had married and was living and working in Aberdeen. There he maintained his interest in football when he became associated with Aberdeen FC after its formation in 1904. Despite living in Aberdeen, he maintained a close association with the Celtic and his old friends of the committee days. It was said of him that the highlight of his football season was the visit of the Celtic to the Granite City. He attended the Ne'erday Old Firm game on 1 January 1910 as a guest of the Celtic directors. He died in Aberdeen in 1929, still a Celtic supporter.

James Cairns

James Cairns was born in Glasgow in 1861 the son of a foreman mason. He first appears on the Celtic committee in 1892. In the National Census of 1891 he is listed as a thirty-year-old, single man living with his mother at Guildry Court in Bridgeton. Like so many of the Glasgow Irish, he found employment on the Glasgow docks, but by the time the Celtic club was being founded he had advanced into the position of stevedore. Unlike other parts of the world where the term relates to an ordinary dock labourer, in Glasgow the title was attached to a highly skilled load master supervising a gang of dockers, whose main task is to load and off-load ships. At the Celtic club AGM in May 1893, he supported Joe Shaughnessy's motion on limited liability. He took the position that, although he regarded himself as a poor man, he felt every club member should be willing to shoulder the responsibility for the club's liabilities equally. In August 1893 while working on the Glasgow harbour he saved the life of the mate of a berthed smack. The man slipped and fell into the Clyde. James Cairns scrambled down the side of the vessel and succeeded in grabbing the man, holding him above the water until help arrived. Voted off the committee at the 1894 AGM, he allowed his name to go into the hat again at the AGM of 1896. In the event he received only twenty-two votes, when thirty-seven were need to gain a position on the committee.

Just days after the Celtic had been officially converted into a limited company, on 20 April 1897, the thirty-six-year-old confirmed bachelor married twenty-one-year-old Rose McKay in St Andrew's Cathedral. Alex Maley, the youngest brother of Tom and Willie was his best man. That probably explains why as a thirty-six year old he joined the recently formed Celtic Harriers cross-country club. Six weeks before his marriage he was in the starting line as the Harriers left on a six-mile run, setting off from Maryhill Barracks. Despite his protestations of poverty at the 1893 AGM, within a year of the Celtic club being converted into a limited liability company, James was living with his young wife in the relatively affluent South Portland Street and was the proud possessor of a very significant 400 Celtic shares. He attended the funeral of JH McLaughlin in 1909, but by 1911, he had moved to Liverpool where he was employed as a ship's agent. He returned to Glasgow where he moved into the booming entertainment industry, becoming the manager of a picture house. He was at the twenty-five year anniversary AGM when Willie Maley was presented with his 300 guineas. At the time, it was mentioned by the *Man in the Know* that both he and James Moore invariably made a point of appearing at the AGMs. He died at his home in Albert Drive, Glasgow in July 1920 from heart failure. His Celtic shares were placed into a trust and remained in the family until the mid 1950s.

Francis Havlin

Francis (Frank) Havlin, sometimes spelt Havelin, Hevelan or even Haveland, was born in Ireland around 1844. He and his family came to Glasgow with the starving masses at the height of the Great Famine in 1847. His father, Patrick Havlin, settled his family in the east of Glasgow at what was then the hamlet of Tollcross. Soon afterwards he found employment labouring in the Clyde Iron Works and moved his family into the village that had grown up around the complex. Francis was raised in the Tollcross area and after leaving school appears to have gained a very valuable apprenticeship as a boilermaker. In September 1872, thirty-year-old boilermaker Frank Havlin married twenty-six-year-old Cecilia Colvin, a Scots-born weaver, at St Paul's in Shettleston. By 1881, the family was still in the Shettleston-Tollcross area and in the National Census Frank is listed as a gasworks labourer living at Great

Eastern Road. At various times he is described as a boilermaker, gasworks labourer, gas stove fitter or a Corporation labourer. Like most people of the era, Frank was a member of a number of associations including the Catholic Union of St Michael's Parish, where he was a member of its committee. Alongside Celtic's Francis McErlean, he was a member of the Fr Beyaert presentation committee when the priest was transferred from St Michael's to Kirkintilloch. He was also the first president of the St Paul's Conference of the Society of St Vincent de Paul based at Eastmuir Parish. Over the space of thirty years he was, at one time or another, a member of all the Irish National organisations based in Shettleston, Tollcross, Bridgeton and Parkhead. Although regularly listed as a labourer, Frank Havlin appears to be largely self-taught, remarkably self-confidant and an eloquent speaker. In August 1893, he addressed the Bridgeton branch of the Irish Nation league on the topic of the Land Question. Frank Havlin joined the Celtic club in 1892, attracted, in his own words, by "the club's commitment to charitable causes". He became a member of the traditionalist faction at Parkhead and was one of the most passionate and outspoken anti limited liability members, completely dedicated to maintaining the club's original *raison d'être*: its commitment to charity.

At the beginning of April 1895, the Celtic club members were called to a special general meeting at the Pavilion Hall. The assembly was called to discuss proposed changes to the club constitution as drafted by vice-president John H McLaughlin. During the meeting, Frank Havlin locked horns with the vice-president, who had engineered very major constitutional changes. The proposed powers included the ability to create new by-laws and to expel a member from the club summarily. Frank argued against a number of the proposals, particularly those that he felt would effectively have given absolute power to the management committee. In particular, he objected to Rule 18, by which the management committee would be empowered, at their own discretion, to insist that members pay their pro rata share of club debt at just fourteen days' notice. Members failing or unable to pay within the allotted time would *ipso facto* cease to be members of the club and would have no further interest in the club. Frank Havlin vehemently objected and said "the successful adoption of such a rule would effectively drive the workingmen from the club". Frank's impassioned speech opposing the implementation of Rule 18 convinced the club members and his objection was successfully carried by a large majority. Had the rules been adopted as drafted, they would have given the modernisers, who dominated the management committee, total control of the club.

As a sideline, John H McLaughlin wrote sports articles for the Glasgow Examiner newspaper and a few weeks after his failed attempt to push through all his constitutional changes at the club, he wrote an article in which he referred to the April meeting. In his article he termed the opponents of his constitutional changes, largely the working class, traditionalist element, as a "contemptible corner" and a "mob", and that: "The only grain of comfort to be extracted from the meeting was that the majority had the good sense to religiously exclude every mother's son of this 'mob' from the committee." At the Celtic club's winter meeting in December 1895, the modernisers again pushed the idea of limited liability. Tom Maley objected suggesting that the half yearly meeting was not the time or place such a motion should be discussed, but as a compromise suggested that a special subcommittee be formed to investigate the pros and cons of limited liability. A counter motion was raised by Mick Hughes and seconded by Frank Havlin, both of whom were determined that no encouragement should be given to the modernisers or to the concept of limited liability. Their amendment that no committee be formed and that limited liability not be investigated was discussed at length. Frank Havlin, while addressing the members on the matter, mentioned John McLaughlin's article, stating that McLaughlin had termed the working-class members of the club "corner boys" and "loafers". After exhaustive argument the Hughes/Havlin amendment was carried by fifty votes to thirty-one and no subcommittee was formed.

After the attempt to advance the limited liability cause was again defeated, again largely by Frank Havlin, John McLaughlin took exception to the terms accredited to him in his article by Havlin during his speech. John McLaughlin claimed it was libellous and took Frank Havlin to court, demanding £100 redress. McLaughlin argued that Havlin's version of the article suggested that he had slandered the members and was therefore unfit to associate with them or to be trusted with the business of the club. Frank Havlin contested the claim and at court defended himself, stating that he had spoken at the meeting from memory and although the exact words may have been different, the inference was correct. He then eloquently voiced the thoughts and concerns of the traditionalist members facing the threat of losing control of their club:

> Working men had been attracted to the club originally because of its charitable aims and had become enthusiastic supporters. The club's primary purpose had been abandoned and what is known as professionalism was introduced by the executive in the system of management dividing the membership into two different camps or parties, one representing the working class element and the other the better-to-do party.

While the court case was still ongoing, the June 1896 AGM was held in the Annfield Hall. Frank was again at his confrontational best, demanding the right to see the books and asking the executive if it were true that non-members were helping to manage the club. For his troubles, at the end of the AGM, Frank Havlin was voted onto the Celtic committee. His election must have been some cause for concern or anxiety for him and his family. As a working man, he could ill afford the time and commitment a position on the Celtic committee demanded. The previous season, the general and business committees met eighty times in total. However, a few weeks later he got some very good news. In what must have come as a great relief to him and his family, John H McLaughlin withdrew from the libel action. The Glasgow sheriff dealing with the case commented that it should never have been brought in the first place and presented McLaughlin with the bill for court costs. Despite his undoubted qualities, the libel action by John McLaughlin was petty and vindictive; £100 might not have meant a great deal to middle-class John McLaughlin, but for Frank, a gasworks labourer, being saddled with a £100 debt would have meant a lifetime of penury and ultimately the poorhouse. The Glasgow newspapers carried the case, pitching it as a David and Goliath story and reported Frank Havlin emerging from the court with flying colours. Only days later John McLaughlin and Frank were rubbing shoulders in the Celtic pavilion both acting as officials during the annual Celtic sports event.

As an ordinary workingman, how Frank found the time to attend the numerous meetings and fulfil the additional commitments expected of a Celtic committeeman is unknown. Similarly, how he felt interacting and working closely with the club's increasingly middle-class office bearers is also unknown; however, at the monthly general committee meeting held on 2 December, Frank Havlin was in attendance and still in a confrontational mood. Treasurer James McKay gave the committee a financial report ahead of the December 1896 half-yearly meeting. It showed that the club's debts were coming down and had been reduced to just £400. In view of the reduced debt burden, Frank proposed that the sum of £50 be sent to the Society of St Vincent de Paul, but the rest of the committee voted down his altruistic gesture. Determined that something should be done for charity, he shamed the committee into splitting £50 equally between the Little Sisters of the Poor, Smyllum Orphanage, the Dalbeth Nunnery, Lanark Hospital and the Whitevale Refuge. Frank's fighting £50 was the largest proportion of the £63 of donations that showed in the club's half-yearly statement. In the event it would prove to be a hollow victory for the traditionalists; the recent revolt of three players and just weeks later the Celtic's humiliating Scottish Cup defeat at Arthurlie, propelled the club towards better business practices and limited liability. At a special meeting in March 1897, limited liability was pushed through and Frank Havlin, no doubt much to his chagrin, was voted onto the committee that organised the share distribution. Like so many of the traditionalist club members, Frank disappears from the history of the Celtic after limited liability and died at his home in Tollcross in March 1906.

Michael Dunbar

Although not a founding father per se, Michael Dunbar was associated with the Celtic for thirty-three years as a player, committeeman and director. His relationship with the club began with his appearance in the first Celtic side versus the Rangers Swifts in May 1888 and continued unbroken until his death in September 1921. Born in Cathcart in 1863, he was the son of a Scots father and Co Wicklow born mother. Although born in Cathcart, he was raised in Busby, Renfrewshire, where his father worked as a printworks labourer. He was one of the famous Hibernians who christened the first Celtic park and was enticed away to Celtic by Tom Maley in June 1888. The licence of a pub in Coatbridge and £300 paid for the goodwill probably had something to do with his decision to join the new club. Mick Dunbar appeared thirty-two times for the Celtic and scored ten goals. He retired from football in 1893 to concentrate on his wine and spirit business then situated in the Gallowgate and was voted onto the Celtic committee the following year. Willie Maley described him as the most affable of companions. The trio of Mick, Willie Maley and James Kelly dealt mostly with the team itself. He was related through

Michael Dunbar

the marriage of his younger brother, Thomas, who played for both Celtic and Rangers, to the family of John Glass.

Mick Dunbar joined the Celtic board as a director in June 1897 on the formation of the public limited company and by the following year, between them, the two Dunbar brothers owned a considerable 550 Celtic shares. Yet another passionate Irish Nationalist, Mick was never a noted orator, but he never failed to attend major rallies and Nationalist platforms and his name regularly appears on the list of subscribers donating money to Irish Nationalist causes. He was one of three Celtic directors on John Redmond's political platform when the leader of the Irish Parliamentary Party visited Glasgow in 1913 to drum up support for the Irish Home Rule legislation. As late as 1918 he was still donating funds to the recently deceased John Redmond's politically doomed Irish Parliamentary Party.

Joseph Scanlan MD

Dr Joseph Scanlan

Joseph Scanlan was born in Glasgow's east end in 1863. His father, Daniel Scanlan, a native of Glenfin, Co Donegal, served for over thirty years as a Glasgow policeman and sheriff's officer. His grandfather arrived in Glasgow in the early 1800s and worshiped in the first little Catholic chapel near the old barracks. Joseph was educated at St Mungo's, St Aloysius and Glasgow University and he qualified as a doctor of medicine in 1883. At the time there were only six Catholic students at the Glasgow institution. He was a close personal friend of the Celtic's first treasurer, Hugh Darroch, and married Hugh's sister-in-law, Sarah Walls, in June 1891 at St Alphonsus Chapel. The wedding ceremony took place just eight weeks before Hugh's death. One of the original club members, Willie Maley in his life story serialised in the Weekly News in 1936, termed Dr Scanlan a "great Celt" and credited the good doctor with much of the success of the first Celtic Sports in August 1890. It was through his offices that a number of the top Irish runners agreed to appear at the first Celtic Park. Dr Scanlan's name intermittently appears in the early history of the Celtic club. One of the earliest mentions was in January 1891 when he was named in the Scottish Sport journal as the Celtic club doctor and has him attending a badly injured Dumbarton player. Although a lifelong supporter, he never served on any of the committees and seldom spoke at the biannual club meetings. At the AGM of 1892, he seconded the proposal to adopt honorary secretary McLaughlin's report, adding that: "It was just such a report as they might expect from a man like Mr McLaughlin, whose qualities had been not only discovered by the Celtic Club, but who had commanded recognition from outside bodies as well." He did speak again during the limited liability debate at the 1893 AGM, when he supported Joe Shaughnessy's motion: "I believe the club would be more prosperous under the new proposal. It was only a matter of justice that every member should have an equal right to incur responsibility and not have the burden on the shoulders of a few as it was at present." While acting as club doctor, he remained in the background, a highly respected and influential club member seen by most as an honest broker. In that guise he would adopt the role of chief enumerator overseeing the voting in of the committee at the AGMs.

After the 1894 AGM, he became embroiled, much to his indignation, in some club politics. Thirty members signed a requisition for an extraordinary meeting to consider alleged irregularities in the election of the committee at the AGM. The special meeting, chaired by John Glass, was duly held in the Mechanics' Hall in Bridgeton to discuss the matter. The signatories alleged that the enumerators at the election had acted carelessly, allowing some members to render two ballot papers. The vote had been conducted under the supervision of Dr Joseph Scanlan and at the meeting he hotly refuted the aspersions, defending both himself and his enumerators against the charges levelled at them. Ultimately, the original vote was declared to be null and void, but immediately afterward the same committee was unanimously re-elected en bloc. On conversion to a limited liability company in 1897, Dr Scanlan became a Celtic shareholder and over the years added to the number of club shares he owned. He remained a popular figure around the Celtic Pavilion and was among the guests at the opening of the luxurious, but fatally flawed, Grant Stand in 1899. Although never a major shareholder, he, and later his family, retained their club shares until the early 1970s.

A member of the Home Government branch of the Irish National League, he was a fervent supporter of constitutional Irish Nationalism. On Saturday 19 March 1892, Dr Scanlan was among the party that accompanied Michael Davitt on his famous Donegal sod laying ceremony in the as yet only half-completed new Celtic Park. After the planting and lunch with the Celtic committee, he, Michal Davitt and John Ferguson joined 15,000 spectators at the old park to watch Celtic play out a 0–0 draw with Clyde. The next day Michael Davitt, again accompanied by Dr Scanlan, addressed a meeting of the Home Government branch in Glasgow. Dr Scanlan was among the branch delegates sent to the National Convention of September 1896 and later that year he was asked to chair a Home Government branch meeting due to be addressed by Tim Healy. The Glasgow Irish were giving the maverick Irish Nationalist MP a hearing after his break from John Dillon's Irish National Federation. Seventeen years later, in June 1913, he was among the leading Glasgow Irish Nationalists who welcomed IPP leader John Redmond to Glasgow as the drive towards Home Rule for Ireland entered a critical phase.

Like so many of the Celtic founding fathers, in addition to his support for the constitutional Irish Nationalism of the IPP, he was a Liberal, taking an interest in welfare reforms, old age pensions in particular. He was very active in local welfare matters, serving on school boards and parish councils. Dr Scanlan was a keen historian, and particularly interested in the history of the Roman Catholic community in Glasgow and Scotland. He wrote and lectured on the subject and as a member of the Catholic Literary Society he regularly gave lectures to the society on subjects usually with an Irish Nationalist or Roman Catholic slant. He was elected the first treasurer of the Gaelic League when it was founded in Glasgow in 1890 and as a talented linguist immediately set about teaching himself the old language. As the medical advisor to the Marist Teaching Order in Glasgow in 1896, he advised that the young pupil teachers accommodated in the overcrowded parochial house at 71 Charlotte Street be rehoused. In August 1898 he was required to administer emergency aid to Celtic founding father Brother Dorotheus. The Marist headmaster had stood on an earthenware bowl when getting out of a bath. The bowl broke and cut an artery in his foot. Brother Dorotheus managed to call for help, but his first aiders could not stem the immense flow of blood. Fortunately, Dr Scanlan was near St Mary's heading to Mass when the emergency happened. He managed to stem the blood flow, but Dorotheus had lost an enormous amount of blood and it took him several weeks to recover. Among his other medical responsibilities, he was the medic to a number of National Forester branches in the east end. Dr Scanlan lived and practised medicine for most of his life in Dennistoun from where he attended Celtic legend Barney Battles during his sudden, fatal illness in February 1905. He gets a mention in Willie Maley's jubilee history of the Celtic written in 1938, when he and Mrs Arthur Murphy, both present at the jubilee dinner, were described as being among the club's oldest enthusiasts. He finally succumbed to the inevitable in January 1950, aged eighty-eight.

Dr Joe Scanlan's eldest son, James Donald Scanlan, was born in January 1899, and like his father he was educated at St Mungo's and St Aloysius College. Like tens of thousands of other young Glasgow Irish men, he answered Archbishop McGuire's call to join the armed forces when he declared the Great War a crusade. He entered the Royal Military Academy at Sandhurst as an officer cadet in 1916 and was commissioned into the Highland Light Infantry in 1917. During the Great War he saw active service in Egypt before resigning his commission in 1919. On his return to civilian life, he graduated with a law degree from Glasgow University in 1923. He was ordained in June 1929 and would serve as Bishop of Dunkeld and later Bishop of Motherwell before returning to his native city as Archbishop in 1964. He conducted the Requiem Mass for the sixty-six victims of the Ibrox Stadium disaster of January 1971. Over 1400 people of all faiths, including the Celtic and Rangers teams, attended the mass in St Andrew's Cathedral, Glasgow. Around the same time, Archbishop Scanlan's sister, Dr Rosemary Scanlan, contributed the family's Celtic shares to a trust fund set up to maintain the archbishops of Glasgow in their retirement. Archbishop James Scanlan died in 1976.

James Moore

Mr James Moore was almost a constant on the Celtic committee between 1892 and 1897. Born of Irish parents in Manchester, England, around 1855, his father John Moore was a hatter to trade. After decanting first to Liverpool, the family moved back to Ireland in 1862 before taking the crossing to

Glasgow ten years later. The Moore family settled in the Gorbals, setting up home in South Wellington Street, before moving to Main Street. Young James followed his father into the hatter trade, a profession that also covered umbrella manufacturing. James was described in the 1881 national census as a twenty-five-year-old umbrella maker. In his youth, James became involved in athletics and was a noted middle-distance runner favouring, the mile. James Moore and his younger brother Thomas, who was also a noted runner, travelled west central Scotland during the athletics season competing for the various prizes on offer. In March 1886, James Moore married Calton girl, Theresa Murphy, the daughter of an Irish metal dealer based in Bellgrove Street. After tying the knot in St Mary's, the newly-weds set up home in Abercromby Street. After moving into the Calton, James became involved with the various associations and confraternities associated with St Mary's Parish. As a noted Catholic athlete living in the parish, James would have been consulted on and involved in the athletics side of the new club and was later described as a close associate of Brother Walfrid. He was deeply involved in setting up the first of the Celtic's sports meetings. When James' running career came to an end, he began to officiate at the sports meetings, very often acting as the race starter. He would later be appointed the official starter for the Scottish Amateur Athletics Association, an organisation of which Willie Maley was a leading member and official. One of the major meetings of the season at which he officiated was the Rangers Sports Day. He was first voted onto the Celtic committee at the 1892 AGM, where he appears to have been the representative of the somewhat neglected athletics side of the club.

At the end of April 1895, James Moore became yet another Celtic committeeman enticed into the spirit trade, when he paid forty-eight pounds a year for the licence of a public house at 6 Forth Street, in Glasgow's Port Dundas district. When his son Thomas was born in 1896, he described himself as a spirit merchant living at 48 Port Dundas Road. During the boom of pedestrianism and cycling in the mid-1890s, the Celtic office bearers decided to promote athletics at the club and turned to James Moore. He was one of the founding members and a leading organiser of the Celtic Harriers and Cycling Club when it was founded in January 1897. The new club drew its members from the Celtic FC athletes, the Hibernian Swimming Club, the Young Men's Society and the League of the Cross branches. James Moore and Pat McMorrow, another Celtic committeeman with an interest in athletics, took the leading roles in promoting, recruiting and running the Celtic Harriers. James Moore was voted into the office of vice-president at the inaugural meeting in January 1897, along with Willie Maley as president and John Glass on the committee. The first run-out for the Harriers took place on 11 February, starting at Celtic Park with Tommy Moore setting the pace as one of the hares. A tea was arranged in St Mary's Hall at the finish. At the first annual meeting of the Celtic Harriers Club in November 1897, James was voted president with JH McLaughlin as honorary president and Willie Maley as honorary vice-president.

On conversion to a limited liability company, James Moore appears to have gained and retained only his one Celtic member's share, while his younger brother, Hamilton-based Thomas Moore, was by 1889, the proud possessor of 100 Celtic shares. It was Tommy Moore, a close friend and running partner of Alex Maley, who tipped Willie Maley the wink concerning the great Peter Somers. Then still a mere youth, Peter was turning out for local club Cadzow Juniors. Peter Somers would go on to become one of the all-time Celtic greats.

James Moore retained a close association with the Celtic club, mostly through his connection with the Celtic Harriers and his role as official starter at the Celtic sports meetings. In 1913, while celebrating the twenty-fifth anniversary of the club, the directors presented James with a medal to mark his long and faithful service to the Celtic club. At the same time, it was announced that the old red cement track would be torn up to make way for additional terracing; somebody remarked that a glimpse of Starter Moore and his red jacket would be compensation for the loss of the track. James Moore would maintain his link to the Celtic club for another twenty years.

A devout Catholic, James was an active parishioner in St Francis, St Mary's and St Peter's parishes. He was a member of the League of the Cross and was involved in most church welfare activities. He was also involved in local politics in the form of canvassing for the Catholic Union candidates at municipal elections. In October 1919, James Moore was one of the founding members of the Knights of St Columba; a Catholic mutual benefit society dedicated to the principles of charity, unity and fraternity. James succumbed to the inevitable in 1933, when he died at his home in Garnethill, Glasgow, at the ripe old age of seventy-seven. Some indication of the high regard with which he was held at the Celtic club can be seen in the very many surviving Celtic personalities who appeared as mourners at his funeral at Dalbeth; among them were Willie Maley, Tom Maley, James Kelly, Arthur Murphy, Tom Colgan, John Shaughnessy, Davie Meikleham and Tom White.

Daniel Molloy

Daniel Molloy

Daniel Molloy, Milloy or even Malloy, was born and raised in Bridgeton to second-generation Glasgow Irish parents. His grandparents settled in Bridgeton, where they were employed as handloom wavers, as early as the mid-1820s. Born in 1862, Dan was probably among those taught by Brother Walfrid at the Sacred Heart School in Bridgeton, when it opened in 1874. By November 1887, Dan, now aged twenty-seven, was married with two children, employed as an ironmonger's traveller and living in Adelphi Street, Bridgeton. He was a popular member of St Mary's Parish, and as a talented fiddle player he often accompanied John H McLaughlin on the piano at the various Church-led functions. Like most of the founding fathers, Dan was involved in the UIL, the INF and the League of the Cross, the latter based at St Mary's. He was among those parishioners from St Mary's involved in the Celtic project from its inception, he was present at the Hibernian versus Cowlairs game at old Celtic Park and was in the George Hotel in Glasgow's George Square for the subsequent reception. The evening of Wednesday 2

January 1889 found Brother Walfrid, Dr Conway, John McLaughlin, Dan Molloy and a couple of players attend a function in the Pinkerton Halls in Main Street, Bridgeton. The occasion was the first annual supper of the O'Connell branch of the Irish National Foresters of which John Glass was a founding member. The company were in a celebratory mood with the Celtic having just beaten top English side Mitchell St John by 7– 1. The night turned into a right auld Irish singsong with Dan Molloy's fiddle playing and Neillie McCallum's singing the highlight of the evening. Dan Molloy would serve on the Celtic committee between 1888 and 1890, where his good nature and jokey personality made him one of the most popular club members in and out of the Pavilion.

In 1891, Dan and his young family emigrated to America where on arrival they settled in New York. There the couple had another two children, both girls. The American adventure failed to work out and in October 1895, the Molloy family returned to Scotland, sailing from New York on the ship *City of Rome* and landing in Glasgow. One of the first things Dan did on his arrival back in the city was to renew his membership at the Celtic club and at the June 1896 AGM, he only narrowly failed to be re-elected onto the committee. Shortly after arriving back in Glasgow, Dan settled in Rutherglen and went into the wine and spirit trade where his light-hearted, comedic character was ideal for a publican. His sudden death on 9 December 1899, aged just thirty-seven, was a great shock to his many friends at the Celtic club. His continued association with the club and its directors is highlighted when he named John Glass, John H McLaughlin and Joe Shaughnessy as trustees in his will, made just three weeks before his death. Buried at Dalbeth Cemetery, his widow Elizabeth and four daughters later moved to Girvan, Ayrshire.

Patrick Welsh

Mr Patrick Welsh,

Patrick Welsh

Finally, Patrick Welsh, or Tailor Welsh as he was known in the east end of Glasgow, has a special place in the folklore of the Celtic club. A west of Ireland man from Co Leitrim, he settled in Glasgow in the mid 1860s and set himself up as a tailor. Having first settled in the Gallowgate, by the late 1880s he and his family had moved to Abercromby Street where they were members of St Mary's Parish. Described as a good Catholic and Nationalist, he was a member of a number of local associations: the League of the Cross, the Society of St Vincent de Paul and of course the Irish National League, where he was for a time the vice- president of the Father MaGinn branch. He was also the vice-president of the Glasgow branch of the Irish National Amnesty Association, an organisation founded by Isaac Butt in 1869 and dedicated to the release from prison of the men of the Fenian Rising of 1867. As a result of the agitation and demonstrations for an amnesty, a number of Fenians were released, among them republican martyr Tom Clarke, who had joined the IRB in 1880. After planning an explosives campaign in England, he was betrayed and arrested in 1883. He spent fifteen years in London's notorious Pentonville Prison before he was released in 1898 as part of a general amnesty for Fenian prisoners. Because of his membership of these associations, Pat would have been well known to the likes of John Glass and John O'Hara.

As a member of the first Celtic committee, it was Tailor Welsh who led Brother Walfrid and John Glass to the Cathcart home of old Sergeant Maley and his sons, Tom and Willie Maley. The Welsh and Maley families were well known to each other since Pat Welsh supported the Maley family when they first arrived in Glasgow from Ireland, after Sergeant Maley retired from the army in 1870. Legend has it that while a young man, Pat Welsh was involved with the Fenians and was being shadowed by the police. While trying to make his escape from Ireland through the Dublin docks, he was discovered by a certain Sergeant Maley of the North British Fusiliers. The soldier took pity on a young, fellow Irishman, who convinced him that he wanted to give up the wild side of Irish politics and settle down in Glasgow. Sergeant Maley reputedly turned his back on young Pat, allowing him to make good an escape. The exact truth of the matter will never be known, but like most legends there is probably at least some basis in fact. For example, the police were apparently shadowing Pat Welsh, but it may have been his brother they were actually more interested in and the Royal North British Fusiliers and Sergeant Maley were in Dublin in 1867 when Pat made good his escape.

If the story as told is true, Sergeant Maley took an almost unimaginable risk to help an unknown young Irish fugitive. Had the military authorities discovered his dereliction of duty, the consequences for Sergeant Maley and his young family would have been completely catastrophic. He would have been awarded a court martial and at best, sentenced to a long period of penal servitude at hard labour, probably in Australia. His wife and children would have been turned out from their army home and he would have lost his priceless military pension. As an example of how serious the military would have viewed the matter, Corporal John Boyle O'Reilly of the 10th Hussars (Prince of Wales) was arrested in 1866 for encouraging fellow soldiers to join the Fenian movement. Found guilty at a court martial, the death sentence was commuted to one of twenty years' penal servitude, which automatically meant transportation to Australia and a lifetime of hard labour. Irrespective of how or where Tailor Welsh met Sergeant Maley, he led Brother Walfrid and John Glass to the Maley bhoys home in Cathcart and the rest as they say is history.

Although Tailor Welsh served on the first Celtic committee and regularly attended club meetings and socials, he appears not to have taken a leading role in the management of the club fairly soon after its establishment. However, his place in Celtic folklore is assured through leading Brother Walfrid and John Glass to the Maley brothers, his association with the Fenians and his legendary escape from the Pigeon House Docks. Pat Welsh died in August 1899 and is buried in Dalbeth cemetery.

Principles and Respectability or Supping with the Devil

In addition to the aforementioned founding fathers, a host of dedicated club members served on various committees over the first ten years of the club's existence. The record of their individual contributions are now largely lost, however, the mere mention of their name in a newspaper report or club document is enough to ensure that their contribution is recorded for posterity and their efforts on behalf of the club clearly recognised.

As described, the original committeemen were all Roman Catholic, not quite all Irish, but all highly respectable parishioners, who were almost to a man involved with the temperance movement, particularly the League of the Cross and the Catholic Young Men's Society. None of the original office bearers or committeemen was directly involved in the liquor trade. That would change and change fairly quickly. The Celtic club's famous or infamous connection to the liquor trade appears to have begun through its attempts to procure or more importantly secure the services of football players. The amateur status of the Scottish game was a pretence that fooled no one. Almost every single football club was paying their players under the counter and offering inducements to keep them at the club. The practice also affected and irritated the English clubs, which were often at the sharp end of some very dubious deals. The English game allowed professionalism and their clubs employed players at very lucrative wages, which of course enticed the cream of the Scottish players over the border. This forced the Scottish clubs, and Celtic in particular, to come up with schemes that would circumvent the SFA's rules regarding payments to players.

It is of course inconceivable that working-class players, like those who gave up positions at Hibernian, Renton or Everton, would come to Celtic simply for the charitable objectives of the club, no matter how laudable. John Glass had a reputation for being able to charm the birds off the trees, but even his gift of the gab had its limitations. In addition to illegally paying players extremely generous cash payments, supposedly by way of reasonable expenses and compensation for injuries and time taken off work, players coming to Celtic would be *set up* by the club. Usually, the player in question would be bought the tenancy of a public house, an establishment that never saw them behind the bar, but from where they drew a weekly cash sum. The pub would be run on the player's behalf by its staff, allowing the player in question to devote his full attention to training and playing football. James Kelly brought in from Renton in May 1888, Celtic's first captain and future club director, was one the first such who developed a sudden passion for a career in the wine and spirits trade. The legendary Dan Doyle was brought to Celtic having been poached from Everton in 1891. No sane person believed that Dan, good Catholic that he undoubtedly was, gave up a very lucrative professional position at Everton for the benefit of his immortal soul. Doyle's subsequent dispute with Everton FC was played out in public, with Dan announcing that he was being paid £3 a week by Everton. However, he had decided to come to Celtic because they had promised him the tenancy of a public house worth £5 a week, plus an additional payment for every match he played in. This was of course highly embarrassing for the officially amateur Celtic club, but they got around the problem by stating that it was not the club, but ardent supporters who had provided the tenancy and the payments were their way of showing their appreciation. Joseph Shaughnessy, the Celtic solicitor and committeeman, represented Dan Doyle at the enquiry. The case was eventually settled when Doyle agreed to pay back some of the advanced wages he had received from Everton. Dan Doyle was one of the Glasgow Irish, born in Paisley and brought up in Airdrie. As far as the Celtic supporters were concerned, he was one of them and Parkhead was his rightful home. Over the period it became almost a custom for star players joining Celtic to be placed in a public house, while club officials too caught the bug as they saw players, like James Kelly and Mick Dunbar, prosper through their tenancies.

The original office bearers were for the most part financially secure and independent enough to be able to devote, even from the very start of the project, a substantial amount of their time and energies to the venture. However, as the success of Celtic accelerated alongside the popularity of the game of football itself, the roles of the officials at Celtic changed from a charitable good deed to literally a full-time occupation. As a result, the same half dozen or so individuals found themselves built into the very fabric of the club, almost permanent office bearers, and as the years passed, effectively indispensable to the running and continued success of the club. During the 1893 AGM, John H McLaughlin was able to report, with some sense of relief, that the new business committee, which had replaced three subcommittees, had met just forty-six times over the previous year as opposed to the eighty-five times the subcommittees had been obliged to meet. Serving on a Celtic committee was always about much more than simply appearing at meetings. Very considerable amounts of time and effort were required to be expended putting into action the committee decisions. A scouting trip to Aberdeen or London might take three days for example.

The Celtic committee itself was for the most part fairly representative and a number of ordinary working-class members managed to get voted onto the committee for varying lengths of time. The lifestyles of the working-class members of the committee ensured they were never able to devote as much time to their duties as the financially independent members. In addition, with one or two notable exceptions, the working-class committeemen often found themselves out of their depth educationally and socially, as their duties brought them into contact with people outwith the club, who would generally be regarded as their social betters.

In order to meet the increased commitment to the Celtic project, the tenancy of a public house for a Celtic office bearer or official solved the same problem of free time and a secure income, as it did for the players. The official could devote all his time to Celtic while drawing an income from the public house. In time, John H McLaughlin, John O'Hara, James Kelly, Michael Dunbar, Willie Maley, Joe Nelis, Arthur Murphy, James Moore and Tim Walls would all take to the wine and liquor trade. It would be strange indeed if such astute men failed to see the commercial possibilities of the public house or whisky shop. In July 1895, the strictly temperance Glasgow Observer published an open letter: "It is to say the least a trifle curious how certain men, players or officials, not in what one could call flourishing financial condition, suddenly blossom into publicans." The association with the disreputable liquor trade would be a stigma the club would be unable to shake off until social attitudes to alcohol itself changed.

Listed are the attendance records of the Celtic office bearers and committeemen elected onto either or both the General and Business committees for season 1894–95.

Name	Position	General	Business
John Glass	President	23	69
James McKay	Hon. Treasurer	23	69
John O'Hara	Committee	21	65
David Meikleham	Leaseholder	19	61
James Curtis	Committee	18	67
Joseph Shaughnessy	Leaseholder	15	63
William McKillop	Hon. President	14	62
John McCann	Committee	21	
Francis McErlean	Committee	20	
William Maley	Hon. Secretary	20	
Michael Dunbar	Committee	20	
Patrick Gallacher	Committee	20	
John H McLaughlin	Vice-President	19	
T.J. Walls	Committee	19	
Arthur Murphy	Committee	16	
James Moore	Committee	14	
James Kelly	Committee	9	
J.M. Nelis	Leaseholder	8	

Chapter Five

Charity versus Profit

As the Celtic team went from strength to strength, their success on the football field ensured that money continued to roll in. However, with the success came moral and financial dilemmas as the charitable principles and objectives of the club came under severe pressure. As the popularity of association football boomed, previously unimaginable sums of money were being generated in what was still officially in Scotland an amateur pastime, but one that was speedily developing into a big business. In order to maintain their club's success and retain their star players, the Celtic committee were forced to offer players more and more illegal payments and inducements to match the increasingly mind-blowing sums offered to them by professional English clubs. Financial and moral pressure mounted too on the club officials, as what began as an act of philanthropy and a part-time hobby, quickly developed into a full-time occupation, which by necessity was taking up all of their time. As the players, office bearers and committeemen syphoned off increasingly larger sums from the profits, the donations to charity fell correspondingly. This led to increasing animosity, suspicion and division at the club, and the AGM of 1891 would be a re-run of the Quillanite rebellion of 1889. Dr Conway's bid to oust John Glass at the 1891 AGM, over the question of monies paid to officials without the prior consent of the membership, failed. Dr Conway then left the club, but much of the suspicion and division remained. The 200-strong club membership polarised into two factions: the *traditionalists* were largely drawn from the ordinary working class members of the club and their aim was to keep the club under the control of its members and true to its charitable origins, and the *modernisers* were mostly the office bearers and better-off members, who increasingly felt that if the club was to reach its full potential it needed to develop a more business-like approach including paying officials. The transition of the club from a committee-run organisation into a professionally managed business was necessary to keep pace with the evolution of Scottish football, which would soon see the introduction of professionalism. The modernisers were regarded by the traditionalists as the "well to do's" – better-off members who appeared to want to take over the club and syphon off money purely for their own financial gain. The modernisers increasingly regarded the traditionalist as a hindrance, working class men who were unwilling or unable to grasp the complexities of running a successful football club. The reshuffle of office bearers and committeemen at the AGM in June 1891 resulted in a new management team at the top of Celtic. Pawnbroker Joseph Nelis replaced Dr Conway as honorary president after beating Stephen Henry by a wide margin; John Glass remained president, William McKillop replaced Francis McErlean as vice-president, Tom Maley took over the post of treasurer from John H McLaughlin, who had stepped in to the post after the death of Hugh Darroch. John H McLaughlin took over from John O'Hara who resigned his position as club secretary, while Willie Maley, still playing for the team, was re-elected match secretary. Although he initially appeared to oppose the more business-like approach, John H McLaughlin, once appointed club secretary, would become the figurehead and spokesman of the modernisers. He would personally take most of the venom from the traditionalists as he put forward deeply divisive proposals that were fully backed by the likes of John Glass, John O'Hara, Joe Shaughnessy, the McKillop brothers and Willie Maley. For the nine vacancies on the committee, twenty-eight names were submitted; Glasgow Irish Nationalist Arthur Murphy was among the successful candidates voted in. One of his first actions as a committeeman was to propose that the club give a donation of £20 to the Irish evicted tenants relief fund.

1891/92 Season

Despite the differences so evident at the 1891 club AGM, the 1891/92 season would be the first really great one for the club. In the league, Celtic began with an away defeat to Heart of Midlothian but then put together a run of nine straight wins taking them up to the end of the year. On 12 December, 6000 spectators watched the Celts retain the Glasgow Cup with an emphatic 7–1 win over Clyde at Cathkin Park. The Celtic party, which included Tom Maley, John H McLaughlin, John MacCreadie and Arthur Murphy, appeared for the Celtic at the Glasgow Football Association social in the Alexander Hotel afterwards. Slightly embarrassed at the margin of the win, Tom Maley gave the acceptance speech on behalf of the club.

The Scottish Cup competition had kicked in at the end of November 1891 and began for the Celts with a 4–2 away win against St Mirren. Kilmarnock Athletic and Cowlairs were both seen off, then at the beginning of February the 5–3 defeat of Rangers saw the bhoys in the final of the Scottish Cup for the second time. The Celts faced the middle-class gentleman of Queen's Park, until recently regarded as Scotland's top football team, twice. The first final was played at a snowy Ibrox Park on 12 March in front of 40,000 spectators, the biggest crowd yet at a final. The crush was such that hundreds of spectators encroached onto the park several times interfering with play. As a result the game, which Celtic won 1–0, was declared a friendly and a rematch was arranged for April. On 9 April 1892, not quite four years after playing their first match, the Celtic took the top prize in the Scottish game when they won the Scottish Cup for the first time. The replay at Ibrox Park, was won more emphatically with a score line of 5–1 for the bhoys. The victory in Scotland's premier club competition sparked a party of epic proportions among Celtic's supporters. Thousands of the Glasgow Irish took to the streets with banners and bands as a raggedy throng of jubilant supporters paraded through the East End. The Glasgow Irish sang and danced the night away both in and outside St Mary's Hall where the Celtic team had arrived in a charabanc for a victory dinner. Not quite seventy-five years later their grandchildren would again parade through the same streets when Celtic won the premier European club competition in Lisbon, the first ever British team to do so. The Scottish Cup winning team was Cullen, Doyle, Reynolds, Gallagher, Kelly, W Maley, Campbell, Dowds, McCallum, McMahon and Brady. Almost twenty years later, Tom Maley would admit that the St Mary's Hall was not the only location the cup visited that night. It was also taken to the sleeping quarters of his own Slatefield Industrial School, much to the delight and excitement of the sleepy-eyed boys. Tom recalled that despite it being late and the boys asleep, the arrival of the cup had an effect better than any alarm bell. The race for the league was lost over a single week in April, with successive defeats to Leith and to the eventual league winners, Dumbarton, by just two points. However, the Charity Cup was still up for grabs with Celtic due to meet Rangers in the final to be played at the beginning of June.

The Three Cup Huddle

By the time of the 1892 AGM in mid May, the capture of the Charity Cup was still just a hope, but with Scottish and Glasgow Cups already secured the meeting was always going to be a joyous one. The Mechanic's Hall was packed as John H McLaughlin, hon. secretary read the club's fourth annual report. The highlights of the season were expanded upon and the team congratulated for their magnificent achievements in winning the two cups. To date, the team played forty-three matches, won thirty-three, drew six and lost four. John H McLaughlin, the club's young secretary had been in the job for a full year and his sharp, active mind had come up with a whole raft of rule changes. It was a sign of things to come. The financial report was submitted by treasurer Tom Maley which showed the income for the previous twelve months had been £4468 and expenditure £4448, leaving a balance of £20. Of the expenditure £140 went to the Poor Children's Dinner Table, £50 to the Evicted Tenants' Fund and £10 to the memorial fund for the late Father Cunningham of Cambuslang. Donations of £10 each were given as wedding presents to both Alec Brady and Peter Dowds. That year had seen the deaths of two of the founding fathers, and wreaths were sent by the club to the families of Hugh Darroch and Michael Cairns. By far the biggest expenditure was on the new ground still under construction at Parkhead, which had already consumed £1189.

In June, the Celts beat Rangers 2–0 at Celtic Park to take the Charity Cup for the first time. In the process the club set a record as the first team to win the three premier Scottish trophies in a single season. With the three Scottish trophies sitting in the club's possession it was a truly magnificent season. The Charity Cup was presented to a club delegation including Joe Nelis, Stephen Henry, Dominic MacCreadie and Willie McKillop at the Glasgow city chambers in George Square. In the absence of the Lord Provost, Baillie Paton made the presentation. He said that this year the sum collected, £1000, was a new record for the competition. Joe Nelis, in accepting the cup on behalf of the club, thought it fitting that the Charity Cup should be in the possession of the Celtic Club, which had been established with the object of aiding charities. In addition to maintaining at its sole expense Free Children's Dinner Tables in Parkhead, the Calton and Bridgeton, during the last three years the Celtic Club had also given over £1200 to charities. A week later the Glasgow Observer was complaining that the allocation of funds from

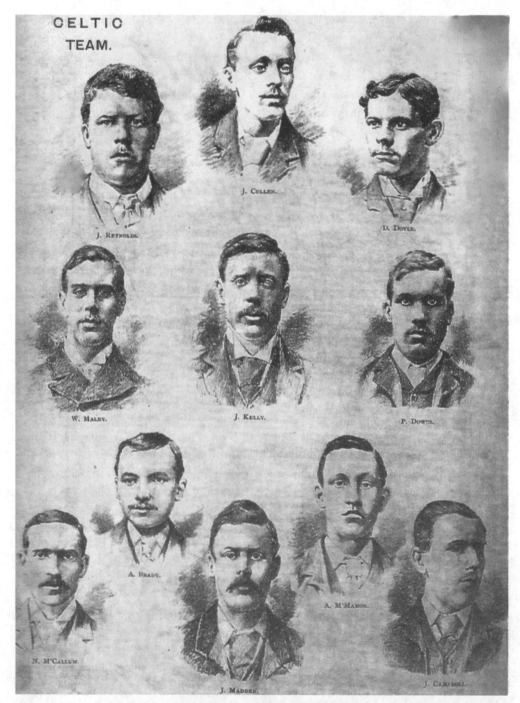

The 1892 Scottish Cup Winners

The first Celtic side to win the Scottish Cup. After the first match was declared a friendly, the Celts won the replay by beating Queen's Park by 5–1 on 9 April 1892. Celtic made changes in their line-up for the replay. Dowds replaced Madden, and Gallagher came in for Dowds. The result was considered a triumph of professionalism over amateurism.

the Charity Cup funds were unfair towards Catholic charities. From the £1000 raised, the Poor Children's Dinner Table received £15, St Vincent de Paul £15, Little Sisters of the Poor £15, Whitevale Refuge £15, Lanark Hospital £20.   In all Catholic charities received just £80, less than a tenth of the total sum raised.

Back in June 1891, the Celtic committee got wind that their landlord was planning a massive rent hike. Absolutely on cue, a familiar Irish spectre appeared at the door in the form of the club's factor. Mr Waddell, a Selkirkshire farmer, impressed at the obvious profits being made by the club, decided the ground rent would be increased from the original £50 pa to an exorbitant £450 pa. Some sources say an even more exorbitant £500 pa. Although there can be little doubt that a significant increase was due to the landlord, the scale of the increase was due to simple greed, or venom, after the first run-in with the club over the use of the ground back in 1888. Whatever the case, it was rent-racking at its worst. The situation undoubtedly brought back to mind tales of the old country, where rent-racking landlords and their factors were the scourge of the Irish people. Prior to the rent hike bombshell, the committee had intended spending some money improving the cinder track for the Celtic Sports meeting, which was just four weeks away. They toyed with the idea of switching the venue to Ibrox or Hampden, but decided to bite the bullet and spend the money.

The committee decided not to bow to Mr Waddell's extortion, gave notice that the lease would not be renewed and immediately began a search for a new home for the club. The committee did not have to look far: barely 200 yards away was a water-filled quarry, which they decided would do just fine. The plot was the property of James Hozier, titled Lord Newlands and a future Grand Master Mason of Scotland. By the middle of August the site had been secured on a ten-year lease and the first turf of the new stadium cut in mid September. The expense of constructing a new stadium was meet by taking on loans guaranteed by four of the wealthiest or most willing club members who became leaseholders; Joe Nelis, Willie McKillop, Davie Meikleham and a Mr George Bradley, later Joe Shaughnessy would replace Willie McKillop. The leaseholders were allotted an automatic place on the all-powerful club business committee. Committeeman James McKay was appointed master of works; he supervised the laying out of the ground and is credited with suggesting the installation of the double track that would prove so profitable for the club in the years to come. Over £4000 would be spent on the project including a new pavilion but some money was saved when the stands from the old park were removed and erected on the new ground. It was the intention that the new ground would be ready for the start of the new football season in August 1892. Once again the club called on its Glasgow Irish supporters to volunteer their labour and over 100,000 cartloads of earth were shovelled into the quarry hole. The new stadium would be ultra-modern and include a stand that could accommodate 3500 spectators, a cycling and running track and a stylish pavilion containing dressing rooms and administrative offices. On 19 March 1892, Michael Davitt, a patron of the Celtic club, was invited to lay the first sod, a divot of Donegal shamrocks in the centre spot of the half-completed Celtic stadium. After the planting and lunch with the Celtic committee, he and John Ferguson joined 15,000 spectators at old Celtic Park to watch Celtic play out a 0–0 draw with Clyde. The new Celtic Park was officially opened on the 13 August 1892 with the club's annual sports day. In a sign of things to come, it was noted at the time that the ceremony was a more secular occasion than the first. Conspicuous by his absence was Brother Walfrid, recently transferred to London after almost thirty years in Glasgow.

After taking on the large debts to finance the new stadium, the Celtic management were determined that the new Celtic Park would pay for itself and no expense was spared to ensure it became one of the top sporting venues not just in Glasgow but the whole of Britain. In December 1893, overhead lighting was introduced with a view to making the stadium available at night. Although it proved a failure, the innovation was ahead of its time and failed simply through lack of technology. The first dedicated press box at a football ground was erected in time for the highly anticipated Scotland v England clash in April 1894. Over 100 reporters attended the game and for the first time they had direct access to telephones. The phones, manned by twenty dedicated operators, allowed the football correspondents to report the 2–2 draw directly to their newsrooms. Yet another innovation was introduced in 1895 when the club installed state-of-the-art turnstiles costing £445 and with the crowds flocking to Celtic Park, not just for the Celtic matches but international football, cycling and athletics, the turnstiles paid for themselves tenfold. It also heralded the start of the once famous war cry of generations of young Celtic supporters, "Hey mister, gonna lift us ower?" The new Celtic Park as a sporting venue brought very significant revenue into the club and the committee took every opportunity to ensure the stadium supported itself and more. The two tracks could be hired for training three nights a week between April to the end of August at a cost of one shilling and six pence a month, or five shillings per season for athletes or three shillings a month or ten shillings a season for cyclists. The park could also be hired for the day by organisations wishing to hold field events. The Post Office, for example, hired Parkhead for its annual sports day.

As the finest stadium in Scotland, Parkhead was regularly chosen as the venue for international games between the home nations. In 1895, the Celtic and Rangers FC, their erstwhile good friends and now the team that had emerged as their greatest rivals, entered into an agreement that would lay the foundation of the "Old Firm" tag, which has been attached to both teams ever since. Rangers had rebuilt Ibrox and it was also being chosen as a venue for internationals and cup finals. Celtic persuaded Rangers to agree that they both would not let out their stadiums for less than the total takings for the stands. This was the first of a number of deals between the Old Firm in which they used their combined power to their own advantage against both the SFA and other teams in the Scottish League. In 1896, the Scotland v England international was held at Parkhead, 57,000 spectators turned up and the gates had to be closed a half-hour before the kick-off. In addition to 100 policemen on duty, the crush was such the Celtic officials pressed 150 kilted soldiers of the Gordon Highlanders, only there as spectators, into service as stewards to help control the crowd.

Between 1894 and 1904, five full international matches between Scotland and England were played at Parkhead bringing in gate receipts of over £11,000. International matches between

Scottish and English league teams over the same period brought another £4000. The funds brought into the club by events like the Celtic Sports meetings staged at Parkhead were also considerable. As their popularity drew increasingly larger crowds, the gate receipts became a vital contribution to the club coffers. Having taken on considerable amounts of debts, the additional income generated for the club by the large crowds attending the sports meeting and the international games, contributed largely to the financial survival of the Celtic between 1892 and the introduction of limited liability. However, not everyone was pleased with the size of the crowds pouring out of Parkhead and wanting to get home. In August 1896, several Glasgow tram conductors appeared in the Glasgow Police Court charged with allowing overcrowding on their trams in the Gallowgate. They collectively entered a plea of mitigation, stating that it was impossible for them to prevent the rush of people from the Celtic Sports meeting getting onto their tram and causing the overcrowding. The classic Glasgow conductor's plea of "Cum oan! Get aff," was apparently to no avail. The police refused to accept the plea saying they should have stopped the tram until sufficient passengers got off. The conductors were each fined a hefty two shillings and six pence.

1892/93 Season

 The new season kicked off on 20 August with a home game against Renton. It was the first game played at the new ground and the occasion was marked with a 4–3 win for the Celts. Johnny Campbell scoring all the goals. The occasion was also marked by the conspicuous absence of three Celtic stars from the previous season's spectacularly successful team. Brady, McCallum and McMahon had, despite the three cups and fistful of medals, debunked south, attracted by the glitter of English gold. At the end of August, the Celtic conducted a North of England tour that involved friendly games against Sheffield United, Middlesbrough, Newcastle East End and Sunderland over 1 to 5 September. The tour produced mixed results, with losses at Sheffield and Sunderland and wins at Newcastle and Middlesbrough. It was noted at the time that the tour was marked by some particularly rough play, even for an era renowned for some ferocious exchanges. Joe Cullen, the Celtic goalie, was left unconscious after a severe kicking at Sunderland. Cullen was Celtic's last line of defence at a time when goalkeeping was an extremely hazardous occupation. Bungling, which involved violently barging a goalkeeper into the net if he had the ball in his possession, was completely legal. The Celtic returned home slightly battered and bruised but much wiser after the tour. Although not as successful as the previous season, the bhoys had marked the move to their new super modern home by winning the Charity Cup and the Scottish League Championship, the latter for the very first time. The bhoys played eighteen games, won fourteen, drew one and lost three. They had conceded 25 goals but scored 54. The league, still considered a minor prize, was won by just one point with Rangers in second place. In the five meetings between Celtic and Rangers that season, honours were even with two wins each and one draw. Rangers took the Glasgow Cup by beating Celtic 3–1 at Cathkin Park, while the Celts spanked the Gers 5–0 at Parkhead to take the Charity Cup.

Four years on from the first Celtic team, most of the original players still held their places, but the likes of Joe Cullen, Jimmy Blessington from St Bernard's and James Davidson from Leith had come in to claim regular places and the new bhoys had greatly contributed to a winning season. Despite the obvious successes, after the previous season's three cups, the league, which was still seen as a minor prize, was no great consolation for the disappointment of losing the two cups. Particularly sore was the defeat in the replayed final of the Scottish Cup. Celtic beat Queen's Park in the first final, but unfortunately the game had already been declared a friendly before the kick-off because of the condition of the pitch. The replay on 11 March saw the Celtic badly roughed up by the supposed gentlemen of Queen's Park with several of the bhoys injured. In the days when the shoulder charge was still acceptable, the Queen's Park physical tactics were described as excellent. The ten-man Celtic side lost 2–1 after Willie Maley was so badly injured he could not continue and in the days before substitutes, no replacement was possible. A disputed second and winning goal for Queen's Park rubbed salt in the wound.

Life for a footballer, particularly a Celtic footballer, was dangerous off the park as well as on it. After the Celtic's 4–2 defeat to second from bottom Abercorn at Paisley on 11 February 1893, the exuberant Paisley supporters invaded the field and set about the Celtic players. During the fracas, Celtic's Johnny Campbell knocked three teeth out of the mouth of an Abercorn fan. The man complained to the police, who brought him into the Celtic dressing room and asked him to identify his assailant. The fan picked out the wrong man when he fingered a bemused and totally innocent Jerry Reynolds. Celtic later complained to the SFA over the incident but amid the laughter, Abercorn agreed to investigate the matter. Abercorn was one of the founding members of the league but was finding it increasingly difficult to live with St Mirren, the other Paisley football team. The Scottish League began a second division for the following season and Abercorn was immediately assigned to it. Season 1892/93 would prove to be the last season of the old disreputable paid amateur and nothing would ever be the same again.

The long running debate over the status of the Scottish game finally came to an end in May 1893 when the SFA agreed to the introduction of professionalism. The governing body had been fighting a rear-guard action against the change since 1885 when it was introduced in England. After a long and at times heated debate the SFA finally dropped the hypocrisy and adopted professionalism. It was the Celtic's man at the Scottish League, John H McLaughlin, who had been the most enthusiastic exponent of the professional game and it was he who made the final successful argument for the motion at the SFA's Annual General Meeting of 1893. The key points from a report of his speech are:

> Professionalism existed; everyone knew it existed and the fact should be recognised. Every sport from which money could be made professionalism had crept in and so there were professional golfers, cricketers and billiard players. It should be legalised and kept under control of the ruling

body thereby ensuring the game derives maximum benefit. Football in Scotland is on the wane due to the top Scottish talent being lured into the professional game in England. He thought the new legislation might put a stop to the talent drain but if not then they were no worse off.

The motion to introduce professionalism was carried by a large majority. At Parkhead, the Celtic committee agreed with the players a weekly wage of £2 with a win bonus for important matches. The following year there were almost 800 players registered as professionals by eighty-three Scottish clubs.

Inequalities were evident right from the start with the smaller provincial clubs paying players ten shillings a week while Celtic and Rangers could afford £2 and £3 a week, double the wage of a highly skilled tradesman. Soon performance bonuses would also play a major part in player remuneration. Professionalism also meant a greater application by players and staff to the job and personal behaviour on and off the park with players now being seen as club employees and therefore representatives. Despite the Celtic's prominent position among the clubs and the leading role taken by its leaders in the Scottish game, by August 1893 there was still no Celtic representative on the SFA committee. The situation resulted in the Scottish Sport journal; often rather grudging themselves when it came to Celtic, to ask why there was such a consistent set against Celtic securing representation on the SFA committee:

Why, there is no club more sneaked after and fawned upon when favours are sought than the Celts. Yet the very clubs that solicit their aid – and very often get it, are amongst those who cast their vote in quite another direction when election time comes around. The Celtic should be directly represented on the committee. They should because of their position and the large stake they have in the concern.

The introduction of professionalism had the immediate effect of cleaning up the game and the day of the paid amateur and of shady under the counter payments was over. With the arrival of professionalism it became increasingly obvious that a decision on the future direction of the Celtic club would need to be made. The question was simply would the club remain purely an amateur organisation solely dedicated to the charitable principles and objective on which it was founded or would a business-like approach be adopted. If the latter was the case then players and staff would be paid salaries commensurate with an ambition to take the Glasgow Irish club to the top flight of professional football. The other side of the argument was of course the more money paid to players and officials, the less would be available for the charities.

At the Celtic AGM of June 1893, the financial and business status of the club came under debate. Despite the club's obvious success on and off the field, the dissatisfaction felt by many club members over the direction of the club regarding expenses versus the lack of charitable donations was debated and again factions formed. The conundrum would continue to cause friction with emotions boiling over at the two major meetings of club members each year. The debate was also driven by the expenditure on the new ground, which had exceeded £4000 and which had put the Celtic Club into serious debt. The leading members of the committee had taken on much of the debt personally, at it must be said a very reasonable 5 per cent interest, but they were increasingly concerned by their personal exposure. The club vice-president, John H McLaughlin, seconded a proposal by Joseph Shaughnessy, now one of the leaseholders of the new ground, to form a limited liability company. The motion was passed by the committee, but was thrown out by the membership led by Arthur Murphy, Joe Nelis and Joseph McGroary.

1893/94 Season

At the beginning of the 1893/94 season the Celtic committee offered their players cash bonuses if the team performed well throughout the season. However, it was agreed that no player's bonus should exceed £5. A number of new recruits had been brought into the squad to strengthen the team including a spare goalkeeper, Dan McArthur, Charley McEleny in midfield and centre forward John Ferguson. The first full season of professionalism, supposedly only a trial, began for the Celtic with a 5–0 win over Third Lanark at Parkhead, an emphatic 4–1 win at Dundee, followed by a 0–0 home draw with Dumbarton. A week later, the Celtic suffered one of their worst ever defeats to Rangers in a 5–0 drubbing at Ibrox. The first four results about summed up what would be a strange, topsy-turvy season for the bhoys. The highest score of the season, 7-0, was achieved in a second round Scottish Cup win at Parkhead against Albion Rovers in December. The free scoring game was witnessed by one of the worse attendances ever at Parkhead with only 1500 supporters turning up. That same month, an experiment with floodlighting was begun at Parkhead. First tried out in a home friendly game against Clyde. Sixteen electric lamps were used to illuminate the playing field, the lights being hung from high poles erected inside the racing track, with a row suspended up the middle of the field. The evening was foggy and not very favourable to the experiment, but there appeared to be sufficient light for the players to follow the ball. The hard fought game ended in a 1–1 draw. The trial did not last long after it was discovered the wires interfered with play with the ball striking them on occasion. It was Joe Shaughnessy's idea and though it was ahead of its time, it was still well worth the try and over 5000 paying spectators turned up that first night against Clyde to have a look. It was just another example of the Celtic trying to wring every penny from the stadium.

On 18 November, the Celts were knocked out of the Glasgow Cup in the semi-final by Rangers. A crowd of 13,000 watched Rangers take the tie by a narrow 1–0 margin at Ibrox Park. The Celtic reached the final of the Scottish Cup after defeating Hurlford, Albion Rovers, St Bernard's and Third Lanark. The final against Rangers was played on 17 February 1894 at Hampden Park. The Celtic went into the game as league leaders with Rangers following up. The Ibrox side were attempting to win the Scottish Cup for the first time in their history. Rangers felt the occasion and went on to beat the Celts by 3–1. Even the partisan Celtic supporters agreed the best team won on the day. Amazingly, although founded fourteen years before the Celtic, this was the Ibrox side's first Scottish Cup win. They had waited so long there was no room on the cup itself for their name to be engraved. A new plinth was dually commissioned and Rangers are the first name on it.

On St Patrick's Day, the Celtic travelled east to play Leith Athletic, effectively as league champions, with Rangers in second place unable to make up the points deficit. Prior to the Celtic game, a number of clubs had complained that owing to the uneven surface of Bank Park, home of Leith Athletic, the visitors were at a disadvantage. The Leith club took the complaints to heart and rented the nearby Hawkhill football ground. The leased ground was as good a playing surface as any in the country, therefore, neither the playing surface or the fact that the Celtic were without the services of a couple of key players, who were on the injured list, were any excuse for the severe reverse which was about to befall them. Around 3000 spectators watched in disbelief as the home team defeated the League champions by a score of five goals to nil. It was the second time in the season that the bhoys had shipped five goals and not at all what the faithful expected on Paddy's Day. Despite their shock defeat at Leith, the race for the league was over and the Celtic's second League Championship title was won by three clear points. Overall, they had played eighteen, won fourteen, drew one and lost three. The drubbing at Ibrox, the home defeat by Hearts and the 5–0 hammering at Leith were all pushed out of minds. The Celts had suffered sore defeats to Rangers in the final of the Scottish Cup and in the semi-final of the Glasgow Cup and they hurt the most.

With the league season over, the Celtic went off on a whistle stop excursion of England. The Celts opened their tour on 7 April by beating London Caledonians 2–1 in front of 5000 spectators at Tuffnell Park. The English champions, Aston Villa, were next and the teams met at Perry Bar in Birmingham on 9 April before 4000 spectators. The Celts left out Doyle, Cullen and Campbell and played Dunbar, McArthur and Divers, whilst Villa were without two of their stars. Sandy McMahon opened the scoring for the Celtic after twenty-five minutes, but just before half-time Villa equalised from a free kick. In the second half Aston Villa, who were playing against the wind, pressurised the Celtic goal and Dan McArthur was forced to save repeatedly. Eventually the pressure told and Aston Villa went ahead. Ten minutes later McMahon equalised with a shot from twenty-five yards to make the score 2–2. Aston Villa went back on the attack and again the Celts buckled under the pressure with the English champions getting their third goal with ten minutes to go. Despite sustained Celtic pressure for the last ten minutes the Villa held on to take the laurels. A draw would probably have been a fairer result but the defeat by 3 goals to 2 was no disgrace in what was an excellent game of football. The Celts played their second game in two days against Bury on 10 April. The evening kick-off at Gigg Lane attracted an impressive crowd of 10,000, who watched an entertaining 2–2 draw, in what was a fairly even match and the result was a fair one. McMahon and Cassidy got the Celtic goals. Amazingly, the bhoys played their third game in three days at Hyde Park, Manchester on 11 April, when they met Blackburn Rovers in another evening kick-off. The game in aid of the Salford Protection and Rescue Society ended in a 0–0 draw and although possession appeared to have been fairly even, the Blackburn goalie was forced to make more saves. So ended the

Celtic's 1894 England tour and on returning home, the players got just over a week off before the return match with the English champions at Parkhead on 21 April. The Aston Villa game was played the same day as the England v Scotland league international at Liverpool. The Celts had four stars away on international duty, Doyle, Kelly, Blessington and McMahon, while Aston Villa had three stars away playing for England. The game saw the return to Celtic Park of two former sons, Willie Dunning and Willie Groves playing in the Villa's colours. However, the absence of so many first team players on both sides and the fact that it was just another game at the end of a very long season, saw a very poor crowd turn up to watch. The Celts totally dominated Villa from the outset, with Willie Maley getting the Man of the Match award for what was described as a magnificent display. Willie Dunning kept the score respectable with his own excellent display. The Celts ran out winners by 2–1 but it could have been so much more.

The Charity Cup was won at Ibrox 12 May with a 2–1 win over Queen's Park, but despite the fact that the cup had been won for the third time in a row, it was scant consolation for losing out on Scottish and Glasgow Cups to Rangers. So ended a funny old season for the Celts, success continued but it was a hard slog. Everyone agreed the 1893/94 season was the most physically demanding yet.

At the club AGM the following month, James Curtis, secretary, and James McKay, treasurer, delivered their reports both of which were received with applause and satisfaction. It had been another successful season, both financially and on the field, but despite the feel good factor, the composition of the committee, club debt and charitable donations sparked some heated debate. With the recent introduction of professionalism and the players' wages and bonuses for the coming season already negotiated, the ordinary members recognised the fact that a tipping point in the direction of the club had been reached. In an attempt to increase their representation on the committee, Stephen J Henry proposed that the business subcommittee be elected from the general body of the membership. He insisted that the club be governed on more democratic grounds and compared the present business subcommittee to the hereditary House of Lords. He felt that since the business subcommittee had the whole management of the club in their hands they should consequently be responsible to the membership. His motion was opposed by JH McLaughlin and others who ridiculed the proposal stating that every committee had the right to elect their own subcommittees. John McLaughlin thought he was bringing football down to the level of politics. Stephen Henry's motion was, after prolonged debate, defeated by a large majority.

The ordinary members were again bitterly disappointed at the lack of charitable donations and voiced their concerns through their spokesman, Patrick Gaffney. Pat was a master wheelwright with premises at Henrietta Street and in the Gallowgate. Although never actually on the committee, Pat Gaffney had been at the celebration dinner for the Hibernian cup-winning team back in 1887 and was an original club subscriber. One of the most passionate anti-limited company members, he proposed at the AGM that the club take on an extra 200 members at ten shillings each and that the £100 raised immediately be given to St Mary's, Sacred Heart, Bridgeton and

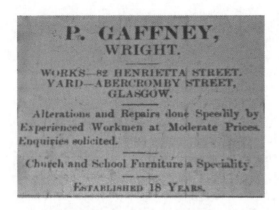

P. GAFFNEY,
WRIGHT.

WORKS—82 HENRIETTA STREET.
YARD—ABERCROMBY STREET,
GLASGOW.

Alterations and Repairs done Speedily by
Experienced Workmen at Moderate Prices.
Enquiries solicited.

Church and School Furniture a Speciality.

ESTABLISHED 18 YEARS.

St Michael's Parkhead Children's Dinner Tables. Speaking for a large percentage of the members, he maintained that the club had broken faith with these charities. An agreement had been made at the inception of the club to give them £5 per week. In fact, the children's charities had received nothing for the last two years. Pat's wife, Catherine, who was a local Catholic schoolteacher, no doubt encouraged Pat in his defiance of the committee. Pat's motion came to nothing after chairman John Glass shot down the idea saying the committee could not see their way to taking on new members, adding that as soon as the club was free from debt the donations would resume. John Glass's put-down was more about club politics and power than finance and charity; an additional 200 members would have effectively doubled the membership and since the majority of the new members would have been ordinary working class men, the infusion would have seriously undermined the power base of the increasingly middle class, office bearers. Unwilling to let the matter drop, Pat proposed that no member of the committee, either ordinary or ex officio, shall, on or after the meeting, receive payment for working directly or indirectly for the club. Pat's motion again had little effect other than another lengthy debate during which the committee repudiated the fact that they had benefited financially from their connection with the club.

The club had recorded a large income of almost £7000, far exceeding any other club in Scotland. Although the income was large, so too was the club's outgoings. In addition to the usual club expenses, such as the £1935 for player's wages, the new football ground was improved to the tune of £1000. The available funds were such the club's liability could only be reduced from £2086 to £1850. The club was left with a balance in hand of just £170. Still, the treasurer James McKay thought the club was in a sound financial position. The members agreed, so much so they voted their treasurer an honorarium of £100. The election of office bearers resulted in the return of the sitting office bearers: John Glass, president; John H McLaughlin, vice-president; James McKay, treasurer; James Curtis, secretary; and Willie Maley, honorary secretary. Serving on the committee were Mick Dunbar, Arthur Murphy, Francis McErlean, Tim J Walls, John O'Hara, team captain James Kelly, former player Pat Gallagher, James Moore and John McCann. New bhoy John McCann was yet another pawnbroker with a shop in the Garngad. The meeting finally ended after midnight.

The irony of James McKay's £100 honorarium set against nothing for the Poor Children's Dinner Tables may have escaped the club members, but the fact never escaped the Glasgow Observer newspaper, which commented:

> *The thing [Celtic club] is a mere business, in the hands of publicans and others. Catholic charities get nothing out of thousands of pounds passing through the treasurer's hands. Can we not get a club that will carry out the original idea of Brother Walfrid? The income of the Celtic club is drawn largely from our own people.*

In reality, the honorariums were essentially bonuses for men who were effectively running, practically full time, a large business concern for no pay. Throughout the autumn, the committee continued to be subjected to a barrage of criticism in the newspapers over the lack of charitable donations. The Glasgow Observer highlighted the fact that a number of Catholic bodies had applied to Celtic for support and all had been refused. On one occasion even the use of Celtic Park was refused. The Poor Children's Dinner Tables, which had received nothing for over two years, also had a direct appeal refused. The Glasgow Observer noted the size of the club's liabilities, but pointed out that when the club started greater difficulties had been faced yet donations were made. Surely it argued £50 or £100 would not swell the debt overmuch. The Scottish Referee noted that Celtic and Hibernian were planning a benefit match for striking miners and suggested some of the proceeds should be diverted to the Children's Dinner Tables, a cause not too much remembered.

1894/95 Season

 Prior to the beginning of the 1894/95 season, the nineteen professional players on the Celtic's books negotiated their bonuses for the season. It was set at ten shillings for a win, and five shillings for a draw for all league games. The committee would decide the cup bonuses as the competition progressed. An old familiar face appeared on the first day of training at Parkhead. Peter Dowds had been brought back to the Celtic after his sabbatical in England. On the first day of the new season, Celtic as league champions unfurled the new league championship flag at Parkhead. The league flag for season 1893/94 was of emerald green silk and included a Union Jack in the top right corner. The press thought it was an improvement on their last championship flag of plain green silk. There is no record of the Celtic supporters' opinions of the patriotic banner.

The new season got off to a stuttering start for the bhoys with an away draw against Dundee, a home win against St Bernard's and a defeat away at Third Lanark. At the end of August, the Celts played an exhibition game against the Gordon Highlanders football team. The Scottish Highland regiment's second battalion had been posted to Glasgow from Dublin and had recently taken over Maryhill Barracks in the north of the city. Over the next two years the Celtic would form a very close relationship with the regiment, which included many Irish recruits after having been stationed at Dublin and the Curragh for a couple of years. Their interest included training the battalion football team, which participated in competitions like the Glasgow Cup and the Army Cup. The Celtic's inconsistencies continued over September with a 3–0 league win over St Mirren, a 2–2 home draw against minnows Battlefield in the first round of the Glasgow Cup and a 5–3 league win over Rangers at Parkhead. The later was a bruising, bad tempered game fought out on 22 September. The Rangers' players' taunts of Papists, Fenians and Irish would not have cooled tempers any. In fact, the atmosphere was so poisonous, the referee called the players together before he allowed the second half to commence. The return game against Battlefield played on 29 September at Langside saw the Celts run out 4–1 winners. The Celtic would go on to win the Glasgow Cup in mid-November by beating Rangers 2–0 at Cathkin Park, Glasgow, in front of 20,000 spectators. Dan McArthur would play one of his best games ever and was carried off the park shoulder high at the end by jubilant Celtic fans.

At the time of the half-year general meeting in November, treasurer McKay's report was upbeat with a gross income of £4500 to date; all going well he thought it could be a spectacularly successful year for the club. The future looked rosy and James McKay in his most sanguine moments was looking forward to seeing the club free of debt at the end of the season, for the first time in its history. However, at the time of the half-yearly meeting the club was £1500 in debt, with just £260 in the bank. James McKay was in fact dreaming his dreams too soon.

In the league, the Celts faltered against a powerful Hearts side at Parkhead on 3 November going down 2–0. An away win over St Bernard on 10 November was followed by a 2–2 draw at home against St Mirren on 22 December. The dropped points meant the bhoys were facing an uphill struggle to make up lost ground over the second half of the season. On 15 December, Celtic was knocked out of the Scottish Cup loosing 2–0 to Hibs but protested that the Edinburgh side had played an ineligible player and the result was nullified. Towards the end of December, the Celtic played three friendlies against English teams, Manchester City and Everton away and Burnley at home. The results, an away draw followed by an away defeat at Everton and a home defeat against Burnley were all disappointing. The general consensus of opinion regarding the tour was that the bhoys had been somewhat bullied and needed to be toughened up. On 29 December, the nullified Scottish Cup tie with Hibernian was replayed in front of 4000 spectators at Easter Road, Edinburgh. They watched the bhoys reverse the Hibernian's previous victory with a 2–0 win of their own. From around Christmas, a prolonged cold spell in the west of Scotland wreaked havoc with the football fixtures programme. Week after week snow and frost made play impossible.

On 19 January 1895, the Celts travelled to the north-east to meet Dundee in the quarter-finals of the Scottish Cup. A very impressive 12,000 spectators watched the game played at Carolina Park. The home fans that braved the chill were rewarded by witnessing their favourites kick the Celtic out the cup after a one goal to nil surprise win. League football finally resumed in mid February but the Celts would have been happy enough if it remained closed. On the day, a powerful Heart of Mid Lothian side inflicted a crushing 4–0 defeat on the bhoys at Tynecastle. Over the remaining seven games the Celtic only dropped two points, drawing 4–4 with Third Lanark and 1–1 with Rangers. However, the dropped points plus those lost prior to the enforced winter break saw the Celtic well beaten by five points into second place in the league by worthy champions Heart of Midlothian.

At the beginning of April 1895, the subcommittee led by John H McLaughlin and set up the previous December to look at club rules and procedures, reported to the general committee. In response to the recommendations, the committee called the members to a special meeting on 3 April held in the pavilion hall at Parkhead. The power brokers at Celtic would attempt to consolidate their power base within the committee and would effectively attempt a hostile takeover, wrapped up in the guise of a new constitution.

In all there were eighteen rules some more contentious and important than others. "Rule 1. The Club shall be called the Celtic Football and Athletic Club," was carried unanimously. Rule 2 was proposed by John H McLaughlin and stated that the office bearers are a president, vice-president, secretary, treasurer and six members who form the committee of management. The whole of the committee had to retire annually, but was eligible for re-election. John MacCreadie objected to the size of the committee and proposed that the number of committeemen be increased to eleven, the idea being to widen the representation. His amendment was carried by a large majority. "Rule 3. From the committee there shall be appointed by the committee of management the following subcommittee – viz., a business committee consisting of the president, secretary, treasurer and another two members. It shall be the duty of the business committee to monthly report to the whole committee the business transacted by them at their weekly or other meetings." Committeeman Tim Walls, recognising that whoever controlled the business committee effectively controlled the club, tabled an amendment that instead of there being two ordinary members in the committee there should be five. John H McLaughlin objected to the proposal stating that it was the business committee who choose the team and that more members would lead to more disagreements regarding the team choice. A member suggested that they should appoint a match committee; while another stated that when such disagreements arose the team selection should be referred to the whole committee. After a vote, a large majority carried Tim Walls' amendment. Rule 4 was the key for the control of the club and would be the most closely contested and debated. It proposed that: "The committee of management should have full executive powers vested in them, including the power to sue and be sued for debts due to and debts due by the club, hereinafter contracted and their actions and decisions shall be binding on the club. They shall have the power to make bye-laws and to remove from the club or committee any member whose conduct in their opinion is objectionable. They shall have full control of the conducting and management of the club and shall be responsible to the general body of members for the same. They shall have powers to fill up any vacancy occurring in the office bearers or committee." Club member Frank Havlin, a gasworks labourer from Tollcross, objected, stating that it would be strange if they allowed a committee to make bye-laws that the members would have to abide by and also protested against the committee having the power to expel a member arguing that a member should have the option of laying his grievance before a general meeting of the club. John H McLaughlin again put the case for the management committee, saying the committee always had the power to expel members and that the committee would be put in an awkward position if a case had to wait three or six months for a general meeting and that some cases may need to be heard in camera or risk being sued. After a lengthy debate the rule was carried as it stood by 43 votes to 38. Rule 7 was passed giving the committee of management the power to add to their number or to the number of the subcommittee, not exceeding three. Rule 8 stated that the office bearers would give their reports twice a year in July and December. Rule 9 covered the procedure for calling an extraordinary general meeting. The management committee could call one any time, while members would need twenty signatures and at least fourteen days' notice. Rule 12 covered subscriptions for new members, the entrance fee (7/6 or 37.5p) plus the annual subscription (5/- or 25p), which must be paid by 1 June. No member could vote in the AGM without having paid. The sums involved were serious investments for the ordinary working class members at the club at a time when 15/- (75p) was considered a decent weekly wage. It was even suggested that the annual subscription should be increased to ten shillings. Rule 17 covered the nominations of office bearers and committeemen, each needing two proposers from the club membership. The proposals needed to be with the club secretary seven days before the AGM and the election was to be conducted by independent ballot.

Rule 18 was probably the most contentious as it proposed that members of the club be equally liable for the club's debt and members could be called at fourteen days' notice to pay their "pro rata" share of the debt. Failure to do so would result in their dismissal from the club. Francis Havlin immediately tabled another amendment stating that the proposal if passed would drive working class members from the club. The new rule was rejected by a large majority with the members recognising immediately that the move would only strengthen the committee and the "well to do" element at the club. Of the rules, and Rule 18 in particular, John McLaughlin later commented: "I had the misfortune to be sponsor for the rules as a whole and this one in particular and had to bear the brunt of the flapdoodle it provoked." The meeting according to the Glasgow Observer ended amicably, but the posturing and obvious power grab by the committee could only have alarmed and increased the suspicions of the ordinary working class members of the club.

On the football field the season ended on a high when on 25 May the Celts again defeated Rangers at Cathkin Park to take the Charity Cup. The bhoys ran out easy winners by four goal to nil, Sandy McMahon getting a hat-trick while James Kelly contributed the other. The Celts had now won the Charity Cup four times in a row equalling the record set by Renton FC between 1885 and 1889. The Glasgow Cup had already been won by beating Rangers 2–0 back in November, so two cups were hidden under the beds of Celtic officials.

Just a couple of weeks after the Charity Cup win the members met for what would be a fractious 1895 Celtic club AGM. Held in the Annfield Halls in the Gallowgate, John Glass presided over a very full attendance of members. First, the office bearers proposed that the press be excluded from the meeting. Stephen Henry proposed and Frank Havlin seconded, a counter that the press be allowed into the meeting. Their proposal was carried and the reporters were admitted. Next Frank Havlin, Ned McGinn and Joe McGroary took exception to secretary John Curtis' minutes of the previous half-yearly meeting provoking a long debate, only brought to an end by appeals from Tom Maley and the chair. Willie Maley then reported on a relatively successful footballing season, highlighting the high and low points. Two cups had been won but a disappointing exit from the Scottish Cup took the shine off the season. The club treasurer John McKay reported another successful year financially, although not quite as successful as they had hoped. A run of poor results and a prolonged winter break caused by bad weather had affected revenues over the second half of the season. Despite this, he announced an income of over £6566, not as large as the previous year, but still over £1000 more than any other Scottish club. Over £250 of members' loans had been repaid and over £420 spent on ground improvements including laying down a permanent composite track. He thought the ground improvements would pay dividends for years to come and highlighted the gate-drawing powers of the ground. Just five fixtures versus Hearts, Queen's Park, Rangers, Everton and Sunderland, yielded a sum of £2380, or an average of £475 per match. The players' weekly wage bill now amounted to £47, up from £35 the previous season, while £200 would be paid to them in the close season's wages. Another £200 would be paid out in wages for the trainer, groundsmen and casual workers. Willie Maley and James Kelly, who to date had been playing as amateurs, each received £100 for signing professional terms. Tom Maley drew attention to the fact that in the balance sheet no donation to the Poor Children's Dinner Table appeared and described it as a gross injustice. The club was originally formed to support East-End charities, and yet out of a princely sum of nearly £7000 not a penny had been devoted to the purpose for which the club had been instituted. Tom Maley's remarks drew applause from the members. John H McLaughlin described the situation at the club as farcical, members were again complaining about the lack of charitable donations, while there was £1400 worth of outstanding debt. Vice-president John H McLaughlin took most of the flak from the traditionalists over the lack of charitable donations and the direction in which circumstances outwith the control of the club or its office bearers were forcing the club. Treasurer McKay's report was carried.

At the committee election, club president John Glass was unanimously returned. John H McLaughlin was re-elected vice-president by a majority over Davie Meikleham, Tom Maley having refused the position. Willie Maley was appointed secretary and James McKay was unanimously elected to the office of treasurer. Twenty-five names were put forward for the eleven available seats on the committee; the following were successful: Mick Dunbar, John MacCreadie, Arthur Murphy, Francis McErlean, Pat Gallagher, James Curtis, Joseph McGroary, John McBride, C Docherty, John McQuade and John McCann. John H McLaughlin was also appointed club delegate to the Scottish League, the SFA and the Scottish Amateur Athletics Union.

A letter from a disgruntled club member was published in the Glasgow Observer on 8 June:

> *Sir, I have before me a copy of the balance sheet of the Celtic Football*
> *Club for the past year. From it I learn that since May 1894 an income*

of £6566 odd has been accrued to the organisation. Of this vast sum more than £2000 has been paid as wages to players, £177 odd spent on entertainment for teams, £210 given as honorariums to players and £26 has been expended on refreshments. Also a sum of £91 has been donated to several more or less deserving causes. But to the Poor Children's Dinner Table, to support which the Celtic club was instituted, I fail to find even a small donation. How is this?

It was the first of a whole series of open letters published in the press all on the same theme.

In addition to the obvious business and or moral divide at the Celtic over the future of the club, the members increasingly became divided along class lines. The office bearers at Celtic had always been better educated and wealthier than the majority of working class members, but as Glasgow Irish, they too had suffered to a greater or lesser degree the same racism, bigotry and marginalisation as their working class contemporaries. For decades the *We Alone* attitude had bound the differing social classes of Glasgow Irish society together in mutual support. However, as they became increasingly associated with the success of the Celtic club, the by now permanent office bearers were drawn deeper into the wider Scottish community by the social aspects of the game and by working with the middle class worthies who controlled the sport. As they became increasingly better connected socially, the ties that bound them to the Glasgow Irish community inevitably loosened. Soon the social differences between the increasingly middle class "moneybags" and the working class "mob" at Parkhead was so pronounced that the Celtic bourgeoisie probably felt they had more in common with the middle class gentlemen running Queen's Park FC than the working class club members at Parkhead. The "them and us" attitude became increasingly pronounced every year until both sides held each other in disdain. In addition to the condescending attitude shown by John McLaughlin towards the working class members who opposed his constitutional changes, future director John McKillop once referred to the general membership as a "rabble".

Despite the two cups won by Celtic that season, it was generally felt that more should have been achieved and that a major reason for the failure was an apparent staleness and lack of fitness among the players, already apparent towards the end of the old year. The committee's response was to advertise for a new professional trainer. By the time the choice was made and the position filled, the season was effectively over and the man appointed, Tom McGuire from Barrhead, started work in July 1895.

Tom McGuire was a former British soldier who had served in India, Afghanistan and Egypt with the 72nd Highlanders, later the 1st Battalion Seaforth Highlanders. During his service on the Indian North West Frontier and in the Afghan campaign, Tom McGuire's regiment had taken part in some of the most famous exploits of the Empire's defenders and Tom held medals for battles at Peiwar Kotal, Charasiah, Kabul and the remarkable 300 mile march from Kabul to Kandahar in August 1880. After seeing service in Egypt including the one-sided fight at Tel-el-Kebir, Sergeant Tom McGuire retired in 1894 by which time the battalion was back in Great

Britain. During his army service, Tom had qualified as a physical training instructor, specialising in gymnastics and fitness and applied for the job at Parkhead. The Army Gymnastic Staff were at the time at the cutting edge of physical training techniques. The military realised the importance of health and fitness and incorporated the latest methodology into physical fitness training. The army of the period expected a soldier to be able to run at speed for more than 1000 yards fully equipped and then be able to fight. Training therefore concentrated on endurance, paying particular attention to leg and lung development, both obviously highly desirable in a professional footballer. A dour, humourless professional, Tom joined the Celtic at a time when the last vestiges of the old paid amateur, club spirit still prevailed and he could not understand why men to whom football was a profession did not approach their training in a professional, business-like manner. Much to the consternation of some players, he introduced a disciplined, structured training regime, which included regular attendance at training sessions, stamina training, ten-mile runs, cross-country running, body building and the legendary laps around the Celtic track. He was also responsible for special diets and for setting up a gymnasium in the upstairs hall of the Celtic Park pavilion. Physical training needed to be full time and the application of Tom McGuire's strict disciplined regime soon showed in the increased fitness levels of the Celtic players.

The sign that the start of the new football season was just around the corner came with the annual Celtic Sports meeting. What was rapidly becoming the premier sporting event in Scotland was held during the first half of August and was eagerly anticipated by all sports fans. The Celtic Sports of 1895, despite the lack of English and Irish champions due to a dispute between athletics associations, was one of the most successful to date. Its success owed much to the current resident infantry battalion stationed at Glasgow's Maryhill barracks. Using his military connections, Willie Maley persuaded the Gordon Highlanders' commanding officer to allow the battalion's sportsmen to step into the breach, while the regimental band provided the musical entertainment. The Glasgow Observer gave a graphic description of the scene at Parkhead on the first day of the sports meeting:

> Sunshine flooded the Celts' vast enclosure, surrounded by the famous dual tracks and deeply fringed by a voiceful throng representing all sorts and conditions of humanity. Flags and bunting fluttered in the breeze and the added charm of variety was imparted to the scene by the band and pipers of the Gordon Highlanders who figured in the arena, their floating plaids and gay ribbons, sombrous bearskins and nodding plumes smacking strongly of martial forays and tented fields.

Among the personalities attending the sports meeting was Councillor John Ferguson and his wife. Wearing a green rosette, the staunchest supporter of Irish nationalism was warmly welcomed by the Celtic committee. Over 20,000 spectators attended the sports meeting and over £450 was taken at the gate.

1895/96 Season

An already impressive Celtic team squad was further strengthened for the campaign of season 1895/96. Defender Barney Battles was brought in from Hearts and centre forward Allan Martin, formerly of Rangers and Hibs also joined the club. Yet another addition was Belfastman Tom "Ching" Morrison, an outside-right brought in from Burnley at the tail-end of the previous season. Determined to reclaim their rightful place as champions of Scotland, the directors set the players' bonuses for the coming season at £10 if they won the league and £5 for every cup won.

The bhoys got off to a reasonable start in the league with three wins including a 4–2 victory over Rangers and a defeat to Hibernian. In the middle of September, the league champions Heart of Midlothian came to Celtic Park. The Edinburgh side brought a trainload of supporters from the capital to cheer them on. The match, despite the early date in the fixture calendar, was widely regarded as a crucial contest in deciding the eventual destination of the league flag. The current champions rewarded their 500 travelling fans' loyalty with a dazzling performance in which the Hearts outplayed the Celts in every department. In the process, they inflicted on the bhoys the club's worst ever home defeat when the Hearts ran out 5–0 winners. It was a very subdued procession of Celtic brakes that trundled their way down the Gallowgate that night. Amazingly, just five weeks later at the end of October, the bhoys recorded one of their highest ever scores against first-class opposition. A crowd of around 10,000 gathered at Celtic Park for the game against Dundee and in a blistering first half the Celts hit six goals without reply. It was reported that Dundee played the second half with just nine players, having lost two through injury, while Celtic hit another five goals to make it 11–0. The scorers on that famous day were: Jimmy Blessington (two), Sandy McMahon (two), Johnny Madden (two), Barney Battles, Willie Maley, Peter Meehan, Willie Ferguson and Dan Doyle. The Celts actually had the ball in the net thirteen times, but two goals were chalked off. The 11–0 victory over Dundee at Parkhead was a remarkable score for Celtic. Just to prove that the high-scoring display was no fluke, two weeks later on 9 November, Celtic beat Third Lanark 7–0. December also saw a comprehensive 6–2 victory over Rangers, after which the game was termed, "another testimonial to trainer McGuire". A few weeks earlier, Charlie McEleney was transferred down south to join two ex-Celts, James Davidson and Jerry Reynolds, at Burnley. Never an enthusiastic trainer, Glaswegian Charlie apparently found it too difficult to adapt to the new disciplined training regime of Tom McGuire.

As professional players grew fitter, so the pace of the game quickened and intensified. The practice of part-time players holding down other jobs and turning out on a Saturday after working a full shift had to stop. This fact was graphically brought home to the Celtic during a Glasgow Cup game against Linthouse at Govan on 21 September. Allan Martin was brought into the Celtic side as centre forward for the start of the 1895/96 season and quickly made the position his own. As a part-timer, he refused to give up his regular employment as a furnaceman in a local iron foundry to go full time. As a result, he was forced to work some horrendous hours

Celtic Sports Supplement 1893

in order to get time off to play football. On the day at Govan, he scored two goals, the first in the first minute and the second in the last minute in Celtic's 7–1 victory. Immediately after the game he collapsed through sheer exhaustion. Subsequent enquiries established that he had worked a double shift in order to get the time off to play.

Tom McGuire also introduced psychology and methodology to the training, methods still easily recognisable today; personal discipline, team bonding and relaxation periods before big games became regular features at Parkhead. The night before the 1895 Glasgow Cup final found the Celtic team, chaperoned by trainer McGuire, relaxing at the Scotia Music Hall in Stockwell Street. McGuire himself was something of a music hall performer and was in great demand for his sword, rifle and Indian club displays. He regularly gave public displays and could be found at numerous events over the close season performing his act. Although there is little record of the interaction between the players and the committee regarding tactics, logic dictates that the trainers must have had some input into the committeemen's team selection and how to get the best out of the players.

A sports reporter from the Daily Record, who visited the Celtic team during a training session at Parkhead prior to the Glasgow Cup final, commented that no team had ever been so well trained and prepared for a game. The Celtic's opponents in the Glasgow Cup final were the flag bearers of the amateur game, Queen's Park. The final would be played at Ibrox on 16 November and the stadium was packed to the rafters. Inside Ibrox, the crowd encroached onto the playing surface and there were still thousands locked outside at the kick-off. By half-time the Celts were down 3–1 with Queen's Park coping better with the heavy, rain-soaked pitch. However, the second half was a different story as the Celtic's superb fitness kicked in. Their strength and superior stamina allowed the bhoys to steamroller the amateurs and go on to an impressive 6–3 victory. The abrupt turnaround left the spectators astounded and it was heralded as a triumph for Tom McGuire and his training regime. A couple of interesting comments were made by a sports reporter and Tom McGuire himself after the Glasgow Cup win: "Trainer McGuire was fearful least his lads would not get a chance to display their fitness, the finish did not satisfy him – i.e., not that he wanted more goals, but rather he wished to see them (Queen's Park) more severely stretched." McGuire himself stated:

> Our players were in the utmost harmony even when one or two slips were made. They faced up the odds without a murmur and it is a pleasing reflection to them and to their committee to hear sounded on all sides the song of praise their display of pure, unadulterated football gained for them.

In the years to come pure, unadulterated Football would become a phrase synonymous with the Celtic style of play.

A few weeks after winning the Glasgow Cup, the club threw a couple of smokers, one for the players and staff and one for trainer McGuire. In appreciation for his efforts over the previous months, Tom McGuire's complimentary concert was held in the Grand National Halls. Among the turns were Wood and Beasley (American comedy duo), A Benson (Irish comedian), Milleno (sword and gun feats) Jimmy Kelly (tenor) and Joe Edmonds (the eccentric banjo comedian). Jimmy Blessington was also down on the programme for a turn. Tom McGuire also contributed to the night with an exhibition of Indian clubs, sword feats, rifle and bayonet exercises. What Milleno thought of Tom McGuire's performance is unrecorded.

In mid-December, the Celtic club members met for the half-yearly meeting. Over 100 members assembled on the balcony hall of the pavilion at Celtic Park. Willie Maley gave his half-yearly secretarial report. To date the team had played thirty-two, won twenty-five, drawn six and lost one. He looked forward to the new Glasgow League due to start in the New Year.

Glasgow Cup Winners 1895/96

Back row: Tom McGuire (Trainer) J. Kelly, A. Martin, D. Doyle, B. Battles, W. Ferguson.
Middle row: J. Madden, A. McMahon, P. Meechan, W. Maley.
Front row: J. Blessington, Glasgow Cup, D. McArthur.

He regretted that the reserve team was not better supported and announced that the sixpenny gate tariff would be reduced to thrupence (1.5p). He hoped in future the reserves would be better supported since it had been proposed to form a Reserve League. He also thanked what he called the "Gallant and Gay Gordons" from Maryhill Barracks. The regiment had come to his aid back in August after a number of athletic stars let him down at the annual sports meeting. He added that it was due to their excellent displays that the sports event was a success. The club owed them a deep debt of gratitude.

Willie Maley finished his report by saying that the team, with just three vital games left in the league against Rangers, Dumbarton and Third Lanark, was about to enter into a momentous struggle for the League Championship, but under trainer McGuire they felt they were in the best possible condition good to meet the challenge. Next up was James McKay with the treasurer's report and after listing an income of £4773 and expenditure of £4731, the latter including £1634 in players' wages, the balance in the account was £33. He assessed the club's liabilities at £1382 with another £65 bill for new turnstiles due on 1 March making the total to £1447. The statement was discussed at length with Joe Shaughnessy pointing out that virtually none of the debt had been paid off since last year, which led to further discussions. Again, the question of limited liability was raised. Those in favour of the scheme pointed to the risk the committee had to bear on behalf of the club; while those against, argued that it would be the end of the charitable purposes for which the club was formed. Tom Maley objected to the question being discussed at the half-year meeting and suggested the AGM or an extraordinary meeting was the right time. The fact that the question of limited liability would be discussed should be widely advertised to give as many members as possible the opportunity to consider the matter. Tom Maley proposed and Stephen Henry seconded that a subcommittee look at the pros and cons of limited liability and at ways to pay off the debt. A direct negative that no committee be formed and that limited liability be not discussed was moved by Michael Hughes and seconded by Frank Havlin. During a prolonged and at times heated debate, Frank Havlin, who had already thwarted the modernisers' plans for absolute control at Celtic the previous April by defeating Rule 18, got into a war of words with John McLaughlin. During the exchange Havlin quoted from a newspaper article written by John H McLaughlin in which he was supposed to have called his opponents within the Celtic membership "corner boys and loafers". John McLaughlin incensed at what he regarded as being misquoted, launched a civil action against Havlin accusing him of libel. In the event, the amendment that no subcommittee be formed was carried by a majority of 50 to 31. The meeting lasted over two hours.

The day after the half-year meeting, the bhoys beat Ranger 6–2 at Parkhead in front of 25,000 spectators. The scorers being McMahon (2), Blessington, Battles, Martin and Tommy Morrison. A week later they saw off Dumbarton with another home win, this time by 3–0. The victories ensured that the league championship would be coming back to Parkhead with a game still to play. It had been an impressive league campaign by the Celts; as the team became progressively stronger they simply steamrollered the opposition, particularly over the second half of the season, winning eleven games in a row. In all, the bhoys dropped just six points over the entire season, all to Edinburgh clubs, but regained the league championship flag for the third time in six years, amassing a total of thirty points. League statistics for the season were: played eighteen, won fifteen, drew none and lost three. Immediately after the Dumbarton game, the Celts travelled to England for a whistle stop Christmas tour, where based at Manchester they would play Everton and Bury. The team shared the train to England with Rangers who were also travelling south on tour.

On 18 January 1896, Queen's Park got their revenge for the Glasgow Cup defeat by knocking the Celts out of the Scottish Cup in the first round. Two penalty kicks helped the Queens beat the bhoys 4–2, while Willie Maley thought it was the Celts' worst performance of the season. In February, the new Glasgow Football League competition kicked in. It was another attempt to fill up the fixture lists and for the Celts it proved a financial success pulling in just under £1000. In its inaugural season only Celtic, Rangers, Queen's Park and Third Lanark took part. The bulk of the games were played in March and April and by the end of the month Rangers had run out winners by two clear points with the Celtic in second place. On a scorching hot day in mid-May, the Celts picked up the Glasgow Charity Cup for the fifth time in a row, setting a new record. Having beaten Rangers 6–1 at Hampden in the semi-final, 11,000 spectators made their way to Ibrox Park to watch the Celts play Queen's Park in the final. The Celts scored first through McMahon only to see Queen's Park draw level. The game finished with the score at 1–1 and extra time was played. James Kelly then put the Celts back into the lead. Thereafter it was a disciplined display by the Celtic defenders, who ensured the victory after injuries to Jimmy Blessington and centre forward John Madden effectively neutered the Celtic attack. The Celtic ran out 2–1 winners after extra time. By the end of the season, the Celts had played sixty games, won forty-two, drawn six and lost twelve. They had scored 185 goals and conceded ninety-nine. In what must have been very pleasant reading for the Celtic management, the sports papers reported that for the season just finished over a half million spectators had passed through Parkhead's gates.

At the Celtic AGM in June 1896, despite the disappointment of being knocked out of the Scottish Cup early, the officials and members were pleased with the team's performance over the season. Although the club had been in existence for barely a decade, Celtic could already justifiably claim to be Scotland's leading side. The Dundee Courier called them beyond question not only the leading professional club in Scotland, but also one of the greatest football concerns in the world. Despite the existence of Dundee Harp, the Celts enjoyed massive support from the Irish who had settled in Dundee and the team news was faithfully published in the Dundee Courier. The Celts' record in the Scottish Cup (one win, losing finalists on three occasions) was less noteworthy than their record in the Scottish League, a competition in which they had yet to finish outside of the top three, winning the title in 1892/93, 1893/94 and 1895/96. Over 150 members made their way to the Annfield Hall in the Gallowgate for the annual gathering and for the most part the meeting was taken up by a detailed report by the treasurer. He could report record profits for the season of over £10,200, a sum unequalled by any club in the whole of Britain. Had the team achieved a decent run in the Scottish Cup, the total would have been ever greater. The greatest expenditures were the players' wages at £2878, an increase of £800 from the previous season, alterations and extensions to the ground including new turnstiles, costing £984, and the repayment of £761 in loans. The club reduced its liabilities from £1581 to just £857 and treasurer McKay announced that had the team made any progress in the Scottish

Cup, the debt would have been wiped out. As it was, he looked forwards to clearing the debt in the following season. After the very definite reversal for the advocates of limited liability at the half-yearly meting back in December, the subject was never raised, but in what was becoming the norm, the questions of club expenses and charitable donations were discussed. At the elections for the club officials, all the old office bearers were re-elected. There were twenty-seven nominations for the committee, those successful with allocated votes were: John MacCreadie (78), Arthur Murphy (73), Pat Gallagher (66), Mick Dunbar (62), Francis McErlean (47), James Curtis (44), James Grant JP (43), Patrick McMorrow (40), Frank Havlin (38), John McQuade (37) and Joe Warnock (37), the latter was a publican and was voted in after a recount. Frank Havlin was the outspoken, working class club member who had thwarted John McLaughlin's attempt to introduce Rule 18. At the time of the AGM, he was embroiled in a civil action having been accused of libel by John H McLaughlin. His election onto the committee was therefore something of a personal snub for the club's vice-president. Among those who failed to be elected was an old opponent of the modernisers, James Quillan. Joe Shaughnessy suggested the new committee should consider giving an honorarium to James McKay and Willie Maley and they both received £75, while James Curtis, who had overseen the reserve team for the last eight years, received £25 for past service.

It was only business, honest!

The annual Celtic Sports meeting was held over two days, 8 and 10 August 1896. The weather for the first day of the meeting was dull and foreboding; it would be an ominous portent of an atmosphere that would hang over the club for much of the season. In addition to the usual track and field events, a special man versus cycle race was planned, as was a gymnastics display by the Gordon Highlanders. The battalion's massively popular military band was also on the programme providing the musical interludes. However, the big attraction was the appearance of Tom Conneff, the Irish-born American champion runner, and JJ Mullen, the famous amateur Irish champion pedestrian and distance runner. Jack Mullen was advertised as running in the two-mile handicap at Parkhead, but was warned by the Irish Amateur Athletics Board not to participate in the meeting, as it would compromise his Irish amateur status. All the usual Celtic personalities and committeemen were on parade for the meeting acting in some official capacity. Tom Maley was umpiring the cycle races and committeeman James Moore was acting as official starter. Some degree of awkwardness may have been apparent in the pavilion when committeeman Frank Havlin put in an appearance grinning from ear to ear. Just a week or so earlier he had won his libel case against John H McLaughlin. The sheriff's decision must have come as a massive relief for the gasworks labourer; a £100 award to McLaughlin would have undoubtedly seen him in the poorhouse. Willie Maley as usual was a very busy bhoy; while acting as clerk of the course and club secretary he still managed to race, coming second in the 100 yards, beaten by a whisker. Opinions varied as to the success of the sports meeting compared to previous occasions, but the talking point of the two-day event was the status of

Tom McGuire

Jack Mullen. He had apparently taken fright at the Irish board's warning and pulled out of the advertised race, but was later persuaded by John Allison of Salford Harriers and Manchester City to take part in an exhibition with Conneff. A convert to Catholicism, John Allison was a top English sports promoter and was described as an advisor to Manchester City with whom Celtic had a very close association. A personal friend of Willie Maley, he was in Glasgow acting as a judge at the Celtic Sports.

As usual the Celtic Sports were judged by the general public to be a great success and further encouraged the general population's interest in sport, adding fuel to the massive explosion in the popularity of cycling and pedestrianism. After the sports meeting, the Celtic committee entertained the officials and the Gordon Highlanders to tea in the Annfield Hall in the Gallowgate. The Celtic Sports would be the last occasion on which the Gordon Highlanders would appear at Parkhead. Willie Maley was in the chair for the event and spoke of the warm and sincere friendship that had grown between the club and the Gordon Highlanders. In his reply, the Sergeant Major reciprocated the sentiments and added that the men who appeared at Celtic Park were all volunteers. They were on duty out of affection and respect for the club, many of them only back that day from arduous military duties. The battalion would shortly be posted to India, but having taken a great interest in the welfare and success of the club, they would follow the Celtic with interest and wished them all success for the future.

Celtic's popular trainer, Tom McGuire, had spent the close season touring around various sports meetings including the Irish National Forester's meeting at Hamilton, giving displays of Indian club, sword, rifle and bayonet exercises. One of his party pieces involved placing a potato in the hand or on the neck of a volunteer from the audience. Tom would then slash the potato in half with his sabre without harming the nervous victim. At the Hamilton meeting, Willie Maley's young brother Alex was competing in the running events and was dragged from the crowd as the hapless volunteer. At the end of July, Tom reported to Parkhead as the players began to filter back ready to start training. The footballers' training regime was obviously interrupted by the preparations for the Celtic Sports, but they got on with it as best they could under the circumstances. On Tuesday 11 August, Tom set off on the short walk from his Bridgeton home to Parkhead, ready to start football training in earnest. En route, Tom stopped off at a local newsagent to buy the morning paper. On turning to the sports pages he was astounded to read that Jack Mullen was being toasted as the new trainer at Celtic Park. When Tom arrived at the park he confronted John Glass, who offered him a position on the ground staff, but Tom said he was a trainer not a gardener and resigned. There then followed a fortnight of "is he, isn't he" as the Celtic management tried to distance themselves from the betrayal of their trainer. The decision to replace Tom McGuire with Jack Mullen astounded most Celtic supporters and sports commentators alike. Mullen, although a very talented runner, had no experience of training football players or managing men and indeed was known in athletic circles as something of an ill-disciplined maverick himself. The Glasgow Observer could not understand the reasoning behind the appointment, stating that Mullen had only previously trained horses and that the Celtic were storing up problems for themselves. How right they were! Even the Scottish Sport weighed in with, "It doesn't follow that because he is a good runner doesn't mean he will be able to manage footballers." Some of the Celtic committee were as shocked as the supporters and when questioned by reporters professed to be ignorant of the facts.

Behind all the shananagains was the fact that the Celtic management had decided to get a slice of the booming athletic and cycle racing craze that was sweeping the country. Just about every organisation from the police, Post Office, local authorities, schools and colleges were all hosting their own athletic or sports meetings and a whole new breed of semi-professional athletes had sprung up, travelling around the country competing for prizes or small cash sums. A posse of bookmakers followed the athletes and the sports meetings became Meccas for illegal betting. At the most important meetings, professional challenge matches with national champions running against each other or champions racing cyclists or horses or against the clock for various athletic records attracted a great many paying spectators. A number of talented athletes were already members of the Celtic club and ran under the title Celtic FC among them committeeman Paddy McMorrow, Tom Moore, the brother of committeeman James Moore, and the three Maley brothers, Tom, Willie and youngest brother Alex. A number of the players were also known to slip on spikes or climb on board a cycle in an attempt to land a decent prize. The founding fathers, never behind the business curve, had decided it was time to build up the athletic side of the club, which to date had been pretty much a side line to the main business of football. As usual they would not let good business sense interfere with ethics or honour, and thought they could kill two birds with one stone. McGuire would be turned out, just as would happen to a player who had failed to make the grade, and Mullen, assisted by Tommy Bonner, could train the football team, oversee the park as groundsman and at the same time be an attraction for the new athletics enthusiasts they hoped to bring into the club. Although there is no smoking gun, Mullen's decision to run first the exhibition race and on the Monday night a two-mile handicap was probably a result of closed-door discussions between the Celtic management and Mullen. The furore over the treatment of Tom McGuire caused a few uncomfortable days at Parkhead and as a smoke screen it was put about that the post was still vacant and that Paddy Cannon the old Glasgow Hibernian trainer had also applied for the job. Although a talented and experienced trainer, at forty years of age, Paddy was now at the end of his athletics career. He was still a world record holder, but he would never attract the top professional athletes to Parkhead and could never be the draw with the public that current Irish favourite Mullen would be. The word on the street was that the job was Mullen's, not only was he the biggest attraction, but he had the powerful Belfast lobby at Celtic backing him including James Grant and Francis McErlean.

Shortly after it was publicly announced that Jack Mullen was the new Celtic trainer, the committee began to look seriously at attracting the athletics and cycling fraternity to Parkhead. At this time athletics and cycling in Scotland were regarded as almost the one sport. Challenge matches were arranged and staged at Parkhead with Mullen, a great attraction in his own

JJ Mullen

right, taking on fancied international runners or the clock. The new ground was itself seen as a major source of income for the club and professional athletic meetings held at Parkhead were another attempt to maximise income. Towards the end of October a race between Irish-American Conneff and Englishman Fred Bacon, the current Champion of the World, was held at Parkhead. The race was actually run at half-time during a match between a Celtic reserve side and an Argyll and Sutherland Highlanders team. In the event, Bacon won the two-mile race in a time of nine minutes and forty-one seconds. Feelers were put out to Glasgow Irish athletes, cross-country runners and pedestrians about coming together under an umbrella club based at Parkhead. As for Tom McGuire, he initially went back to the public displays and got a few shows at the Scotia theatre, but within the month he was working with the Scottish Manufacturing Company making cycles in Hosier Street, Bridgeton. Obviously feeling sorry for Tom, *the Man in the Know*, advertised for a new position for him as a "Drill Sergeant or Disciplinarian for schools". The Celtic players had a whip around for their popular, though strict trainer, while the National Foresters in Tom's hometown of Barrhead arranged a smoker, and Jimmy Blessington put up a silver cup as a raffle prize. Despite his poor treatment from the Celtic management, Tom never held a grudge. In September 1899, when the Celtic's latest trainer, Dan Friel, broke his ankle, Tom McGuire came back to Parkhead to take over team training while Dan recovered.

1896/97 Season

The 1896/97 season therefore started with the Celtic embroiled in controversy, but it was nothing new for the club management and they knew it would soon blow over. As far as the football was concerned, they were very confident that the latest Celtic side would make a better show in the Scottish Cup and retain the Scottish League title, to make it four wins out of five in the competition.

In the corridors of power, the Celtic's cause was also advancing with John H McLaughlin stepping up from vice-president to president of the Scottish Football League. The Celtic began the season with a formidable array of players to choose from – goalkeepers: McArthur and Cullen; backs: Meehan, Doyle, Dunbar and Orr; centres: Kelly, Russell, Battles, McEleny, O'Rourke, J King and Farrell; forwards: Blessington, McMahon, Madden, Ferguson, Morrison, Divers, Crossan, Henderson and Hutchison. The latest signings, Davy Russell and Alex King both from the Heart of Midlothian, were added to the list. Still not satisfied, Larkhall-born Paddy Gilhooley, a robust centre forward playing with Cambuslang Hibernian and Henry McIlveny, back at Parkhead for the second time, would join the team later in the year. In addition, there were a number of part-timers to provide reserves for a second eleven. Everyone at the club was confident and upbeat and everything looked on course for another very successful year.

The Scottish League champions started the new season with an away defeat to Hibernian in the league, but recovered to record six straight wins, mostly against the less powerful sides. However, there was trouble brewing in the leaderless dressing room. The players had been left pretty much to their own devices as Jack Mullen juggled three balls at once: the team, the park and his own training and running commitments. The latter often took him away from Parkhead for days on end. Team captain James Kelly was coming to the end of his career and no longer one of the boys, was already planning his retirement and a new career in local politics. Even Willie Maley inserted his finger into yet another pie when he planned and carried out a massive expansion to his sports outfitters shop over the summer of 1896. With Tom McGuire and his disciplined ways gone, a number of players got a bit carried away with their affluence and celebrity status. Others felt their real or perceived grievances over pay and criticism of their play were being ignored. Of course, in the absence of a disciplined management presence in the dressing room, the ubiquitous barrack-room lawyers put in an appearance, egging the malcontents on from the back of the crowd. At the end of September, the Celtic lost a friendly game 3–2 at home to Sunderland and from then results began to tail off, although they were now playing the more powerful teams in the league. After a 1–1 draw in the Glasgow Cup final, on 21 November the Celts lost the replay 2–1 to arch rivals Rangers in what was a bruising encounter. One of the walking wounded was Sandy McMahon, although his injury seemed fairly minor at the time, it refused to clear up and the "Duke" would be out of action for months. His loss was a severe blow to the Celts both on and off the field as he was forced to spend much of his time in Manchester receiving treatment.

Reporters from the Glasgow Evening News and its sports paper, the Scottish Referee, not for the first time that season, accused the Celtic players of being over-aggressive during the Rangers game. The entire team took exception to the comments, and before kick-off the following week against Hibernian at Parkhead, they demanded that the reporters in question be ejected from the ground, insisting they would not take to the field until they were gone. The committee of course refused their demand and three players, Peter Meehan, Barney Battles and John Divers, stuck to their guns and refused to strip for Jack Mullen. The pavilion was cleared as the committee tried to cajole the players to relent but they would not be persuaded. The dressing room revolt delayed the start of the game by fifteen minutes and ultimately the Celts appeared minus Meehan, Battles and Divers. Willie Maley, now largely retired from playing, and travelling reserve Barney Crossan filled two of the positions, and committeeman Davie Meikleham was dispatched post haste to Cathkin Park to collect Tommy Dunbar, who was playing there with the reserves. The bhoys were forced to play with a man short until the start of the second half when Tom Dunbar arrived at Parkhead by hansom cab. The game eventually ended in a creditable 1–1 draw, but Tom Dunbar took a terrible ribbing because the ten-man Celtic side were leading 1–0 until Tom took to the field. The committee stated they would suspend the three malcontents, who according to John Glass would "never be allowed to kick a ball again for them". Their pay was docked and the committee asked the Scottish Football Association to exercise its prerogative and confirm the suspensions, which it did. The dressing room revolt and the suspensions caused irreparable damage to the cohesion, spirit and morale of the players and the team was effectively destroyed.

The half-yearly meeting was held in the Annfield Hall on the evening of 9 December. Rather surprisingly given the recent events, it proved to be quiet affair with few members making their way to the Gallowgate. The committee were obviously expecting trouble and rumour had it that several members wanted their say on the recent player revolt. In anticipation, the sporting press were excluded on a vote. In the event the incident was never even mentioned. Willie Maley, yet to fully grasp the seriousness of the situation, started the meeting off with a report highlighting the success of the August Sports, both amateur and professional. So far the football team had played nineteen games, of which they had won eleven, lost three and drawn five. The Glasgow Cup had already been disposed of, but although they made it to the final, fate decreed that they should relinquish it to Rangers. The League competition was reaching its final stages with the Celtic still well in contention. Although it would be a stiff finish he was hopeful that another League flag would be their reward. The forthcoming match with Rangers was exercising the whole attention of both the committee and the players. He ended his report by referring to the Scottish Cup. He hoped that when summarising at the end of the season, he would be able to add what had long been missing from his reports, the capture of the Scottish Cup. James McKay then announced a record income for the half year of over £5800, over £1000 more than the corresponding period in the preceding year. He further stated that over the year extensive improvements on the Park had been completed and that £1000 of debt had been cleared. He hoped that by the annual meeting in June 1897, he could announce that not only had the outstanding debt of just £400 been cleared, but that there was a substantial balance in favour of the club. The members present were well pleased with the results and both reports were passed. All told, the meeting lasted just over an hour. With no sense of impending disaster, or any mention of limited liability for once, the meeting passed without dispute or rancour, with the players' revolt seemingly ignored.

Once the details of the meeting leaked out, the press too were impressed with the state of the club's finances. They highlighted the fact that the huge sums now being generated by all football clubs were in sharp contrast to sums from just a dozen years ago when £1000 would have been regarded as an extraordinary income. As for the Celtic club, "It is a matter for congratulation that the club debt is now within sight of being wiped away altogether, as the annual general meeting should see the club free men, owing no man a penny." On the club balance sheet was further proof of Frank Havlin stirring the pot. At the monthly committee meeting held a week previously on 2 December, Havlin proposed a £50 donation to the St Vincent de Paul Society, but his motion was voted down by the rest of the committee. Determined that something should be donated to charity, he shamed the committee into splitting £50 equally between the Little Sisters of the Poor, Smyllum Orphanage, the Dalbeth Nunnery, Lanark Hospital and the Whitevale Refuge. Frank's fighting £50 was the largest proportion of the meagre £63 of donations that showed in the club's half-yearly financial statement.

This rare photograph was probably taken in mid December 1896. Seated far right is the old Celtic stalwart Willie Groves. "Darlin' Willie," was brought back to Parkhead from Hibernian to reinforce the side after the three-player revolt of 28 November, but only managed two games before his health broke down. The irrepressible Dan Doyle is pictured in the centre of the sitting row. Prone to going absent without official leave, Dan and Pat Gilhooly, standing second player in from the left, would shortly add to the woes of the Celtic management when both players failed to appear for the Scottish Cup first round game against Arthurlie. Celtic trainer and professional athlete J.J. Mullen is pictured standing behind Willie Groves with the ubiquitous trainer's towel over his shoulder.

(Photograph courtesy of Marie Rowan)

Despite the dressing room unrest and the unavailability of the players involved in the revolt, by the end of the year in the league the bhoys had won ten, lost two and drawn four and were sitting at the top of the table albeit only on goal difference. An increasing concern was a growing injury list and their record for the season so far against arch rivals Rangers. The bhoys had drawn twice and lost twice to the light blues, and both defeats were costly. The first saw them surrender the Glasgow Cup in the replayed semi-final, while the latest was a serious setback which saw them defeated by 2–0 in the league. The dropped points saw their lead at the top of the table disappear as they were pulled back into the chasing pack with only two games left to be played. It also saw veteran Willie Groves going off seriously injured to join the ever-growing queue in the treatment room. Still, the team appeared to be going well enough; sometimes it was a bit of a stagger, but with the exception of the Glasgow Cup defeat, things appeared to be on more or less on course. In the Scottish Cup, the Celts had been given a very favourable first round draw, away against the non-league amateurs of Arthurlie. After the disappointment of their first round exit to Queen's Park in the previous year's competition, the Celtic's progression into the second round was taken as a foregone conclusion.

As the old year drew to a close, the Celtic management's attention was firmly focused on things other than football. As part of the ongoing campaign to encourage Scottish athletics, or more specifically Scottish athletics with Celtic Park as its epicentre, they were focused on the now imminent Celtic Professional Sports meeting. To be held at Parkhead over 4 and 5 January, Celtic's Jack Mullen was the main draw at the event. He would race against a host of international champions including the famous Fred Bacon. Also on the bill was Paddy Cannon of Stirling, the old Glasgow Hibernian trainer, and still a world record holder. On the first day, the heats were held for the 120-yard sprint and the two-mile handicap, with prizes of £30 and £15, respectively. To inject some fun into the event on the second day, the committee planned a 100-yard sprint race for footballers. The stars would race in their team strips and the committee hoped the appearance of the footballers would encourage spectators to attend. Glasgow's new resident infantry battalion, the Argyll and Sutherland Highlanders from Maryhill Barracks, would provide the entertainment. The advertisements for the event promised an imposing military display. Jack's preparations for the two-day event began a week or so earlier and included a four-mile race for a £50 purse at Parkhead on Christmas Day. On the day it rained and only a few hardy annuals turned out to watch the race run in a heavy downpour. Apparently, the park bookies were giving 5/4 against Mullen, who ran out an easy winner in a time of twenty minutes and thirty-four seconds.

CELTIC HARRIERS,

A Public Meeting for the Formation of a Cross-Country and Cycling Club in Glasgow, under Catholic auspices, will be held on WEDNESDAY, JANUARY 13th, 1897, at 8 p.m., in the Grand National Halls, Main Street, S.S. All interested in Athletics are requested to attend.

C. Q., Secretary, pro tem.

In yet another strand of the Celtic's strategy to encourage athletics, the Celtic Harriers Club, a cross-country/cycling combination was formed over the New Year period. The project was driven forward by the combined efforts of certain officers of Celtic FC and the Hibernian Swimming Club. As usual, workaholic Willie Maley took on the lion's share of the organising, while Celtic committeemen James Moore and Pat McMorrow did the recruiting and cajoling. Around 150 members of the Young Men's Society and the League of the Cross, some already members of Celtic FC and the Hibernian Swimming Club, signed up for the project. The Glasgow Observer noted that there had long been a need for a Catholic cross-country club in the city and that many of the young men were already members of Clydesdale, West Olympic, Queen's Park, Maryhill and other local harrier clubs. Such sterling Glasgow Irish runners as Tom Moore (brother of James), Shanley, Bell, Alex Maley, McMorrow and Conville would enlist under the banner of the Celtic Harriers. It was planned to include a cycling section in the Harriers where Tom Maley and John and Joe Shaughnessy, sons of the Celtic committeeman, would take an active interest. Interestingly, Charlie Quin (*Man in the Know*) who was himself sporty also got involved as the club secretary, pro tem. The Celtic Harriers would be based at Parkhead where the Celtic committee put the entire training facilities at its disposal. A formal meeting took place in mid-January when the new club's constitution was set out and office bearers elected. As expected the power brokers at Celtic FC assumed dominant positions as the Celtic Harrier's office bearers and on the committee; Willie Maley, president, James Moore, vice-president, Pat McMorrow, team vice-captain, while John Glass was voted onto the committee. One of the first matters agreed was that the club strip would be a white shirt with a green shamrock badge and black knickers trimmed in green in winter and white in summer. The first training practice would take place at Parkhead on 27 January.

While Willie Maley was busy setting up the Harriers and Jack Mullen was preparing for his professional races, the sullen Celtic footballers were pretty much left to sulk over Christmas and New Year. With the three Celtic rebels still suspended, a half dozen regulars injured and the remainder of the team still mourning the missing shillings in their reduced pay packets, the morale and disenchantment among the players reached an all-time low after their Ne'erday 1–0 defeat by Hibernian. The Hibs game had been a friendly and a raft of team regulars was missing, either through injury, sickness or had been given the game off. Dan Doyle was one of the missing, but in his case he may have awarded himself the day off. Independent-minded Dan was prone to going absent without prior notification to or permission from the committee. Stalwart James Kelly was also off on the day but with permission, he was planning his election campaign for the Blantyre School board. In fact, the scratch Celtic side played relatively well against Hibernian's strongest eleven and were unlucky not to have gained a draw. The injury hoodoo struck yet again when Pat McElney's long-term injury broke down, adding another name to the doctor's list. As a reward for the improved performance against Hibs, the committee treated the players to a night out at a Christmas pantomime.

GLASGOW LEAGUE CHAMPIONSHIP.

RANGERS v. CELTIC.

At IBROX PARK, at 2.30, on
SATURDAY, Jan. 2, 1897.

THERE IS SOMETHING NEW UNDER THE SUN!
To witness this great match, John Houston, the famous weather prophet, will travel specially from Kirkcudbright. At half-time and at full-time he will scientifically cause to be discharged with a loud report, synchronously with the referee's whistle, his world-renowned patent automatic GUN, ingeniously constructed on new and novel clock-work lines, and encompassed within the limited precincts of what he himself describes as "a small house (portable), three feet square."

COME IN YOUR HUNDRED THOUSANDS.

The New Year's football campaign would begin in earnest on 2 January with the Celtic's first tie in the Glasgow League competition. The Glasgow League comprised of Celtic, Rangers, Queen's Park, Clyde and Third Lanark and the teams played each other home and away. The competition was intended to fill in gaps in the teams' fixture lists and therefore it ran from November until May. The game against Rangers at Ibrox Park would be the Celtic's chance to break a disappointing run of results against a very powerful Ibrox side. Due to the injury situation, the Celtic committee decided to wait until the day of the game before announcing their team. On the day it was McArthur, Doyle, Orr, Russell, Kelly, King, Morrison, Blessington, Gilhooly, Ferguson and Crossan. Over 26,000 spectators, including an impressive number bedecked in green and white, made their way to Ibrox. The sports commentators were amazed at the turnout for the little regarded Glasgow League competition and were unsure if it was the holiday, the football or Mr John Houston, the famous weather prophet's widely advertised demonstration of his automatic timing gun that brought them out. The Celtic won the toss and in a first half that was described as hard, fast and furious, the Celts, despite holding their own managed to lose two goals. In the second half Rangers dominated from the start, pressed home their advantage and scored another goal to make the score 3–0. In what turned out to be the best Old Firm game of the season, Rangers proved too strong for a weakened Celtic side. In a precursor to the fatal injury of Johnny Thomson in an Ibrox goalmouth thirty-four years later, Dan McArthur received a very serious head injury from the boot of a Rangers' forward. The incident caused a scuffle in the penalty box as the Celtic players thought that Tommy Hyslop should have pulled out of the challenge. Dan was carried unconscious to the pavilion where his wound received stitches from the club doctor. The massively versatile Alex King replaced the Celtic keeper in goal for the last twenty minutes of the game, which was already well lost. The final result was 3–0 to the Gers with the Celts finishing with ten men on the park. The Celts had now lost three games in a row to their greatest rivals. Amazingly, in each of the defeats the bhoys had lost a key player. Sandy McMahon had gone off during the Glasgow Cup final, Groves in the Scottish League game and in the latest, Dan McArthur. The Celtic goalkeeper would be out for the rest of the season. The sports commentator writing in the Glasgow Observer the following Saturday thought the Celtic side was a disgrace. He thought the situation was intolerable with many of the players unfit to wear the Celtic colours. Something had to be done to strengthen the team's weak spots before the supporters could return to Ibrox, Cathkin or even Barrhead with any confidence.

The Arthurlie Humpf

The Celtic's challenge for the Scottish Cup of 1897 would begin on 9 January with a first round match against the non-leaguers Arthurlie FC. Founded in 1874, the club was one of the oldest in the country and was based in Barrhead near Paisley. The visit of the Scottish League champions was a dream tie for the football minnows. The amateur side had only managed to get to the first round of the cup by way of a qualifying competition. All the football pundits including the Celtic management and players regarded lowly Arthurlie as a pushover and it would appear that the committee's eye was taken off the ball in the run up to the game. The Arthurlie ground, Dunterlie Park, was a short ten-minute walk from the railway station and was only capable of accommodating a crowd of 3000. The Arthurlie committee contacted the Celts after the draw had been announced and for £75 offered to swap the venue from Barrhead to Parkhead, but the Celtic management declined the offer. They made the judgement that the match at Parkhead would not attract £150 worth of spectators through the turnstiles, so they preferred the half gate from Dunterlie Park, which would probably only amount to about £30. With the Scottish League champions coming to town, the Arthurlie committee were determined they would make the most of the occasion. They put up goal nets and erected four new pay-boxes for the tie. As always the punters were squeezed with the club increasing the entry fee to six pence, the first time that figure had been levied in Barrhead. The club treasurer expected a cash bonanza of £60 or £70 at the gate. The game caught the imagination of the Barrhead community and a local hatter promised the Arthurlie players a new hat each if they scored three goals against the Celtic. Inspired and driven on by their supporters, the Arthurlie amateurs put in extra training for the biggest game in the history of their club. They felt they would put on a good show and winked that they might have a surprise in store for their visitors. The surprise was more of a shock and was known locally as the "humpf".

It was a much depleted Celtic squad that reported to Celtic Park on the Friday morning where a head count was taken of those fit enough to play. Davie Russell added to the committee's worries when he reported that he was having a problem with his eyes, which appeared inflamed and sore. Between the missing and the injury list no definite eleven could be selected, but a number of players were instructed to make themselves available to travel to Barrhead, while some key individuals were warned that they would play. The Celtic players were dismissed after being instructed to assemble in Glasgow's Central Station on Saturday morning where they would be marshalled by Willie Maley and the committee. Maley and a number of the players then went to visit John Divers, who had gone down with a serious cold, which had developed into pneumonia. On the Saturday morning the committee looked on with dismay as the Celtic squad began to assemble in Central Station. Such was the depleted state of the squad with injuries and suspensions, the committee, with just hours to go till kick-off, had, with a few exceptions, no idea who would pull on the Celtic colours. To add to their woes, Dan Doyle had done one of his disappearing acts, which given the circumstances of the game was half expected, and it appeared that Pat Gilhooly had decided to follow suit. Both were absent as the carriage doors closed and the train pulled out of the station. When the team arrived at Barrhead, the committee still had no idea who would play or in what position they would play. John Glass apparently had a premonition of disaster and felt a shiver run down his spine as the full magnitude of the situation dawned.

The Celtic players who arrived in Barrhead on the day of the match were more like a disorganised bounce game squad than a professional football team. With six regulars, Madden, Dunbar, McMahon, McArthur, Russell and Orr, unavailable and three regulars still suspended, plus Doyle and Gilhooly missing, it was always going to be something of a scratch side that would be donning the green and white stripes on the day. The players chosen to play must have been among the most reluctant and unenthusiastic ever to wear a Celtic jersey. On occasions much less critical than this, Willie Maley would strip, but even he saw the writing on the wall and took a back seat. When Willie Maley finally handed the sports reporters the Celtic team sheet some though it was a joke. Were Crossan and John King really playing at full back? Where were Doyle, Russell and Gilhooly! Such was the chaos and reticence in the Celtic dressing room, some of those chosen to play were still getting stripped when the game started, Celtic having only seven men on the park. The team that eventually took to the ploughed field that was Dunterlie Park was Cullen, John King, Crossan, Farrell, Kelly, Alex King, Morrison, Blessington, McIlvenny, Henderson and Ferguson.

The Arthurlie surprise could be seen as soon as the players left the pavilion. The infamous humpf was a steeply sloping portion of the ground that peaked in a corner. When Ching Morrison first saw it he asked Willie Maley how he was supposed to climb it. In addition, the Arthurlie committee had their groundsmen narrow the playing area to help constrict the Celtic's close passing game. The scratch Celtic side started brightly enough and with the slope in their favour, created several chances. However, it was Arthurlie that scored first, against the run of play, but the Celtic equalised shortly afterward through Harry McIlvenny. Just before half-time Arthurlie scored a second goal and again it was against the run of play. In the second half the Barrhead men had the slope and enthusiastically set about putting the Celts to the sword. When Arthurlie applied concerted pressure, the playing conditions, lack of team cohesion, organisation, effort and enthusiasm soon began to tell. With Sandy McMahon and Jimmy Orr watching from the touchline, the Celtic side effectively collapsed. Arthurlie scored twice more before Ferguson scored a very late second for Celtic. The reigning Scottish League champions were outfought and outplayed and the final score did not flatter the home side. John Glass was so sickened by the Celtic display, for the first time ever he left the game before the finish. Were it not for Cullen in the Celtic goal the score could have been very much worse. The game ended in a stunning 4–2 defeat that saw the Celtic crashing out of the Scottish Cup. The astonishing score reverberated not only throughout Scotland, but also throughout the whole of Britain and Ireland. Despite all the manpower difficulties, the side Celtic cobbled together in the Dunterlie pavilion should have been good enough to see off the amateurs, but too many players simply went through the motions of playing. Their reward would be a place of infamy in the annals of the Celtic club. That said, the management of the time should also take their share of the shame. To their credit, it was later reported that the committee had been given information that would have allowed them to lodge a protest. This may have resulted in the game being replayed, but at the insistence of John H McLaughlin, the Celtic committee very wisely decided not to contest the result.

Within days of the Arthurlie defeat, the newspapers were reporting that the Celtic committee had met to discuss the attitude and conduct of the players. The behaviour of some of the players over that New Year period and the earlier revolt of the Parkhead three, convinced the committee that they had lost control of the dressing room. The situation was completely unacceptable and they resolved to enforce a more rigorous discipline in future. It would be interesting to have heard Tom McGuire's opinion on the reintroduction of discipline. Even the newspapers recognised that something had to be done to regain control of the Celtic dressing room, commenting, "The Arthurlie result could be a blessing in disguise if a more rigorous discipline might be introduced". The enactment of the committee's new hard-line policy was felt in the dressing room immediately: Henry McIlvenny and John King were scapegoated and paid off. Peter Meehan was transferred to Everton and soon after Ching Morrison was dispatched back to Burnley. Barney Battles and John Divers also left the club at the end of the season, but both would return to Parkhead in the autumn of 1898. Doyle and Gilhooly were each fined and docked a week's wages for not turning up after being picked to play. A number of other players also had their wages reduced. Only Cullen, Kelly, Blessington and Alex King came through the debacle with their footballing reputations unsullied. Forty years later, Willie Maley described it as the greatest sensation in Scottish football and it probably still is. For years afterward, it

FOOTBALL NOTES.

THE SCOTTISH CUP TIES.

THE CELTIC CRUSHED BY ARTHURLIE.

The close of the New Year holidays brought a renewal of activity in football circles. No League matches were on the card, interest being centred on the struggle in the first round of the Scottish Cup ties.

No fewer than sixteen ties were played off, and one of the results was sufficient to make football players open their eyes with astonishment.

The disaster which befell the Celtic at the hands of the Arthurlie comes as a climax to the misfortunes which the Western club has suffered during the present season.

In nearly every match they have played this winter the Celts have been unable to tell their team an hour before entering the field, but their ill-luck on Saturday beats their record.

One after the other came reports that Doyle, Russell, and Orr could not play, and Gilhooley could not come. Ten men only would have been put on the field had not M'Ilvenny at the last moment put in an appearance.

Thus Arthurlie, who played their usual men, had to be met with a team from which almost all the first eleven were wanting.

The Celts played well, and worked indefatigably, but the Arthurlie rear ranks proved too many for them.

The Celts were weak at back, and did not show up well when they came within shooting distance. The home team proved themselves superior from start to finish.

The loss of the match will be a big blow to the Celts, and will mean also a good round sum in money to them.

Dundee Courier Jan 1897

was said the name of Arthurlie could only be whispered in the corridors of Parkhead. As a final twist of fate, the Celtic was again drawn against Arthurlie in the first round of the Scottish Cup in January 1898. This time there would be no slip-up with the Celtic winning 7–0.

The Arthurlie result was final confirmation for the power brokers at the Celtic, not that any was needed, that the club had to be properly and professionally managed. Rule by volunteer officer bearers and committeemen, answerable to the general membership, could no longer be tolerated. The game of football had morphed into an arm of the entertainment business and if the Celtic was to prosper, it could only do so by introducing proper business management structures. For the pragmatic office bearers and power brokers at the club, that meant conversion to a limited liability company. With most club members and neutral observers recognising that something had to change at Parkhead, the players' revolt and the disaster at Arthurlie were catalysts for change. The power brokers at Parkhead recognised the shift in opinion and grabbed the opportunity with both hands. What was required was a stratagem to surmount the moral argument put up by the die-hard traditionalist members.

Although the Celts were now out of the Scottish Cup and had already lost the Glasgow Cup to Rangers, there was still the Scottish League, the Glasgow League and the Charity Cup to be won. If the team could be quickly pulled together and with a number of the injured returning to fitness, they were more than capable of salvaging something from the season. In mid-January, the Celts still sat on top of the Scottish League, ahead of Hearts on goal difference both on 24 points, followed by Hibernian and Rangers with only a couple of points separating the top four teams. With only two games left to play in the league programme, there was a long break of six weeks before the first of them, Dundee at Parkhead on 20 February. The Celtic management therefore had at least some breathing space, time to regroup in their attempt to retain the league flag. The first game after their shock exit from the Scottish Cup was a Glasgow League encounter against Clyde at Parkhead on 16 January. The 3–0 defeat by Rangers on 2 January had seen the Celts get off to a bad start in the Glasgow league, but with seven games to be played there was still a long way to go.

As a result of the player clear-out after the Arthurlie debacle, an injection of new blood was urgently required to see the Celtic through what was left of the fixture list. The Glasgow League had already kicked off so a number of young players, Slavin, Conachan, O'Rourke, Carlin, Neilson and Monteith, were promoted into the senior squad from the reserves in an attempt to spark some life into the side. To reinforce the reserves, Willie Maley turned to the Army and a number of players from the Argyll and Sutherland Highlanders, the Highland Light Infantry and the Royal Marine Artillery were drafted in to help fulfil the reserve team's Combination League commitments. Initially things went quite well and the Celts took a commanding lead in the Glasgow League, but from what seemed like an unassailable position they managed to let slip from their grasp what was then seen as a very minor prize. Their worse performance was a 4–0 defeat by Queen's Park at Parkhead.

The Celts also managed to squeeze in a couple of forays into England in mid-February with friendly games at Sunderland and in London against the Corinthians and Woolwich Arsenal. On Thursday 18 February, a special meeting of the general committee convened to discuss a subcommittee report. Over a year previously, John H McLaughlin had announced that the Scottish Cyclists' Union had offered £500 for the use of the club ground for three days in July 1897, provided the cycling track was brought up to international standard. The subcommittee formed to look at the cost of improving the Parkhead stadium's cycling track had now submitted its findings. After the power brokers on the committee read the report, they decided this was just the lever or pretext they were looking for to force the subject of limited liability. They decided to strike while the iron was hot and the club members were summoned to an extraordinary general meeting just six days later.

After a prolonged break, the Scottish League finally got going again on 20 February when the Celtic would face Dundee at Parkhead. It was a crucial game from which they had to take full points if they were to retain the league championship. On the day Celtic's misfortunes continued when minutes before kick-off, John Neilson, already stripped for the game, admitted that he had played a league match for Abercorn against Dundee. The admission meant that he was ineligible to play. Some of the committee were willing to take the chance and play him anyway, but John McLaughlin would not hear of it. A young reserve player, Jimmy Carlin from Paisley, only at the game as a spectator, was ordered to strip. For much of the game Celtic pinned Dundee into their own half of the pitch, but try as they might they could not make their dominance pay with a goal. As the second half ebbed away and the bhoys pressed ever more desperately for a winner, Dundee broke away to score in the very last minute. The sucker punch gave Dundee a 1–0 away win and scuppered the Celtic's chances of retaining the championship flag. The defeat dropped the Celtic back into fourth position in the league behind Hearts, Hibernian and Rangers with one game left to play. The loss of the league championship was yet another bitter blow to the Celtic supporters. The mix-up over the eligibility of John Neilson, the last thing needed at the start of a vital game, was yet another example of mismanagement and added yet more grist to the power broker's mill.

Despite their worries and concerns for the club, the day after the defeat by Dundee, in a show of Irish solidarity, several of the Celtic committee attended a large gathering of the Irish National Amnesty Association held in Glasgow. Over 2000 Glasgow Irish assembled in the Grand National Assembly Hall in the south side of the city to hear speakers demand the release of Irish political prisoners held in English prisons. Most of the Irish nationalist organisations based in Glasgow were represented including most branches of the National League, which had sent delegates. Among the Celtic personalities in attendance were John Glass, Hugh and Arthur Murphy, Mick Dunbar, Pat Welsh, Michael Hughes, Joseph F McGroary and Tim Walls.

To the precipice and beyond

On the night of Thursday 25 February 1897, only around 100 members of the Celtic Football Club assembled in St Mary's Hall, having answered the summons with very little notice. The members were meeting in an atmosphere of despondency having just days earlier suffered yet another disappointment as they watched the Celtic surrender the league flag to Heart of Midlothian. The sporting press were excluded from the meeting and the club secretary was ordered to prepare a report for issue later. On the agenda was nothing less than the future of the Celtic Football and Athletic Club. John Glass presided and announced to the members present that the subcommittee formed to look into the Scottish Cyclists' Union proposal had reported back. The situation was simple enough: the Scottish Cyclists' Union had offered £500 for the use of the stadium, but it could cost £900 to put the track into a fit state to host the World Cycling Championships. John Glass then put the real reason for the meeting before the membership. Despite the relatively healthy state of the club's finances compared to previous years (£600 in debt), those office bearers and guarantors who had taken on personal liability for the club's debts had decided that they were not prepared to take on any more without the protection of limited liability. A number of them had intimated privately that they were prepared to leave the club, at the same time withdrawing all financial support. Some had dropped hints to the press and it was reported in the Scottish Sport that:

> The patience of some of the long-suffering guarantors and in the case of
> at least one of them – a most important one too, he has intimated that he
> will resign his entire connection with the club, rather than enter into the
> increased obligations involved in the improvements without the safeguard
> of a company. This action is not a matter of bluff for his ultimatum has
> been already written and is a serious matter.

The Scottish Sport thought that faced with the alternative of losing their guarantors, who were referred to as "men of sense and substance", or floating a company, the Celtic membership should not hesitate to declare for the company. This was indeed a very serious matter; the men threatening to walk away were in reality the only people capable of running the club, which was now a major enterprise employing a couple of dozen people and generating a very large income, not only for the club but also for the local area. Only they had the free time, the financial independence and, after managing the club for the best part of ten years, the business acumen, footballing and sporting know-how and contacts. Few of the Celtic club members would be able to step into the breach and take over the running of the club. Most were tradesman or labourers, not greatly educated and by necessity working long hours. After a prolonged debate, it was agreed, reluctantly for a large proportion, that a subcommittee be formed to draw up the article of association, which would be put to the membership for their consideration at a later meeting. The subcommittee comprised John Glass, John H McLaughlin, Joe Shaughnessy, Willie Maley, Mick Dunbar and James McKay, all regarded as modernisers. Tom Maley, Michael Hughes and Joseph F McGroary represented the traditionalists, while pragmatists Stephen J Henry and John MacCreadie could be seen as representing the middle ground. Two other members, Mr F Houchin and Mr J Furie, served on the committee, their position regarding the matter are unknown. If the traditionalist members thought they had kicked the subject back into the long grass, they were sadly mistaken. The power brokers had the bull by the horns and were determined not to let go. Again they forced the issue by preparing the document and having it ready for presentation within three days. After consideration by the general committee the scheme for limited liability would be put to the general membership on 4 March.

The fork in the road had finally been reached. The nub of the matter was simple enough: the members were being asked to decide whether the club should remain a community-owned and controlled asset, run by volunteer committees and purely a vehicle for raising charitable funds, or whether it should be converted into a limited liability company owned by shareholders and run by an elected full-time board of directors whose business aim was to make profits for the shareholders. The conundrum for the traditionalist members was not the financial sense of a limited company per se, which most admitted made business sense, but how to safeguard their control of the club and how to ensure any new organisation remained true to the club's founding charitable principles, while at the same time ensuring the club's continued success. In reality, the men best able to ensure the continued success of the club were the moneybags – the very men the traditionalists feared were trying to take over the club for their own financial benefit. Clearly when it came to any share issue those who could afford to buy the most would gain control of the club. On the evening of 4 March 1897 in St Mary's Hall, just yards from the old League of the Cross Hall where it all started almost ten years previously, the Celtic club members gathered to decide the fate of the club. John Glass again presided and announced the nine articles of association: (1) That a limited company be formed, to be called "The Celtic Football and Athletic Co. (Limited)." (2) That the nominal capital of the company be £5000, in 5000 ordinary shares of £1 each. (3) That each present member of the Celtic Football and Athletic Club be entitled on applying therefor to one fully paid up share in the company. (4) That every holder of ten shares in the new company shall be entitled to one vote and every holder of more than ten shares to an additional vote for every ten shares over and above that number.

(5) That each of the present members of the club be entitled to one vote for the fully paid up share to be allocated to him and that the annual subscription of such members shall not exceed five shillings per annum. (6) That the company take over the whole debts and liabilities of the club as at the 1 April 1897, in exchange for which the company shall be entitled to the whole assets thereof. (7) That after paying a 5 per cent per annum dividend, the directors shall have the power to give to such charities as they select such sum or sums as they think proper. (8) The qualification for directorship shall be the holding of one share in the company. (9) That the first directors of the company shall not exceed seven in number.

After some debate over the voting rights where some members, still suspicious of the motives of the moneyed members who they thought were trying to buy the club, the nine articles were unanimously adopted. The articles were then remitted to the general committee, which was instructed to carry out the work for the formation of the new company. It was agreed to hold the next meeting of the club on 6 April when a progress report on the formation of the new company would be submitted. Just when the members thought that the contentious subject had finally been put to bed, a surprise motion was submitted. It was proposed, seconded and agreed to present John Glass with an honorarium of £100 cash and 100 fully paid shares in the new company in recognition of the services rendered by him to the club since its inception. The general committee was also instructed to begin immediately the building of the new track and the question of a paid manager for the new company was considered, but the decision put off until the next meeting of the club.

So the dice was finally cast: faced with the simple choice of losing their guarantors, men of substance and proven business ability, or floating a company, the membership really had no choice. Willie Maley in his 1938 Celtic Jubilee book described the members' options even more starkly: "The matter came to a head at a special meeting in 1896 when, the 'Heads' stated distinctly that the club must be placed on a sound footing or else close down." The offer of a free share worth a pound would also have been a massively attractive incentive for the working class member to vote for a limited company. To a labourer, one pound was a serious amount of money, the equivalent of well over a week's wages. Public opinion on the decision was mixed; in general the sporting press thought the move was inevitable and in the best interests of not just the club but, since the Celtic were major promoters of athletics and cycling, Scottish sport in general. The Catholic Church wasn't so sure. The Church saw the formation of the Celtic company as a betrayal, a hostile takeover of their original idea and the loss of a major source of charitable revenue. Article seven in the company constitution stating that after paying a 5 per cent dividend any charitable donations would be at the prerogative of the directors, rubbed salt into the open wound. To very many of the churchmen it appeared that a group of corporate profiteers had single-handedly turned the charitable foundations on which the club was based into one with completely opposite values based around the accumulation of personal wealth and aggrandisement. The *Man in the Know* thought with Celtic Limited an accomplished fact, the membership should have every reason to be proud of their work. He also thought the honorarium given to John Glass was a bit over the top. While stating that he had the greatest respect for

Mr Glass and admitting that he had been a very hard-working member in the early days of the club, to increase at a stroke the new company's liabilities from £600 to £800 was unfair. He also thought it unfair that equally hard-working members who had done as much were passed over. The additional £200 of debt, so readily accepted when it came to the honorarium for Mr Glass, put the sum that required to be raised for the cycling track improvements into context and reinforced the question mark over the motives of the power brokers at Celtic.

The last of the season's Scottish League games was played on 13 March against St Mirren at Love Street. The match was meaningless with only pride to play for, but the result was a disappointing, if not unsurprising 2–0 defeat at the hands of the Paisley Buddies. The sports hacks decided that St Mirren had not played that well but the transitory Celtic side was even worse. The makeshift Celtic forward line never jelled and missed several chances that may have changed the outcome. In the Celtic defence, Dan Doyle got some little credit, as did Davy Russell and James Kelly. Jamie Conachan got a mention as the best, just, of the poor Celtic forwards. However, Orr, Neilson and Pat Slavin were named and shamed and described as – *miserable*. The loss saw the Celts confirmed in fourth position in the league behind winners Hearts, Hibernian and Rangers. It was the lowest place they had ever occupied at the end of a season. The game also turned out to be the last Scottish League appearance for the Celts' player and legend James Kelly – a few days later he was voted onto the Blantyre School board and a month later became a director of the new Celtic Football and Athletic Company. It was also a bad day for John Glass personally, who had his home broken into while in Paisley with the team. The thieves stole some jewellery and the Second XI cup won by the reserves back in 1891. The Glasgow Observer reported the break-in and sourly commented: "good thing they never got the £100 eh!" The remaining fixtures for March and early April were played out, including a four-day tour in the north of Ireland with games against Cliftonville and Belfast Celtic on their programme. Both resulted in victories for the bhoys and by the time they returned to Glasgow the new cycle track, which had been at the centre of the limited liability debate, was already complete and ready to be signed off by the contractors.

At around eight o'clock on the evening of Tuesday 6 April 1897, the last general meeting of the old Celtic Football and Athletic Club was called to order in the Gallowgate's Annfield Hall. After some discussion and minor amendments, the articles of association were formally adopted and the formal transfer of the old club to the new limited liability company was completed. The Celtic Football and Athletic Club, born out of the beautiful idea that something should and could be done to alleviate at least some of the dire poverty and want in the East End of Glasgow was gone, a victim of its own success. A provisional board of seven directors with the powers to issue shares was elected comprising: JH McLaughlin, John O'Hara, John Glass, Tom Maley, Michael Hughes, Mick Dunbar and James McKay. On a motion from Joe Shaughnessy, it was unanimously agreed to recommend the board to appoint Willie Maley secretary of the company. The first meeting of the new provisional directors would be held on 8 April.

No one could ever accuse the Celtic management of being slow off the mark and the new directors set out their stall for the new business right from the start. The directors immediately turned their attention to the team, which they felt comprised veterans, shirkers, youngsters and cripples. In fact, plans for the new team were already well progressed. John Glass and his lieutenants had begun sounding out targeted players almost immediately after the post mortem on the Arthurlie debacle and there were rumours in the sporting press of big English signings for a new look Celtic team as early as the end of February. The power brokers at Celtic had obviously been confident and anticipating victory over the traditionalists in the limited liability vote. Now in mid-March, the sporting press were informing their readers that the Celtic management was planning dramatic changes to the team and it was the worst kept secret in football that a number of very expensive professionals then playing in England had already been secured. The Celtic directors were winking at the press and dropping hints that the new signings would be in place for the Charity Cup competition due to begin in May. The winds of change also blew through the institution itself. The informal club atmosphere of committees and old boys at Parkhead was quickly swept away as one sports commentator put it: "the Celtic pavilion is becoming more exclusive every match, the man with the friends who once passed them in on a nod, can't pass in himself." Even the most faithful of Celtic supporters, the members of the Celtic Brake Clubs, felt the chill. Within a few weeks of the formation of the new company, the brake clubs became embroiled in a dispute with the new directors over cut-price tickets bought in bulk. Despite the assurances of Mr James Moore, the then secretary of the United Celtic Brake Clubs, who witnessed the exchange, directors John Glass and John McKillop refused to honour a verbal agreement given by James McKay, when secretary of the old club, to sell season tickets to the brake clubs at a reduced price. Despite a prolonged exchange, the directors refused to yield and the Celtic supporters were forced to choose between supporting the team and walking away. Not for the last time while in dispute with the Celtic management, the faithful supporters choose to bite the bullet, placing loyalty to the club and team over principle.

The month of May was largely given over to the charity competition, but the last of Celtic's Glasgow League games spilled over into May. The Glasgow League title normally meant very little to the Celtic, but the penultimate game was against Rangers and that always meant something. On Saturday 1 May the two Glasgow giants clashed at Parkhead. Over 20,000 spectators, a record for the competition, turned out to watch the two clubs' sixth meeting of the season. For the Celtic faithful, it was their first look at some of the Celtic's much-vaunted new Anglo-Scot signings. The Celts paraded four of their new men: Hugh Goldie (Everton), Willie Orr (Preston North End), George Allan (Liverpool) and Adam Henderson (Preston North End). The reappearance of Dan McArthur in the Celtic goal after months on the injury list was welcomed and seen as a good omen, while the new bhoys, who had only arrived in Glasgow the night before, showed no signs of fatigue as they took to the park. The game, played on a blustery May Day, would be one of the Celts' best performances against Rangers over the entire season. The sides were well-matched and the game ended in a fair 1–1 draw, all the new bhoys played well, Dan McArthur was back to his best and Adam Henderson scored Celtic's equaliser on his debut. The Celtic fans left Parkhead hoping a corner had been finally turned and looking forward to the next meeting with their greatest rivals in just over a week's time. The new found optimism would not last long; just two days later 10,000 watched in horror as the new look Celtic were drubbed 4–0 at home by the amateurs of Queen's Park. The final game in the Glasgow League competition was an evening kick-off and the Celtic fielded exactly the same side that achieved the draw with Rangers, but now the team looked tired and uncertain and were completely outclassed in every department. The decisive defeat saw the Celts slip back into third position in the Glasgow League behind the new champions Queen's Park and Rangers. The faithful left Parkhead scratching their heads, what now for Rangers and the Celts' last chance of a trophy, the precious Charity Cup?

By the time of the first round Charity Cup game on 11 May, the Celtic had added yet more new players to the side. Johnny Campbell had been fetched back to Parkhead from Aston Villa bringing with him two of his pals, Jim Welford and Jack Reynolds. The team that would meet Rangers on the day was McArthur; Doyle and Welford; Reynolds, Russell and Orr; and Blessington, Allan, Campbell, King and Henderson. The attendance for the evening game, played at Hampden Park, exceeded all expectations with over 21,000 passing through the turnstiles. The game got off to something of a nervy start with both sets of players anxious not to make an early mistake. From the kick-off Rangers did most of the attacking, but were held at bay by some stout, vigorous tackling from the Celtic backs. After twenty minutes of total dominance, Rangers got their first goal when they broke away from a rare Celtic attack to score. Rangers maintained the pressure and within minutes of the restart McArthur was forced to save from a long-range shot. Almost immediately afterwards another Rangers shot struck the post and with McArthur helpless the rebound was forced across the Celtic goal line taking Ranger's lead to 2–0. The loss of the second goal spurred the Celtic for a few minutes and King fired a fierce shot just over the bar. However, Rangers were soon back on top subjecting the Celtic goal to severe and sustained pressure. Rangers looked set to break through again, but half-time, for them, came too soon. Immediately on the restart, Rangers were back on the attack and within five minutes had a goal ruled off side, struck the Celtic bar and had their forwards miss two easy scoring opportunities. After seven minutes of constant Rangers pressure, Celtic's new left winger, Adam Henderson, broke away, raced up field, skipped passed the final Rangers defender only to be brought down in the box. Jerry Reynolds stepped up to score from the resulting penalty kick to make the score 2–1 to Rangers. Inspired by the goal the Celts came more into the game and for ten minutes or so gave as good as they got. The spectators were enjoying an exciting, keenly contested game with the attacking play flowing from end to end. Unfortunately, the Celtic revival did not last and Rangers were soon back subjecting McArthur's goal to sustained pressure. Rangers got their third goal after Dan Doyle completely missed his kick and the ball went in past a surprised and helpless Dan McArthur. A fourth Rangers goal was scored with around fifteen minutes to go. In what was one of the most one-sided games ever played between the clubs to date, Rangers ran out easy victors by 4–1.

The sore defeat came despite the appearance of the new English "Dons" as they were being termed. In fact, the Celtic side probably contained too many new players, most of who were already burned out after a long English season and whose unfamiliarity told in their disjointed performance. The Daily Record sports hack enthused at Rangers' triumph and thought their performance was "nothing short of marvellous" and "one of the cleverest and most merited victories they had ever achieved". For the Celts, the loss of the Charity Cup, which they had held for the last five years, was a particularly painful blow. To rub salt in the wound, it also meant that Rangers, having already won the Glasgow Cup and Scottish Cup, now had a golden opportunity to equal Celtic's record of three cups in a single season. The triple cup triumph had been achieved by the Celts in the 1891/92 season. Some small consolation for the Celts was to be had when it was announced that the large crowd had produced record gate receipts of over £580 for the charity fund. For the faithful, it was the last of a long list of humiliations at the hands of Rangers that season. Over the course of the season the Celts' record against their greatest rivals was crushingly one sided and made sad reading: played seven, lost four, won none and drawn three.

In mid-May, Rangers crushed Third Lanark by 6–1 to win the Glasgow Merchants' Charity Cup. It had been a wonderful season for the Ibrox men both on and off the park and their financial income for the season for the first time overtook that of the Celtic. This season marked their emergence as the confirmed foremost challenger to Celtic; unfortunately, it would also mark the beginning of the end of the old inter-club friendliness. For the Celtic faithful, the trauma of the 1896/97 football season had one last ignominy: in mid-May the Celts travelled through to the capital to meet Heart of Midlothian in a friendly match. Somehow or other they managed to arrive with a player short. With no travelling reserves, they were forced to ask Hearts to borrow one of their players. The sporting press of course gleefully made the most of the indignity.

So ended the worst season in the short history of the Celtic. In the space of just eight weeks over November 1896 to January 1897 the Celtic team had imploded. Although the signs were there before the rebellion of the Celtic three, the incident was undoubtedly the trigger that set off the explosion. The top players were the super stars of their day and to a large extent the problems that emerged in the 1896/97 season can be seen as a result of a number of these stars adopting an attitude that suggests they thought they were bigger than the club. They thought that their popularity with the fans made them *untouchable*, but their selfish attitude saw a very powerful team, easily capable of sweeping the board of honours, self-destruct. The committee moved swiftly to regain control of the dressing room but it was in the immediate term too little, too late. The team spirit was gone and with it any chance of rescuing the season. JJ Mullen would also be a victim of the axe, being replaced as trainer for the start of the new season by Dan Friel brought in from Third Lanark. Jack went back to Belfast before taking himself off around the world plying his trade. Jimmy Quinn bumped into Jack Mullen in 1913 when his running days were well over; he was working on the Belfast to Ardrossan ferry. The season 1896/97, which had started so full of promise, degenerated into the club's worst to date; they finished fourth in the league with no cups in the cupboard. It was the first season since 1890/91 in which Celtic had failed to win a single honour.

Tammany Hall and its Bosses?

The principal responsibility of the provisional board of directors voted in by the old club membership at the beginning of April was to oversee the mechanics of converting the club into a company including the issuing of shares. The plan initially was to raise £5000 in share capital with 5000 £1 shares. Each of the existing 201 club members were entitled to one share, plus there was the additional 100 shares so generously given to John Glass, making the initial distribution 301 shares. The remaining 4699 shares were offered for sale at ten shillings per share to club members. Inevitably, most went to those who could afford to buy them, the moneybags. Among those members and power brokers who ended up with significant numbers of the first issue were: John Glass (100) (his brother Peter Partick also acquired 200), Joe Shaughnessy (300), James Kelly (200), William McKillop (200), John McKillop (200), James McKillop (100), John H McLaughlin (150), Michael Dunbar (150) (his brother Thomas also took 100), Thomas Colgan (150) (his brother John took 100) and John O'Hara (100). The biggest single acquisition of 400 shares went to James Grant, an engineer based in the north of Ireland, who also owned a number of public houses in Glasgow. Described as a genial Irishman from Co Antrim, he first sat on the Celtic committee in 1896. A year later, another block of 5000 shares would be issued to raise funds for the club, and again the vast majority of the shares went to the same moneyed individuals, who took the opportunity to increase their holdings in the company. When the dust settled, James Grant remained the largest single shareholder with 801 shares, followed by Joe Shaughnessy with 601 and James Kelly with 473. The complex matrix of family and business relationships could also affect the power balance, with Grant being able to call on the 500 shares now held by the Colgan brothers. The McKillop brothers' shareholdings totalled 1300, but fell short of the Grant–Colgan combination by just one share. The Glass brothers could muster 802 shares, while the Dunbar brothers held 550. Some of the ordinary, working class members kept hold of their one share for sentimental reasons, many were passed down the generations and are still framed and hanging in pride of place in many homes throughout the world. Many others were forced to sell their share over the years as life and its travails took their toll. The vast majority of the available shares would coalesce around the same moneyed individuals who had taken the lion's share of both issues. These men would create family dynasties at Parkhead and control the destiny of the Celtic for almost 100 years. As early as mid-June 1897, the worst fears of the traditionalists were becoming very apparent.

In mid-May, the new cement cycling track at Parkhead was formally opened with the Northern Cycling Club's Grand Cycling Carnival. It was a roaring success with over 20,000 spectators rushing through the turnstiles, despite the fact that the final of the Charity Cup was being played at Hampden. More success was to follow just a week later when 30,000 turned up for the Merchants cycling meeting. Over the two weekends, almost £1100 was taken at the gates and the track was largely booked up to the World Cycling Championships at the end of July. The profits from the first month of the new cycling track being opened had more that paid off the Celtic's £400 outlay. Such was the popularity of cycling, in 1897, Glasgow could boast fifty-nine cycling clubs. Those in the know reckoned that the track would prove to be a veritable bonanza to the company, bringing in big revenue during the close season. At the beginning of June, the last balance sheet of the old Celtic club, covering its last eleven and a half months ending 15 April, was issued to shareholders. Despite what was a disastrous season, the results were satisfactory. The gross income amounted to £7851, £2252 less than the previous year. The major source of income was the league and £2699 was taken at home fixtures. Friendly fixtures brought in £889, amateur sports £572 and professional sports £443. Members' subscriptions and season tickets amounted to £313. The largest expenditure items were players' wages at £2931, sports and tracks £752, travel and hotel expenses £524 and honorariums £295; £200 of loans were repaid and £77 was donated to charity. Liabilities balanced out at £1190 including £967 due at the bank. The *Man in the Know* was fairly scathing towards the club members when he commented:

> That a club with an average income of £8000 and such little debt should
> be driven into limited liability, does not say much for the members who
> allowed such a thing to occur. However, as the bulk of the members by
> their own action have deprived themselves of having the slightest say in
> the company's management, they will have plenty of time to repent their
> action.

His comments were a bit unfair since earlier he felt the articles of association and the voting system in particular was a fair one. It is interesting to compare the end of season revenues for the other senior Glasgow clubs: Rangers £10,156, Queen's Park £5,740, Third Lanark £3, 656 and Clyde £2,269. It is also interesting to note that for the first half of the season the Celtic received £5,850 and in the second half only £2,039, less than half the amount of the opening portion and probably the real cost of the player revolt and the lack of discipline in the dressing room. The seal was set on the season when at the beginning of July the Lord Provost presented the Glasgow Charity Cup to Rangers. Willie McKillop, representing Celtic, watched heavy hearted as the prize that had been in the Celtic's possession for the last five years was formally surrendered. In what was the Ibrox side's greatest season to date, they now had the big three cups adorning their trophy room. Colonel Merry, in his capacity as chairman of the charity committee, announced that as a result of the season's competition £1400 had been disbursed amongst the various charities. Since the start of the competition in the 1876/77 season a grand total of £17,860 had been distributed.

In mid-June the first AGM of the new Celtic Football and Athletic Company took place in the Annfield Hall. There was little business to discuss, the last financial statement of the old club was read and it was noted with some satisfaction that the major portion of the liabilities of the old club, including the £967 due to the bank, had been paid off. It was the first opportunity for the new shareholders to flex their muscles and a new board of directors, which reflected the new power brokers in the company, was voted in. The new board were: Mick Dunbar (514 votes), John Glass (493), James Grant (486), James Kelly (473), John McKillop (470), John H McLaughlin (461) and John O'Hara (417). Out went the traditionalist representatives, Tom Maley with 112 votes and Michael Hughes with sixty-three. James MacKay was also voted off mustering 150 votes. In came James Grant, John McKillop and James Kelly. John H McLaughlin was voted into the position of chairman and unashamedly gave a short speech predicting great prosperity for the new company. The first action of the new board was to formally appoint twenty-nine-year-old Willie Maley secretary of the new Celtic Limited Company on a salary of £150 per annum. He would hold the position for the next forty odd years, becoming in the process a Celtic legend. He was also given an honorarium of £40, as was James McKay for past service to the club. So that was that, the outcome towards which John Glass, John H McLaughlin, Joe Shaughnessy and William McKillop had been working for years had finally been realised. The *Man in the Know* thought the new board was just what would be expected and alluded to backstairs deals: "Two of those rejected (Tom Maley and James McKay) had years of service to recommend them, but this availed nothing against the methods which reminded one of the Tammany Hall and its bosses."

The new office bearers and directors were, depending on your opinion on limited liability, either visionaries, examples of an increasingly successful, business-oriented, socially mobile, professional Glasgow Irish middle class, who saw the potential of the club and were determined to maximise that potential, or, as the Roman Catholic Church and those who opposed the move saw them, moneybags, betrayers of their community, men who would line their own pockets while taking the bread from the mouths of hungry children. It is interesting to compare the occupations or professions of the office bearers of the first Celtic committees and the first board of the limited liability company. The former comprised a doctor, lawyers, teachers, pawnbrokers, a hairdresser, a builder and a cooper. The first Celtic Football and Athletics Company board famously consisted of six publicans and one glass (John Glass).

Realisation of what they had been force to do also dawned for very many of the old members, their doubts and fears were expressed by the *Man in the Know*:

> *Though the vast majority of the old members are not at all satisfied with the selection, they only have themselves to blame, in handing over the club to a few moneyed individuals they cut a rod to beat themselves and now must endure the whipping with the best grace they can muster.*

From the modernisers' side of the fence, the move to limited liability status appeared a natural progression, the next logical step in the continuous evolution and advancement of the club. The Celtic club in fact was only following a trend already well-established in England of successful clubs being converted into limited companies. The company status allowed the directors to raise sums of money, never before imagined, to invest in the club without the sword

Lord Newlands

of Damocles hanging over the heads of the guarantors. The prime example of this came just eight months after becoming a limited company, when at the December meeting of shareholders the Celtic management announced that they were deep in negotiations with their landlord Sir James Hosier over the purchase of the land on which the Celtic stadium was built. The directors stated that an additional £5,000 worth of shares would need to be issued to help fund the purchase. Hosier, titled Lord Newlands, had no intention of selling the land and the Celtic's lease still had years to run, but sensing the eagerness of the Celtic, perhaps with old ghosts breathing down immigrant necks, he agreed to sell the land at an exorbitant £10,000. The price was far beyond the real value of what had been a water-filled clay hole and many shareholders were willing to move yet again, but John Glass, the main instigator of the plan, was willing to pay the massively inflated price to gain the freehold from the Master Mason. It was the last time the Celtic would suffer the avarice of a landlord, but Lord Newlands took his pound of flesh.

There is little doubt that the Celtic power brokers held a gun to the heads of the membership when they threatened to walk away from the club in March 1897. The question is where would their departure have left the Celtic club? There must be some grave doubt as to whether the Celtic club could have survived as a major force in the Scottish game in the long term had the members called their bluff. That the Celtic had a large and passionately loyal fan base there is no doubt and by 1897 the club had already established its own corporate identity, which in itself was a powerful draw in an age of altruism. However, the problem was not simply the financial viability of the club, but it was who among the Glasgow Irish had the interest, the time, the financial independence and the business and footballing expertise to step into the breach. In the interim, the club may have closed down while a new management team was assembled. If new office bearers and committee did manage to pick up the reins, perhaps under the leadership of Tom Maley and Joe Nelis, the development of the club would almost certainly have stagnated. Amateurs would have been managing the Celtic club on a part-time basis at a time when the game itself was progressing and developing and morphing into an arm of the booming entertainment industry. Had the club brought in outside, non-Glasgow Irish expertise, much of the club's Catholic and Irish identity would have gone and with it much of what tied the fan base to the club. That the club would have survived in some form there is little doubt, but the Celtic club in the form we know it would not have existed. With the loss of the most powerful engine of change that was the Celtic club, Rangers FC would in all probability also have stagnated. With the loss of the country's two most powerful clubs and their intense rivalry, who knows how the Scottish game would have developed over the next century. During the Charity Cup presentation ceremony in July 1897, Colonel Merry, the veteran chairman of the charity committee made a very telling statement when he commented on the changing state of the game since the inception of the Merchant's Charity Cup in 1876, "football is no longer a pastime; rather it has become a huge, commercial undertaking". Within just a few years of the Celtic's move to limited liability status, most major Scottish clubs had followed their lead; Rangers FC converted in May 1899.

The Celtic Football and Athletics Company Ltd

For the Celtic faithful, after the disasters of 1896/97, the start of the new 1897/98 season could not come quick enough. By August 1897, considerable sums of money had been spent on assembling a new Celtic team, resulting in an illustrious squad of internationally renowned players christened the *English Dons*, who assembled for pre-season training at Parkhead. The club had appointed long-term club secretary, Willie Maley, as its new full-time manager and Dan Friel had been brought in from Third Lanark as the new trainer tasked with maintaining discipline in the dressing room. There was to be no repetition of the player revolt or the Arthurlie fiasco. Perhaps the expectations were just too high, for despite some successes the season proved to be something of a disappointment. The Scottish League was won for the fourth time with the Celts going through the eighteen-game fixture list without a single defeat and conceding only thirteen goals, but none of the coveted cups were won. An early exit in the second round of the Scottish Cup beaten 3–2 by Third Lanark was a particular disappointment. The premier Scottish prize had last been won by the bhoys way back in the heady days of 1892. The faithful consoled themselves with winning the Scottish league championship and convinced themselves that the team needed time to gel.

On 31 May 1898, the Celtic Football and Athletic Club Limited published its first full yearly report: income £16,267, a record for a British football club, expenditure £14,872 with balance £1395. The receipts from football alone amounted to £9600 with players' wages absorbing £3500. That season additional ground improvements and extensions cost £4453. A dividend of twenty per cent was declared and £105 was voted for directors' fees. If the new directors thought they would be applauded for the massive dividend they were mistaken. According to the *Man in the Know* the announcement caused widespread grumbling among the members, who wanted just five per cent and demanded that the remainder be given to charity. He thought people strange: the directors had given over £529 to the dividend while £230 had been raised for charity. He added: "I think charity and its objectives have not been forgotten." Given the spectacular end of year results, the miniscule outstanding debts and undoubted financial viability of the old club were brought sharply into prospective. The results increased suspicions as to the motivation of the power brokers who had driven the move to limited company status. The colossal twenty per cent dividend was a massive public relations disaster for the new directors. The difference between twenty per cent and five per cent would mean very little to the ordinary club member with his one share, but not so for the moneybags with hundreds of shares, who made a killing.

Season 1898/99 proved to be another let-down for the hard to please Celtic faithful; the Scottish League was lost with the Celts falling back into third place, but the Glasgow League was won. The much-treasured Charity Cup was recaptured from Rangers, with a 2–0 win at Ibrox, but the bhoys were knocked out of the Glasgow Cup, beaten 2–1 at Celtic Park by Rangers. The highlight of the season was undoubtedly the victory over Rangers that saw the Scottish Cup back at Parkhead at last. A crowd of 25,000 turned up at Hampden Park on 22 April to watch only the second ever 'Old Firm' Scottish Cup final. The Celts just edged the best of the play in what was a dour midfield struggle over the course of the first half. At half time the sides went into the pavilion with the score still 0–0. Ten minutes or so after the restart, the Celts went into the lead thanks to a headed goal from Sandy McMahon. Twenty minutes later Johnny Hodge scored a second. Rangers claimed he was offside but the referee dismissed their appeals. Celtic held on to their two-goal lead to run out winners and claim the Scottish Cup for only the second time in the club's history. The winning side was McArthur, Welford, Storrier, Battles, Marshall, King, Hodge, Campbell, Divers McMahon and Bell. Like the proverbial Glesga bus, you wait ages for one and another comes along right after. After a wait of seven years, the Celtic retained the Scottish Cup the following season by beating Queen's Park 4–3 at Ibrox. The forward line was unchanged from the previous cup winning side, but the new line up in defence was McArthur, Storrier, Battles, Russell, Marshall and Orr. The Celtic's record for the 1898/99 season was played sixty, won forty, drew twelve and lost just eight.

At the AGM of June 1899, the Celtic board declared an income of £15,380, somewhat less than the previous record breaking year, but with a balance of £1395 the directors were able to issue an impressive dividend of ten per cent. The Glasgow Observer commented:

> There is no doubt that the Celtic Club just now is being ably and economically managed, and indeed the future prospects are so good that any shares which come into the market are being snapped up at a pretty smart premium.

That the new directors and major shareholders did very well financially out of the Celtic company is beyond doubt. In addition to very healthy returns on their shareholdings, the annual bonuses for the directors were also well worth having. However, much of the profit came from the cult of the Celtic itself. In addition to extracting dividends and fees, the spin-offs from being Celtic personalities, mainly in the form of pulling clientele into their pubs and businesses, were very lucrative indeed. The motivation and altruism of the first directors would be very touchy subjects at Parkhead for the next sixty years or so as the questions cascaded down the generations and onto the shoulders of their descendants. The Celtic power brokers were also making advances in Scottish football's corridors of power. For years the Celts had been shamefully overlooked on the various Associations, but now there was a reaction and that summer saw John H McLaughlin elected president of the SFA: John Glass, president of the GFA, and Willie Maley, secretary of the new Inter-City league. The Celtic team would continue to misfire over the next few seasons while the new professional organisation at Parkhead bedded itself in. The practice of spending large sums on established stars would fall by the wayside and Willie Maley would introduce a policy of nurturing home-grown talent. The scheme would take some time to come to fruition, but the practice would prove its worth and would stand the club in good stead for many years.

It is worth pausing at this point to consider the charitable ethos of the new limited liability company. On conversion, the new Celtic management team immediately set about putting the club firmly on a commercial footing. The *raison d'être* had changed from charitable fund-raising to making profits for the new shareholders. However, irrespective of that fact, the directors were living and operating in an age of civic responsibility and philanthropy and could not have ceased charitable contributions entirely, even if they wanted to. In addition, over the previous ten years the club's office bearers, now largely the company's directors, had vociferously trumpeted the charitable ethos of the club, so much so that the Celtic club and charity were even then pretty much synonymous. What did change, and in fact had already begun to do so prior to the conversion, was how the Celtic management in the main delivered the charity. Instead of handing over cash sums to the various good causes, the team, or individual players or indeed the football ground itself, were used as tools to raise money. The Celtic team coming to play at a local park, a star player turning up to draw a raffle or the free use of Celtic Park was at least as lucrative for the good cause as a £10 or £20 cash donation sent from the club. The Celtic had always played charity games, but this became the rule of thumb for the new Celtic company when it came to charity: what made best business sense or what was more convenient or practical, sending £10 or taking a Celtic side to play a game? If they chose to play the game, the team itself may achieve some gain, by trialling new players, testing players coming back from injury, etc. The Celtic management were also relieved of the workload of organising and staging the event, and handling and distributing the funds.

Just a fortnight after the new company came into being, the Celtic went to Belfast where on 20 April they played a friendly match against Belfast Celtic, the proceeds of which went to the Sisters of Mercy's Mater Infirmorium Hospital in Belfast. On 4 July, Celtic went to Kilsyth to play a charity game for one of their own. Alex Drain from Kilsyth had played for the Celtic reserves on a number of occasions, but failed to make the grade. A miner to trade, he turned out for the East Stirlingshire team while working the pits at Kilsyth. In mid-June, his back was broken during a cave-in at the pit and he was not expected to survive. The Celts took a full strength team to Kilsyth to play the benefit for his family of five children. The area was home to very many Glasgow Irish and a sizable crowd turned out to watch their favourites. A fortnight or so later, the Celtic took a full strength team through to Broxburn to play another benefit game. This time, the game was played in aid of a young miner blinded in an explosion in the pit. At the beginning of September, in the middle of a very busy week at the start of the new 1897/98 season, the Celtic went down to Greenock to play a match in aid of St Mary's RC school, Greenock. A strong Celtic side played a local select at Morton's Cappielow ground and a large crowd enjoyed the bhoys' 3–2 victory. Throughout the season the Celtic played a number of friendlies, usually in aid of some good cause or other, while two of the last games of the season would be in aid of Catholic charities, one played at Parkhead for James Kelly's old village church in Renton and the final game saw the Celts trek all the way to Aberdeen to aid the Catholic Charity Association. An example of just how lucrative a Celtic charity match could be, can be seen in August 1898. The directors sanctioned the Celtic reserve team to play a select side from the giant Singer's Factory at Clydebank. One of the employees at the factory had died suddenly and the game would be played for the benefit of his widow and children. The match was played gratis at Celtic Park and a very considerable £50 was raised for the family. Under the old club arrangements, it is most unlikely that such a sum would have been donated to a widow's charity fund. The Celtic did of course continue to send occasional cash donations to good causes when it was more convenient. In March 1898 the directors donated £25 to an Irish Relief Fund when famine again visited the west of Ireland. One of the worst affected areas was that of Pettigo, Co Donegal, ancestral home of future Celtic stalwart, Hugh Hilley. The fund would help the starving and destitute of the west of Ireland to make a new start; many went to the Americas, but some, like the Hilley family, preferred to make the short trip across the North Channel to Scotland.

'Nothing succeeds like success'. 'Mr. Secretary Maley: "Leave this to me"'.
Scottish Sport, 24 August 1900

Scottish Sport August 1900

The Celtic Football and Athletic Club Ltd over the following decade or so became the wealthiest, most powerful team in Scotland and the most successful team in Great Britain. Playing attractive, entertaining football, the various Celtic football teams achieved undreamt of success on the field, but their success was underpinned by a single-minded, at times ruthless, approach to the business side of the game. Driven by its chairmen John H McLaughlin and later James Kelly and the board of directors, the Celtic club acquired a reputation for astute and ruthless business practices. Never behind the business curve, the Celtic committeemen and later the directors were consistently at the forefront of innovation and change as they strove to maximise income streams. This ranged from professional athletics and cycling, to floodlights and state-of-the-art tracks, to hiring special trains and renting out the stadium and the tracks, to the installation of the first press box with dedicated telephones for reporters.

In 1906 the directors allowed the first concession at Parkhead when they agreed to a score of boys from the Cameo store in Cathcart, bedecked in Celtic colours, to sell cigarettes, fruit and confectionary to the crowd. Scotch pies and Bovril would come much later, but you always had to bring your own kerry-oot of McEwan's Pale Ale, Guinness or Tennent's lager. Within just four years of moving to their new ground, the stadium itself was bringing considerable sums into the club. Such was the success of the club's sports meetings, very large crowds regularly made their way to Parkhead to what was considered to be among the best athletics events in the whole of Britain. The Celtic directors' well-deserved reputation for business acumen among the hard-headed businessmen of the day, fully complemented their club's footballing reputation. Having said that, business foresight was sadly lacking when in May 1904 the Grandstand and Pavilion at Parkhead burned down. Unfortunately, the £6000 structure and fittings were only insured for £2000. The directors decided not to have it replaced but instead erected a covered standing area that would in time become a Parkhead legend in its own right, the famous or infamous "Jungle". Another bad business idea was the Grant Stand, a two-storey construction built at his own expense by director James Grant. The stand was opened in October 1899 by Councillor John Ferguson, but proved to be something of a white elephant. Built with a large glass frontage, the windows often steamed up and became something of a standing joke. James Grant eventually offloaded it to Celtic a few years later at a considerable personal loss.

Over the first twenty-five years of its existence, the Celtic club had not only cemented its place as the leading club in Scotland but also one of the leading clubs in the whole of Great Britain. In 1903, the club changed its shirt from vertical stripes to the now world-famous green and white hoops. In 1904 the bhoys took the hoops to a wider audience when they became the first Scottish club to tour Europe where they got a wonderful reception. Over the period they won eight Scottish Cups, eleven League Championships, including six in a row between seasons 1904 and 1910, nine Glasgow Cups and eleven Glasgow Charity Cups. Season 1907/08 was the greatest yet for the Celts when they won every competition entered. It would be almost sixty years before the Parkhead faithful would see the same feat not only repeated, but also in terms of achievement surpassed with the capture of the European Cup in 1967. The club established a reputation for playing fast, attacking, attractive football, a reputation that it still enjoys to this day. The success of the Glasgow Irish club was not always applauded quite as generously as it might have been by those close to home, but the club was widely admired and celebrated outwith west central Scotland. Football played the *Celtic way* ensured the team was in great demand and regularly toured the country playing friendly and exhibition matches. On one occasion while playing in England they were billed as the *Greatest Team on Earth*.

A number of the players who graced the Celtic colours in the club's formative years became legends: James Kelly, Neil McCallum, Johnny Campbell, Peter Dowds, John Madden, Sandy McMahon, Jimmy Blessington, Dan McArthur and the immortal Dan Doyle all entered Celtic folklore. Likewise, the players of the first truly great Celtic team, which straddled the first decade of the new century and won six League championships in a row between 1904 and 1910, also became legends in their own lifetimes and immortals in the Celtic Hall of Fame: Davie Adams, Willie Orr, Willie Loney, Alex Bennett (the first man to score while wearing the green and white hoops), Jimmy Hay, Davie Hamilton, Donny McLeod and Peter Somers all still live on in the folk memories of the Parkhead faithful.

As the Celtic Football Club approached its quarter century, most of the founding fathers of the club, Irish Nationalist almost to a man, were now gone, some at a relatively young age. Dr

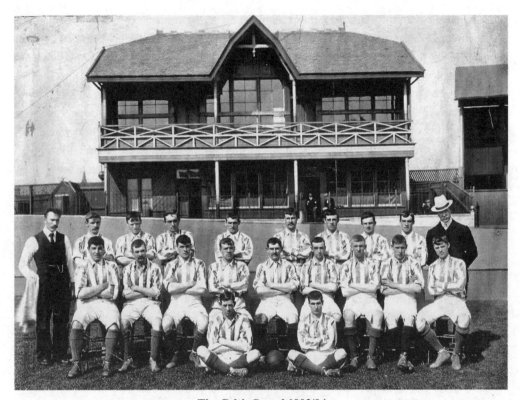

The Celtic Squad 1903/04

John Conway the first honorary president died aged 35, Hugh Darroch, the club's first treasurer aged just 32, Hugh Murphy in 1903, John O'Hara in 1905. Michael Davitt, John Glass, Joseph Shaughnessy and the leader of the Glasgow Irish John Ferguson all passed in 1906. Frank Havlin, the working-class members' champion and bane of the office bearers also died in 1906, predeceasing his old adversary John H McLaughlin by three years. John H McLaughlin died in 1909 after twenty-two years of service to the club, twelve years as chairman. Celtic legend Tom Maley called the Scottish Football League his monument. Only one element of the club's success story could perhaps be seen as a disappointment: since the club's transfer to a limited company in 1897 the club had donated just £2000 in cash to good causes. Although, over the same period the team played innumerable charity matches and the directors gave freely and often of their time and their wallets, thus helping to raise considerable sums for all kinds of good causes. The Scottish football club with a distinct and proudly Irish Catholic flavour was already a Glasgow institution. With the origins of the club so distinctly Irish, it became a tradition that any Catholic Irishman passing through Glasgow went to see the Celtic play. That tradition of Irish support is continued today with thousands of Irish supporters regularly travelling to Glasgow to watch the Celtic.

By the eve of the Great War, the Celtic Football Club, a Scottish team based in Glasgow, playing their football in Scotland and comprising mostly Scottish players, was still regarded by most people, certainly in west central Scotland, as an Irish team. The reason for this was simply because over the course of twenty-five years the Celtic Football Club itself had emerged as a definition of Irishness and was the single greatest ethno-cultural focus for its Irish and Glasgow Irish supporters. For the consciously Irish, Catholic community in Glasgow, the club provided a sense of their own identity. The general public's perception of and grudging attitude to the success of the Celtic club, whose directors were all Irish or Scots-Irish Roman Catholics, was a reflection of the enmity long endured by the Glasgow Irish community as a whole. The football club's cultural and religious heritage and the political beliefs of its founding fathers and the vast majority of its supporters ensured it was regarded by the Scottish establishment with barely disguised animosity and suspicion, particularly when it came to the politics of Ireland and particularly regarding Irish Home Rule. As the very high profile standard bearer of the Glasgow Irish, the attitudes experienced by the Celtic club in many ways reflected the ambiguous position of the Glasgow Irish in Scotland and the Irish nation as part of the Union of Great Britain and Ireland. Irrespective of that fact, by 1913, such was the force generated by the Celtic's sporting success, supported by their massive fan base, both the Scottish footballing and wider Scottish community would just have to come to terms with the fact that led by the Celtic Football Club, the Glasgow Irish community had emerged from the shadows and were now demanding their rightful place in the sun.

Chapter Six

The Gathering Storms

The Storm in Europe

In the last decades of the nineteenth century and the first of the twentieth, a number of major political changes took place in continental Europe. Prussia's victory under its Iron Chancellor, Otto Von Bismarck, in the Franco-Prussian War of 1870–71, upset the delicate balance of power that had kept Europe broadly at peace since Waterloo in 1815. The crushing defeat of the French in just eight weeks saw Paris besieged, starved and then captured. In the subsequent peace settlement, the French were humiliated, suffering the loss of two provinces, Alsace and Lorraine, and made to pay an enormous cash indemnity of five billion francs to the victors. As a direct result of the victory, Bismarck was able to fulfil his ambition to unify the separate German states under the leadership of Prussia and to see Germany emerge as the most powerful nation on mainland Europe. The Franco-Prussian War certified the army as the agent and symbol of Germany's national destiny, and it ensured that soldiers would enjoy elite status in the state that emerged out of the conflict.

In the years that followed the victory over France, the new Germany rapidly industrialised and by 1900 had surpassed Great Britain as the most powerful industrial nation in Europe. The German industrial base was staggering; in just thirty years steel production had multiplied by twelve, coal by five, manufacturing by four and exports had multiplied by a factor of three. It was by far the most advanced nation in the world in the new field of chemical production. Much of its new wealth was invested in infrastructure including a superb railway system. Over the same period, under Prussian influence, militarism was institutionalised in the Imperial German state, shown in the immense influence and prestige that the army commanded in German politics and society. The disciplined military ethos permeated almost every facet of German society from schools, to workplace and sport and social clubs. Most German public holidays or festivals took on a military flavour with the German national holiday held on Sedan Day, celebrating the victory over the French in 1871. The German army on full mobilisation was a colossal five million men and was almost entirely free from civilian political control and matters of command, military planning, personnel, organization, training, and justice remained in practice the exclusive prerogatives of the army's commander-in-chief, the German Keiser. The powers of the German parliament (Reichstag) were limited to approving the military budget. Despite the fiercely nationalistic nature of German society, like elsewhere in Europe, social unrest threatened the stability of the German state as the working classes became organized and increased their representation in parliament. Fear of German industrial and its military might also forced socialist France, with an aging population of around forty million, to seek an unlikely alliance with reactionary Czarist Russia. This resulted in an agreement that they would come to each other's aid in the event either was attacked by Germany.

In response to the Franco-Russian military pact of 1894, the Germans were forced to consider and plan for an attack by these nations simultaneously. Germany's solution to the spectre of a war on two fronts was devised by Count Alfred von Schlieffen, Chief of the German General Staff from 1891 to 1906. His recommended counter was simply to attack first. Germany recognised that it was not strong enough to combat both countries at the same time, therefore the plan relied on Germany's ability to defeat either individually but that country had to be defeated quickly before the other could come to the aid of its ally. He recommended that the French should be tackled first, believing that monolithic Russia would need six weeks to fully mobilise and launch an offensive. The Germans believed that if they could repeat their success in the Franco-Prussian war of 1870–71 when they crushed France in just thirty-three days, the bulk of the German army could then be rushed to the eastern front to confront the Russians. Curiously, the German war planners barely considered the implications of the involvement of Great Britain, despite her being regarded as Germany's biggest obstacle to attaining the status of a world power.

Among their spoils of victory from the Franco-Prussian War, the Germans annexed the French/German frontier provinces of Alsace and Lorraine. Count Schlieffen, well aware of the intensity of French feeling over the lost territory, surmised (correctly) that in the event of war the French would first move to retake their lost provinces. He built this supposition into his plan and proposed a German fighting withdrawal on the frontier, while a massive right hook, composed of the bulk of the German army, swept through neutral Belgium and into France, bypassing on either side of Paris to take the French forces being drawn into Alsace and Lorraine from the rear. The plan could be likened to a revolving door: if somebody pressed heavily on one side, the other would swing round to hit him on the back. A vital component of Schlieffen's plan was that the right wing of the armies must bypass Paris to the west with the "right sleeve of the right hand man brushing the channel". He estimated the campaign would take thirty-nine days and much would depend on the vaunted German railway system's ability to move men and materiel quickly and efficiently.

In 1914, Great Britain had for one hundred years been the sole and undisputed global superpower and was the possessor of the greatest Empire the world had ever seen. Her possessions straddled the globe and at its zenith included nearly a quarter of the land surface and one quarter of the world's population. The British diaspora largely populated colonial America, Canada, Australia and New Zealand. With colonies and naval bases on every continent, through the might of the Royal Navy, the long arm of British political influence was felt worldwide. Great Britain's imperial power was at its zenith, but after two vicious little wars with the Boer farmers, its thirst for colonies had abated and the empire was being viewed more as an economic block. On the run up to war Britain was no longer the world's leading industrial country. From the 1870s, Britain's industrial and commercial strength had declined relative to the United States of America and Imperial Germany and both nations had overtaken Britain industrially. However, Britain bolstered by being the world's banker and by a booming shipbuilding industry remained the leading power in the world thanks to its financial resources, productive capacity, imperial possessions and the might of the Royal Navy.

At the forefront of British strategic thinking on Europe was Belgium and the Low Counties or more specifically their channel ports. In 1839, Britain and the other major European powers including Prussia (Germany) signed a treaty guaranteeing Belgian neutrality. High on Britain's list of considerations for doing so was to safeguard the Belgian ports. The ports were vital to Britain's military and commercial interests since they could be used as a springboard for invasion and were important gateways into Europe for trade. In 1898 and 1900 an increasingly belligerent Imperial Germany passed Navy Bills, which meant it could build a battle fleet that would undermine the global supremacy of the British Royal Navy. This antagonised and threatened Great Britain and resulted in a naval arms race between them. Britannia had ruled the waves unopposed since Napoleonic times; however, although it still possessed the most powerful navy in the world, much of its fleet was spread across the oceans of the world, protecting its vast empire and trade routes. Control of home waters was a matter of national survival for the British: immediately prior to the outbreak of the war Britain imported sixty per cent of its food. A powerful German fleet in the North Sea, which could outgun the British Home Fleet, left Britain open to blockade and starvation or invasion by a massive German army, which it could not possibly match in size.

The British had not been involved militarily in Europe since the Crimea in 1854–6, but the conflict with Russia was confined to a very small and distant area. For the most part, the British were content to leave the Europeans to squabble among themselves as long as no one nation completely dominated. Now one nation was dominant and increasingly belligerent as Germany began to flex its military muscle demanding its place in the sun and its share of the spoils of empire. The Germans, coming late to the game of imperialism, had already caused diplomatic problems for the French in Morocco in 1905 and again in 1911 in an attempt to gain African colonies. The Germans had also managed to antagonise the British by supporting the Boers during the war in South Africa, persuading Britain that Germany and not its historic enemy France, was its current and greatest threat. This decision saw Britain ally itself with its two old adversaries, Russia and France. The *Entente Cordiale* of 1904 saw Britain and France reinforce diplomatic and later military links, smoothing the way for similar links with Russia in 1907. By the beginning of 1914, the major European nations stood in two opposing camps: Britain, France and Russia known as the *Triple Entente* on one side, and Germany, Austria-Hungary and Italy known as the *Triple Alliance* on the other. Any incident involving any of these countries would see a chain reaction, dragging all the nations, like prisoners manacled together at the ankles, into war.

On St Vitus Day, 28 June 1914, in the Bosnian capital, Sarajevo, a consumptive nineteen-year-old Bosnian student assassinated the heir presumptive to the Austro-Hungarian throne. The assassin was part of a disparate Serbian nationalist gang (the Black Hand), organised by Serbian military intelligence. Archduke Ferdinand and his wife Sophie were being driven from an official reception when Gavrilo Princip stepped off the pavement and fired the fatal shots into the official car killing both royals. It was their wedding anniversary. Archduke Ferdinand represented the once great, but now in terminal decline Austro-Hungarian Empire. Headed by its eighty-four-year-old Emperor Franz Josef, this ancient empire was made up of a conglomerate of states populated by German, Slavic and Italian peoples. The ailing empire had been held together for decades largely by loyalty to the ruling Hapsburg dynasty. The court comprised over seventy archdukes and archduchesses with old Franz Josef as feudal chief and head of the family. The empire was more like a medieval feudal kingdom and the populations more akin to tenants on the vast estates of the ruling nobles. Prior to the unification of Germany under Bismarck, Austria as the major Germanic power, dominated the collection of smaller states that made up the German Confederation. In 1866 Austria and Prussia went to war in a dispute regarding Schleswig-Holstein. The Prussians defeated the Austrians in just seven weeks and from then on assumed the role of the senior Germanic state. During the first decade of the twentieth century, the Austro-Hungarian's were flexing military muscle they no longer possessed in an area that is now known as the Balkans. The region was extremely volatile, populated by many different ethnic groups including the Serbs, a Slavic race closely related to the Russians. Each group harboured ancient enmities against the others going back centuries. Serbia was an independent and expanding state that had only recently doubled its territory after a successful war against another ailing empire, that of the Ottoman Turks, which had dominated the region since the late Middle Ages. The withdrawal of the Ottoman Turks left a power vacuum into which both the Austro-Hungarians and the Russians, through their Slavic cousins the Serbs, wished to step.

In 1908 Austria-Hungary arbitrarily annexed Serbia's neighbour, Bosnia-Herzegovina, in a sudden move that antagonised both Serbia and Russia. The Russians wanted to back their Slavic brothers, but Germany sided with their Austrian cousins, told the Russians to accept the annexation and to warn Serbia to calm down. If not, Austria-Hungary would attack Serbia with full German support. The Russians, still recovering from the disastrous Russo-Japanese War of 1904–5, were unprepared for such a conflict and backed down. The fiercely independent and, as a result of their successful recent conflicts, highly antagonistic Serbs were furious; they had dreams of a Slavic federation in the region and resented Austrian influence and interference in their backyard. Serbia felt the large Slavic population of Bosnia-Herzegovina should be ruled by a greater Serbia and control of the country would also give the landlocked Serbs much needed access to ports on the Adriatic. The assassination of Archduke Ferdinand was both a show of solidarity with the Slavs of Bosnia-Herzegovina and a declaration of intent aimed at Austria-Hungary and Turkey. The shot Gavrilo Princip fired into the Archduke's limousine is often called "the fuse that set Europe ablaze"; that is a slight exaggeration but the assassination certainly did not help the situation. What it did was to provide the excuse for Austria-Hungary to slap down the upstart Serbians and cement its own influence in the region. Princip's bullet was also called "the first shot of the war". Interestingly, the registration number of the Archduke's car was A. 111118. This could also be read as 11.11.18, the date the last shot of the war in Europe would be fired.

At the beginning of the twentieth century, to most people the name *Turkey* meant the exotic decadence of the infidel Turk, of Christian slavery, kasbahs and harems. Those more learned thought of the vast but declining Ottoman Empire, then known as the *Sick man of Europe*. The Ottoman Empire once comprised mainland Turkey, its possessions in the Balkans, which in the north almost reached Vienna, the Dodecanese Islands and the coastal regions of the Arabian subcontinent, which in the west included Israel, Syria, Libya, part of Arabia and Yemen. In the east, the Turks held sway over the Persian Gulf, Iraq and the Emirates. Six hundred years of expansion had resulted in a vast empire populated by a great mixture of nationalities and races. There were Arabs, Armenians, Kurds, Persians and Serbians all with different cultures, languages and religions, most of whom were extremely difficult to control, each having their own national and religious aspirations. In 1908, a revolution instigated by the Committee of Union and Progress, better known as the *Young Turks*, based in Salonika and with the support of the Turkish military, forced the despotic Sultan into constitutional change and to establish an elected Chamber of Deputies. Between 1908 and 1914, the Young Turks progressively gained more power and influence, usually as a result of some national emergency. However, Turkey continued to slide into decline, with major revolts in Arabia in 1908 and by the Albanians and Kurds in 1909. Despite their best efforts the Young Turks could not prevent significant swathes of the Empire being lost through nationalist ambition and foreign expansionism. This humiliation led to a virtual Young Turk dictatorship, and from January 1913, the Young Turks assumed absolute power in a bankrupt Turkey.

Recognising Turkey's strategic importance, the Germans carefully fostered relations with Turkey, including the formation of a German Military Mission to help organise and train the Turkish army and state visits in 1889 and 1898 by the Kaiser himself helped to nurture the relationship. German diplomats in Constantinople were instructed to maintain close personal ties with the major players in the Young Turk government and to reinforce at every opportunity German support for the regime. Relations between the British government and the Young Turk government were at best cool. British public opinion, which supported Turkey against Russia in the Crimea, had tired of what they now saw as a corrupt, despotic and cruel country with an appalling record of atrocities against their minority groups, particularly the Christian Armenians. Although British influence in Constantinople was on the wane, the Turks still greatly admired the Royal Navy and in what was a major capital expenditure for Turkey, two new battleships were being built in England for the Turkish Navy. The ships, the *Sultan Osman* and the *Meschedieh*, would be ready by August 1914 and their future Turkish crews were already training in England.

The British still hoped to avoid the coming war with Germany and blindly continued to pursue their foreign policies as if that would be the case. In what was a monumental failure of strategic and political forethought, the British failed to recognise the staggering consequences of a Turko-German alliance and the ramifications for Russia of German control of the Dardanelles. The narrow Dardanelles strait controlled the entrance to the Sea of Marmara and thus the Black Sea, and could be likened to the neck of a bottle, a bottle into which mighty Russia could be effectively and easily corked. Half of Russia's exports, including nine-tenths of its grain, passed through the Bosphorus and the Dardanelles. Britain had already gone to war over control of the vital waterway when it supported Turkey against Russia in the Crimean War. That campaign was fought to prevent Russian control of the strategic straits, which would have threatened Britain's trade route to India. The continued decline of the old Ottoman Empire ensured that future guardianship of the Dardanelles would be in the minds of western diplomats and statesmen from then on. After the Crimean War, it was decided by the major European powers that no single nation should have absolute control of the region and that the Ottomans should themselves retain possession of the vital waterway. A key clause in the Treaty of London of 1841 and reaffirmed after the Crimean War was that in "the event of a European war, foreign war vessels are not to be allowed passage through the straits as long as Turkey remained at peace".

By the mid-summer of 1914, the diplomatic situation was reaching crisis point. The Turks were still reluctant to be drawn into the coming conflict, but were being sucked further and further into the German camp. The Germans, who knew at this stage that the war was inevitable, were pulling out all the diplomatic stops to make sure it happened. On 28 July, Austria-Hungary declared war on Serbia and two days later Russia ordered a general mobilisation in support of the Serbs. Alarmed at the Russian mobilisation, Turkey followed suit the next day. Even with the whole of Europe on the very edge of the precipice, the British still refused to recognise the inevitability of the war. By failing to take a strategic overview of the situation and acting to secure at the very least Turkish neutrality, they allowed the Turks to continue their drift towards the Germans. The British and the French failed to understand both how concerned the Turks were regarding their perceived threat from Russia and the importance of the Dardanelles to Russia itself. In the event of war, Russia's access to the Mediterranean through the Dardanelles would be the only contact route with its allies, Britain and France. On 3 August, the British government at the insistence of the then First Sea Lord Winston Churchill, requisitioned the two Turkish battleships recently completed in British yards. The move caused outrage in Constantinople as much of the funds to build the ships had been raised by public subscription. As far as the Turkish government was concerned it was a final act of betrayal by its old friend, now allied to Turkey's implacable enemy Russia. Of course the Germans took full advantage and in a public gesture of solidarity sent to the Turkish navy two German battleships, the *Goeben* and the *Breslau*, complete with German crews. One of the requisitioned Turkish battleships would be renamed *Erin*. The decision to commandeer the Turkish ships would have far reaching consequences for many sons of Erin and their Glasgow Irish cousins in the not too distant future.

The Storm in Great Britain

In London during that long, hot summer of 1914 the events in central Europe were far from the minds of British politicians. Among their concerns were a series of prolonged and increasingly militant labour disputes and unofficial strikes. Between 1910 and 1914, the working class in Britain and Ireland launched successive waves of mass strikes of unprecedented breadth and ferocity against all the key sectors of capital, strikes that blew apart all the carefully promoted myths about the passivity of the British working class and of the stability of comfortable middle-class England. The mass strikes in Britain and Ireland can be traced back to the depression of 1908–09. In the previous year the unskilled working class in Belfast had united across the sectarian divide to launch a general strike that had to be put down by extra police and troops. In 1910 there were 581 disputes in Britain with 660,000 working days lost, in 1912 alone, working days lost totalled over 34 million. This largely unknown period of British social history is known in labour circles as the "Great Unrest". The upsurge in unofficial and often spontaneous strikes was led by the workers, who had formed themselves into strike committees.

Ignoring the increasingly conservative trade union bureaucracy, the power and confidence of the strike committees grew over the period. In contrast to the largely peaceful, union-organised strikes of the latter half of the nineteenth century, the pre-war mass strikes extended rapidly and unofficially across different sectors – mines, railways, docks, transport, engineering and building. As the unrest persisted, direct action by strikers saw widespread acts of sabotage, attacks on collieries, docks and railway installations. In response to the increasingly violent clashes between strikers, employers and strike-breakers, the government deployed the forces of the Crown. In the resulting clashes with the police and the military, the strikers saw at least five comrades killed and many more injured. The government became increasingly concerned that the nationwide strikes threatened to go beyond working-class demands for better pay and conditions and morph into a revolutionary movement that could directly confront the state.

The first shots in this phase of the class war were fired in September 1910, when over 30,000 miners struck in South Wales over pay – despite opposition from their trade union leaders. They remained on strike until the end of the summer of 1911. In Clydebank in March 1911, 11,000 workers at the American-owned Singer factory went on strike in support of twelve women polishers. The woman had come out themselves in protest at the company streamlining work practices that saw them required to work harder but be paid less. The Singer factory employed a very large number of the Glasgow Irish, so many that the Celtic Football Club was concerned enough to be worried about the effect on their gate. Encouraged by local socialists, the Singer strike of 1911 was an example of early working-class solidarity crossing the traditional religious divide in west central Scotland as Protestants and Catholics walked out together. In the event the strike was eventually broken when the workers agreed to go back under conditions that meant the girls would suffer no loss, the management accepted the principle of collective bargaining and there would be no victimisation on the return to work. After the workers went back on 10 April, over 400 were sacked including the strike committee leaders. Also on strike later that year were the Glasgow seamen and dockers, who were taking part in a national walkout, as syndication saw different trade unions actively support each other. During strikes in Dundee in December 1911, extra police and soldiers from the Black Watch had to be sent to keep order.

Another example of class solidarity was seen in Liverpool when tugboat workers, Mersey ferry workers, coopers (barrel-makers) and labourers at the giant Stanley Dock tobacco warehouse, Cotton Exchange porters, brewery workers and workers at the rubber plant all struck. When 4,000 railway workers struck – against the wishes of senior rail trade union officials – the docks were closed and no freight trains ran out of Liverpool at all. Most goods could only be moved with the agreement of the strike committee and the authorities were powerless to intervene. Predictably, the government's response was to draft an extra 2,400 police and 5,000 troops into the city. The government also ordered two navy warships up the Mersey. Liverpool was a deeply divided city with regular sectarian riots, but some 80,000 people marched behind Orange and Green bands to a mass meeting called in support of the strike on 13 August. The police and troops repeatedly attacked the crowd, which culminated in *Bloody Sunday*: the violent dispersal of a peaceful mass demonstration by the workers. The strikes united Protestant and Catholic workers, at least for a short while in the city, which at the time was riddled with sectarian violence. In response to the state-organised violence, the workers overcame traditional divisions to defend their communities during several days of *urban warfare*, which saw them erect barricades and barbed wire entanglements. The following day four rail unions threatened a national rail strike unless rail companies agreed to negotiations. The government offered rail bosses "every available soldier in the country" to resist the ultimatum and on 17 August a national rail strike was declared in the famous "liberty telegram", which proclaimed: "Your liberty is at stake. All railwaymen must strike at once. The loyalty of each means liberty for all." Later, five prison vans carrying some of those arrested at a rally, escorted by army cavalry, were attacked and furious attempts made to free the prisoners. In the melee the soldiers killed two dockers. Liverpool Territorial soldiers were ordered to hand in the bolts of their rifles: the local authorities were worried that the rifles might be turned against police and regular soldiers. At Llanelli in Wales, soldiers from the Worcestershire Regiment were rushed to a railway embankment in the town where a crowd of striking railway workers had disabled a train by dowsing its fire. A local magistrate arrived to read out the Riot Act to the crowd, which had been stoning the soldiers. The officer commanding the detachment then ordered a small squad of soldiers to open fire up the embankment. Three men were hit, two died. As the militancy continued, in 1912, the British government was forced to take even more elaborate precautions, deploying troops against the threat of generalised unrest and putting whole areas of the country under martial law. In 1913, over 11 million strike days were lost and there were more individual strikes than in any other year of the *Unrest*, including in hitherto unaffected sectors like semi- and unskilled engineering workers, building workers, agricultural labourers and municipal employees. In March 1913, another strike in Dundee saw 30,000 millworkers stop work. To maintain law and order the local authorities ordered detachments of the local regiment, the Black Watch, onto the streets. Later that year a strike at Leith docks saw an attempt made by some of the strikers to blow up one of the walls of the docks. In response, the local authorities asked the senior naval commander to send six gunboats to anchor off Leith docks. Strikes and social unrest became so common even schoolboys went on strike.

As part of a nationwide action, schoolboys in sixty-two cities in Britain and Ireland emulated their elders and went on strike. Among their demands were shorter school hours including a half day on Wednesday, the cessation of homework and corporal punishment, which came in the form of the cane or in Scotland the tawse, and pay for school monitors. Some even demanded cushions for their school seats. On 15 September 1911, the Glasgow Herald reported that striking youths in the east of the city collected after school in the Calton and after holding a meeting on Glasgow Green with their fellows from the South Side, marched through Bridgeton and the Calton singing popular songs and shouting their demands. A rowdy element among the strikers broke scores of widows in several schools including St Ann's RC school in Crownpoint Road. Public schools in Green Street, Cubie Street, Campbellfield Street, Calton and Hozier Street all suffered a similar fate. In Maryhill, striking schoolboys from St Mary's RC School and Oakbank School joined forces to parade around the district shouting their demands. While they were passing North Kelvinside Higher Grade School around fifty to sixty boys left their lessons and attempted to join the strikers, but the timely arrival of two burly Glesga polis sent them scurrying back to their lessons. An indignant North Kelvinside headmaster later denied the newspaper report that any of his pupils had tried to join the strikers. In Govanhill, Victoria School, Calder Street School and the Holy Cross School were the prime targets of the strikers, with windows smashed in all three. Similar outbreaks of schoolboy militancy were witnessed throughout Scotland principally in Dunfermline, Dundee, Dumbarton, Greenock and Paisley. The schoolboys' strike petered out after a few days with the authorities for the most part taking the view that it was a high-spirited escapade. Their demand that the cane and tawse be removed was painfully denied with the forceful application of a number of stokes to some ringleaders.

The lessons learnt during the Unrest convinced many trade unionists of the need for amalgamated unions. For the militant strike committees this syndication was a means to achieve their militant ends, but the trade union leadership saw that they could not survive without adopting the position as well. Espoused by Glasgow Irish radical Willie Gallacher among others, syndication was basically a plan for turning trade unions from defensive organisations into organs with which socialists could attack the capitalist state itself. After individual unions amalgamated, the intention was that workers' cooperatives would take over industry, the trade unions would assume the management of industry and run it for the benefit of the workers. Eventually all industrial workers would be united in one super union capable of launching a social and political revolution. The National Union of Railwaymen was one of the first to instigate the process and by 1913 had brought most rail unions together. Unfortunately for the syndicalists and despite a triple alliance of transport, mining and rail unions agreeing to mutual support, the individual unions remained separate entities. However, a new more militant, politically combative form of trade unionism had emerged that was fully capable of not only defending workers' rights but also advancing those rights by taking the battle to the capitalists.

Yet another thorn in the side of the Liberal government was the increasingly violent women of the suffragette movement, who were now blowing things up, throwing themselves in front of racehorses and having to be force-fed in prison to prevent them starving themselves to death. The aim of the movement was to gain the parliamentary franchise for women on the same terms as men. By 1884 all male householders could vote, as could men with educational or professional qualifications who were not householders in their own right. Woman had made some political gains during the previous fifty years and could vote in municipal elections. The first modern women's rights movements originated in the 1860s and by 1900 the National Union of Women's Suffrage Societies (NUWSS) carried the political rights banner for females. In 1903, a difference over the aims for the emancipation of women saw the NUWSS split and the formation of the Women's Social and Political Union (WSPU) led by Mrs Emmeline Pankhurst. She believed that women should be pressing for immediate equality with men in the existing system of voting. Between 1903 and 1906, Pankhurst, now joined by her daughters, Christabel and Sylvia, worked closely with the ILP believing the socialists to be the best vehicle for the advancement of her cause. This despite the fact that the socialists in the form of the ILP were themselves split over the issue of women's voting rights. Socialists and trade unionists in particular had difficulty identifying with a movement or cause that was led by well-to-do middle-class women and which, if successful, would mainly benefit that class of female. Middle-class women with the vote would for the most part naturally favour the conservative and unionist parties. Trade unions were also completely hostile to the idea of female equality in the workplace. By 1906, the lack of any real enthusiasm for or commitment to the suffragettes' cause from the ILP was glaringly apparent. Mrs Pankhurst became convinced that women must seize the initiative themselves if they were ever to secure their political goals. Frustrated by the lack of progress and the prevarication of politicians, the suffragettes resorted to more militant tactics. The Liberal Party was also divided over female suffrage. Some opposed it altogether, while others although sympathetic, were unsure how to advance the cause. Their main dilemma was the political consequences for the Liberal Party were they to drive the enfranchisement through. It appeared that the conservatives and unionists were those most likely to benefit from the change.

Many suffragettes were later closely associated with the socialist movements and Sylvia Pankhurst, youngest daughter of Emmeline Pankhurst, split from her mother's organisation to form the Worker's Socialist Federation. Emily Davison, who threw herself in front of the King's horse during the 1913 Epsom Derby, is another example of a committed socialist. She had been actively collecting money for the dockers' families a year before her death under the horse's hooves. James Connolly and the Irish Citizen Army were among the few organisations that wholeheartedly endorsed women's suffrage and treated women as equals. In Scotland, the suffragettes with headquarters in Glasgow were equally militant. The King's portrait in the Royal Scottish Academy in Edinburgh slashed, the Wallace Monument and Burns Cottage damaged, the stand at Ayr Racecourse burnt down, and golf courses and bowling greens vandalised. Shop windows were smashed along Sauchiehall Street and postboxes all over Scotland were damaged. Ethel Agnes Mary Moorhead was the Roman Catholic daughter of an army surgeon who had settled in Dundee. She became notorious throughout Britain for her militancy and was imprisoned on several occasions. Coatbridge schoolteacher and future Irish Republican rebel Margaret Skinnider was also a committed suffragette. The actions of the suffragettes greatly embarrassed the government, particularly when the imprisoned women began hunger strikes, which the government countered by force-feeding and with later what became known as the *Cat and Mouse Act*, which allowed them to release the women when they became ill then re-arrest them once they had recovered. On the outbreak of the Great War, the suffragette leadership called off the campaign for the duration. Thereafter, many of the Glasgow suffragettes turned their attention to broader political campaigns; Agnes Dollan, for example, became involved in the fair rents campaign of 1915.

The Storm in Ireland

Despite the problems of industrial unrest, militant women and an increasingly belligerent Germany, it was Ireland, the running sore of British political life that most occupied the minds of the British political elite. Almost daily, the explosive political situation in that bitterly divided island appeared to deteriorate. Many of the ancient sores and some not so old, still festered. As usual the political situation in the auld country was right at the top of Glasgow Irish political concerns. Seared into the Irish psyche are countless examples of English and British brutality and injustices, both real and imagined. The very reason central Scotland and Glasgow in particular had a large ethnic Irish community was largely down to centuries of English economic mismanagement and misrule in Ireland. Throughout the later nineteenth and early twentieth centuries Home Rule or the *Irish Question* had bedevilled successive British Parliaments. By the turn of the twentieth century, Ireland as a whole was for once a relatively prosperous part of the United Kingdom. There had been some major advances in Catholic civil rights throughout the nineteenth century and by 1914 the Irish Land Acts had ensured that many small landowners were native Roman Catholics. More and more Catholics were also achieving high office in the professions and in the political and military establishments both in Ireland and in Britain. Education was finally reaching the masses and on its back a wave of cultural nationalism swept through Ireland.

An entire generation of young, mostly middle class, were not only fervently proud to be Irish but overtly anti-English with their Gaelic allegiance manifest in all aspects of Irish

AN ULSTER "PARADISE."

(The Ulster Unionist Council have intimated that they will not interfere with Mr. Churchill's Belfast meeting if held in the Celtic Park Football Ground—a place which is known locally as "Paradise.")

MR. CHURCHILL: "Fancy, Redmond, no Orangemen there! No wonder they call it "Paradise!"

Reynold's Newspaper 4 February 1912

culture, particularly language, sport, traditional music and the theatre, all of which were flourishing. Indeed, Scotland was by the turn of the century also rediscovering its own national identity. Over the previous two hundred years, the nation had been so completely absorbed into the Greater Britain project that it had largely lost its own individual sense of nationhood. Now the Scottish cultural revival, much of it newly invented, provided the momentum for its own vociferous Home Rule movement. The call for the decentralisation of political power from Westminster was such that, ever the arch imperialist, Winston Churchill considered a federal system with each of the four home nations having their own devolved assemblies. At the beginning of February 1912, he visited Belfast to deliver a speech in support of Irish Home Rule, but the Unionist town council refused him the use of Belfast City Hall. As he tried to gain entry, his car was attacked by a Unionist mob that blocked his path. Irish Nationalist MP Joe Devlin had already offered him the use of the Belfast Celtic football ground (Also known as Paradise) as an alternate venue. His visit to Celtic Park prompted one of Rudyard Kipling's more outrageous racist comments. A staunch Unionist and close personal friend of Sir Edward Carson, in a letter to a friend Sir Charles P Crewe written in mid-February, he noted his pleasure at Churchill being denied the use of Belfast City Hall and in confining him to West Belfast. He then went on to describe the Belfast Celtic's football stadium (Paradise) as a *Kaffir Reservation*, a very obvious allusion to the native Irish, whom he regarded as being racially inferior.

In addition to the question of political freedom for Ireland, the social and industrial unrest experienced on the British mainland was also, much to the dismay of the government, also rearing its ugly head in Ireland. In particular, socialism and militant Irish trade unionism was manifest in the form of the Irish Transport and General Workers' Union (ITGWU), which was formed by Liverpudlian Jim Larkin. Sent to Belfast in early 1907 as a union activist by the National Union of Dock Labourers (NUDL), Larkin successfully organised unskilled Belfast labour and led a number of industrial actions in the city. Unnerved by his militancy, in 1908 he was transferred to Dublin by the NUDL. There he immediately set about reforming the Irish branch of the Independent Labour Party. Within the year he organised three strikes, in Dublin, Cork and Belfast. Alarmed at his tactics of 'blacking' goods whereby dockers refused to handle the goods of strike-breaking employers, Larkin was suspended by the NUDL, who refused to finance his

James Connolly

planned actions. This led to his involvement in the formation of the ITGWU, which represented largely unskilled or semi-skilled labour, dockers, carters, labourers and factory hands. Jim Larkin was the first person to attempt to organise unskilled workers in the city. The ITGWU also opened branches in Belfast, Derry and Drogheda. Its political programme included an eight-hour working day, provision of work for all the unemployed and pensions for all workers at sixty years of age. In addition, it sought compulsory arbitration courts, adult suffrage, nationalisation of the Irish transport system and Irish land reform. Larkin was the union's secretary and edited its paper, the Irish Worker and People's Advocate, which had a circulation of 20,000 and was arguably the most effective propaganda sheet at that time in Ireland. By 1909, he and the ITGWU had largely broken away from British trade unionists after they were expelled from the TUC. The ITGWU would not be re-affiliated until 1911. His combination of socialism, Republicanism and trade unionism became known as *Larkinism*. In July 1910, Edinburgh-born Marxist-socialist James Connelly joined Larkin. He became Larkin's second-in-command, taking the socialist-Larkinite message back to Belfast. After forming the ITGW Larkin confronted the Dublin capitalists and City Corporation and after a prolonged and increasingly violent series of strikes, the result was the Dublin Lockout. In August 1913, the ITGWU began the dispute with the Dublin United Transport Company over trade union recognition. More than 400 employers banded together to lock out 15,000 workers in an attempt to smash the syndicated ITGWU. A further 10,000 workers were laid off as a result of the dispute. The prolonged dispute saw the economic life of the city come to a standstill. The dispute ended in February 1914 with over 100,000 people, one-third of the Dublin population, taken to the very edge of starvation. In support of their trade union colleagues, British unions and socialist organisations collected over £110,000 for the strikers. The Dublin relief fund set up by the Lord Mayor raised less than £6500 to help the families of non-unionised families. During the seven-month-long dispute, strikers had been viciously attacked by baton welding Dublin Metropolitan Police (DMP), resulting in a number of deaths. In response, the workers formed a socialist militia known as the Irish Citizen Army.

The idea of a strikers' militia was first mooted by Captain John White, a recently retired British Army officer, Boer War veteran and Ulsterman. After retiring from the army he settled in back in Ulster but was disgusted at the Carsonite version of Loyalism as demonstrated by the Union Jack waving UVF. He moved to Dublin where he became involved in the Civic League and suggested forming the militia, at the same time offering his professional skills. It was he who at a later meeting read a telegram from Sir Roger Casement offering his support for the proposed citizen's army. Although the strike was eventually broken and the workers went back to work in February 1914, the threat of the citizen's army remained. The strike was one of the few examples in Irish history where class solidarity outweighed sectarian and national divisions, as Catholic and Protestant workers manned the barricades together. During the strike, the citizen's army was never armed with anything other than hurling sticks and bats, but the potential to rally and unify the masses worried the government considerably. It was reorganised and retained in 1914 by Captain White but in mid-1914 he joined the mainstream Irish Volunteers and James Connelly assumed command of the citizen's army. Years later, Lenin would praise the citizen's army as being the first Red Army. The defeat in the Dublin Lockout was a very significant reversal for the trade unionists in Ireland and the ITGWU was almost destroyed. Larkin took himself off to America to raise funds, while James Connolly attempted to rebuild in Ireland. The six-month lockout was on the surface about labour union recognition from Catholic Irish bosses, but the Dublin Lockout of 1913 could be seen as much more than just a labour dispute. In many ways it reflected the political, intellectual and moral battles being fought for the souls of nations throughout Europe. With Ireland on the cusp of Home Rule and more political freedom than it had enjoyed in over a century, the dispute was also the clash of two sets of political and social values. On one hand, there was the new Irish Catholic ruling class in waiting, conservative, capitalist, imperialistic and content to remain within the Empire. On the other, there was a loose coalition of Marxists, socialists, advanced Nationalists, suffragettes and trade unionists, each with their own political and social goals and visions for a post Home Rule Irish society.

Prior to the outbreak of the Great War, mainstream Irish Nationalist political opinion was very similar to that of modern Scotland prior to devolution and the establishment of the Edinburgh parliament, i.e. it was felt that the "English" had mismanaged and neglected the country and the Scots could do just as well, if not better, looking after their own interests. However, like most ordinary Scots now, most Irish people then, including the vast majority of Irish Nationalist politicians, were not Republicans and were reasonably content to remain within the overall British constitutional and imperial framework. Like just about everything in Anglo-Irish relations, there are paradoxes when it comes to Ireland and its place in the British Empire. Was Ireland Britain's oldest colony or part of the controlling power? Was it at the centre of power or just another peripheral country to be exploited? The answers to those questions differed from person to person, depending on who and what you were and what personal benefit was gained from being part of the British Empire. And therein lies the rub, for it was only on an individual basis, as opposed to a nation or kingdom, that the questions could be judged. Overall, Ireland, particularly the south, never came to regard itself as an integral part of the British homeland in the same way as Scotland or Wales, and it was therefore never treated as such, particularly when it came to the maintenance of law and order. Ireland's location and strategic importance meant it was vital to Britain's interests that it remain part of the Union, but because Ireland's political position was constantly in flux, its status within the British Empire was constitutionally ambiguous and the majority of its inhabitants were ambivalent, therefore its position within the Empire was, for better or worse, unique.

At the beginning of the twentieth century, Dublin and Belfast, with their impressive Georgian city centre municipal buildings, most certainly looked and felt like great imperial cities. Their citizens would most certainly have been aware of the British Empire and that it was central to most of their lives. Just like today's European Union, for the man in the street, the Empire was not something that was thought of every day, but it was there in the background, controlling and influencing very many facets of everyday life. There are paradoxes and contradictions when it comes to Irish opinion of and participation in the Empire. The Irish were for the most part fully signed up to the British Imperial project, of that there is no doubt; tens of thousands of Irish soldiers helped to win it and thousands of Irish administrators helped run it, but at the same time the Irish were also a significant force for subversion. For the Catholic Irish, the Empire could be an agent of liberation and social advancement, yet at the same time a force of oppression. Despite Ireland being drawn into the Union politically in 1800, the majority of the population being Roman Catholic meant they were excluded from the process until Catholic emancipation in 1829. Even then they continued to be excluded economically for much of the century. This economic exclusion at home forced Irish Catholics to embrace the opportunities for political and social advancement provided by the Empire. By the end of the nineteenth century the Irish, including very many Catholic Irish, were firmly embedded in colonial administrations throughout the Empire and despite the fact that many of the colonial statesmen and their administrations were sympathetic and supportive of Irish Nationalism, they were seen by many advanced Irish Nationalists as flunkies of British Imperialism and oppression. This was particularly true of the governance of Ireland. Even though the Irish sent representatives to both houses of the British parliament in London, as did the Scottish and Welsh, Ireland was administered by what was seen by the Irish, as a colonial government based in Dublin Castle and known simply as the Castle. The Irish administration was a strange mix of metropolitan and colonial governance, which was in many ways a throwback to the subjugation days and of the old Ascendancy parliament. On the eve of the Great War, the Castle was presided over by a Lord Lieutenant, at the time the Earl of Aberdeen, while the country was actually run by the Chief Secretary, Augustine Birrell. The Castle and the government offices, which stood in the most prestigious streets of Dublin, was a very potent symbol of British Imperialism. Whether an Irishman found that comforting and assuring or tyrannical and intimidating was really down to the individual. Ireland and the Irish undoubtedly benefited from the Imperial connection, most particularly industrial Belfast and Ulster, Dublin and the south much less so.

The capital city of Ireland, Dublin, had been the centre of British rule for over 800 years. In 1911, Dublin's population was, eighty-three per cent Catholic, thirteen per cent Church of Ireland, two per cent Presbyterian and Methodist and two per cent others. Unlike industrial Belfast, Dublin was a cultural, administrative and business centre, with its economy driven largely by commerce. The port was a major transit point for goods in and out of Ireland, particularly cattle and horses, which were exported to England. With the exception of the brewing (Guinness) whiskey, confectionary and biscuit (Jacobs) industries, which employed large numbers of Catholic women workers, there were few opportunities for mass employment. By the beginning of the twentieth century, Irish Roman Catholics had made some inroads into the lower levels of banking, insurance and accountancy, and in the southern provinces an economically powerful Catholic middle class had emerged based largely around Dublin.

These upwardly mobile people, having achieved some success and status, most certainly would have felt part of and proud of what was the greatest empire the world had ever seen. For the vast majority of the Dublin citizens, the exact opposite was true; on the eve of the Great War there was little evidence of any economic growth in Dublin. Indeed, most of the traditional industries in the city were struggling to survive, let alone prosper. Even by the standards of the times, the citizens of Dublin were marked by profound divisions in social class, religion and wealth. The rich and poor existed side by side and for tens of thousands of the poor, the brutal reality of daily life meant living in tenement slums, long-term unemployment, being starved into ill health and begging on the city streets. The high-density slums of Dublin were among the very the worst in the United Kingdom. The conditions of the poor were largely ignored by those who prospered and by those responsible for the management of the city. By the turn of the twentieth century, that meant the Catholic and Nationalist professional and business classes, who had taken control of Dublin Corporation. Although some improvements had been made, particularly to infrastructure, like roads and sewerage, little had been done to alleviate the conditions in the slums, largely because many of the corporation members actually owned the slum properties. The Roman Catholic Church did not help much when they objected to and often blocked any social welfare provisions or improvements instigated by Protestant-led organisations, describing them as proselytising.

As the traditional skilled manufacturing industries, such as weaving, declined there were few industrial developments or industries in the south of Ireland that could maintain a skilled workforce. This had led to a preponderance of small-scale, unskilled or semi-skilled employment opportunities paying very low wages. This, in turn, led over the course of the later part of the nineteenth century to a large-scale exodus of skilled Protestant workers north to Belfast or across the Irish Sea to Britain. Contrary to popular belief that the southern Irish Protestants were Anglo-Irish gentry and Protestant farmers, the vast majority were in fact urban dwellers, with the high social and political status of the former tending to dominate the popular image. Despite the massive drop in numbers, Protestants still dominated Dublin's political, social and economic life well into the nineteenth century. Unlike in Belfast where sectarianism and racism were overtly and regularly violently endemic, in Dublin the sectarianism was more understated, more an unspoken, but implicit understanding of distinctiveness. As a result there were very seldom violent religious confrontations in the city, but that said, sectarianism and racism defined the city just very bit as much as in Belfast with Dublin's Irish Roman Catholic population feeling very much like second-class citizens in their own city.

Although by 1911 Protestants only formed around fifteen per cent of the population in Dublin, they still remained a massively influential and disproportionately powerful force in the city. They completely dominated banking, senior business management and higher professions such as the law and medicine. The new railway companies and larger engineering and manufacturing companies that existed in the south tended to be controlled by the old Protestant commercial elite. Protestants also managed to provide sixty-six per cent of the city's Justices of the Peace, while in Ireland as a whole the figure was forty-two per cent. Although never quite as poor as the Roman Catholics, Dublin Protestants also had their share of working-class poor. However, as Dublin Protestants became less numerous, group affiliation based on religion became more important than wealth or social status. As in Belfast and Ulster, the Protestant working class formed the backbone of the Loyal Orange Order in Dublin. As the Home Rule crisis deepened, around 400 Orangemen joined the Dublin Volunteer Corps, also known as the Loyal Dublin Volunteers. Their commander was a retired army colonel, Henry McMaster, who was also grandmaster of the Orange Order in the city, which comprised eleven Orange Lodges, including one in Trinity College. The corps had about 100 rifles, and planned to defend the middle-class townships against imaginary rampaging Catholic mobs, if Home Rule was ever introduced. Some members had registered as reservists with the Ulster Volunteer Force, which promised to provide guns and ammunition for Dublin, if hostilities broke out. By the outbreak of war their membership had swollen to around 2000 of which some 600 would enlist, a considerable number into the 9th (Service) Bn Royal Inniskilling Fusiliers (Tyrone UVF). Around eighty men signed up with the 7th (Service) Royal Dublin Fusiliers, 10th (Irish) Division. On the eve of the Great War, Dublin was a powder keg, a seething mass of intense and bitter political unrest as befits a city riven by social, religious, political and economic differences. Irish Nationalists, Unionists, Republicans, socialists, Marxists, suffragettes, very often led by middle-class poets, playwrights, artists, teachers and dreamers, all driven by their own ideologies, were all intensely active in the city. Up to this point the differences, although bitter and deep, with the exception of the violence experienced during the Dublin Lockout, were conducted in a civilised, dignified and decidedly British manner. In the background, the presence of thousands of soldiers quartered in the city at the Royal, Portobello and Wellington Barracks stood by ready to enforce civil authority, be it British Imperial or Irish municipal authority.

During the industrial revolution, Belfast had boomed alongside the industrial cities of the British mainland. From a town of just 20,000 souls at the time of the Union, by the eve of the Great War its population had increased to around 400,000. By the end of the nineteenth century, Belfast had already far outstripped Dublin both in population and in wealth. Belfast was a major player on the British industrial landscape and was widely regarded as the third city of the Empire after London and Glasgow. Industrialisation was the engine of Belfast's remarkable growth and the principal contributors to its development were shipbuilding, linen and heavy engineering. On the eve of the Great War, the city was sending more than double the amount of taxes to the British treasury than the rest of Ireland put together. The wealth created by Belfast spread throughout the north of Ireland with towns like Portadown, Lisburn, Derry and Lurgan all flourishing. It was these booming industries that drew very many of the southern Irish Protestant working class north. The citizens of Belfast were divided by religion: by 1911, thirty-four per cent were Presbyterian, thirty per cent Anglican Church of Ireland, twenty-four per cent Roman Catholic and seven per cent Methodist. The figures produced and drove an acute sectarian divide and tension that was particular to the city. Yearly sectarian riots, usually around 12 July, drove the people to seek safety in numbers and produced religious ghettos, the Roman Catholics in the south-west and Protestants dominating much of the rest of the city.

Like most Victorian and Edwardian cities, Belfast too had its working class of both religious persuasions living and working in appalling conditions. Although shipbuilding had brought the city to international renown, the Ulster linen mills employed the greatest number of workers and brought in the greatest wealth. The Ulster linen mills were, even for the period, notorious sweatshops. Having usurped Dublin's position as the epicentre of Unionism, Protestant Belfast was unique in that it was an Irish city that revelled in its Britishness, and as a major player on the British industrial landscape, it was largely dependent on its connections to the United Kingdom and its Empire for its prosperity. Dublin Castle may have been the centre of the British government's administration of Ireland, but Belfast was undoubtedly the focal point of Loyalism and Unionism.

Dublin Castle 1900

Chapter Seven

A Nation Once Again?

In order to understand something of the political and business atmosphere in which the directors and supporters of Celtic Football and Athletic Club Ltd operated during the Great War, it is necessary to understand the political traditions and reputation of the club and its supporters  over the first twenty-five years of its existence. The club's founding fathers and later its directors were politically very active and outspoken on very many topics including social welfare, education, land reform both in Ireland and the Scottish Highlands and British Imperialism. From the turn of the twentieth century, the Glasgow Irish had been flirting with the socialist policies of the Scottish Labour Party to which they were naturally drawn; however, the glittering prize for most people with Irish Nationalist sympathies was still Home Rule for Ireland. For the Glasgow Irish, all these political subjects were heavily influenced by their Roman Catholic religion and their Irish heritage. As the founding fathers led the Celtic to its pre-eminent position in Scottish football, the club itself became a highly visible vehicle and propaganda tool, which was advertising and promoting the political beliefs and aspirations of the Glasgow Irish community, the vast majority of whom supported Home Rule for Ireland. The cornerstone of their political beliefs, *constitutional* Irish Nationalism, is manifestly clear in their membership and adherence to the agenda and philosophies of the Home Government branch of the Irish National League (INL) and its successor the United Irish League (UIL). Like the INL and UIL, the main political focus of the Glasgow-based Home Government branch was Irish ¬– rather than Scottish or British – land reform and self-government for Ireland, while the protection of the interests of the Irish in Britain was secondary. From around 1903, the UIL was effectively under the control of John Redmond, the leader of the Irish Parliamentary Party (IPP). The Home Government branch came to dominate Irish politics completely in Scotland and its weekly meetings were known as the parliament of the Glasgow Irish. It raised considerable sums of money for the IPP and brought all the major Nationalist politicians of the time to Glasgow; Parnell, Davitt and John Redmond came and they were very happy to do so, recognising the importance of Glasgow Irish support. Rallied by the Irish Nationalists' mouthpiece, the Glasgow Observer, the Glasgow Irish vote conditionally went to the Liberal Party, which promised to deliver both Home Rule and land reform. By 1914, this latest generation of Glasgow Irish had been supporting the aims of the IPP for the best part of twenty-five years, first under Charles Stewart Parnell and for the last fourteen years under the leadership of John Redmond. Very many had grown up with the dream of Irish Home Rule, which now seemed at last to be within touching distance.

By the eve of the Great War, very large strides in Irish land reform had been taken and much of the land was back in the hands of the Irish people. Home Rule for Ireland was about to be put on the statute book and although the volatile separation question had still to be answered, much of what generations of Glasgow Irish Nationalists had dreamed of appeared to have been achieved. At the Celtic club, despite the loss of the likes of John Glass, Joe Shaughnessy, William McKillop and John O'Hara, Irish Nationalist sentiment remained immensely strong having been built into the very fabric of the club. It should be carefully noted that the Irish Nationalism as practised by the club's founding fathers, later the directors of the Celtic club and by the vast majority of club supporters over the period in question, was of the non-violent, constitutional change variety, completely in tune with the politics of the Irish Parliamentary Party as led by British constitutionalist John Redmond. Irish Nationalists' political aspirations had been since the mid nineteenth century to achieve by peaceful means some form of self-government (Home Rule) with a parliament in Dublin. The vote was largely in the hands of an expanding Glasgow Irish middle class, who were at the time prospering and who were themselves comfortable enough with the dual identity of being both Irish and British. However, the horrific experiences and grievances of the Irish immigrants who had arrived in Britain had been seared onto the folk memory of their children and grandchildren and the Irish Home Rule Bill was universally supported within the Glasgow Irish and indeed the entire British Irish community. Their political support in parliamentary elections was given entirely to the Liberal Party, which, as far as the Glasgow Irish were concerned, was de facto the IPP.

John Redmond

Mr John Redmond was the current leader of the Nationalist IPP. Born in Co Wexford, the son of an Irish Nationalist MP, he was educated by the Jesuits at Clongowes Wood and later at Trinity College, Dublin. The Redmond family were among the few members of the Catholic landed class who had managed to hold onto their land through the period of the Penal Laws. His connections with the smaller landed gentry made him less of the fierce and relentless enemy of the landlord class than, for instance, Michael Davitt, who was the son of a small farmer evicted from his home while a child. However, Redmond did take part in the Land War (1879–82) and the Plan of Campaign (1886–91) and was briefly imprisoned in 1888 for incitement. By the turn of the twentieth century, he had united and taken over the leadership of the IPP and was seen as the Irish political successor to the immortal Daniel O'Connell and Charles Stewart Parnell. He lacked the charm of the former and the political guile and ruthlessness of the latter, but he was immensely popular in his own right. The IPP existed purely to deliver by constitutional means Irish Home Rule and land reform and was in most other aspects fairly conservative. Redmond, for example, denounced Irish agricultural labourers in a speech at Rathfarnham near Dublin, for forming a trade union to protect their own interests. On the granting of local government in 1898, a measure that first enfranchised the Irish working class on local bodies,

John Redmond made a speech counselling the labourers to elect landlords to represent them – a speech described by Michael Davitt in the House of Commons as the "speech of a half-emancipated slave". In the years immediately before the outbreak of the war, John Redmond and the IPP opposed any concessions to the suffragette movement mainly as a political expediency, although John Dillon, the deputy leader of the party, appears to have been simply sexist. He was quoted as saying to Irish suffragette Hanna Sheehy-Skeffington: "Women's suffrage will, I believe, be the ruin of our Western civilisation. It will destroy the home, challenging the headship of man, laid down by God. It may come in your time – I hope not in mine." In 1912 John Redmond was lampooned in the national press because of the IPP's support in defeating a parliamentary Women's Conciliation Bill. He realised that any franchise reform would lead to general election reform, which in turn would lead to the redistribution of parliamentary seats and this would favour the more affluent Unionists. He came in for a great deal of criticism, with the English press in particular accusing him of gaining the emancipation of Irishmen at the cost of its refusal to English women. Prime Minister Asquith and John Redmond with a combined majority in Parliament, had no notion of allowing women's suffrage and when this became obvious, feminists on both sides of the Irish Sea, including the IWFL, were outraged. The result was that nineteen Irish women's organisations were represented at a mass meeting in Dublin in June. The militancy in Ireland swung into action with a whole series of attacks on property; windows were smashed in the GPO, Customs House and Dublin Castle. When Prime Minister Asquith went to Ireland in July 1912, the first incumbent Prime Minister ever to do so, English and Irish suffragettes organised demonstrations to show their displeasure. Even before his arrival in Ireland, he was forced to change his travel arrangements after reports of a suffragette demonstration at Euston Station in London. After arriving in the Irish capital on 18 July, a woman threw a hatchet into the open carriage in which both Asquith and John Redmond were travelling as it passed the GPO. The hatchet grazed John Redmond's ear, drawing blood. Later a woman tried to burn down the Theatre Royal in Dublin to prevent Asquith from speaking there. Both women were sentenced to five years' imprisonment. There is another version of the hatchet incident in which it was claimed that it was Helena Moloney, an extreme Irish Republican, who threw the hatchet. Suffragettes also targeted the Ulster Unionist Party and set fire to buildings in the north of Ireland when they discovered that Unionist leader Sir Edward Carson also opposed votes for women.

John Redmond M.P.

It is important to understand exactly where John Redmond stood in the context of his subsequent, unequivocal support for the British during the Great War and to recognise the overwhelming popular support both he and his political position enjoyed in the first two years of the war. Redmond was deeply opposed to the use of physical force as a means to political ends and as a great admirer of the British House of Commons, he was committed to political change by constitutional means. He was convinced of the power of a still evolving constitutional

John Redmond 1914

British democracy and was sure he could gain land reform and Home Rule for the whole of Ireland on his terms. By 1914, most constitutional Nationalists considered their aims for land, local government and educational reforms were well on the way to being achieved. Although Protestants in Ireland continued to dominate landownership, the ability of tenants to buy their holdings through the land acts of 1881, 1903 and 1909 saw millions of acres back in the hands of the native Irish. On the subject of Home Rule, Redmond considered it politically, financially and practically undesirable that Ireland should be wholly independent and outside the most economically powerful organisation on earth, the British Empire. Much the same economic reasons apply to modern day Britain and Ireland and their continued membership of the European Union. His vision was that Irish Home Rule was an interim step to All-Ireland autonomy. In his own words:

> *I mean the restoration to Ireland of representative government in accordance with the constitutionally expressed will of a majority... I mean that the internal affairs of Ireland shall be regulated by an Irish Parliament ... that all Imperial affairs ... and common interests of the Empire shall continue to be regulated by the Imperial Parliament as at present... The Irish say to England, "Retain every guarantee of the entire strength of the Empire and give up that which you have shown yourself incompetent to fulfil satisfactorily."*

Therefore, his vision was one in which an Irish parliament based in Dublin would be responsible for all internal Irish matters, but the Irish would retain representation and an Irish voice at Westminster, largely as exists with the devolved parliaments of the Scots and Welsh today. He further expected that in time Home Rule would evolve into full autonomy on a dominion model similar to those of Australia and Canada.

In March 1911, John Redmond was the keynote speaker at a St Patrick's Day lecture in Glasgow where as a massively popular figure among the Glasgow Irish, over a thousand Nationalists packed into the hall to hear him speak. Willie Gallacher, the Paisley Irish radical and future communist MP, was in the audience as was Tom Maley and his wife. In August 1911, Redmond's vision of Home Rule saw demonstrations in support by the Ancient Order of Hibernians at Stirling and the National Foresters at Pollokshaws near Glasgow, where 15,000 and 7000 supporters turned out, respectively. Much to the consternation of the fledgling Scottish Labour Party, who felt the Glasgow Irish should be concentrating on their own problems of working conditions and social deprivation, the Glasgow Irish vote consistently went to the

Liberal Party, encouraged by John Redmond and the IPP. The Liberal Party dominated Scottish politics of the period and in the 1910 general election had won fifty-seven out of seventy seats in Scotland, a number of which they held through the qualified support and tactical voting of the Glasgow and Scots Irish. The Liberals were seen as the party most likely to challenge the aristocracy, landowners and the interests of big business as represented by the Conservatives. No one could therefore have any doubts as to John Redmond's unambiguous political philosophy and his adherents must by definition have supported his imperial Nationalism and constitutional monarchism. When Redmond took over the IPP after the death of Parnell, the party was split and had been largely ineffectual for a decade. Having reunited the party, by 1914 the IPP had eighty-four sitting MPs and held the balance of power at a hung Westminster parliament.

The IPP had been in a loose allegiance or coalition with the British Liberals since the turn of the twentieth century and had been responsible for or agitated for a whole raft of measures, which fundamentally changed the lives of the British and, in particular, the Irish poor for the better. The Wyndham and Birrell tenant land purchase acts were, without exaggeration, the most radical change in Irish life and had a fundamental affect on land ownership in Ireland. Before the acts, the land was largely owned by landlords, many of them absentees. With the 1903 Wyndham Act, Irish tenants using cheap British government loans, which were to be repaid over seventy years, bought land from their landlords. In 1870, ninety-seven per cent of the land was owned by Protestant landlords and fifty per cent was owned by just 750 Ascendancy families. By 1914, almost seventy per cent of native Irish famers owned their own land. While the acts were brought in by a Conservative government in an attempt to stifle the clamour for Home Rule, it was IPP agitation that forced the Conservatives into what were very major concessions. The Local Government Act put power back into the hands of the people by abolishing the old landlord-dominated grand juries and replacing them with councils, which administered local affairs and were run by Irish people. The councils were very important in that they established a grass roots political class, which showed itself capable of running Irish affairs, and stimulated the desire for more power to influence Irish affairs on a national level. The Labourer's and Town Tenants Acts improving housing, the Evicted Tenants Act, Old Age Pensions and Housing of the Working Classes Acts and the Congested Districts Board, which provided work for deprived areas in the west Ireland, were all major steps forward. With these very obvious advances of the various Irish causes, which many once thought impossible, John Redmond's prestige and influence had grown and he was universally acknowledged as the "voice of the Irish people". His opinions commanded attention throughout the English-speaking world and thanks to the Irish diaspora particularly in America, he wielded considerable power and influence in the corridors of power and not only at Westminster. He believed his cause was right and through political argument had gained the support of a vast majority, not only in Ireland, but also in the whole of Great Britain.

However, Redmond failed, as did most Nationalist politicians, to recognise and adequately address the depth of opposition from one million Ulster Protestants and the lengths to which they and their Conservative Party allies were prepared to go to thwart the democratic aspirations of the majority of the Irish people. John Redmond was so focused on achieving the nirvana of Home Rule itself, he rarely spoke publicly of Ireland's future under Home Rule. His occasional comments suggest he envisioned most of Ireland remain a rural, traditional society in which peasant virtues were safeguarded and promoted, which was very similar to that of his arch-enemy Éamon De Valera when Taoiseach in the 1930s and 1940s. This of course fed the fears of industrialised Ulster, which visualised that under Home Rule, Belfast City Hall would lie derelict and there would be cows, pigs and sheep grazing in Donegall Place. By nature and instinct, Redmond was a conservative, therefore in the most likely event of him winning a majority in the new Home Rule parliament, the policies of his new Irish conservative government would have leaned in that direction. The veteran Nationalist and old Celtic hero, Michael Davitt, predicted a new Irish National Assembly controlled by Redmond and his National Conservative Party when he published a fictional account charting the first steps of the Irish National Assembly of 1910. In it, he depicted that the Irish Conservative government would be defeated by the National Democratic Party with the support of the Independent Labour Party because of its policy to allow the Catholic Church to control Irish education. By 1914 John Redmond had apparently succeeded where both O'Connell and Parnell had failed and was about to deliver Home Rule. He had played the English at their own political game, in their own parliament and had seemingly won. John Redmond had taken the majority of the Irish people to the threshold of self-determination and through Home Rule to the promise of nationhood once again. John Redmond was at the peak of his political power and popularity.

A different Vision

There were at the time three other Nationalist organisations with their own visions of a New Ireland. First, there was a militant labour movement under Edinburgh Irish socialist and former British soldier James Connolly. He was motivated by the Marxist belief that socialism could only be achieved when a country was sufficiently industrialised for the proletariat to be strong enough to overthrow the bosses and their capitalist oppression. Born of Irish parents, Connolly believed the British establishment deliberately kept the south of Ireland agricultural and poor to serve the needs of the wider British economy. To Connolly, complete independence from Britain was essential if Ireland was ever to become a socialist state. By linking trade unionism with his aim of establishing a socialist workers' republic, he brought many of the urban working class, who previously had little interest in politics, into the Republican and therefore, by definition, the separatist fold. This was a re-emergence of the idea for a Republican revolution after a hundred years and was a growing force pushing for independence from Britain. James Connolly had many adherents in central Scotland with connections to the Catholic Socialist Society, which at one stage discussed the formation of a citizen's army in Glasgow. As far as the Unionists and Redmond's Nationalists were concerned, Connolly wrote in the socialist newspaper Forward in March 1911:

We can detest them both. In fact, they represent the same principle in different stages of social development. The Tories are the conservatives of Irish feudalism; the United Irish Leaguers are the conservatives of a belated Irish capitalism. It is our business to help the latter against the former only when we can do so without prejudice to our own integrity as a movement.

The second was Sinn Fein (*We Ourselves*), a movement founded by Arthur Griffith in 1905. Interestingly, it was Mary Lambert Butler, a cousin of Sir Edward Carson, who suggested the name to Griffith. His constitutional idea was for a dual monarchy, mimicking a similar concept that had worked well for Austria and Hungary from which the plan took its title, the *Austrian Solution*. The idea was akin to a federal system in which the separate, but equal, kingdoms of Ireland and Britain were governed separately under the same monarch. The movement rejected Connolly's ideas of socialism and the violent overthrow of capitalism, although at times they did cooperate. They also rejected the IPP's constitutional approach. Arthur Griffith advocated a system of peaceful resistance in which an independent Irish parliament would be set up in Dublin to govern Ireland in defiance of the British Government. In effect, the Irish Government would carry on the management of Irish internal affairs as if it were already independent, ignoring the usual British institutions, such as the courts and civil administration, as though they never existed. Although a former member of the IRB, Griffith was not really a Republican and Sinn Fein did not want an Irish republic. He was happy enough to see Ireland remain within the British Empire as long as it was to the material benefit of the Irish people. While he had initially denounced the 1912 Home Rule Bill as a "grotesque abortion" of the national demand, he quickly rallied and called on separatists to make preparations for becoming the principal party of opposition in the Irish parliament. His organisation would later get the blame for the Easter Rising despite never actually supporting or taking part in it. The organisation had almost disappeared by 1914 although Griffith still published his newspaper Sinn Fein on an occasional basis but he was on the verge of bankruptcy.

Thirdly, there was a small, but dedicated number of men, not all Irish and not all Catholic, who believed that only a fully independent and Republican Ireland would be acceptable. (*Republicanism has never been an exclusively Catholic enterprise.*) The Irish Republican Brotherhood (IRB) was a secret, non-sectarian, oath-bound organisation founded in Ireland in 1858 by James Stephens. The organisation believed the only way to overthrow British rule in Ireland was by force of arms and in 1914 the organisation was actively working to that end. The IRB in 1914 was no longer a mass organisation, as it had been in the 1860s. It had about 1300 members, mostly elderly Fenians organised into small *centres* throughout Ireland and in British cities with large Irish immigrant populations, like London, Liverpool and Glasgow. Although much reduced in numbers, its influence was felt across a broad cross section of Nationalist organisations that it had infiltrated, from cultural organisations, the Gaelic League and GAA, to the political party Sinn Fein, to the Irish Industrial Committee and most significantly, from

1913, the Nationalist militia, the Irish Volunteers. Its influence, therefore, was felt far beyond its own ranks.

Ulster Will Fight!

In the decade prior to the outbreak of the Great War, the province of Ulster with its large Protestant minority was the epicentre of opposition to the Home Rule Bill in the form of Unionism. Unionism is simply a belief in the constitutional bond between Britain and Ireland and the movement dates from the Home Rule crisis of 1885–86, when a formal Irish and Orange Unionist organisation emerged. The Unionists were a minority outside Ulster in the north-east. In the other three provinces, Unionist farmers and workers had always been in a minority and their numbers had fallen further over the course of the nineteenth century and they were further undermined by land reform. Without the backing of a large Protestant population and political supporters, they could not campaign as effectively against Home Rule as Unionists in Ulster. As a result, around the turn of the twentieth century, the leadership of the Unionist anti-Home Rule movement began to change from southern Anglo-Irish landlords to the northern commercial and industrial middle classes. Unionism enjoyed the support of a number of Irish institutions, including the Irish Conservatives, the Church of Ireland and a lately resurgent Orange Order. Landed and commercial capitalists, the southern Anglo-Irish gentry, northern industrialists and imperialists also supported Unionism. The new, young middle-class Unionist leaders felt that the British Conservatives were ignoring their concerns and that the landed elite no longer had the necessary social and political influence to protect their interests. They had a lot to lose, including power, land and a privileged position largely based on racism, nepotism and sectarianism. As a consequence, the Ulster Unionist Council was formed in 1905 and would provide the basis for Unionist opposition to Home Rule between 1912 and 1914. A vital feature of Ulster Unionism during their campaign against Home Rule was the way class divisions were bridged by the common commitment to defend the Union. This happened only in Ulster. While most Unionists were upper and middle class in the other three provinces, Ulster was completely different. Here Unionism crossed the class divide and included people from all classes of society, landlords, farmers, businessmen, agricultural labourers and urban manual workers, many of whom were just as poor as their Catholic neighbours.

The political situation in the Protestant north of Ireland had grown increasingly tense as the Unionists watched the Home Rule Bill make its slow progress through the British Parliament. Dublin Castle may have been the centre of the British government's administration of Ireland, but Belfast was the focal point for Loyalism. In September 1911, the Unionist leader, Sir Edward Carson, a Dublin-born Protestant lawyer and British MP, told an Orange Order meeting at Craigavon House: "We must be prepared … the morning Home Rule passes, ourselves to become responsible for the government of the Protestant province of Ulster." In the early 1880s Edward Carson had represented tenant farmers in the Land Courts set up by Gladstone's 1881 Land

Act. His performance so impressed Nationalists in Waterford that they asked him to stand for Parliament. Carson, a firm supporter of the Union, politely refused. He genuinely believed that Ireland would be worse off with Home Rule and hoped that opposition in Ulster would kill the bill for the whole of the country. In 1892 he was elected a Unionist MP for Trinity College, a seat he held until 1918. Although a staunch Unionist, he was liberal in other areas and in addition to championing land reform he supported the demand for a Catholic University. Edward Carson was in many ways the respectable face of Ulster Unionists promoting the cause at Westminster and at public meetings. His principal lieutenant and chief organiser was Ulsterman James Craig. The son of a self-made whisky millionaire, staunch Orangeman and MP for East Down, Craig was once described as the very epitome of Ulster intransigence. His strength lay in his organisational ability and feel for grass roots opinion among the Protestants of east Ulster. He is now recognised, much more so than Carson, as the founding father of Northern Ireland.

Sir Edward Carson

From the British Conservatives and Ulster Unionist's perspective, most feared that Home Rule was simply a stepping-stone to full independence and believed that Ireland should never be allowed to be politically independent from Great Britain. Aside from the powerful landowning and business elites with their own vested interests, Unionists thought that Ireland was an integral part of the British economy and could not be allowed to go its own way since that would cause massive disruption to the economy of both Ireland, especially industrial Ulster, and Britain. For northern Protestants in particular, Belfast was the symbol of the benefits of the Union, the one industrialised city in Ireland that being export-based benefitted enormously from free trade within the British Empire. Prime among the concerns of the Ulster Unionists was the belief that under a Nationalist-controlled Dublin government, Ulster's commerce and industry would be unfairly taxed to subsidise the poorer south. From an Imperial point of view, many thought that if Ireland were allowed to break free from the Union, it would have a disastrous effect on the unity of the rest of the British Empire. How could Britain hold the Empire together if it could not prevent the break-up of the Union? The British Empire by this time had evolved into and was being increasingly regarded more as a trading block, a commonwealth, as opposed to a nationalist adornment. Many traditionalist Unionists feared Irish independence meant the end of the British Empire with dire consequences for the wealth and prestige of the nation.

The old strategic *back door* argument also still held good. In the event of a major war, where would Ireland stand? What would happen if it was invaded and overrun or sided with the enemy? Many in the British establishment thought an increasingly powerful United States of America would be the next enemy, with the nightmare scenario that an American fleet would be welcomed into Irish ports. The Ulster Protestants, of course, added the religious dimension with their fear of an independent Catholic Ireland being controlled by Rome. To them "Home Rule meant Rome Rule" because of the strength and influence of the Roman Catholic Church in the south of Ireland, which was predominately Catholic. On 30 September 1912 (Ulster Day), the Ulster Unionists organised a huge rally in Belfast at which 218,000 men and 220,000 women signed the Ulster Covenant, some supposedly in their own blood, that they would never accept Home Rule. One of the effects of this quasi-religious ceremony was to raise their campaign to the level of a Protestant crusade, placing it above mere politics. At Belfast Town Hall immediately prior to the signing ceremony, a Rev William McKean preached a militant sermon using the text: "Keep that which is committed to thy trust" (1 Timothy 6:20). After which he went on: "The Irish question is at the bottom a war against Protestantism. It is an attempt to establish a Roman Catholic ascendancy in Ireland." The old fears still haunted the dreams of the descendants of the Protestant settlers: the cause of Irish self-government was interwoven with centuries-old memories of Catholic dispossession and Protestant ascendancy on the one hand and Popish plots and moonlit cattle raids on the other. Many ordinary Protestants feared that a Dublin parliament would take the opportunity of righting old wrongs and settling old scores.

The Ulster Covenant was also signed in towns and cities throughout Britain. Glasgow like Belfast was very dependent on exports and feared any threat to Imperial unity that could jeopardise trade. Home Rule was therefore always going to be a concern in the city. While the majority of Glaswegians remained detached from the political furore, the signatures of 5000 Ulstermen and women resident or working in Glasgow were added to the Covenant at a number Orange and Unionist halls. In Coatbridge, over 1000 Ulstermen signed at the Conservative Club, which remained open late to allow shift-workers to sign. In and around Motherwell, yet another 200 from an estimated 5000 Ulstermen resident in the area signed on the first day, while Orange flute bands paraded through the Union Jack strewn streets. In 1914, a similar Unionist Covenant in support of the Ulstermen would attract over two million signatures on mainland Britain. The Daily Mail condemned the British Covenant: "All members of that treasonous and seditious conspiracy known as the 'British Covenant' are in support of armed revolution in Ulster."

While the vast majority of the opposition to Home Rule came from the Protestant Ulster Unionist community, very many middle-class Roman Catholics throughout the whole of Ireland also opposed any form of Home Rule. They were personally doing very well in the current political system and saw no reason to change what was working for them. This opinion was strongest among the middle-class Catholics in Ulster, where it was widely recognised that in the event of a Dublin government coming into being, middle-class taxes in Ulster would rise. The Catholic working class in the north were also fearful for their jobs with many Ulster firms threatening to pull out of Ireland in the event of the introduction of Home Rule. On the other side of the coin, not all northern Protestants opposed Home Rule; on 24 October 1913, Home Rule supporters held a meeting at Ballymoney, Co Antrim, where the hall was reportedly full a half hour before it was due to start. The meeting was deliberately for Protestants only, so Unionists could not claim that it was in reality packed with Catholic Home Rulers. The audience represented a cross section of the townspeople, while many from the farming class were also in attendance. All the speakers were prominent Protestants and included Alice Stopford Green,

Captain Jack White and Sir Rodger Casement. The meeting unanimously passed a series of resolutions pledging to oppose Carson and disputing the narrow claim that differences of creed necessarily separate Irish men and women into hostile camps. A local Justice of the Peace, John Dunsmore, made the points that three-quarters of Carson's provisional government were landlords and linen lords, that bigotry was the bedrock on which the linen industry was built and that wages in that industry in Ulster were half those in Lancashire. Ulster loyalty and low wages went hand in hand.

John Redmond and the IPP's bitterest opponents at Westminster were the British Conservatives, a party that represented the landowning aristocracy and the upper and middle classes. The Conservatives held a vast majority among the hereditary peers, who sat in the British House of Lords, and the party had used its influence to have the peers veto the two previous Home Rule Bills sent up by the House of Commons. Lloyd George, the Liberal Chancellor of the Exchequer, called the House of Lords "Conservative poodles". After the January 1911 election, which resulted in a hung parliament, the Liberal administration, which favoured Home Rule for Ireland, remained in office only thanks to the IPP, now holding the balance of power. John Redmond recognised the need to negate the power of the Lords and forced the Liberals to introduce the Parliamentary Act of 1911, effectively removing the House of Lord's veto over bills raised by the House of Commons. The British upper chamber, despite its Conservative majority, could now only delay parliamentary legislation by two years; therefore the successful passage of an Irish Home Rule Bill was only a matter of time. Under the leadership of Redmond, in May 1914, Irish political agitation had at last secured the final passage of a Home Rule Bill and only Royal Assent was needed to make it law. The bill had been forced through the House of Lords by the Liberal Party at the third attempt despite the vehement opposition of the Protestant Ulster Unionists supported by the British Conservative Party.

At the root of all the politics, the economics and the religious differences in Ireland, the fundamental problem was and is one of race. Despite the determined efforts of constitutional Nationalists to present a picture of an Irish nation divided only by politics and religion, it was never the case. Strip away the religion and the politics and you are left with two distinct peoples, the British Irish and the Gaelic Irish. This particular generation of Ulster Protestants saw themselves as very definitely British first and Irish second. The Duke of Wellington, born into an Ascendancy family in Dublin, reputedly once said, "Just because you're born in a stable doesn't make you a horse." The British Empire was at the peak of its power and prestige and was recognised as the world's superpower. In an era of rampant nationalism among all the nations of Europe, this generated an enormous sense of pride in all the British peoples, including those of British descent in the great white dominions, Canada, Australia and New Zealand. Unfortunately, it also created an enormous sense of racial superiority in all the British peoples. In the north of Ireland, the Ulster Protestants regarded themselves as racially superior to their Irish Catholic neighbours. They created and maintained a distinct society, and were still very much the inheritors of the old Plantation settlers. It was entirely the norm for Ulster Protestants to go through their entire lives never having any meaningful interaction with a Roman Catholic.

They were imbued with the Calvinists' certainty that God was on their side, since the deity had come to their aid on numerous occasions when all seemed lost – the siege of Derry and the Protestant wind of 1798, for example. Why? Because they believe God has a divine purpose for the Presbyterian tribe planted in Ulster. God is on their side and he is the ferocious, wrathful God of the Old Testament, who condones enmity, annihilation and retribution: "For he is our God; and we are the people" (Psalm 95). The belief was then and is still today both a source of strength and weakness of Ulster Protestantism. Today, the chant, "We are the people," is most often heard at Ibrox Park where it is a favourite of the Rangers supporters, very many of whom are the descendants of Orange Ulstermen. Ironically, very few of them know the origins or meaning of their favourite war cry.

On 1 January 1913, Sir Edward Carson moved an amendment to the Home Rule Bill in Parliament to exclude permanently the nine counties of Ulster. At the same time, Ulster Unionists formed the 85,000 strong paramilitary Ulster Volunteer Force (UVF), recruiting mostly from Orange halls. The Unionists feared that the British government would coerce Ulster into accepting Home Rule and would use the army to enforce its policies. Three-quarters of all Protestant males over the age of sixteen in Ulster had signed the Covenant and almost half of those joined the UVF. It is worth at this point understanding something of the role of the UVF and why it came into being. The UVF was formed as much to instil some discipline into the notoriously violent ranks of the working-class Loyalists as to be a very powerful bargaining tool helping to put pressure on national politicians and the Liberal government. It was very important for the Unionists to present Ulster as united and loyal but also disciplined, sober and upstanding, in what in many ways was a PR exercise in the fight for the support of the British people. Orange-instigated riots with Catholics burnt out of their homes were the last thing Carson needed. The UVF would fulfil that role, being essentially a grown-up version of the Boy's Brigade or Boy Scouts. Although the UVF was organised and trained as a quasi-military unit, the senior leadership of the Unionists never envisaged a civil war, but in the event of a Unilateral Declaration of Independence (UDI) the UVF would operate as an Ulster police force. The UVF had started out as something of a joke with most of the volunteers marching about with wooden rifles, cricket bats and hockey sticks, but some did have an assortment of rifles and pistols and slowly a disciplined force began to take shape. In June 1913, they suffered a severe blow when in Hammersmith, London, the British government confiscated over 4500 rifles destined for the UVF.

When it came to physical force, the senior political leadership was split into doves and hawks as far as arming the UVF were concerned. Pressure to arm came from the grass roots so the senior political leadership, fearful of the disintegration of Ulster Unionism, acquiesced to the militants. Carson, like Redmond, was a dove and neither wanted to arm their militias, indeed Carson later tried and failed to prevent weapons being landed at Larne, ordering that they be taken back or dumped. When Sir Edward Carson visited Glasgow in October 1913, he warned in his speech that the government was provoking forces that neither they nor he could control if they wanted and that he would not control if he could. The political aims of Carson and the

UVF were supported by the British Conservative Party, then in opposition at Westminster, and, moreover, for party political reasons, positively encouraged by them. The Conservative leader, Andrew Bonar Law, himself a Scottish Presbyterian with Ulster roots, was well aware of the forces he was unleashing when he played the infamous *Orange Card*. In what was a staggering level of irresponsibility, arrogance and hyperbole he declared, "I can imagine no length of resistance to which Ulster will not go, which I shall not be ready to support and in which they will not be supported by the overwhelming majority of the British people."

To ordinary Englishmen, the Irish problem was incomprehensible and under normal circumstances they were about as interested in the goings on in Ireland as they were in the goings on in Outer Mongolia. The Home Rule debate had been staggering on with various degrees of intensity for over twenty-five years and most ordinary Englishmen could not have cared less. For the most part their interests were strictly parochial: jobs, taxation, pensions and education. From time to time the IRB tried by bomb and bullet in England to force the issue but this generally had the opposite effect to that desired, and they were viewed by the English as mad Irishmen committing terrorist outrages. With Unionist politicians recognising that some form of devolved Irish parliament in Dublin was an inevitability, the role of the UVF changed; it was now seen as a Unionist army that would if necessary fight the British Crown to secure Ulster's place in the Union (*a strangely confused concept of loyalty*) or to secure an independent Ulster. The formation and arming of the paramilitary UVF was a significant cranking up of pressure on the British government as Carson and Craig made physical force a part of Irish politics once again. In political terms, the UVF was a throwback to a more brutal era, nothing remotely like them could be envisaged as having been spawned in modern England. It reaffirmed for many Englishmen that Ulster Protestants were just as bad as the Irish Nationalist plotters and bombers, both groups were menacing, seditious and violent. Ironically, the Ulster Unionists wanted to be British, yet their behaviour was seen by most on the mainland as very un-British.

On 27 August 1913, the Belfast Telegraph reported that Sir Edward Carson had lunch with the German Kaiser in Hamburg. In November 1913, an Irish churchman in the Loyalist Journal wrote:

> *It may not be known to the rank and file of Unionists that we have had the offer of aid from a powerful continental monarch who, if Home Rule is forced upon the Protestants of Ireland, is prepared to send an army sufficient to release England of any further trouble in Ireland by attaching it to his dominion, believing as he does that, if the King breaks his coronation oath by signing the Home Rule Bill he will, by so doing, have forfeited his claim to rule Ireland. And should our king sign the Home Rule Bill, the Protestants of Ireland will welcome this continental deliverer as their forefathers, under similar circumstances once did.*

The visit of Sir Edward Carson to Germany where he meet the Protestant German Kaiser sent a very powerful message to the British Government and as the Protestant churchman had hinted in his article, Protestants threatened with Popery had removed a King before, which was a message not lost on the British King. The Ulster Unionist's dalliance with the Germans and their apparent willingness to replace the English King with a German Kaiser later led to them being labelled *Huns*. Sir Edward Carson would later try to distance himself from the meeting when offered a place in the 1915 coalition government, but his friend Rudyard Kipling gives an insight into the Unionist mindset at the time when he wrote: "I believe that if Ulster was pushed to the brink, it would call for support from Germany. An Ulster handed over to the Celt means an appeal for outside intervention as in 1688. That is what I fear horribly."

A Hun was originally a member of a Dark Age Mongolian tribe that swept through Europe raping, looting and burning as it went. They clashed with the Celtic tribes of Gaul; the Romans regarded them as barbarians. The ferocity and mercilessness of the ancient Huns led to the name *Hun* becoming a byword for ruthlessness and savagery. The term was quickly attached to German soldiers in 1914 after their ruthless and savage behaviour, particularly during their advance through Belgium when, for example, they wantonly destroyed the medieval Catholic University of Louvain. A large proportion of the supporters of the Rangers Football Club were then supporters of Ulster Unionism. By the start of the 1917/18 Scottish football season just about every professional footballer would be involved in full-time war work or serving in the armed forces. With every football club in Britain in the same position, having lost most of their star players, the football authorities allowed a system of temporary or short-term transfers that permitted players to turn out for local teams near where they were posted or stationed. It was a complete lottery as to where a player might be posted by the military authorities. If a player happened to be posted within reasonable traveling distance to a local club, then by a gentleman's agreement he turned out for that club. A star footballer turning out for a small provincial club meant an automatic increase in attendance and a much-needed injection of funds. After watching the Celtic win four League flags in a row, the management at Rangers Football Club, now under the control of a decidedly Orange/Unionist management team, decided to mount a determined and deliberate effort to deprive the Celtic of yet another League flag. For the 1917/18 season, Rangers' scouts ruthlessly trawled the minor clubs for star players enticing them to guest at Ibrox. The practice of a rich powerful club using its financial muscle to the definite disadvantage of smaller clubs was widely seen as dishonourable. It was almost a return to the bad old days of the paid amateur. The result was an all-star Rangers guest team that managed to win the Scottish League title by one point from Celtic, whose players were drawn largely from young local talent. The unashamedly Celtic-biased *Man in the Know* writing in the Glasgow Observer newspaper was so incensed at Rangers' strategy that he described it as "Hunnish" behaviour. The derogatory and now considered bigoted title, *Huns*, is still attached, mainly by Celtic supporters, to the supporters of the Rangers football club, the vast majority of whom still support Ulster Unionism.

Over the remainder of 1913, the politicians argued over Carson's amendment bill. The Unionists now pushed for an Ulster Protestant enclave of nine counties to remain permanently within the United Kingdom. The outraged Irish Nationalists, of course, objected and various permutations of four, six and nine counties and temporary exclusion periods were bandied back and forth. By March 1914, the British Liberal government was losing patience with the Unionists but it recognised that if the Home Rule Bill was enacted as it stood, rebellion and civil war in Ireland were a very real possibility. As a final throw of the dice it proposed that the electorate of each Ulster county, plus the cities of Belfast and Derry, vote on whether they wished to opt out of Home Rule for six years. The government thought it had been more than reasonable and even those politicians in the cabinet who had some sympathy with the Unionists rallied behind the proposal. Winston Churchill remarked, "If the Ulstermen reject the offer it would be because they prefer shooting to voting and the bullet to the ballot." Only four Ulster counties had solid Protestant majorities and Carson rejected the offer out of hand, declaring it nothing but a stay of execution. The government now felt it had no option but to proceed with the bill, which would complete its third and last passage of the Commons within a few months. In an attempt to get ahead of the ball, a decidedly worried British Government introduced a total ban on the import of arms into Ireland. The government, having belatedly decided to assert its authority, issued instructions the Royal Navy to dispatch battleships and cruisers to Irish ports and additional infantry battalions to be moved to Ireland to reinforce security at arms dumps and military barracks throughout the island. The action was designed to pre-empt any move by the UVF or any other paramilitary organisation against military establishments to seize weapons and ammunition. The arrest of UVF leaders was discussed but John Redmond advised against it as he thought it would create Unionist martyrs.

On the night of 24/25 April 1914, just one month after the infamous, Curragh Mutiny, in which a small number of British Army officers threatened to resign rather than take military action against Ulster, the Ulster Unionists dealt another body blow to the British government. Bolstered by the impression that the army would not interfere and with the connivance of local government officials, at the port of Larne in the north of Ireland the UVF landed 20,000 rifles and three million rounds of ammunition. Operation Lion launched at a cost of £60,000 involved hiring two ships, the *Fanny* and the *Clyde Valley* (the latter was renamed the *Mountjoy II*, after the ship which supposedly broke the boom at Londonderry in 1690), to transport German arms from Hamburg to the north of Ireland. With the gunrunning ships approaching Larne, the courage of the Unionist leadership, including Carson, faltered and orders were sent that the weapons were not to be landed, they were to be taken back or dumped. The operational commander on the ship refused to obey the orders and sent his own message informing the leadership that he was coming in like it or not.

The main operation took place early in the morning of the 25 April 1914, when the two ships landed the weapons (Mannlichers and Mausers) in Larne. The remainder of the cargo, another 15,000 weapons and 2 million rounds of ammunition were landed later at Bangor and Donaghadee. Whereas the illegal importation of the arms and ammunition was without any doubt an open secret, particularly at the very highest echelons of Unionism both in Ireland and in Britain, particular care was taken not to publicly flaunt the landings in the face of officialdom. No attempts were made by the Royal Irish Constabulary or the British Army to

UVF machine gun mounted on car

prevent the landing or to seize the arms. The operation to offload and distribute the cargo went like clockwork with the UVF actually taking over the entire port. Within hours the arms and ammunition were distributed throughout the north of Ireland and issued to volunteers, who, armed with permits issued by sympathetic local magistrates, now held the weapons legally. The UVF now had weapons and they were prepared to fight Britain to remain a part of it and their war cry, the old Churchill slogan, "Ulster will fight and Ulster will be right," overnight became much more realistic and threatening. The UVF was rapidly becoming effectively trained and very well organised with many retired British Army officers assuming command appointments. Now they were also very well armed and the mockery stopped. The formation and arming of what was a large, illegal, Protestant private army gave its political masters an enormously powerful bargaining tool when it came to dealing with the British government. By the beginning of May 1914, the political situation in the north was a tinderbox. Only a spark was needed to cause the explosion, which would result in a full-scale Protestant rebellion against the Crown, despite their professed loyalty. In fact, their loyalty was now conditional – they remained loyal only on the condition that the Government supported the Unionist position on Home Rule.

Soldiers Are We

At the beginning of November 1913 at the Wynn's Hotel in Dublin, a number of prominent Nationalists sat down to plan the formation of the Irish Volunteers, among them were Patrick Pearse, Éamonn Ceannt and Sean MacDermott, all IRB members. The Nationalist Irish Volunteer movement was duly formed under the leadership of Antrim-born and Belfast-educated Professor Eoin MacNeill. Although heavily influenced from the outset by the IRB, MacNeill, a respected academic and co-founder of the Gaelic League, who had suggested the move in an article "The North began", was not one of them. Much less politically homogeneous than the UVF, the Volunteers included those who sought a constitutional solution under the British Crown, i.e. *Home Rule*, and those, like the shadowy IRB, who wanted an independent Irish Republic. Numbering at its peak at around 180,000, the Irish Volunteers were more numerous than the UVF, though they were very poorly armed and generally less well trained in comparison. Like the UVF, many of the Irish Volunteers were former British soldiers; some estimates put the figure as high as 38,000. Many of the men were former non-commissioned officers, the backbone of the British Army, but they were desperately short of commissioned officers with recent military experience. The most senior military advisor to the Volunteers was former regular army officer Colonel Maurice Moore. He was a descendant of John Moore, president of the Connaught Republic as appointed by General Humbert in 1798, and it was said of his father, George Henry Moore, that he succoured the people of Mayo during the famine years. Maurice Moore was born at Ballyglass, Co Mayo, and joined the British Army in 1874. He saw action in the Kaffir and Zulu Wars and at Ladysmith, Colenso and Spion Kop (the Kop at Annfield football ground is named after this battle) during the Second Boer War. While serving in South Africa as Commanding Officer 1st Bn Connaught Rangers, his revulsion at the concentration camp tactics and ill-treatment of Boer civilians led him to write several anonymous articles describing the brutalities he had witnessed. His articles were published in the Freeman's Journal and brought the atrocities to the attention of the British public, causing outrage. He retired from the army in 1906. Moore was fluent in the Irish language, speaking it as a matter of course with his men in the Connaughts. He supported the Gaelic League and in 1903 started schools in Mayo teaching Irish language and history. His support for the introduction of Irish as a compulsory subject for the National University of Ireland brought him into conflict with the Catholic Bishops.

An IRB leader with Ulster Quaker roots, Bulmer Hobson, immediately recognising the potential of such a force, seized the opportunity and helped organise the public launch of the new force on 25 November 1913. The IRB hoped to infiltrate it and use it as the nucleus of an Irish army in a future rising. By the beginning of 1914, there were, unbelievably, five military organisations in operation on the island of Ireland: the British Army, the UVF, the Irish Volunteers, the Irish Citizen Army and the Fenians of the IRB. John Redmond, who was the nominal political leader of the Irish Volunteers, was unhappy at Nationalists resorting to arms but once it had happened he moved quickly to take control of the volunteer movement. He demanded half of the seats on the provisional committee, effectively placing the organisation in his control. As the alternative was to split the movement, his demands were conceded, much to the anger of the IRB. While the moderates did not like the idea, they were prepared to go along with it in order to prevent the very popular Redmond from forming his own similar organisation, which would siphon off most of their support. In a number of British cities, London, Manchester, Newcastle and Liverpool, the resident Irish also formed Irish Volunteer Brigades. As was the case in Ireland, the IRB heavily infiltrated the Irish Volunteer movement. In Britain, many of the members were old Fenians who had participated in the Dynamite Campaign in Britain during the 1880s.

With large, well-established Irish organisations, like the United Irish League, the Ancient Order of Hibernians, the Irish National Foresters, the Gaelic Athletic Association and Sinn Féin, to draw on, Glasgow and its environs formed the first of two Irish Volunteer battalions in mid-January 1914. A meeting had taken place in Bute Hall in Norfolk Street in the city when all the Irish associations gathered to consider forming an Irish Volunteers Corps for the west of Scotland. High-ranking IRB man and Forester's official James McLaughlin from Renfrew chaired the meeting, with Eamonn Flynn, a former player and official of the Sarsfield Hurling Club and a prominent member of the Scottish provincial board of the Gaelic Athletics Association, acting as convener and secretary. Although there was some debate over the aims of the organisation and the exact role the volunteers were to be asked to assume, several Home Rulers and the AOH delegate expressed fears that they would actually be asked to fight. A vote resulted in forty-three for setting up the corps and thirteen against. Among those voting in favour of the move was another IRB man, Dan Branniff, who was representing Sinn Féin at the meeting. He avoided mentioning the Republican advantages of such an organisation, and Branniff instead emphasised the point that the Volunteers had helped in the smooth running of the 1782 Grattan Parliament. Thus the Sarsfield or 1st Glasgow and West of Scotland Regiment of Oglaigh na hEireann (Irish Volunteers) was formed. A provisional committee of fifteen, comprising delegates of the various Irish groups such as the UILGB, the Gaelic League, the Catholic Socialist Society, the National Foresters and Sinn Féin, was set up to oversee the expansion of the Volunteers. Subsequently, companies were raised and based in Baillieston, Uddingston, Coatbridge, Wishaw, Bridgeton, Maryhill, Paisley, Port Glasgow and Greenock. The Corps headquarters were in Anne Street, off Jamaica Street in the city centre. Around the same time a second battalion was formed in Gourock based on forty individuals. Details of where to enrol and the times of drills were published in the Glasgow Observer with the following poem:

> Then arouse exiles of Erin, shake the sleep dust from your eyes;
> Tis your country calls for service, volunteers demand supplies.
> Give your best to drill and arming, for be sure this thing is true,
> When war clouds gather o'er her, Ireland's claim is first for you.

Despite the obvious Nationalist nature of the organisation, the Glasgow and West of Scotland Regiment were at pains to stress that they were non-political and non-sectarian and that any Irishman who loved the old country was welcome in their ranks.

Despite the rhetoric and the best of intentions, the movement was slow to get off the ground. It was only in April 1914, after a visit to Glasgow by greatly respected Lawrence Kettle, professor of National Economics at University College Dublin and former Irish National Party MP, and the unequivocal backing of the Glasgow Observer and Glasgow Star that the movement took off. In the east end, Bridgeton's G Company was one of the most active in the Corps. The driving force behind it was thirty-two-year-old local man, John Joseph Hinchey. A married man with one child, immediately before the outbreak of the war he was employed as a commercial traveller. His home was at Clydeview Terrace, overlooking the football pitches on Glasgow Green. JJ Hinchey was the company secretary, the *Mr Fix-it* of the organisation, it was he who enrolled the volunteers, issued the rulebooks, took the subscriptions and organised the training. Another member of the Glasgow Irish Volunteers and one of the younger members of the IRB

Charles E Carrigan

in Scotland was Charles Edward Carrigan. Born of Irish parents at Denny, Stirlingshire, Carrigan at the age of sixteen was president of his local branch of the United Irish League (UIL), which supported the Irish Parliamentary Party. He later severed his connection with the UIL and went on to join the IRB. He helped to form the first branch of Sinn Féin in Scotland, the *Eire Og Craobh*, in 1905 and was its first chairman. The branch was very active and advertised its activities in the Glasgow Observer. It also organised Gaelic classes and held lectures on Irish history and on the contemporary political situation. Seen as a threat by the United Irish League, Sinn Féin's policies were loudly opposed and its leaders often had difficulty making themselves heard at UIL meetings. At Hamilton in 1907, a very large number of Irish Nationalists gathered to hear Irish Nationalist MP, TP O'Connor speak at the Hamilton Hippodrome Music Hall. Dan Branniff, wearing his Sinn Féin hat, travelled through from Glasgow and attempted to make a speech decrying the Irish Parliamentary Party but having received a hostile reception he was escorted off the platform. In the years leading up to the Great War, Sinn Féin in Scotland never threatened the dominance of the UIL. Growing up among the Glasgow poor of all denominations, like so many others, Carrigan developed a strong socialist ethic and was a member of John Wheatley's Catholic Socialist Society. His left-wing tendencies came to the fore when he openly criticised Sinn Féin leader Arthur Griffith for siding with the management during the 1913 Dublin Lockout. Since the formation of the Volunteers, Carrigan combined his role as Scottish representative on the Supreme Council of the IRB with serving in A Company of the Glasgow Irish Volunteers. Later evidence suggests that he led an IRB campaign of infiltration, placing its men into a number of Glasgow Volunteer companies.

By May 1914, the 300 strong 1st (Glasgow) Battalion Irish Volunteers Corps was parading through the city and practising shooting in the east end at Bridgeton, just a few hundred yards from Celtic Park. They had appointed both drill and signalling training sergeant majors and formed a corps of bugles and drums. They were not the only ones parading or practising shooting. By 1914, there were over 100 Orange Lodges in Glasgow, a quarter of the British total, from which Glasgow's Ulster Volunteer Force detachment could draw recruits. They too drilled and trained and on 9 May while opening their new 600-seat Orange Hall in Cathedral Street, they paraded with 400 men. It is difficult to calculate with any accuracy the strength and commitment to arms of the British-based volunteers of either persuasion. Suggestions are that its early association with the advanced Nationalists of the IRB hampered the Glasgow and West of Scotland Regiment and that its subsequent progress as an organisation was not greatly impressive. It was only when John Redmond took over the Irish Volunteers in May 1914, that the full weight of the UILGB political machine swung behind the volunteer movement in Scotland and by June, the West of Scotland Regiment based in Govan could muster over 440 men and the movement was reportedly spreading like wildfire. A large proportion of the volunteers were former soldiers and all command and training appointments within the organisation were held by ex-military men. In July 1914, intelligence reports estimated the maximum strength of the two west of Scotland volunteer regiments at around 3000. That number was drawn from a potential manpower pool of around 45,000 Glasgow Irish nationalists of fighting age.

While politically active enough to join the organisation in the first place, the vast majority of the Glasgow Irish who put their name on the muster rolls were miners, steelworkers or labourers employed in heavy industry or the building trade. These occupations involved toiling long hours at physically demanding work that left them with little energy or time to pay very much more than lip service to political causes of whatever hue. In the Irish pub or their local Hibernian's social club they threw a few ha'pennies into the tin for the boys and staggered back home to work and family commitments. The most enthusiastic of the volunteers may have attended a few drills and turned out on public parades but it is more than likely that the vast majority would have failed to show in the event of a shooting war in Ireland. That is not to say there were not men and women from Scotland who were able and more than willing to fight, like the Scottish contingent that fought during the Easter Rising, but they were the smallest of minorities.

Margaret Skinnider

Foremost among that minority was the Sinn Fein and IRB's top man in Glasgow, Charles Edward Carrigan. Charlie Carrigan led a sizable Scottish contingent over to Dublin prior to the Easter Rebellion of 1916. Charlie was destined to die in a hail of British bullets outside the General Post Office in Dublin. Also present in Dublin that Easter was Coatbridge-born Margaret Skinnider. A mathematics teacher Margaret was living in Buccleuch Street, situated in the faintly bohemian district of Garnethill, just a stone's throw from St Aloysuis College, while teaching in a Catholic school in the south-side. A very modern woman, Margaret Skinnider was an active suffragette, a member of the Glasgow branch of Cumann na mBan (*The League of Women*) and a member of the Glasgow Irish Volunteers. Shortly after the outbreak of the Great War, she joined Celtic director Colonel John Shaughnessy's Glasgow Citizen's Defence Force where she learned to shoot in a range set up in the west-end. She spent much of 1915 in Dublin working with Countess Markievicz before returning to Glasgow and her mathematics pupils. Prior to the Easter Rising of 1916, Margaret carried ammunition and explosives across to Ireland from Glasgow on the cross-channel ferry. During the Easter Rising, Margaret was deployed as a dispatch rider and sniper and would be wounded in action at St Stephen's Green. Meanwhile the long, glorious summer of 1914 kept the Glaswegians sweating and flocking to the parks in their droves, while the Volunteers, Green and Orange, continued to drill and practice their shooting skills. In Westminster, Dublin and Belfast their political leaders took Ireland to the very brink of civil war.

Machine Guns versus Pikes

The Home Rule Bill was finally passed in May 1914 but the Ulster Protestants refused to accept the bill as it stood. Tabling an amendment they demanded that the northern counties of Ireland be excluded. King George V intervened in the crisis calling a conference at Buckingham Palace in July 1914 in a doomed attempt to find a solution.

On 22 July while walking back from Buckingham Palace and passing Wellington Barracks, some men of the 1st Bn Irish Guards rousingly cheered John Redmond and Belfast nationalist John Dillon MP. The battalion was ninety per cent Roman Catholic and was overtly Irish Nationalist in its political sympathies. The noise brought hundreds more guardsmen to the windows and doors of the barrack blocks. On spotting the politicians they too joined in the cheering, waving blankets and bed sheets. John Redmond acknowledged the Irish guardsmen's rousing rendition of "A Nation Once Again" with a smile and a wave. The Army hierarchy was still very sensitive to any show of political favour after the Curragh fiasco and the following day the entire battalion was paraded by its commanding officer, Lieutenant Colonel the Honourable GH Morris. A Galwayman with a broad Irish accent, Morris was very popular with his men but on this occasion he rebuked them for their demonstration of support for the Nationalist politicians. While recognising that they were entitled to their individual opinions, he recommended that they should be kept private. He ended the rebuke with a wink: "You are all or nearly all, racing men who like a good bet from time to time. Back what horse you like but keep your tips to yourself."

With the Home Rule Bill passed by the British parliament it was now a question of trying to appease the Unionists, and determining what would it take to get them on board and prevent civil war in Ireland. By this stage the Unionists realised that Home Rule and a Catholic-dominated parliament in Dublin was a certainty. Their aim now was to establish a Protestant-dominated enclave consisting of as many of the northern counties as they could persuade the Liberals to give them and which would remain a permanent part of Great Britain. John Redmond voiced the opinion of the nationalist majority in the House of Commons to the concept of partition when he stated "Not a single sod of Irish soil and not a single citizen of the Irish nation shall be excluded from the provision of Home Rule." The idea of the nationalist Catholic population subjected to an Orange Order controlled, autonomous statelet in the north of the island was the stuff of nightmares. In the north of Ireland, Unionist plans for rebellion were finalised: Sir Edward Carson prepared to form a provisional government and arrangements were made with Scottish sympathisers to evacuate women and children and to receive supplies in the event that Ulster was blockaded. They even planned to issue their own currency.

After watching the Larne gunrunning episode, the Nationalists decided they had best get some guns too. The decision to purchase weapons was taken at a meeting in Alice Stopford Green's rooms in London's upper-class Westminster. The ad hoc group of London-based, liberal-minded, Nationalist supporters were all Anglo-Irish Protestants and very of the much upper and upper middle class. Alice Stopford Green was the daughter of a Protestant Archdeacon of Meath. Alice was an ardent Nationalist but still managed to be a great friend of the very cold-blooded Unionist, Arthur Balfour. Other members of the group were Sir Roger Casement, an Ascendancy Protestant and recently retired British diplomat, who would later be hung by the British; Sir George and Lady Young; Sir Alexander Lawrence; Lord Ashbourne; Mary Spring Rice, the daughter of Lord Monteagle and niece of the British ambassador in Washington; Conor O'Brien, a cousin of Lord Monteagle, Sinn Féiner, local Irish Volunteer leader and Redmonite; Darrell Figgis, journalist and tea merchant, and Robert Erskine Childers, soldier, journalist, author and politician. Between them and their friends they managed to raise almost £1524, a pittance in comparison to the £60,000 fortune available to the UVF, but enough to ensure the German arms dealers took them seriously.

Erskine Childers

Erskine Childers was an upper-class English adventurer, born in Mayfair but raised in Ireland by his mother's family, the Bartons of Glendalough. He joined the British Army as an enlisted man in 1898 and served in South Africa with the Honourable Artillery Company during the Boer War. In 1903, he became something of a personality when he wrote a classic espionage novel, *The Riddle of the Sands*, about a German invasion of England. The O'Rahilly, born in Ballylongford, Co Kerry, was an independently wealthy, Nationalist supporter and founder of the Irish Volunteers, who had spent some time living in Europe. In his capacity as the grandly titled *Director of Arms* he came to London to advise the gunrunners (*despite knowing very little about arms*) on European arms dealers. On 27 May, in an escapade that could easily have been a chapter from his novel, Erskine Childers and Darrell Figgis departed for the continent to organise the purchase of the weapons. The pair turned up at the door of Magnus Bros in Hamburg, the same people who had supplied the guns to the UVF. After pretending to be Mexicans, they concluded a deal for the supply of 1500 rifles (11 mm Mausers) and 45,000 bullets including illegal dum-dum bullets offloaded by the suppliers to people who knew no better. (*The bullets were never issued.*) In June, Erskine Childers went to Dublin where he met Eoin MacNeill and Bulmer Hobson, and between them they thrashed out a plan for landing the weapons in Ireland.

On 9 July, Arthur Griffith wrote an article for an Argentinian Irish newspaper. The article was a plea to the 35,000 strong Irish diaspora in Argentina to help organise the importation into Ireland of arms and ammunition for the Irish Volunteers. After the success of the Unionist gun-running operation, the need to arm the Nationalist Volunteers was both desperate and immediate. The sense of panic and foreboding coming from one of the Irish Nationalist leaders can be detected throughout the article, while the inclusion of pikes (spears) at the end of his list of weapons available, serves to highlight the frantic need. He emphasised the point that situation in Ireland had progressed beyond sending money to buy arms. Money was no longer any good;

it was weapons and ammunition that the Volunteers required. Amazingly, he went on to give detailed numbers and sailing patterns of British naval vessels assigned to anti-smuggling patrols off the Irish coast. According to Griffith as of the beginning of July 1914, the membership of the Irish Volunteers stood at 160,000 with the total number drilling regularly about 110,000. Of the 110,000, 80,000 might be regarded as physically effective. About 10,000 of these were ex-privates and non-commissioned officers of the British Army, of whom about half had recent battle experience. There was also a sprinkling of men who had seen service in the American army and the French Foreign Legion. There were even a few desperate characters, who had recently been fighting in the Balkans. The Volunteers were therefore well served with non-commissioned officers, but they were lacking commissioned officers with military experience. Griffith put the numbers at three colonels, two majors, twelve captains and twelve lieutenants, all with British Army experience. In armaments, he thought the volunteers had access to about 2000 modern rifles and perhaps 10,000 sporting guns and shotguns, 10,000 revolvers and around 2000 pikes. Around forty per cent of the volunteers understood how to use the weapons. There was some cavalry available, around 1000 in all, but no artillery. Some progress was being made in organising cycling, ambulance and signal corps, but no general service corps responsible for logistics existed whatsoever. With their own plans to smuggle in weapons and ammunition well advanced, he thought with a bit of luck the total number of weapons would soon be revised upwards. In the north, the UVF were conducting training exercises with machine guns and planning to deploy aircraft.

Unlike the UVF's *Operation Lion*, which was a model of military planning, the volunteers organised a typically amateurish venture in keeping with the poets, dreamers and adventurers they undoubtedly were. The weapons would be picked up from a German tug by two yachts rendezvousing in the English Channel and landed at Howth harbour nine miles from Dublin. One yacht, *Kelpie*, would be sailed by Conor O'Brien, his sister and a barrister friend (who knew nothing about sailing) and two sailors from the west of Ireland. The second yacht, *Asgard*, would be crewed by Erskine Childers, his invalid American wife Mary (Molly), Mary Spring Rice and Captain Gordon Shephard. Educated in Eton and Sandhurst, Gordon Shepard was the son of Sir Hale Horatio Shephard, then the Advocate-General of the presidency of Madras. A serving British Army officer in the Regiment of Fusiliers, he was at the time attached to the new-fangled Flying Corps. Two Donegal fishermen, who were to be told nothing of the mission, made up the crew. Late evening on 12 July, both yachts duly arrived at the rendezvous point near the Roentgen Lightship and picked the weapons up from the German tug. O'Brien took less rifles than he was expected to (600) leaving Childers to take 900 rifles, which was an extra 150. The additional weight made the *Asgard* dangerously overloaded, so overloaded in fact that the last two boxes of precious ammunition had to be thrown overboard. Two nights later, the *Asgard* was off Plymouth and slap bang in the middle of the British Naval Review – 232 British warships that covered forty nautical miles. At one point they were almost run over as a warship bore down on them only to alter course at the last possible moment. Saturday 18 July found them rounding Land's End and the next morning they put into the Welsh port of Milford Haven;

Molly Childers, with rifle, and Mary Spring Rice aboard the Asgard.

Gordon Shephard's military leave was over and he had to get back to his barracks. Before he caught the train for London he decided to take Mary Spring Rice shopping and for lunch in Milford Haven. Meanwhile, the smugglers nervously awaited Mary and her shopping on board the *Asgard* sitting in a British port piled high with illegally imported weapons.

It took them another week to make Ireland and by Saturday 25 July they were just ten miles from Howth. That same Saturday, 5000 Ulster Volunteers, fully armed including with four machine guns – in short, a full infantry brigade equipped for active service – marched through the streets of Belfast with no official interference. The following day as arranged, around a thousand volunteers under the command of Bulmer Hobson and the O'Rahilly, commanding B Company, 3rd (Dublin) Irish Volunteer Battalion, left Dublin as if on a routine route march. Accompanying the volunteers on the march to Howth, a distance of about nine miles, were Arthur Griffith founder of Sinn Fein, Eoin MacNeill, the poets Padraic Colum and Thomas MacDonagh, Cathel Bruga, Darrell Figgis and a detachment of Boy Scouts (Fianna na hEireann), with two handcarts loaded with heavy cudgels. According to the plan at 1000 hours on the Sunday morning a motorboat would come out of Howth to let the Asgard know that all was well and that it could enter the harbour. The deadline came and went; two hours later there was still no sign of the motorboat. Mary stood on the highest part of the boat in a bright red skirt, the signal that they were about to approach, but still nothing. They could see into the harbour and the place looked deserted so they decided to take a chance. With Molly at the wheel, *Asgard* swept into the harbour and tied up at the quay. A group of men emerged from behind some sheds, among them Captain Gordon Shephard (amazingly on leave again), who helped to tie up the yacht.

The volunteer column from Dublin arrived at around 1300 hours and made their way to the pier where Childers' yacht was already tied up. Gordon Shepard organised the Boy Scouts in offloading the precious cargo and within an hour the volunteers set off back to Dublin with 900 pretty obsolete rifles and a quantity of ammunition, most of which could not be used with the rifles. The only interruption was when four coastguards in a rowing boat came towards the *Asgard*, but on seeing the volunteers, they decided discretion was the better part of valour and retired. Unbelievably, the amateurish plan had worked, though on reflection no one could quite understand how it had worked. The volunteers made their way back to Dublin with a spring in their step, their new rifles slung over their shoulders and attached to the cross-bars of their bicycles. The O'Rahilly, in a mood of euphoria, later wrote: "For the first time in a century one thousand Irishmen with guns on their shoulders were marching on Dublin town." Unfortunately, no one could see what the now heavily armed column of a thousand soldiers looked like to anyone in authority. Unlike the Unionist gunrunning escapade, which took place in the dark of night and was deliberately planned to avoid a major confrontation with the authorities, here we had a thousand armed men plus hundreds more civilian followers marching in broad daylight to the seat of the British government in Ireland.

Armed Irish Volunteers en route from Howth to Dublin

Only dreamers or deluded schemers would think their public display would not instigate some kind of reaction from the authorities. Erskine Childers and his wife blissfully put back to sea and sailed off back to England, where he spent the remainder of the Great War as a British naval officer, winning the Distinguished Service Cross. While the armed volunteer column made its way to Dublin, Captain Shephard and Mary Spring Rice made their own way back to the city, where they went to the Arts Club for afternoon tea. Less than three weeks later, Captain Shephard would deploy with his unit to France as part of the British Expeditionary Force and by 1917 he was the youngest Brigadier General in the Royal Flying Corps. He was killed in a flying accident at Auchel in January 1918. After the war, Erskine Childers again became embroiled in Irish politics and was elected to *Dáil Éireann* in 1921. He opposed the Anglo-Irish Treaty and was executed in November 1922. After shaking hands with every member of the Free State firing squad, he told them to take a couple of steps closer to make it easier for them. Conor O'Brien would land his consignment rifles at Kilcoole on 1 August unopposed and without incident.

Back at Howth, with the telegraph wires cut, the local Coastguard had to send a man by bicycle to Baldoyle to raise the alarm. The Assistant Commissioner of the Dublin Metropolitan Police (DMP), to whom the incident was reported, not only called out the Dublin police, but also quite illegally called out two companies (120 men) of the 2nd Bn King's Own Scottish Borderers (KOSB) based at Portobello Barracks in Dublin. The Scottish battalion had arrived in the city almost two years earlier and was the home service battalion of the regiment. At this time, British infantry regiments comprised two regular battalions. One battalion remained at home in the UK, while the other served overseas in one of the many British colonies. After a period of time, sometimes as long as twelve or fifteen years, the battalions would swap over. The home service battalions were generally manned by poorer quality men, the sick, the infirm and recruits, many having just completed their basic training. Inexperienced officers or second-rate old officers commanded the battalions, while the more able officers went to the foreign service battalions policing the Empire. The home service battalions were usually well under strength with numbers regularly falling well below fifty per cent of the war establishments of just over a thousand all ranks.

Meanwhile, the Irish Volunteers were on their way back to Dublin and had reached the village of Raheny where the road was blocked by a contingent of DMP. Far from impeding their march or attempting to seize the weapons, the constables cheered the Volunteers as a halt was called. While the men rested the Volunteers showed off their new weapons to the equally enthusiastic policemen. According to some press reports, the policemen and Volunteers joined in a rendition of "A Nation Once Again" as the march resumed. At the Malahide Road another contingent of police, backed up by the soldiers of the KOSB confronted the Volunteers. In yet another farcical incident the Volunteer leaders, Hobson, Figgis and MacDonagh, engaged the police officers in debate while the Volunteers filtered away with their weapons. In the middle of the police operation, a number of the Dublin policemen refused to obey the order to disarm the Volunteers and were themselves placed under guard. The police did manage to seize a dozen or so rifles, but it was soon apparent to them that they were wasting their time and they beat a rather embarrassed retreat. The soldiers of the KOSB commanded by Captain Cobden also about turned and made their way back to barracks. As the soldiers marched back to Dublin, Volunteer supporters heckled them along the way and at some point on the route back they were met by another force of the KOSB numbering about a hundred men. The crowd, continuing to scoff and jeer, trailed the soldiers back the three miles or so into Dublin. The crowd harassed and heckled so closely, that there were moments en route when the soldiers in the rear ranks turned to make lunges at their tormentors with their bayonets. As the column approached O'Connell Bridge the size of the hostile crowd grew, swelled by people congregating around the tram terminus at Bachelor's Walk, who stoned and bottled the soldiers. In an attempt to break away from the crowd, the officer now commanding, Major Alfred Haig, who had just joined the column, ordered a rearguard to block the narrow causeway at Bachelor's Walk while the main body continued back to barracks. It remains unclear to this day exactly what happened, but apparently without orders, shots were fired by the rearguard, resulting in the deaths of three unarmed civilians. Over thirty more were injured, from bayonet wounds received in the close quarter affray, one dying in hospital weeks later. One of those killed, Mrs Mary Duffy, had a son serving with the Royal Dublin Fusiliers.

The reaction to the Dublin shooting throughout the country was immediate, and the deep feeling of resentment and indignation was echoed by an outraged John Redmond when he addressed the House of Commons on the matter: "Let the House clearly understand that four fifths of the Irish People will not submit any longer to being bullied, or punished, or shot, for conduct which is permitted to go scot-free in the open light of day in every county in Ulster by other sections of their fellow countrymen." The Glasgow Irish were, of course, incensed and the Glasgow Observer's headlines screamed for justice. Even in England the incident drew bewildered comment: "Why, should they shoot the people in Dublin when they let the Ulstermen do what they like?" More important than these deaths, tragic as they were, was the failure of the British administration to act impartially in enforcing the law.

The most immediate significant consequence of the events along Bachelor's Walk was that within days of the incident, tens of thousands of until then uncommitted Irishmen joined the Irish Volunteers. John Redmond demanded and got an immediate judicial enquiry but as events on mainland Europe took the country into war, Bachelor's Walk became more or less a local news story. On 29 July, three of the people killed, Mary Duffy, James Brennan and Pat Quinn, were given what amounted to a military funeral as the cortèges were escorted to Glasnevin Cemetery, Dublin, by thousands of Irish Volunteers including an armed honour guard. Also in attendance was Mary Duffy's son dressed in his British Army uniform. The KOSB were confined to barracks and plans set in operation to move them out of the country, but as elsewhere, events overtook them. As far as the KOSB were concerned, perhaps some indication of their mindset regarding the incident can be gleaned from the regimental history written after the Great War. There the author devotes just sixty-two words to describe the incident and is unsure whether two or three civilians were killed. He then devotes 150 words bemoaning the effects the incident had on recruitment and how the subsequent fatal accident enquiries wasted hours, labouring ad nauseam over the incident and how it interfered with the battalion's ability to mobilise for war. Dubliners took to calling the battalion the "King's own murderers.

THE IRISH VOLUNTEERS
(By John O'Dowd, M.P.)

Now God be praised, our flag, upraised,
Floats high o'er tower and steeple;
No more were slaves: that banner waves
Above a conquered people.
Our flag, long crushed in mire and dust,
In Freedom's light appears;
Twill guarded be right gallantly
By the Irish Volunteers.

See that bold mass of marching men,
Who come from hill and valley;
They gather from city and town and glen-
An uprisen nation's rally!
"Our new-born Freedom to maintain,
Through all the coming years"-
This is the motto, this the aim
Of the Irish Volunteers.

Then here's to Redmond, our leader grand,
To Dillon and Devlin glorious,
And here's to each man of their fighting band,
Who carry the flag victorious.
They have failed each plan of the Tory clan,
They've scattered the gloom of years,
O these are men to lead the van
Of the Irish Volunteers.

We have won our fight for Ireland's right,
By valour and love and brav'ry;
New Liberty's light has pierced the night
Of Ireland's cruel slav'ry.
We've burst the chain, 'tis rent in twain.
We've dried dark Rosaleen's tears.
Three cheers for Redmond, and here again
A toast to the Volunteers.

Chapter Eight

The Celtic On the Eve of War

By the time of its twenty-fifth birthday celebrations in season 1913/14, the Celtic Football and Athletic Club, founded by the Glasgow Irish community had succeeded beyond the wildest dreams of its founding fathers and faithful supporters. The Celtic was arguably the most powerful and wealthiest football club, certainly in Scotland, if not in the whole of Great Britain. For the Glasgow Irish and indeed the entire Irish community in Scotland, the massively successful Celtic Football Club was a source of enormous pride and inspiration. As a club, Celtic's long term commitment to constitutional Irish Nationalism was also a very overt display of Glasgow Irish civic and social responsibility, at a time when Ireland and the Irish were being seen as a destabilising force within the union of Great Britain and the Empire. That the Celtic supporters themselves had much to do with the success of the club there was no doubt. As early as 1900 the supporters were being widely acclaimed as being like none other. The Glasgow Herald newspaper put much of the success of the club down to its supporters: "Enterprise, of course has a lot to do with the Celt's success but there must be other causes at work. These are not to be found on the surface. One, and perhaps the most important is the loyalty of the Celtic supporters."

To the Glasgow Irish, the club had become much more than simply a football team; the Celtic club itself had become the physical embodiment of the Glasgow Irish identity, the very essence of their community. On conversion to a limited company in 1897, the community-owned asset had passed into the hands of private business but it no longer mattered who owned or controlled the club, the Glasgow Irish had created it, built it and nurtured it and now they unconditionally supported it. The club had become the single greatest ethnic and cultural focus of the community and had transcended the mere playing of sport. Although obviously rejoicing in the success of the team, whether the team was successful or not was of little consequence, for the team's sporting battles were merely representative of the community's struggles in life and they, like the club, could not be given up. That was why the Celtic's style of play mattered almost as much as the final result, for the team was a reflection of the best characteristics of the community and its principles. It was not simply that the team must win at all costs; it was the manner in which they won. The option of whether the Glasgow Irish would or would not support the Celtic was removed from them at birth. Irrespective of whether you were a man or a woman, young or old, football follower or not, being born Glasgow Irish meant you were born to and always would, irrespective of where you happened to be in the world, support the Celtic.

Willie Maley

At the birth of the Celtic club it was once said of the first team captain and future chairman James Kelly "no Kelly, no Keltic". Twenty-five years later it was being said "no Maley, no Celtic, as we know it". By 1913 and the club's silver jubilee celebrations, Willie Maley was widely regarded as Mr Celtic. He had been associated with the club since its inception and had guided the club, particularly in football matters, to the very pinnacle of the game. He was recognised throughout British football as the spokesman and very public face of the football club. He was the guardian and custodian of the Glasgow Irish community's greatest and most cherished achievement, the Celtic Football Club. His personal celebrity among the Roman Catholic Glasgow Irish gave him enormous influence among the community, particularly among the club's active supporters. He was also involved in a number of local and national sporting bodies outwith football and served on their various committees. This allowed him to exercise his influence beyond the Celtic club and football and he was a recognised sports authority. As a former athlete, he maintained a close interest in athletics and remained involved with the Scottish Amateur Athletics Association. In recognition of his service to the Celtic club, at the 1913 AGM the board of directors voted him an honorarium of 300 guineas, a very considerable sum. In his reply, Maley stated, "To work for the club had become a labour of love… the club is a part of my very existence."

The story of the Maley family connection with the Celtic is well known to any Celtic supporter who, as the club song goes, knows the history. It was Willie Maley who was at home the night Brother Walfrid, John Glass and a certain old Fenian called Pat Welsh came to Cathcart to knock on the door of an old soldier, Sergeant Thomas Maley. The trio were trying to get together players for their new football team and it was actually Willie's older brother, Thomas Maley that they had come to see. Tom Maley had something of a reputation as a footballer having played for Hibernian, Partick Thistle and the old 3rd Lanarkshire Rifle Volunteers. The trio, knowing little about football themselves, were interested in his football contacts in addition to his footballing skills. Tom Maley was not at home when they called but during the small talk with the family, nineteen-year-old Willie, who had also played a bit of football but was really more interested in athletics, was invited to come along with his brother to have a look at the new set-up. The two Maley bothers, with the approval of their father, did indeed make their way to Parkhead and decided to throw their lot in with the new club. Both Maley brothers played in the select team that represented the club in the first game against Rangers Swifts in May 1888.

Willie Maley was the third son of Sergeant Thomas (O'Malley) Maley of the Royal North British Fusiliers, who was originally from Ennis, Co Clare, where Sergeant Thomas Maley's father, Charles O'Malley, was the land steward on the estate of Lord Inichiquin. In 1846, young Thomas, aged just sixteen, ran away from home to join the army and enlisted into the 21st Regiment of Foot, the Royal North British Fusiliers. Although service in the ranks of the army was always looked down on by the middle classes and in Ireland by the small farming classes, it was not the case with the working classes of Britain or Ireland and literally millions of Irishmen

Sgt Thomas Maley

served in the army during the course of the nineteenth and early twentieth centuries. Thomas Maley served for most of his adult life as a professional British soldier, seeing action in the Crimea at Alma, Inkerman and Sebastopol. He later served in Malta and the West Indies at Bermuda. By the mid-1860s, their foreign service tour over, the Royal North British Fusiliers were back in Britain. Willie Maley was born in 1868 in the army barracks at Newry, and two of Willie's elder brothers were likewise born in army quarters, the oldest Charles, later Father O'Malley, in Barbados and Thomas Edward Maley was born in the army barracks at Portsmouth.

Retiring from the regular army in 1870, Sergeant Thomas Maley took his richly deserved pension and settled his family in Glasgow, living first in the Gallowgate with Tailor Welsh. There he utilised his military experience by gaining employment as a military drill instructor with the 3rd (Renfrewshire) Volunteer Admin Battalion. The volunteer battalion had several out-stations and Sergeant Maley was the permanent staff instructor, first to the drill hall at Thornliebank (25th Corps) and three years later to the Cathcart (23rd Corps). In 1880 the battalion was consolidated and retitled the 3rd (Renfrewshire) Volunteer Corps with the 23rd Corps becoming (G) Company. In 1887, in yet another re-designation, the unit became the 3rd (Volunteer) Bn, Argyll and Sutherland Highlanders. This regular reorganising and retitling of units not only affected the volunteers. In 1877, Sergeant Maley's old regiment, the Royal North British Fusiliers, was retitled the Royal Scots Fusiliers. Willie Maley's mother, Canadian-born Mary Ann Montgomery, was herself from a military family. Her Scottish father Alexander Montgomery was, like Thomas Maley, a career soldier, who had attained the rank of sergeant major serving with the Royal Engineers. Willie Maley was born in Ireland, but he was raised from infancy in Cathcart near Glasgow and considered himself to be most definitely Scottish, but with proud Irish Catholic roots. So much so, despite some objections in the press, in 1893 he accepted a Scottish international cap and played football against Ireland.

To understand something of the man Willie Maley would become, it is important to understand the early influences in his life and the environment in which he grew up. Central to these was his father and his position as the permanent staff military instructor attached to a Volunteer Force battalion. This fact would have ensured that all the Maley boys were heavy influenced by the military and immersed in the Volunteer Force's military, but very social lifestyle. Although volunteer bands sprang up during the Napoleonic conflict, the Volunteer Force for the most part emerged in response to the French invasion scares of the late 1850s. The volunteers had evolved from private and very exclusive military clubs, membership of which entailed the payment of membership and annual subscription fees and had at first been totally self-sufficient. The movement became very popular because it was stamped with the seals of patriotism and respectability and to be a part of the Volunteer Force carried a good degree of social status. The men who had joined the old Volunteer Rifle battalions were for the most part middle class: solicitors, bank staff, accountants, civil servants, businessmen, teachers, students and artisans. They joined with a sense of national service and were prepared to sacrifice both time and money purely for the satisfaction of knowing they served. Over the years, the War Office became more involved in the organisation and provided increasing levels of support. The composition of the force also began to evolve and from its beginning as an exclusively middle-class military movement it became as much a *social and recreation* movement. The Volunteer battalions became extensions of the social structure of the times with the middle class officers being for the most part men of authority and social standing in their communities. Often they encouraged men with similar interests and their employees, subordinates and tenants to join their battalion and their particular company within the battalion, very often turning the battalions and its companies into private clubs with busy social calendars. Individual companies assumed secondary titles, which continued after the creation of the Territorial Force in 1908. Most battalions still had companies unofficially titled, such as the bankers, civil servants, artisans, students, merchants and the likes. Social causes also featured, most popular being the total abstainers.

The role of Sergeant Maley, who remained in the same position until he retired in the early 1890s, was that of the resident expert and advisor in all things military. The position of the permanent staff military instructor was more a way of life than simply a nine-to-five job. It would have been he who organised all aspects of military training (drills) for the company. This would range from basic weapons training for recruits to field and rifle range training for the entire company. He would have been responsible for the security and maintenance of the company's weapons and the armoury including the unit's ammunition. He was the on-the-spot advisor to the company officers and non-commissioned officers in all matters military. As the permanent staff instructor, he would have been the first point of contact for anyone wishing to communicate with the company and his place of duty would have been at the drill hall. He may even have been responsible for the upkeep of the drill hall itself. He would have been the senior member of the sergeants' mess after the volunteer company sergeant major and would undoubtedly have been responsible for organising all the social function for the mess and for the company. It is not a great leap of imagination to envisage how involved the young Maley boys would have been in their father's work. They would have spent most of their free time at the drill hall, running about wearing the uniforms and helping their father to clean and maintain the weapons; the boys could probably handle and shoot the weapons better than most of the volunteers. Although there is no evidence to date of Willie joining the Volunteers, Tom Maley did join, being promoted to non-commissioned-officer rank. It would be strange if Willie didn't follow his big brother into the volunteer's ranks. The Maley family would have been expected to attend the battalion's regular social functions, such as outings, dances and sports events; in fact Sergeant Maley probably helped to organise many of them. The Volunteer sports, shooting competitions and training events were major news items and regularly featured in the newspapers and often took up a half page in the Scottish nationals. In addition to its military function, the volunteers' drill hall was also a focal point for the local community. It was used for very many of their social events like fetes, dances and community meetings. Sergeant Maley was their first point of contact, and he would have been involved to some degree with most of the village and parish organisations. His position as the permanent staff instructor therefore carried with it a good deal of social status and Sergeant Maley would have been a well-known and respected personality within his local community.

In addition to the honour and respect afforded a Victorian father as the head of his household, Sergeant Maley's social position within the local community would have ensured that he was regarded with a great deal of pride by his sons. Some indication of the authority old Thomas Maley had over his boys can be seen when he persuaded Tom Maley to stop playing for Hibernian FC. Old Tom felt the Hibernian club was not inclusive enough and was hindering the integration of the Irish Catholics into the wider Scottish society. When the Celtic deputation, led by Brother Walfrid, arrived at the Maley's Cathcart home in December 1887, it was Sergeant Maley that they first had to convince. After listening to the plan presented by Brother Walfrid and John Glass, in Willie Maley's own words: "My father gave them his hearty support." Had old Sergeant Maley not allowed his sons to become involved in the project, the story of the Celtic would have been very different.

Reflecting the increasing interest in sporting participation in wider society, the Volunteer Force provided the first opportunity for lower middle and respectable working class to have an active involvement in sport, particularly football and athletics. The military were among the first organisations to take up football and the football team of the 3rd (Lanarkshire) Rifle Volunteers formed in 1872 were one of the founding members of the Scottish Football Association. Soon after Sergeant Maley's arrival at Thornliebank and later at Cathcart, both Volunteer units began to enter football and athletic teams in local and national competitions. Willie Maley retained a life-long interest in athletics and first kicked a ball after watching his father's volunteer battalion team play. It is therefore unsurprising, considering the family connection with the volunteers that both Willie and Tom Maley turned out for the 3rd Lanark Rifle Volunteers football team. Tom was a regular, but Willie, then more into athletics, was known as a *ham and eggs* man, a reserve who turned up hoping to get a game.

Sergeant Maley finally retired from the military in 1892 after over forty-six years' service. Throughout his time with the Volunteers, old Sergeant Maley was a very well known and respected figure in the Cathcart community and on his death in May 1896; he was buried with full military honours, which included a firing party and a military band. As the cortege approached Cathcart village from the Holy Cross Chapel at Govanhill, the coffin was taken from the hearse and carried on the shoulders of the burial party through the village, where many of the shops had closed. The news of Sergeant Maley's passing and details of his military funeral were published in the Glasgow Herald and in the Glasgow Observer. All the Maley boys were therefore steeped in the army traditions of two famous Scottish regiments, but the three older boys in particular maintained a deep affection for the Royal Scots Fusiliers. Willie Maley retained possession of his father's medals during his own lifetime and regarded them among his most prized treasures. The Maley family had prospered after settling in Scotland.

With his regular army pension and secure employment, Thomas Maley was able to set his sons firmly on the road to success; Charles would enter the priesthood under the old family name of O'Malley; Thomas Edward Maley would train as a schoolteacher, becoming an industrial school superintendent and very successful football manager. Willie was trained in accountancy and had opened his own very successful sports shop in the Gallowgate, before turning to what would become his life's work, managing the Celtic. The Maley's youngest child, Alexander, was born at Cathcart and he too would eventually find his way into football management at Clydebank, Clyde and Hibernian.

In the military's male-oriented world, the ethics of duty, self-discipline, hard work, respectability and self-improvement were instilled into all the Maley boys and would remained with them throughout their lives. Despite the family's obvious Irishness and their undoubted prolonged and active support for constitutional Irish Nationalism – all four brothers were known to have spoken on Nationalist platforms – the sons of old Sergeant Maley most certainly felt they owed a large degree of loyalty to the land that had adopted them. The army had imbued the self-improvement ethic into Sergeant Maley and his boys and Scotland and Britain had provided them with the opportunity to succeed. Like most of the respectable classes, with their success came a feeling that they were stakeholders in the country and in the enterprise known as the British Empire. The Maley boys may have been proud of their Irish roots, but they were also very proud of their dual nationality and British heritage and saw no paradox in the fact.

William Maley

Soon after joining the fledgling Celtic club, Willie Maley, utilising his accountancy skills, took on the role of player/secretary. The role of secretary involved organising the Celtic clubs fixtures and liaising between the club committee and players. He shared in the early footballing success of the club and regularly featured in the sports writer's columns, given what would today be called the *Man of the Match* award. He himself played down his footballing prowess, which by any standards was considerable. Indeed, he was a good enough player to get a couple of international caps for Scotland. In 1896, he effectively hung up his boots, though he did on several occasions step back into the breach for the club when called upon to do so. For example, during the three-player rebellion in November 1896, he pulled the green and white shirt back on. His entry onto the field was described by a sports hack: "Secretary Maley came spanking onto the field in a never-say-die fashion, rolling up his sleeves." In 1897 soon after the club was converted to a limited liability company, Willie Maley was officially appointed secretary/manager with a very generous salary of £150 pa. His first season in charge saw Celtic win the League by a comfortable margin, but go out of the Scottish Cup to his old comrades, the 3rd Lanark Volunteers. A man of many facets, Willie Maley was a footballer, football manager, athlete, cyclist, accountant, a businessman, the father of two boys and a devout practising Roman Catholic. Willie Maley did, at least initially, have other interests in his life, including an ongoing love for athletics; he was also something of an entrepreneur owning a very successful gentlemen's outfitters, but it was the Celtic club that would come to completely dominate his life.

Willie Maley had, over the previous quarter century, stamped his personality on the club like few other individuals have ever done at any other similar institution. He had the reputation of being a stern, strict disciplinarian, very much in the mould of an army sergeant major. Discipline, both personal and institutional, was the bedrock on which good military units are founded and discipline was the stock-in-trade of sergeant majors. After his military upbringing, it is hardly surprising that he would absorb some of its influences. Willie Maley had learned many of the attributes of a good sergeant major and carried them into his role at the Celtic Club. It was the sergeant majors that made the soldiers "jump to it"; it was their responsibility to see that the men and their equipment set and maintained high standards. Willie Maley certainly ensured the players maintained his standards when it came to playing for Celtic. He once said: "The player who cannot conduct himself on and off the park has no peg for his suit at Celtic Park." He expected them as representatives of the club to behave in a dignified manner both on and off the field. Sergeant majors taught their soldiers all the facets of their warlike trade. Likewise Maley ensured his players knew their trade; as a matter of policy young players were fed out to smaller clubs to ensure they got experience playing at a reasonable level.

As an authority figure a sergeant major did not expect to be popular, but if a soldier was treated fairly, as well as sternly, he could earn the soldiers' respect. Despite his reputation for being a stern, typical Victorian authority figure, like most sergeant majors, Maley's bark was worse than his bite and he could usually see some good in a man. Few players would have admitted to actually liking their imposing and domineering manager, but most would admit to holding him in great respect. A sergeant major had to be a man of unusually strong personality, self-confident and with untiring energy. No one would ever accuse Willie Maley of lacking in any of the aforementioned characteristics as he imposed his iron will on the Celtic club. In order to inspire confidence, it is vitally important that sergeant majors are above reproach and while, unlike Maley, they may not have been particularly well educated, he like they had been there and done that and those under them appreciated that they knew what they were talking about. Willie Maley had seen and done it all in the world of sport, in football management and in business. As a footballer of international standard he represented Scotland; he was the most successful football manager in Great Britain, which at that time probably meant the world. He owned a number of successful businesses and as a former record-breaking athlete; he organised and stage-managed the internationally renowned Celtic Sports Meeting.

Good sergeant majors are completely devoted and fiercely loyal to their regiment, its traditions and its family ethos. They see themselves as very much the guardians of a very precious institution and spend their professional lives maintaining its standards and dignity and reinforcing its spirit of family. Having been massively influenced by the military environment in which he was raised, Willie Maley introduced and encouraged the same ethos of devotion to duty and fierce family loyalty into the Celtic club. Although, he was completely committed to

THE MALEY BHOYS

RSF

SGT THOMAS MALEY

A&SH

THOMAS E. MALEY

WILLIAM MALEY

ALEX S. MALEY

FR CHAS O'MALLEY

the success of Celtic Football Club, he realised that the success of the club was not only about winning football games, it was also about how the institution was perceived by the wider public. It was vitally important to Willie Maley that the club, representing as it did the hopes and aspirations of his community, achieved and maintained the highest possible reputation for excellence. Only by doing so could its representatives sit alongside the footballing and wider Glasgow establishment figures, meeting them on equal terms. As a supporter himself, he fully understood that the club represented much more than simply football to its Glasgow Irish supporters. He therefore devoted his life to ensure that the club officials and players achieved and maintained the standards he set. It was a very high benchmark and he was often accused, mostly behind his back, of being egocentric or of being a dictator. There is indeed a very thin line between despotism and benign dictatorship but the perception is usually in the individual's personal experience.

Politically, Willie Maley, like the vast majority of the Celtic board and club supporters, was both an Irish Nationalist and a Liberal, the latter not only because of its promise to deliver Home Rule for Ireland, but because of the party's commitment to social reform. As early as 1889, the Celtic were demonstrating socialist tendencies by financially supporting striking handloom weavers and later supporting miners and dock workers engaged in strike action by contributing to the strike funds. With regards to their Irish Nationalism, it is very important to understand that Willie Maley, the Celtic board and the vast majority of the Celtic supporters were constitutional Nationalists and did not support the wilder men on the fringes of Irish politics. Willie Maley once described the Fenians as "foolish fellows, only doing harm to themselves." They endorsed the politics and policies of the Irish Parliamentary Party, led by Mr John Redmond, and by the eve of the Great War had done so for the best part of twenty-five years. The Celtic club had, of course, sent its own delegation to the Irish Race Convention in 1896. In May 1909, Willie Maley organised the travel arrangements for the Home Government branch delegates to the United Irish League conference in Manchester, while his brother Tom was at the same time lecturing at UIL meetings. In 1911, a delegation of players and officials from Celtic returning from their European tour diverted to London where they meet Irish Party MPs at Westminster. In June 1913, John Redmond and the leadership of the IPP visited Glasgow to drum up support for the Irish Home Rule Bill. Finally, after decades of trying, Ireland was on the very brink of achieving Home Rule and it had been achieved by reasoned debate and not by the bomb and bullet. At a meeting in the city centre no less than three Celtic directors; James Kelly, Mick Dunbar and Colonel John Shaughnessy were all on John Redmond's platform. Also on the platform with Celtic connections were Dr Scanlan, S. J. Henry, Pat Gaffney and Arthur Murphy.

Despite his unquestionable support for the aims of constitutional Irish Nationalism, it is important to understand that Willie Maley would have regarded himself as very definitely British and like his entire family, he was with a small "I" an imperialist to the bone. So much so that as club secretary, undoubtedly with the full approval of the committee, he oversaw the design, purchase and flying of the Scottish League Championship flag for season 1893/94. The club's second League Championship flag was of emerald green silk with a Union Jack in the top left quarter. In the opinion of the Scottish Referee sports paper, the new flag was a great improvement on the Celtic's previous championship flag, which was just plain green silk. Unfortunately, there is no record of what any of the Glasgow Irish thought of the flag. The year previously, the club had made a special commemorative medal that was presented to Jack Kibblewhite of Swindon for breaking the four-mile record at the Celtic Sports. The badge was a Scottish as opposed to an Irish design, having a lion rampant on one side and the Glasgow coat of arms on the other. He also maintained a lifelong affection for the royal family. In 1903, Willie was chosen to play for Scotland against the Auld Enemy at Richmond. While James Kelly as the team captain was introduced to Duke and Duchess of Teck and their daughter Mary who would marry the future George V and become Queen in 1910, the rest of the team missed out. Bitterly disappointed, the lost opportunity to shake hands with royalty rankled Willie for years. He finally managed a royal handshake in February 1940 when he shook hands with King George VI at the start of yet another war. The fact that the antiquated Bill of Rights prevented a Roman Catholic from marrying into the royal family seems never to have occurred or troubled him.

When the latest Celtic squad won the 1913/14 League Championship and Scottish Cup double, forty-six-year-old Willie Maley was at the peak of his power and influence, both at the Celtic club and in Scottish football generally. He was by far the most successful manager of the most successful team in Britain. Unfortunately, his total commitment to the Celtic had cost him his marriage, although as a Catholic he realised divorce was out of the question. In addition to his own extensive business interests and what was a time-consuming full-time job at Celtic, he was also involved with the Scottish Junior Football Association and the Scottish Amateur Athletics Union. As a devout Roman Catholic he attend to his duties and spent a considerable portion of his time supporting Church-led charities. The Celtic's workaholic manager was long separated from his wife and living with his widowed mother and two teenage sons, Charles and William, in Glasgow's upmarket west end. Living nearby was the family of his brother Tom. The old Celtic favourite was managing the English side Bradford Park Avenue, but his family remained in Glasgow while he commuted back and forth. The youngest brother, Alex was also in football management with second division side Clydebank FC, while the oldest brother, Father Charles O'Malley, was regularly in Glasgow, visiting from his parish at Ayr.

The Celtic and the Army

Like most people who professed Irish Nationalist sympathies, Willie Maley and the Celtic officials would have had very strong feelings about the history of the English or British in Ireland. By the summer of 1914, John Redmond was on the verge of successfully forcing the Irish Home Rule Bill through the British Parliament and onto the statute book at the third attempt. The political situation in Ireland had reached a potentially explosive crescendo with opposing Nationalist and Unionist forces resorting to arms and a bloody civil war looked almost certain. The crisis would have been a great cause of concern for the Glasgow Irish and the personalities at Celtic football club. Like the vast majority of the club's supporters, the Celtic board had family and friends living in Ireland. The latest incident at Bachelor's Walk would have brought to the fore the very mixed feelings most of the Irish and Glasgow Irish harboured about the army and its role in Ireland. It must also be said that many directors and staff at Celtic Park also had long-standing affiliations to the British military and did not see any conflict of interest in the fact. Soldiers were once a very common sight at Celtic Park since they were, from the club's earliest days, allowed free entry into the stadium when in uniform. Considering Willie Maley's military connections, it should come as no surprise to learn that British Army bands regularly played at Parkhead before games and often provided the entertainment during the annual Celtic Sports Meetings. At the very first Celtic Sports Meeting in 1890, the band of the Lancashire Fusiliers based at Maryhill Barracks entertained the crowd, while the following year it was the turn of the pipes and drums of the local Highland Light Infantry volunteers based at Main Street, Bridgeton.

Celtic teams regularly played military teams and over the years the club poached several players from barracks around the country. Typical examples include Andy Lynch poached from the Scottish Rifles while at Glasgow's Maryhill Barracks in December 1897 and Willie Nichol poached from the Seaforth Highlanders in 1911 while stationed at Fort George and playing for Aberdeen FC. Often the football team of the resident infantry battalion stationed at Maryhill would be used for trial games as Willie Maley gave potential Celtic players a run-out. One such was the immortal Patsy Gallacher, who scored a hat trick against an army select in his second trial game at Maryhill barracks in 1911. After Rangers FC started a cricket team in 1913, Celtic followed suit. The Celts' first game was against an army select at Maryhill barracks. Willie Maley, Peter Johnstone and Alex McNair were the stars in the Celtic side, which won by one run. The military barracks at Maryhill in the north of the city was the base for the resident infantry battalion posted to Glasgow. The Celtic club very frequently used the barracks with the gymnasium providing probably the best sporting facilities in the city. The football team played many bounce games there while the Celtic Harriers also used the barracks and its facilities as a start and finishing point for their runs.

Many former players and staff had been soldiers, including Tom McGuire, Celtic's old trainer. Tom served in India, Afghanistan and Egypt with the 72nd Highlanders, later the Seaforth Highlanders. Both John Shaughnessy and Willie McKillop held commissions in the

Volunteers and in Shaughnessy's case he commanded a Territorial Force battalion. In the mid-1890s the Celtic club had a very close association with the Gordon Highlanders then stationed at Maryhill barracks. The battalion received fulsome praise from Willie Maley in his half-season statement in December 1895, for coming to his assistance when there were no English or Irish champions on display during the Celtic Sports Meeting back in August. The Highlanders had provided the musical entertainment and a number of regimental sports champions to compete in the games. On 4 April 1896, the Gordon Highlanders pulled the Celtic officials out of a very tight spot when over 55,000 spectators turned up for the Scotland versus England international held at Parkhead. The crowd was such the gates had to be closed forty-five minutes before kick-off with large numbers still locked outside. Three-quarters of an hour before kick-off the crush inside the stadium was such the crowd swarmed over the barricade at one corner of the ground game. The number of police and stewards on duty at the ground were insufficient to control the crowd. The situation had become very dangerous and with large numbers on the pitch, the game itself was in danger of being cancelled. At that time the Celtic allowed ladies, priests, ministers and soldiers in uniform free entry into the ground and a large body of Gordon Highlanders had come down from Maryhill to attend the game. Seeing the dangerous situation develop and organised by their sergeants, 150 kilted soldiers came to the aid of the police and Celtic stewards. With the help of the soldiers, the crowd were ushered back off the playing field and the overspill arranged along the cycling track. On the day, with Jimmy Blessington the only Celt in the Scotland side, the auld enemy was beat 2–1. Later, the assistance rendered by the Highlanders caused some controversy with the newspapers accusing the soldiers of moonlighting as stewards for the Celtic. A terse statement issued by both the club and the battalion's commanding officer categorically denied any such arrangements.

The same Gordon Highlanders performed the duties at the military funeral of Willie Maley's father when old Sergeant Maley was buried with full military honours in May 1896. The association with the Gordon Highlanders was such that the Celtic trained the battalion's football team and allowed Army Cup games to be played at Parkhead. The Gordons reciprocated by providing a fifty-man military drill squad, a pipe band and gymnastics display team for the Celtic Sports in August. It would be the last time the Gordon Highlanders appeared at Celtic Park, having been posted to India. Prior to their departure, the Celtic committee held a social at the Annfield Halls to see them off. Willie Maley proposed a toast to the Gordon Highlanders and Sergeant Major Robinson in reply remarked that the men who appeared at Celtic Park had volunteered for the duty out of affection and respect for the club. On arrival in India, the battalion formed its own Celtic supporters' club. Three years later, Sergeant Major Robertson would win a Victoria Cross in South Africa. No doubt many of the Celtic supporters from the Gordon Highlanders were among the casualties referred to by John Ferguson during his anti-war speech in March 1900 in Glasgow.

Willie Maley's Irish heritage would have instilled very strong feelings about the history of the English or British in Ireland. He would also have had very mixed feelings about the army and its role in Ireland, but given his military background he could recognise better than most the good and bad aspects of the army. Thomas E Maley while the superintendent of the Slatefield Industrial School would direct hundreds of the orphaned and wayward boys towards a life in the military, recognising that it was once of the few opportunities such boys would have to make something of their lives. Despite the apparent inconsistency in loyalties, the Maley family and most of Celtic's working-class supporters could fully appreciate the circumstances in which tens of thousands of Irish and Glasgow Irish, despite their natural Nationalist sympathies, voluntarily took the King's shilling.

Taking the Shilling

(Courtesy National Army Museum)

To understand why hundreds of thousands of Irish nationalists found themselves serving in the British Army over the course of the nineteenth and early twentieth centuries, despite the ambivalent relationship between the nations, one must understand something of the social and economic circumstances in which they found themselves over the period. Central to this was, of course, the volatile relationship between Ireland and England.

From time to time Irish Nationalist propaganda of various political hues denounced Irishmen who enlisted into the British Army as traitors to their country and enemies to its people. However, the stigmatisation and vilification of individual Irish or British soldiers and war veterans were never prevalent or popular among the general population in Ireland and even less so among the Glasgow Irish. Any animosity or criticisms such as there was, were aimed at the politicians or at the military as an arm of the state and done so in general terms. It was usually instigated or motivated as a political response to a particular episode of British Imperial expansionism, such as the Boer War, and was largely conducted by middle-class intellectuals, who relieved of the pressure of finding something to eat, had time to think deep thoughts and to produce the propaganda. The poorest of the working class, particularly those forced to survive in the slums of the Victorian and Edwardian cities, recognised and understood that joining the army, however patriotically or politically uncomfortable, if it was ever the case, was a legitimate escape route from squalor, deprivation and want.

One of the very few avenues of escape from the suppression of human dignity in mid-eighteenth century Ireland was to sign on for foreign military service, either with a European power or with the British Honourable East India Company. In the mid 1790s, the removal of the ban on Irish recruits had a significant impact on the composition of the British Army. By the time of the Napoleonic Wars there were so many Irishmen in the British Army, the Duke of Wellington would comment that fully half of his army in the Peninsula were Irish Roman Catholics, and without them no victory in Europe would have been possible. The contribution of the Roman Catholic Irish to the British Army's success in the Napoleonic Wars was obviously colossal and their performance on the battlefield formed the basis of the reputation subsequently enjoyed by the Irish fighting man. Prior to the establishment of identifiably Irish regiments, the reputation of the *Fighting Irish* earned in the Peninsula and at Waterloo ensured there was always a place for an Irishman in any British regiment.

In 1830 when the population of Ireland was a third of that of Great Britain, Irishmen made up 42 per cent of the British Army. In the mid-nineteenth century, the British Army Board operated a general recruitment policy of enlisting two-thirds of men on the British mainland and one-third from Ireland. Between 1841 and 1845, 18,800 Irishmen were recruited in Ireland. In 1846 alone, the Irish figure was 4952 and in 1847 the figure reached 6316. Over the two famine years of 1846 and 1847, an extra 7000 men were taken into the army from Ireland to help alleviate some of the suffering. In addition, all military barracks in Ireland were renovated as part of a public works programme to help provide employment. Watching soldiers eating regular army meals was a massive inducement to a starving man, while Queen Victoria's shilling and regular army pay might literally mean the survival of his family. Most Irish recruits were immediately sent to regiments serving in India and elsewhere in the Empire. The aforementioned figures are for men recruited in Ireland, and do not take into account the thousands of Irishmen who had moved to the mainland and enlisted once the extra quota from Ireland had been filled. Willie Maley's father was among those young Irish recruits who enlisted in Britain in 1846.

By 1868, 24 per cent of the army was Roman Catholic Irish; again this figure does not include the Glasgow Irish or British Irish, who in this period would still very much consider themselves to be Irish. By 1878 there were eight Irish regiments of foot: the Royal Irish Regiment, the Royal Inniskilling Fusiliers, the Royal Irish Rifles, the Royal Irish Fusiliers, the Connaught Rangers, the Leinster Regiment, the Royal Muster Fusiliers and the Royal Dublin Fusiliers. Of these the Royal Inniskilling Fusiliers, the Royal Irish Rifles and the Royal Irish Fusiliers traditionally recruited among the Protestant poor in the north of Ireland. The remainder recruited in the Catholic south of the country and were commonly referred to as the "Southern Irish Regiments."

The percentage of Irish Roman Catholics in the army dropped around the start of the twentieth century, but numbers were still very significant. The 1911 National Census of Ireland gives some insight into the religious breakdown of the Irish regiments shortly before the outbreak of the Great War. Although Irish regiments that traditionally recruited in Ulster would attract fewer Roman Catholics, the southern regiments and the Irish Guards would be broadly similar to the Connaught Rangers. The census return of the 2nd Bn Connaught Rangers then based at the Curragh in Co Kildare shows: Roman Catholics 505 (77.3 per cent), Church of England 131 (20.6 per cent), Methodist sixteen (2.45 per cent) and Presbyterian one (0.15 per cent) to give a total of 653.

While penury was undoubtedly the major push factor for the Irish and Glasgow Irish to join the army, it would be a mistake to consider it as being the only factor. By the beginning of the twentieth century very many Irish and Glasgow Irish families of all social classes had a long tradition of military service, having had grandfathers, fathers or uncles who had served in the armed forces or had brothers or cousins currently serving. Raised on tales of regimental do and dare in far-flung exotic places, it is unsurprising that the excitement and romanticism of army life would appeal to an adventurous young lad, desperate to get away from the squalor of the slums or the sheer tedium of the family smallholding. Very often generations of the same family served with the same regiment, establishing a very deep affiliation and affection for it. After the recruits left their families, if they had a family since a considerable number of soldiers were orphans, they found a new family in their chosen regiments and its battalions.

On joining the army, a man became a part of something bigger and very often much better than what he was leaving. Finding a place within the organisation increased his feeling of self-worth and the battalion became his new tribe. Once a man was accepted into the regimental family and assigned to one of its battalions, his battalion quite literally became his life. Every facet of his ordered, disciplined day revolved around the battalion and its regimental traditions. It is one of the more remarkable aspects of the British Army's unique regimental system that men develop a lifelong loyalty to their regiment. Even to the point where an Englishman joining an Irish or Scottish regiment wore the kilt or shamrock badge with as much pride as the natives. Similarly, an Irishman or Scotsman joining an English regiment was absorbed into and became part of that regiment.

Each British regiment with its unique history, traditions and insignia provided a tribal unity and loyalty that for the most part transcended the traditional animosity between Protestants and Catholics and religious affiliations took second place to regimental loyalty. A man's religious beliefs, if he had any, mattered very little in combat; of much more importance was would the man stand by his comrades in the line of fire. The last thing on a combat soldier's mind while in action is the religion of those supporting him. The famous or some might say infamous Highland Light Infantry (HLI) was regarded as Glasgow's own regiment. With its regimental depot at Maryhill barracks in the north of the city, the HLI recruited mainly from the Glasgow slum dwellers of both sides of the city's religious divide. It was probably the most volatile mix of Highlanders, Glasgow Irish and Scottish Lowlanders it is possible to imagine, yet as policemen all over the Empire could testify, if you fought one of the HLI you had best be prepared to fight them all. The soldiers most certainly did argue and fight, sometimes viciously, among themselves within the battalion, but it would not be about religious theology. Arguments between factions within the HLI would more likely be among Celtic and Rangers supporters and about the merits or latest performances of the Tims or the Gers. By the middle of the 1900s, there were Celtic supporters clubs within most of the Lowland regiments and the Celtic results, usually in the form of the Glasgow Catholic Observer or Glasgow Star newspapers, were sent to barracks throughout the British Empire. Over the years, tens of thousands of the Glasgow Irish served with the HLI, passing through the once infamous Maryhill Barracks gates. Irrespective of their religious or sporting affiliations, when push came to shove, the soldiers of the HLI stood shoulder to shoulder against all comers.

Maryhill Barracks Gates c1900

(Glasgow City Archives and Special Collections)

It was this process of institutionalised loyalty that bound soldiers to their units and to each other and which crossed nationalities, politics and religious affiliations. Regimental and caste loyalty proved the biggest threat to any Irish soldier's Nationalist sentiment as lifelong friendships were forged, sometimes in the most trying of circumstances. When soldiers were deployed in aid of the civil powers, usually against strikers or evicted tenants, they did so with personal misgivings and the sympathy of the soldiers would most certainly have been with their class. However, they were there as an arm of the state and would do their distasteful duty to the best of their ability. Problems usually arose when, stuck in the middle, they themselves were attacked in the course of their duty. At that point the attitude of the soldiers would undergo a fundamental change. If rioters or strikers were attacking the military, the soldiers would act to protect or defend their caste often with catastrophic results, both for the civilians and the reputation of the military.

To some men who took the shilling, the army offered adventure and foreign travel and an escape from the grinding tedium of a family smallholding or from the hard physical graft of a lifetime cutting peat. To others it was the chance to escape the sordid, overcrowded conditions of the city slums and regular periods of unemployment. For others a broken heart or a pregnant sweetheart's father with a shotgun proved the deciding factor. Very many young men who found themselves on the wrong side of the law were given the choice of a prison sentence or a period of army service by sheriffs or judges. If asked, most men probably could not tell you exactly why they joined up, it being a combination of all or none of the aforementioned factors. By the turn of the twentieth century, most recruits came from the urban poor where sheer economic necessity made the decision to enlist easy as regular trade downturns meant unemployed and growing sons were often an unbearable financial burden on families already existing close to the breadline. When asked why did you enlist? A favoured reply was: "I listed for me pound!" The soldier's pound was his daily bread ration. James Connolly, socialist, Irish Republican martyr and former regular British soldier would later called it "economic conscription". Tom Barry, future Chief of Staff of the IRA wrote of his service in the British Army:

> *In June 1915, in my seventeenth year, I had decided to see what this Great War was like. I cannot plead I went on the advice of John Redmond or any*

other politician, that if we fought for the British we would secure Home
Rule for Ireland, nor can I say I understood what Home Rule meant. I
was not influenced by the lurid appeal to fight to save Belgium or small
nations. I knew nothing about nations, large or small. I went to the war for
no other reason than that I wanted to see what war was like, to get a gun,
to see new countries and to feel a grown man.

For the Irish or Glasgow Irish servicemen, a posting to the Emerald Isle meant they were forced to confront their divided loyalties. While at no point did their military service lessen their feeling of Irishness or if they were among the politically minded minority, their Nationalist aspirations, bonds of loyalty to both their comrades and to their battalions and regiments most certainly complicated matters. The majority of young working-class British and Irish males who joined the army were very poor, badly educated and had little or no interest in politics. It is very difficult to see the larger political picture when you are literally starving or have no shoes on your feet. They saw the army as a job; on occasion it was a very unpleasant job, particularly when ordered to support bailiffs or police enforcing the law, but to the ordinary soldier, soldiering was their occupation and nothing more. The average British soldier of the period was completely apolitical. Just before the outbreak of the Great War, one Sinn Féiner described the type of man who joined the Royal Dublin Fusiliers: "They were poor, had no politics and took no interest in them. They were not interested enough in politics to wish to stay at home, they joined to be with their pals."

A number of Ireland's greatest Nationalist, and indeed Republican, heroes spent some time in the service of the Crown or were the sons of British soldiers. James Connolly executed by the British after the Easter Rising served with the 1st Bn the King's Liverpool Regiment. Although there is some ambiguity around his early life, it is most likely that he was born to Irish parents in Edinburgh's Cowgate and legend has it that he was taught Irish Nationalism by an old Fenian uncle who had also served in the British Army. By the age of fourteen, Connolly, unemployed yet again, faced the common dilemma of working class males: *take the King's shilling or starve*. He chose to follow his eldest brother John Connolly into the army. After completing his military training in Liverpool, he was posted with his battalion to Cork in 1882 and served in Ireland for almost seven years. Of men killed while serving in the British Army at the start of the Great War he said: "I am not writing this because I glory in the tales of the British dead. Those poor rank and file were and are no enemies of mine, of my class, nor of my nation."

Thomas Clarke was a driving force behind the 1916 Easter Rebellion. He was born in 1857 of Irish parents and first saw light of day in army quarters at Hurst Castle on the Isle of Wight. His father, James Clarke, was a British soldier who attained the rank of sergeant in the Royal Artillery. Soon after his birth, his father was posted to South Africa with his regiment and remained there for the next ten years. The family returned to Ireland in 1867 and settled in Dungannon, Co Tyrone. Tom Clarke joined the IRB in 1880 and after spending some time in

America, he returned to Britain where he planned an explosives campaign in England. Betrayed and arrested in 1883, he spent fifteen years in London's notorious Pentonville Prison. He was released in 1898 as part of a general amnesty for Fenian prisoners. Like Connolly, he too was executed for his part in the Easter Rising.

Michael Mallin

Michael Mallin was another former British soldier executed for his part in the Rising. He was born in 1875 in the Dublin slums and while his mother had Republican sympathies, like so many Nationalists, her siblings were all British soldiers. In 1889, just short of his fifteenth birthday, Michael followed his uncles into the army, joining old Sergeant Maley's regiment, the 1st Bn Royal Scots Fusiliers (RSF), as a bandsman. After seeing service in Dublin, Glasgow, Shorncliffe and Aldershot, the battalion was posted to India in 1896. The RSF later saw action on the famous Northwest Frontier during the Tirah War. The battalion would remain in India until 1908 when it moved to Rangoon. Michael Mallin completed his twelve-year engagement in 1902 and returned to Ireland thoroughly disenchanted with Imperialism. He found work as a weaver and became involved in trade unionism before joining the Socialist Party of Ireland. In 1909 he was elected onto its committee. After supporting the workers during the Great Lockout, in 1914 he joined the Irish Transport and General Workers Union. Utilising his military training, he became involved in the training of the Irish Citizen Army, being appointed Chief of Staff in 1914. Throughout 1914 and 1915 he continued to drill and train the citizen's army, often giving lectures on military tactics and operations. On Easter Monday 1916, Michael Mallin led a contingent of a few dozen men and women from Liberty Hall to take St Stephen's Green. On arrival, the Tricolour was raised above the adjacent Royal College of Surgeons. The position held out against determined attack until the surrender order from Pearce and Connolly arrived on 30 April. Michael Mallin was tried by British court martial on Friday 5 May and sentenced to death. The former British soldier and Chief of Staff of the Irish Citizen Army was executed by his old comrades at dawn on Monday 8 May 1916.

By the eve of the Great War most of Celtic's supporters were second-and even third-generation Glasgow Irish; however, the fact that they had been born in Glasgow or Scotland did not detract from their commitment or sympathies for the predicament of the auld country. Regardless of that fact, the exact same socio-economic circumstances that saw the Irish serve in the British Army also saw the Glasgow Irish voluntarily serve in considerable numbers. Like their Irish cousins, they too would have had divided loyalties and many tipped their hat to their cultural roots and chose to serve with Irish regiments, travelling to the regimental depots in Ireland to enlist. However, most joined local regiments, which in west and central Scotland meant the Highland Light Infantry (Glasgow and Lanarkshire), the Royal Scots Fusiliers (Glasgow and Ayrshire), the Argyll and Sutherland Highlanders (Glasgow, Argyllshire, Renfrewshire and Stirlingshire), the Cameronians (Scottish Rifles) (Glasgow, Hamilton and Lanarkshire) and the Royal Scots (west and mid Lothian). Many also chose to serve with the Scots and Irish Guards and the units of the cavalry, artillery, engineers and in the army service corps. The latter was where most trade training was available, including sought after and very valuable motor mechanic and driving experience. The Royal Navy and Naval Reserve forces also attracted considerable numbers of the Glasgow Irish since there was a regional Naval Reserve depot based at Govan. Precise recruitment figures for the numbers of Glasgow Irish enlisting in the regular army are unavailable since they were recorded simply as being British.

The ordinary soldier's loyalties were completely polarised, focusing mainly on his regiment and battalion and his mates. It was not that they did not feel the unrest and disquiet in their native land or class, it was just that they felt above it, detached from it and felt they owed a personal allegiance to their adopted caste of professional soldiers. Day to day, most young soldiers then, like now, were more interested in alcohol, football and girls, not necessarily in that order. The average Irish or indeed Glasgow Irish recruit who joined the British Army in peacetime could be described as Catholic, desperately poor, apolitical and of an adventurous spirit.

The Celtic's 1914 European Tour

For the successful 1913/14 league championship and cup-winning Celtic squad, the highlight of the year was the annual end of season Continental tour of Europe. The team were due to set off from Glasgow on 14 May 1914 for a five-match jaunt around Germany, Austria and Hungary. A fortnight before, Willie Maley and the Celtic directors took in the English FA Cup final between Burnley and Liverpool at Crystal Palace in London. Maley was planning an exhibition match between the Scottish and English cup holders to be played probably in September. After watching an uninspiring final in which Burnley took the honours, the consensus of opinion was that the Scottish champions could give the English cup holders two goals of a start and still come up trumps. Little did they know at the time but the two national cup holders would be meeting much sooner than September. The bhoys set off for the Continent the day after beating Third Lanark 6–0 at Hampden Park to win the Glasgow Charity Cup. The following fourteen players were included in the party: Shaw, Dodds, McGregor, Young, Johnstone, McMaster, Jarvis, McAtee, Gallacher, McColl, McMenemy, Browning, Crone and the final place was taken by Frank Kelly, the son of Celtic chairman, James Kelly. The twenty-two-year-old was training to be an accountant but as a talented outside right with blistering pace, he supplemented his pay by playing football, mostly with Motherwell FC. In addition to Willie Maley, directors James Kelly, Mick Dunbar and John McKillop and trainer Willie Quinn assisted by Celtic legend Jimmy Quinn made up the party.

The Celtic tour was conducted during the annual military manoeuvres on the Continent and throughout their trip the Celtic party saw and were highly impressed by the military might of the German and Austro-Hungarian Armies. From the first morning when their train crossed the Rhine at Wessel, until they re-crossed the river a fortnight later, the Celtic party saw regiment after regiment conducting training exercises. Their train was inconveniently crowded with soldiers and en route between cities the train was held up to allow free passage of troop trains. Soldiers appeared to be everywhere. In Vienna, the team went to the open-air baths where they dined in bath sheets and met several batteries of artillery, who were cooling down after a hard day's training, as was a regiment recruited in the Tyrol called the Bersaglieri, who were sharpshooters. In Budapest, they came across regiments of Moravians and Honveds and the team followed a Bohemian regiment as it marched accompanied by its band to Sunday Mass. When in Berlin they missed the review of the elite Prussian Guard due to the weather, but were suitably impressed as it goose-stepped down the Unter den Linden. In Potsdam, the Celts marvelled at the giant and distinctly menacing Zeppelin airships flying overhead. Both German cities they likened to military camps. Military officers were even crowded into their hotels. One stood to salute the Celtic as the hotel played the British national anthem in their honour. The Celtic tourists thought both the German and Austro-Hungarian soldiers were "well set up" all very fine fellows and much more impressive than the French soldiers that they had seen previously Unlike the British who maintained a small 247,000 strong volunteer army, a half of which was posted overseas to police the empire, the major Continental countries retained vast conscript armies, totalling in the millions.

Budapest Cup Medal

John McKillop left the tourist's party at Dresden. Unwell for some time the Celtic director was booked into a health spa at Marienbad, where he hoped to take the cure. En route to Budapest from Vienna, the Celtic party was stopped at a customs post when Peter Johnstone's cases were searched. The magnificently attired customs officials discovered that he had ten extra packs of cigarettes. The officials were all for confiscating Peter's favourite smoke until someone noticed that he was part of the famous Celtic team. After posing for photographs and signing autographs, his supply of Woodbines was safe and the Celts continued on their journey. On arrival in the Hungarian capital on 17 May, the Celtic played a friendly against local side Ferencvaros, which resulted in a 2–2 draw. Willie Maley then discovered, much to his annoyance, that the Celtic were scheduled to play a charity game against the English FA Cup winners Burnley. The game would be played for a trophy put up by a local businessman and grandly titled the Budapest Cup. The match turned into a very physical encounter, beyond what might be considered as typical of a Scottish or English cup game. A sports commentator suggested that a war correspondent should have sent in the match report and the encounter was nicknamed by those who saw it the Battle of Budapest. The match finished in an ill-tempered 1–1 draw after Burnley was awarded a controversial late penalty. As the players were leaving the pitch, Peter Johnstone got involved in a scuffle with Burnley's Jimmy Lindsay. The Ulsterman was mouthing off and Peter took exception to his comments. The pair had to be prised apart by club officials. The subsequent newspaper headlines highlighting the brawl, made unpleasant reading for the Celtic directors. After the game the Hungarian officials wanted a replay, but neither team were keen and agreed that the rematch would be played back in Great Britain either at Parkhead or at Burnley. The officials withheld the cup until the outcome of the replay was decided, but presented both sides with their medals. The next two games saw two victories for the Celtic tourists; the bhoys scored six goals against both Weiner Athletic in Vienna and Hertha FC in Berlin. On 30 May, the Celts were defeated 1–0 in a bruising encounter with the Leipsic Sports team in Leipzig. McAtee, McMaster and Patsy Gallacher were rested with Crone, Jarvis and Francis Kelly, son of the Celtic director, coming in as replacements. From the kick-off, the bhoys had all the play but the goals they scored were chalked off. According to one eyewitness, the referee seemed more interested in the success of the Leipsic team than anyone else. In fact, the goal that won the game for the Germans was plainly fisted in, but allowed to stand. It was a battered and bruised Celtic side that staggered into the pavilion after the final whistle. Jimmy McMenemy in particular took some brutal punishment from a very physical German side. Two days later the Celts were back in Berlin where they beat Preussen FC 4–0 in the final game of the tour.

Soon after getting back from the Continental tour, the team and club officials went off on their summer break. For the players it was a casual month with some going on holiday. Wing wizard Patsy Gallacher went back to his home village of Ramelton, in Co Donegal, while goalkeeper Charlie Shaw went to Saltcoats for a fortnight. However, the players retained by Celtic for the new season continued to be paid over the close season and that meant putting in guest appearances at the numerous sports events throughout west central Scotland. Several players also appeared as five-a-side teams to play in the football competitions that were part and parcel of most sports events. The bigger the event, the better the prizes and the more powerful the Celtic combination. For example, the winning Celtic five who turned out at the Pollock Sports day included two youngsters, Joe Cassidy and Joe O'Kane. Cassidy was already on the Celtic books, but was farmed out to Ayr United, while young O'Kane was a Maryhill boy who Willie Maley had his eye on but had yet to sign. Meanwhile, the five who turned out for the Celtic at the two-day Rangers Sports meeting, Dodds, McColl, McAtee, Browning and Gray, were all members of the first team. For a successful five-a-side team, the prize was usually along the lines of a canteen of cutlery, pocket watches, clocks or travel cases. Willie Maley, ever the workaholic, was talent hunting along with Jimmy McMenemy at the replayed Junior Cup final at Cathkin Park on 7 June. On Wednesday 10 June, Maley along with a number of club directors, attended the City Chambers where they were presented with the Celtic's twelfth Glasgow Charity Cup. The following weekend he was at the East Kilbride Sports meeting judging the athletics.

At the end of June, Willie Maley took a break and spent a week or so on holiday at Tomintoul in the Scottish Highlands. His last few days there were spent contemplating the deteriorating political situation in Ireland and the assassination of the Austrian Archduke and his wife in Sarajevo on 28 June. He recalled that at one stage it was feared that the Celtic's 1914 Continental tour would be cancelled because of the deteriorating health of the Austrian Emperor Franz Joseph. He never thought the eighty-four-year-old monarch would survive his latest bout of illness and no one dreamed that it would be his heir and nephew that the Austro-Hungarians would be burying. Although the Celtic tourists never visited Sarajevo, they did meet at dinner several Bosnian and Herzegovinian diplomats in Budapest on state business. The Celts thought them oriental looking with their olive skins and red turbans, but they seemed gentlemanly enough. The Celtic party also picked up their mood of dissatisfaction with the Austro-Hungarian interference in Bosnian affairs. As Glasgow Irish, it was difficult not to feel some sympathy for small nations struggling with the aggression of a large imperialist power. Some of Maley's friends and acquaintances thought the murder of the Archduke and his wife was the price of empire and the Austro-Hungarians had to pay for their annexation of two small warlike states. Although he never imagined that any conflict in the Balkans would affect Great Britain or Ireland, it was feared that the Celtic would not see the Prater and Vienna next summer. On Willie Maley's return to Glasgow, the rest of July was spent finalising the programme for the Celtic Sports Meeting. The world-renowned athletics meeting had been an annual event at Parkhead for the last twenty odd years and more or less ran itself. Only the current crop of touring international athletic stars of the track and field needed to be signed up, which involved a number of trips around the county including one to London. By the beginning of August 1914 everything was in place for the Celtic Sports Meeting. Only the weather, which after a glorious summer had apparently broken, and the latest incident in Ireland, where the army had opened fire killing three unarmed civilians in Dublin caused the Maley brow to furrow.

The 1914/15 Celtic Team

By the start of the new 1914/15 season, Willie Maley's second great Celtic team was settling into the task with most of the players now well established in their team positions. The success of this latest Celtic squad was further proof and justification of Maley's philosophy of evolutionary change and his policy of bringing local talent into the club as opposed to paying large transfer fees for established stars. The current pool of players emerged from the 1913/14 season as Scottish Cup holders and Scottish League champions from a three-year transition period of poor results, as judged by the club's own very high standards. The first team regulars included Charlie Shaw, the ever-reliable goalkeeper. He transferred to the club from Queen's Park Rangers for the start of the previous season in a rare cash transfer for £500. Small for a goalkeeper at just 5ft 6in tall, he possessed safe hands and commanded his penalty box with the authority of a much bigger man. Born in Twechar, twenty-nine-year-old Charlie was married and in addition to playing professional football he and owned a tobacconist and newsagents at Bridgeton Cross railway station, just a half mile from the stadium at Parkhead. In the right back position was Alex McNair from Bo'ness. Known by fans as "the Icicle", the nickname was a compliment to his intelligent, cool-headed play under pressure. Brought into the team in 1904, Alex was a model of consistency and one of the veterans of the current side. He was a survivor of Maley's first great team, which won six League Championships in a row and every competition it entered in 1908. A married man with five children, Alex lived in Larbert near Stirling and travelled daily through to Glasgow. At left back was Joe Dodds, a brickworks labourer from Carluke, who was brought

Scottish Cup Winners 1914

Back row (left to right) W. Maley (Manager) J. McMasters, J. Dodds, C. Shaw, A. McNair, P. Johnstone, J. McColl, J. Quin (Trainer) Front row (left to right) A. McAtee, P. Gallacher, J. Young, J. McMenemy, J. Browning.

into the team in 1909 as a centre half. Joe was moved rearwards to left back on the departure of Jimmy Hay in 1911. The move was a stroke of genius as he and Alex McNair formed one of the greatest defensive pairings in the history of the club. Prior to joining Celtic full time, Joe, like his three brothers, was a member of the Territorial Force of part-time soldiers based in Carluke. The right half was Ayrshireman "Sunny" Jim Young from Kilmarnock. Jim joined the Celts on a free transfer from Bristol Rovers in 1903. The current team captain, he was another veteran of Maley's first truly great team, the six-in-a-row 1905 to 1910 championship-winning side. The epitome of the greatest team Scotland and Britain had ever seen, by 1914 Sunny Jim was already a Celtic legend with the Parkhead faithful having put in eleven years of outstanding service to the club. Centre half Peter Johnstone was a former Fife miner and diehard Celtic supporter. The ultimate utility player, Peter was signed to replace the great Peter Somers at inside left in 1908. He was a great favourite with the Celtic fans, who admired his courage and obvious commitment to the cause. He was dropped back into the midfield in August 1913. Married with two children, Peter was another Celt who took to retailing, but unlike the vast majority of his contemporaries who opened public houses, Peter had recently opened a newsagents shop in the Gallowgate. This was probably the influence of his in-laws, who were pro-temperance leaning. At left half, Johnny McMaster was a time-served electrician from Port Glasgow, who joined the Celts from Clydebank Juniors in May 1913. Despite a slight deafness, he was rock steady, seldom getting the praise his quiet effective performances deserved. A married man with two children, he lived in Glasgow while playing for the Celts. At outside right, Andy McAtee was a coal miner from Cumbernauld. Brought into the side in September 1910, the former Croy and Mossend Hibernian winger was as fast as a gazelle and possessed a blistering shot. Both characteristics stemmed from massively powerful thighs, which at the time were likened to oak trunks. Married at the end of October 1913, Andy was living with his new wife in the village of Condorrat just a mile from his family home in the village of Smithstone. At inside right, Patrick (Patsy) Gallacher was born in the poorhouse in Ramelton, Co Donegal, but was brought up in Clydebank. The diminutive footballing wizard was the darling of the Celtic faithful and the brightest star in a team of all stars. A carpenter to trade, he was brought to the Celtic club in October 1911. Nicknamed the "Mighty Atom", Gallacher may have been small but he was as hard as nails and possessed legendary ball control. Hard working and possessing boundless energy, Patsy was an enormous asset to his team in defence as well attack. By 1914, he was already well on the way to becoming, in the truest sense of the term, a Celtic legend. At centre forward, Jimmy McColl was brought into the side for the 1913/14 season's Scottish Cup final replay at Ibrox. His two goals against Hibernian helped secure the cup for the Celts and his place in the first team. The fearless style of play of the twenty-one-year-old boy from St Anthony's reminded the fans of the Mighty Quinn in his heyday. He was soon to be christened "Sniper" in recognition of his prestigious shooting ability. Small for a centre forward, McColl made up for his lack of height with enormous courage. Rutherglen-born, inside left Jimmy (Napoleon) McMenemy was rescued from a tedious, labouring job in a glass factory to become one of the Celtic all-time greats. He signed for Willie Maley up a Union Street tenement close in 1902 and fought his way into the team the following year. "Nap", as he was known to the fans, had all the attributes of a great footballer: fast, excellent ball control, passing and heading ability, good vision and a fierce shot. Napoleon led the line for the six-in-a-row championship-winning side and his name would have been first on the Celtic team sheet. The regular outside left was Johnny Browning. Largely underrated, he was quietly effective on the left wing at a time when wing play was a very large part of the Celtic game. Born in Dumbarton, this *Son of the Rock* was a baker to trade and had fought his way into the team midway through the 1912/13 season. Nicknamed the "Smiler" on account of his dour personality, Johnny was brought into the team from that remarkable school of footballers, the Vale of Leven. Despite his apparent dourness, he reputedly did a good Harry Lauder impersonation and was something of a character in the dressing room. Smiler Browning would be a fixture at outside left for the next seven years.

For a professional footballer, to have secured a regular place in the Celtic team was a life-changing event. Every player in the current squad came from a working-class background and football was their escape from the grinding poverty and squalor associated with their class. The majority of the players were unskilled labourers; many were miners and after their footballing careers came to an end with few exceptions they returned to the pits or to backbreaking manual labouring. While at the Celtic club the players were the best-paid footballers in Scotland with most receiving between £5 and £6 per week plus win bonuses. The Celtic's wage bill for season 1913/14 was £5800 for a squad of twenty-two players. In comparison the next wealthiest team in Scotland, Rangers, paid out £5300 for a playing squad of twenty-five players. The Celtic directors believed in quality rather than quantity and would rather have had a first squad of sixteen first-class players at £6 per week than twenty-five moderate players averaging half that sum. Despite the Celtic club's political affiliations and Irish Roman Catholic heritage, with the exception of the very first Celtic team, the club adopted a policy of employing players and staff irrespective of their creed or political leanings. The double-winning Celtic squad reflected the religious diversity with a mix of Roman Catholics and Protestants.

In winning the 1913/14 League Championship Celtic had lost just three times, conceding just fourteen goals in thirty-eight matches, the lowest ever in Scottish football. In what would become his final season, the great Jimmy Quinn's swansong cast a shadow over the club and the supporters doubted if they would ever see his likes again. Signed in 1902 from junior side Smithston Albion, Jimmy Quinn won six League Championship medals between 1905 and 1910 and five Scottish Cup winner's medals (1904, 1907, 1908, 1911 and 1912). First capped for Ireland in 1905, he won eleven full international honours and made eight appearances representing the Irish League. The mighty James had, with one exception, been out of action for the double-winning season and Celtic struggled to find a quality centre forward let alone a replacement for the living legend. Bernie Connelly, George "Dod" Whitehead and the magnificently named Londoner, Ebenezer Owers, brought in from Clyde FC, were all given a go, but in some way or other were found lacking. Finally, young Jimmy McColl, signed from St Anthony's in September 1913, was brought back to Parkhead and quickly made the position his own. The 1913/14 Scottish Cup was won at Ibrox Park when the bhoys defeated Hibernian FC after a replay in an all-Irish final. Hibernian FC was, like the Celtic, founded and supported by the immigrant Irish community, in this case from those who had settled in and around Leith and Edinburgh. Ibrox Park was situated in the south of the city and was the home of Celtic's old friends, but now greatest rivals, Glasgow Rangers. The stadium, a bastion of Irish Protestantism, had never before or since seen or heard the likes of it. Both sets of supporters, 40,000 strong and bedecked in emerald green, sang songs like "God Save Ireland" and "Wearing O' The Green". The Celtic were lucky not to lose the first game, but thanks to two goals, one each from McColl and Browning, they overwhelmed Hibernian in the replay a few days later by four goals to one. The victory gave the bhoys their ninth Scottish Cup and their third League and Cup double.

The only disappointment in what was a great season was their exit from the Glasgow Cup at the hands of Third Lanark FC (originally, the 3rd Lanark Rifle Volunteers) after a goalless draw at Parkhead and a fluky late goal at Cathkin Park. Sweet revenge came in the form of a 6–0 drubbing of the "Warriors" in the Charity Cup final played at Hampden when McMenemy (2), Dodds, McColl, McMaster and Johnstone all got a piece of the action. In what was a truly wonderful season, the bhoys played a total of fifty-three games, won thirty-eight, lost six and drew nine. They scored 112 goals for and conceded twenty-four goals against. In the League only, the statistics were eighty-one goals for and an amazing fourteen against. For twelve successive games between 1 January and 21 February 1914, the Celtic never had a goal scored against them. Patsy Gallacher, the "Mighty Atom", was the top scorer with twenty-one goals from thirty-seven starts and Charlie Shaw played in every one of the thirty-eight League games. The players who contributed to the success in large or small measure with appearances were: Shaw (thirty-eight games), McNair (thirty-two), Dodds (thirty-six), Young (thirty-four), Johnstone (thirty-six), McMaster (thirty-three), T McGregor (thirteen), Davidson (five), Loney (two), McAtee (thirty-six), Gallacher (thirty-seven), McMenemy (twenty), Browning (thirty-seven), McColl (seventeen), Quinn (one), Owers (fourteen), Whitehead (seven), Connelly (eight), Crone (seven), A McGregor (one), Cassidy (one) and Hill (two).

In addition to the first team regulars, there was a string of reserve players ready to step into the breach. At this time Celtic had no reserve team as such, but the highly transitory second string got run-outs at friendly, charity, benefit and minor cup games or were loaned out for spells to other teams. Celtic had a particularly close relationship with Ayr United and dozens of players came and went between the clubs over the war years. Curiously, Willie Maley's eldest brother, Charles O'Malley, was a parish priest in Ayr, but apparently he showed very little interest in football. Also in the 1914/15 Celtic squad was Thomas McGregor, a quality fullback and standby for McNair or Dodds. Born in Laurieston, Stirlingshire, Tom was a first-class footballer, who even as a reserve managed to get into the Scotland squad. Standing in for McNair, he played in all the games during the European tour including the bruiser at Budapest against Burnley. Glaswegian Henry Jarvis was a wing half who came to Celtic in 1912 from Cambuslang Rangers. An electrician to trade, he worked full time at Fairfield Shipyard. As the understudy for the ever-reliable Jim Young, Henry spent a lot of his time on short-term loans. Edinburgh-born boy wonder, Michael Gilhooly signed for Celtic as a sixteen year old in 1912 from Glencraig Celtic and was showing immense promise as a centre half. Against a regular halfback line of Young, Johnstone and McMasters, he was facing an uphill struggle to establish himself in the team. Maley recognised him as a very definite talent but he was yet to get a run-out in a League game. The eighteen-year-old pulled on the hoops for friendlies or benefit games. Alex Gray was born in Bainsford near Falkirk and was a close neighbour of Alex McNair. Brought into the team from Stenhousemuir in 1912, he had been recommended to Celtic by old bhoy Willie McOustra. When the Celtic signed Alex, Willie McOustra commented: "Well, Willie, you have got some good players from the village, but you've got one of the best tonight." Alex was a fast, tricky left-winger, whose only problems were the reliability of Johnny Browning and the reputation of Billy Crone. Fed out to Ayr United for the previous two seasons, he was now back training at Parkhead and working in the Parkhead Forge as an iron moulder. Billy Crone was a Belfast bhoy brought to the club from the Celtic's great friends and namesake Belfast Celtic. "Handsome" Billy arrived at Parkhead in mid-1913 as cover for Patsy Gallacher and Jimmy McMenemy. Billy brought something of a reputation with him but was struggling to live up to the hype. Joseph O'Kane, a young centre forward from Maryhill, was just in the process of coming to the club. Willie Maley was not quite sure about him just yet, but he would get a run-out and would soon be off to Clydebank on loan.

Last, but by no means least, was the legendary Jimmy Quinn. The Celts just simply refused to let him go. After years of physical abuse, his body was almost constantly breaking down injured. His best days were well gone but such was his persona and status, the club kept him, hoping against hope that he could make a comeback. Such was his reputation with fans of all clubs, the sports writers often speculated and hoped for the return of the Mighty Quinn as he was famously and affectionately known. For the Celts, he was guaranteed a place in the first team whenever he was fit enough or whenever he could be persuaded, often against his better judgement, to step into the breach when the need was greatest.

Outwith the squad at Parkhead, there were a number of players who remained on Celtic's books but who were loaned out to various clubs; Alex McGregor was at Dumbarton, James Wilson went to East Stirling while Willie McStay, Bernie Connelly and Joe Cassidy were all at Ayr United. It was to be expected that a couple of the youngsters, Michael Gilhooly and Joe O'Kane, would be farmed out to other clubs for the season. This *farming out* was the usual procedure for Celtic, not only did it get the players in question senior games and experience, but it saved Celtic from having to pay them. Several players who had been on the Celtic books during the 1912/13/14 seasons were let go, including Willie Angus from Carluke. A great friend of Joe Dodds, Willie simply could not break into the first team and had been farmed out to Vale of Leven along with Willie McStay. At the beginning of August 1912, Willie McStay was taken on by Ayr United while Willie Angus was not picked up. *The Man in the Know* commented: "No club seems anxious to pick up young Angus the Carluke lad. He could give point to some players already signed." Willie Maley thought Angus was talented enough, but was too quiet for the rough and tumble of senior football. Willie Angus went back to junior football picking up the captaincy at Wishaw United. Likewise, outside left young Archie McMillan, brought in from Kirkintilloch Harp, was freed to go to Ayr United. For the bhoys the season was due to start on 15 August with a difficult away game against a young, Heart of Midlothian team at Tynecastle.

The Celtic Board of Directors 1914

Much had changed at Parkhead over the close season. The club had a new chairman, since Celtic player legend James Kelly had resigned the post just a couple of days previously. James Kelly was one of the Celtic originals; he was the team captain in the club's very first game against Rangers and had led the new Irish outfit to undreamt of success over its first ten years. By the time he retired from the game in 1897, he had already been on the Celtic committee since 1891 and on the formation of the new limited liability company, his initial holding of 200 shares ensure him a place on the first the board in June 1897. He took over the position of chairman in 1909 on the death of John H McLaughlin. James Kelly was yet another Celtic publican, having gained his first licence by way of a helping back-hander from John Glass, as an unofficial signing on fee back in 1888. By 1914, he had prospered through his association with the Celtic and now owned several public houses. Married to the daughter of founding father Francis McErlean, James Kelly raised his family of six sons and four daughters in the Lanarkshire village of Blantyre. Politically, James Kelly was a Liberal and a long time supporter of Irish Nationalism and the constitutional politics of John Redmond's IPP. He was on the platform

when John Redmond and the leadership of the IPP visited Glasgow in June 1913 to drum up support for the Irish Home Rule bill. His resignation had come somewhat out of the blue as far as the Glasgow sporting press were concerned and there was some talk of a rift in the boardroom, but it was denied by the club. The *Man in the Know* reported the reason for the resignation was simply to allow Kelly to concentrate on his responsibilities as a local councillor, justice of the peace and other public works. He also pointed out that Kelly retained his place on the board. Alongside Willie Maley and Mick Dunbar, James Kelly as a player of international status took most to do with the team itself including its selection. James Kelly would create a dynasty at Parkhead that would control the club for the next seventy years.

The new man in the chair at Celtic Park was Glasgow Irish solicitor Thomas White. Born in Glasgow in 1880 to an Irish father and Scots-Irish mother, he was educated at St Aloysius and Glasgow University where he studied law. He lost his father James White while still young

and his mother Jessie ran a successful scrap metal business in the east end of Glasgow on her own. Something of a boy wonder, Tom White while still in his early teens, was a fervent Irish Nationalist and a frequent speaker on Nationalist platforms. By the time he was twenty-three, he was the vice-chairman of the HGB and also the chairman of the Glasgow Star and Examiner newspaper, the former, had been started by the HGB as a direct competitor to the Glasgow Observer. Tom White was already a director of the newspaper, when he became the chairman taking over from Joe Devlin, the Irish Nationalist MP, when he became the general secretary of the United Irish League. A pupil of John Glass, on the death of the founding father in 1906, Tom White joined the Celtic board aged just twenty-five and represented the club on the Glasgow Football Association, becoming its vice-president and later its president. As a recently qualified solicitor, he married in 1910 and set up home in Monteith Row. Like so many of the leaders at Celtic, he was an early convert to socialism and was in 1910 an election agent for the Scottish Labour Party. Later that year he would refuse the chairmanship of the HGB when old Celtic committeeman Arthur Murphy resigned the position over the Irish Nationalist/Liberal/Scottish Labour schism that split the membership. Tom White's support for the labour party reflected a growing dilemma in the minds of the Glasgow Irish as their divided loyalties and new political sympathies reflected their ethnic drift and ever quickening integration into mainstream Glasgow society. When James Kelly resigned, Tom White was the sitting vice-president of the SFA. He would preside over the Celtic for a record thirty-three years and, like James Kelly, would found a dynasty at Celtic. However, most modern day Celtic supporters will be surprised if history regards the last generations of the old families as particularly distinguished members of the Celtic board, unlike their illustrious predecessors.

In 1914, in addition to James Kelly and Tom White, the Celtic board also included former player Mick Dunbar, who in 1914 was unmarried and living in Armadale Street, Dennistoun, with his schoolteacher sister. Willie Maley had first met Mick when he and his brother Tom Maley travelled to Alexandria to watch a game of football between two village teams. From that point the pair were great, life long friends. A regular in the very first Celtic side, Mick Dunbar contributed greatly to the early success of the football team. When he hung up his boots he remained a part of the management team at the club. He and his brother Tom Dunbar were successful publicans with three establishments in Glasgow's east end. Although not politically outspoken, Mick Dunbar never failed appear at the numerous political rallies and meetings and could be relied upon to put his hand into his pocket for the causes of Irish Nationalism. Alongside, James Kelly he was on the platform when John Redmond and the leadership of the IPP visited Glasgow in June 1913. He was completely committed to the constitutional politics of John Redmond and his Irish Parliamentary Party and their objective of Irish Home Rule. First voted onto the Celtic committee in 1894, he was later voted onto board in June 1897. At the club he, along with Willie Maley and James Kelly, took most to do with the football team itself.

Irishman Thomas Colgan joined the Celtic board in 1905 on the death of John O'Hara. Yet another publican, he had long-standing Irish Nationalist credentials, having been a member of the Home Government delegation to the Irish Race Convention in 1896. Tom Colgan was himself something of a sportsman, taking an active interest in athletic and football. As a young man he was a sprinter and he played football for St Malachy's College, Belfast. He had been on the periphery of the Celtic club for some years and was among the original shareholders of the new limited company. By 1898, he and his brother John, who was a successful Antrim cattle dealer, held a considerable 500 club shares between them. In 1903, Tom Colgan married the daughter of fellow director James Grant, but tragically his young wife Mary Ellen died in childbirth just nine months later aged twenty-seven. Tom Colgan was also involved with the Celtic's ethnic cousins the Belfast Celtic being a shareholder in and director of the club.

Described as a genial, big-hearted Irishman, James Grant was first voted onto the Celtic committee in June 1896 and as the biggest single shareholder (400 then 800) was elected onto the board of directors in 1897. A wine and spirit merchant, he held several licences throughout the city including the Grant Arms in Argyle Street and the Old Vic in Govan Road. Like most of the leading Celtic personalities he was a member of the HGB of the UIL, but in 1896 moved to the Govan branch of the UIL. Straightforward and bluff to a degree, he believed in calling a spade a spade. He knew little of football and took little to do with the team. On conversion to limited liability he took over the responsibility for the stadium from James McKay and was

responsible for the improvements and extensions at the ground. His main claim to fame was building the famous or infamous Grant Stand at Parkhead. Although he had spent much of his working life in Glasgow, he maintained a home in Toomebridge, Co Antrim, where he was a local justice of the peace. Having been ill for a number of years and having undergone a number of operations, by 1914 James Grant was terminally ill and spent most of his remaining time at his home in Toomebridge. His shares in the club would remain in the Colgan and Grant family until the 1990s.

Glasgow solicitor John Shaughnessy was the son of founding father Joseph Shaughnessy, who had died in 1906, and his Scottish wife Mary McDonald. John was born in Rutherglen in 1868, and he and his siblings spent their summers with their mother's family in the Scottish Highlands. He followed in his father's footsteps by attending St Mungo's and St Aloysius College in Glasgow and he later studied law at Glasgow University. In his youth, John Shaughnessy

was himself something of a sportsman, playing junior football for his local team Rutherglen Glencairn. He played at outside left in the team that won the now defunct South Side Junior Cup and the Cambuslang and District League in their first season 1896/97. Two of his Glencairn contemporaries, Jimmy McMenemy and Alex Bennett, would go on to play for the Celtic. He and his siblings were also immersed in the Celtic club from a young age and were active members of the Celtic Harriers and the Celtic cycling club. In 1897, John Shaughnessy joined the Volunteer Movement, the Victorian version of the Territorial Army, and was accepted for a commission with the 1st Volunteer Bn Highland Light Infantry (later 5th Bn HLI). Just eighteen months later he transferred to 3rd (Lanark) Rifle Volunteers. John Shaughnessy served with the volunteer battalion from 1899 and between then and 1907, he was promoted through the ranks until he became a major and was appointed company commander. Over the previous eight years, John Shaughnessy had attended and passed a number of military courses including musketry instructor at Hythe, tactics, military engineering and supply and equipment. Although he could not be considered a crack shot, he took an active interest in shooting and was a member of the Darnley Range Committee. The Haldane Army reforms of 1908 heralded the end of the volunteer movement including the old 3rd (Lanarkshire) Rifle Volunteers. The volunteer battalion was disbanded, only to immediately reform with the new title of the 7th Bn Scottish Rifles Territorial Force (TF). As a recently promoted lieutenant colonel, John Shaughnessy assumed command of the new formation. He took the battalion to their annual camp at Troon in mid-July 1909 and every year thereafter until his retirement in 1913, after sixteen years' military service. After his retirement, John Shaughnessy remained a member of the National Reserve.

Like his father, John Shaughnessy was very active in local politics, particularly school boards, and he was the first Roman Catholic to gain a position on the Cathcart school board. Also like his father, he was a member of the Liberal Party and he was a natural bridge between Liberals and Irish Nationalists at a local level. Alongside Mick Dunbar and James Kelly, he was the third Celtic director on the Irish Parliamentary Party's political platform during John Redmond's June 1913 visit to Glasgow. With deep roots in the Celtic club and a substantial number of shares in the company, John Shaughnessy was voted onto the Celtic board in 1911. As a Celtic director, he represented the Celtic club on a number of associations including the Glasgow Football Association.

John McKillop was another of the original members of the club and was voted onto the board in 1897. He was the brother of Celtic committeeman and honorary club president, William McKillop, who died in 1909. A restaurateur by profession, he along with his brother had established the famous Grosvenor Restaurant situated in Gordon Street in Glasgow. John McKillop had taken the lead in running the family business while his younger brother got involved in the Celtic project and later became an Irish Parliamentary Party MP. Now aged sixty, John McKillop was unmarried and spent most of his time on the golf course at Lethamhill, near Riddrie, while yet another younger brother, James McKillop, also a Celtic shareholder, looked after the business.

The McKillop firm was probably Glasgow's most famous and highly regarded restaurateurs and caterers and were often chosen by the City Council to organised and provide for official functions. A fervent Celtic supporter, John McKillop knew little of the technicalities of the game and left the running of the Celtic team to Maley, Kelly and Dunbar, however, he was involved in the business side of the company. In 1914, John McKillop had been desperately unwell for some time. He had accompanied the Celtic team and party during their recent European tour, but halfway through he went to take a cure at a Continental spa. Back in Glasgow, by the autumn of 1914 his condition was deteriorating.

At the beginning of August 1914, the Celtic management were looking forward to the start of another football season with a good degree of confidence. The Celtic football team were the current Scottish League champions and Scottish Cup holders and with a perfect balance of experience and youth in the side there was no reason why the Celtic could not repeat the successes of the previous season. More immediately, the management at Parkhead were largely concentrating on the forthcoming annual Celtic sports meeting. Everything was in place for the event, which after twenty odd years almost ran itself. It had been a glorious summer, but lately the weather had broken, mostly showers, but also occasional heavy driving rain replaced weeks of unbroken sunshine. With an eye on their sports meeting attendances Willie Maley and the directors hoped the squalls were not the end of the summer.

Chapter Nine

Armageddon

While the British government's attention was focused largely on Irish Home Rule and the boundaries of Fermanagh and Tyrone, in far off Sarajevo the Serbian bullet that killed Archduke Ferdinand of Austria-Hungary at the end of June, had also knocked over the first in a row of very important dominoes. Austria-Hungary's reaction to the assassination of its heir (who was not greatly liked by the Emperor Franz Josef or his government) was three weeks in the cooking. The Austro-Hungarians decided that the Serbian government was implicated in the assassination and decided to stamp their authority upon the Serbians by crushing the nationalist movement in the region and cementing Austria-Hungary's influence in the Balkans. It did so by issuing an ultimatum to Serbia that effectively nullified Serbia's sovereignty. Austria-Hungary's expectation was that Serbia would reject the ultimatum, thereby giving it a pretext for launching a limited war against Serbia. The Serbians had Slavic ties with Russia, an altogether different proposition for Austria-Hungary. After its earlier backdown over Bosnia-Herzegovina, Austria-Hungary did not expect Russia to be drawn into the dispute, other than through diplomatic protests. However, it sought reassurances from its ally, Germany, that it would come to its aid should the unthinkable happen and Russia declare war. Germany readily agreed, even encouraging Austria-Hungary's warlike stance by issuing the "Blank Cheque".

The already teetering dominoes began to topple. On 28 July, Austria declared war on Serbia, mobilised and within forty-eight hours was bombarding the Serbian capital, Belgrade, from warships on the Danube. Russia mobilised its vast army in support of the Serbs, Germany mobilised its armies in support of Austria and declared war on Russia on Sunday 1 August. Russia looked for support from its ally France, and France looked to Britain. Strategically important to both sides, Turkey hopped from leg to leg still unsure which way to jump. Although the British were allied to both France and Russia, it was a loosely worded agreement that only placed a "moral obligation" to come to the aid of the French. As late as 31 July, the British Prime Minister, Herbert Asquith, had told the Archbishop of Canterbury that Britain would not intervene in any European conflict. There had been little sympathy in Britain for Serbia up to this point and only a few people could have told you anything about it, including exactly where it was. Just about anyone who was anyone pleaded with the government not to become involved, including the Governor of the Bank of England, who warned Lloyd George of a possible financial collapse. With the exception of the armaments industry, big business desperately wanted to stay out of it and at the beginning of August the Independent Labour Party organised a number of anti-war demonstrations around the country, including one on Glasgow Green.

Published weekly on a Saturday, the Glasgow Catholic Observer of 1 August, was not yet quite in tune with the magnitude of the events. The newspaper supported Catholic Austria's belligerent ultimatum to Serbia issued on the 23 July. It thought the Austrian tough stance was "a victory for the right side", one which would bring hostilities to a speedy end and prevent a European war. A couple of days later, a surprise announcement from John Redmond would necessitate some fancy journalistic footwork from the editor. The newspaper's first wartime edition of 8 August carried an article, "A Catholic View of the Situation and Prospect", justifying the British decision to go to war from a Catholic point of view. The article was written by a well-respected Catholic academic and made it clear to the Glasgow Irish that the war was in fact a "Just and Honourable conflict". The *Man in the Know*, had only the Celtic on his mind and was looking forward to the new football season just a fortnight away, and more immediately to the annual Celtic Sports Meeting, the first without cycling in the programme.

That same day the Glasgow Herald carried three full pages of war news. In addition, it noted that three Italian warships had left the Clyde having been ordered back to the Mediterranean. In Rothesay, an Italian ice-cream seller was fined £2 or fourteen days in prison for opening his shop on the Sabbath. He chose to pay the fine. It also commented that the tension in Europe was not effecting the holiday mood in Glasgow, with crowds of holidaymakers heading "doon the watter" for the August bank holiday. The flow was also going in the other direction; the end of the Glasgow Fair holiday and TF units returning from their fortnight's camp saw traffic brisk at railway stations with extra trains laid on to cope with demand. All the newspapers carried articles on the importance of safeguarding Britain's food supplies and of the Royal Navy's control of the sea. Food prices were already rising throughout Britain, with some of the highest hikes seen in Dublin. The Rangers Sports Meeting started at Ibrox and would continue on Monday with Celtic entering a team in the five-a-side competition.

In the days immediately before the war, the mood in Glasgow was, according to the Evening Times newspaper, "Excitable". So much so it ran a couple of special editions devoted entirely to the war on Sunday 2 August. The newsboys did a roaring trade, some travelled out to Kirkintilloch and Lenzie where they were charging double. Despite the newspaper vendors being closed, it being a Sabbath, 200,000 copies were sold. While the newspaper boys were making a killing, that evening, 2 August, Germany presented a note to the Belgian government demanding passage of their army through Belgian territory, in order, it said, to pre-empt a French attack on Germany. Belgian neutrality was embodied in the Treaty of London (1839) and was guaranteed by Britain and France and recognised by all the great powers of Europe, including Prussia (Germany). The Belgian King appealed to the British for diplomatic intervention to safeguard Belgian integrity. In response, Britain's ambassador in Berlin warned Germany that Belgian neutrality must be respected or Great Britain would declare war. The Germans were astounded and dismayed that Britain was prepared to stand by the Belgians over what they called a "scrap of paper", but even if the Germans had wanted to stop, their war plan was too far advanced to halt. With France another of the guarantors of Belgian neutrality and having received a promise of armed support from Britain, the Belgian authorities promptly rejected the German demand. The rejection played right into German hands, since their War Plan had always included the invasion of Belgium anyway. In Italy, the socialists, pacifists and republicans pressurised the government to remain neutral and on 2 August the Italian Prime Minister announced that Italy would not honour its Triple Alliance obligations, much to the surprise of the Italian army's High Command.

On 3 August, Germany declared war on France. Britain ordered a General Mobilisation. That day in the House of Commons, in response to Edward Carson's offer of the Ulster Volunteers, John Redmond made his own dramatic pledge in which he offered Irish Nationalist support to the British. It was clear that he was supporting Britain because it was in Ireland's interest to do so. He opened his speech by highlighting Ireland's past grievances against Britain, but insisted that the recent change in Britain's attitude towards Ireland, particularly the governmental support for Home Rule, had created an entirely new situation. The Home Rulers, he declared, stood with Britain against German militarism in the hour of crisis:

> To-day two large bodies of Volunteers exist in Ireland. I say to the Government, that they may to-morrow withdraw every one of their troops from Ireland. Ireland will be defended by her armed sons from invasion and for that purpose the armed Catholics in the South will be only too glad to join arms with the armed Protestant Ulstermen. Is it too much to hope that out of this situation a result may spring which will be good, not merely for the Empire, but for the future welfare and integrity of the Irish nation? Let the Irish Volunteers and the Ulster Volunteers defend Ireland while the British army concentrated on the Germans in Flanders.

Of course, if the British government wanted to withdraw the army garrisons, and they did, leaving Ireland to be defended by the Volunteers, they would need to provide, arms, ammunition and training for the Irish Volunteers. John Redmond's offer to help guard Ireland was very well received by the British and Irish public alike and both he and Sir Edward Carson were loudly hailed in the national newspapers for their statesmanship. The Home Rule Act had already passed through the different stages that had stood between it and its final passage into law by receiving the royal signature. The next six weeks would see both sides locked in a final round of negotiation and struggle. The imminent passing into law of the Home Rule Act provided the British government with an opportunity to transform attitudes in Nationalist Ireland towards Britain. Although anti-English sentiment had by no means disappeared, throughout the island of Ireland attitudes had softened and any show of confidence in the Irish people and respect toward Irish nationhood would have been eagerly accepted and reciprocated.

The Glasgow Herald on 3 August reported that 5000 dock labourers at the Glasgow harbour, 1900 loading coal, were likely to be laid off due to trade disruption. The giant Singer factory at Clydebank, which employed thousands of Glasgow Irish, also announced short-time working. So many Celtic supporters were employed at Singers and as dock labourers that the Celtic board were concerned at the possible effect on the gate. With many of the Glasgow Irish members of the reserve or the TF and likely to be called up, the Celtic directors were immediately concerned for the Celtic Sports Meeting due to start in five days' time and at one stage considered cancelling the event. They decided, however, that the Celtic Sports Meeting should go ahead as planned. It was felt that the sports were just the thing to take the people's minds off all the talk of war. Willie Maley made arrangements to have the latest war news communicated to the crowd by megaphone and on message boards. At the second part of the Rangers Sports meeting held that evening, the Celtic five-a-side team of Dodds, McColl, McAtee, Browning and Gray beat Rangers in the semi-final, but lost to Clyde in the final.

In Glasgow city centre that night, despite the incessant heavy rain, the streets were very busy with people eager to hear and discuss the latest news as it was posted on bulletin boards on the newspaper office walls. The first of two contingents of mobilised naval volunteer reservists, 250-strong, marched behind a mounted police escort from the offices of the Mercantile Marine in James Watt Street, via Main Street (Anderston) and Waterloo Street to Glasgow's Central Station, entering by Hope Street. A large crowd awaited them inside the station and the press was such that several women were crushed and a number fainted. After the singing of patriotic songs the reservists departed for Portsmouth. The crowd leaving the station coincided with the arrival of the newsboys on the streets selling a special edition of the Evening Times. Extraordinary scenes were reported as the newsboys were swamped with thousands of people eager to read the latest developments.

On the morning of 4 August, Sir Edward Carson sent a telegram to the headquarters of the Ulster Volunteer Force:

> All officers, non-commissioned-officers and men who are enrolled in the Ulster Volunteer Force, and who are liable to call out for service by His Majesty for service in the present crisis, are requested to answer immediately to His Majesty's call, as our first duty as loyal subjects is to the King.

That same day in Dublin, Coroner Byrne presiding on the Bachelor's Walk enquiry delivered his verdict. He found that the three people killed during the incident on Bachelor's Walk on 26 July (one was the mother of a serving soldier), had died from bullets fired from rifles of the King's Own Scottish Borders (KOSB). He added, "We strongly condemn the actions of the military in firing on unarmed citizens, as we are of the opinion that the circumstances existing at the time did not justify such action." The jury considered that the government should compensate the relatives of the dead. That day the Germans decided they could wait no longer if maximum advantage was to be gained from their sweep into northern France and declared war on Belgium. While the declaration note was being delivered to the Belgian authorities, German troops had already crossed the Belgian frontier and were attacking the fortress city of Liege. The line in the sand had been crossed and while swords were drawn throughout Europe, in Constantinople the Turkish government was in a quandary; terrified of mighty Russia, they decided to sit on their hands for the moment and just for the moment the Germans decided to let them.

With the start of the new 1914/15 Scottish football season less than a fortnight away, the latest squad of Celtic players reported for training to the club stadium in the east end of Glasgow. The current Scottish League Champions and Scottish Cup holders had their double to defend and were about to have the close season cobwebs and excess pounds blown off by trainer Willie Quinn. It was a new look Celtic Park that greeted the players who reported for training that first morning. The old red cement cycling track built in 1897 for the Cycling World Championships, innovative in its day, had been dug up, the space converted into additional terracing at a cost of £3000. Both cycling and athletics had played a large part in helping to establish the fledgling club both financially and as an Irish-Scottish sporting institution of international renown. Thankfully, old race starter and Celtic stalwart James Moore, resplendent in his red jacket, would provide some continuity with the glory days of athletics and cycling at Celtic Park when he appeared for the annual Celtic Sports Meeting.

The bhoys swapped news of their holidays, compared close season training regimes and wondered at the latest outrages perpetrated by the mad women suffragettes, such as trying to blow up Robbie Burns' Cottage. The possibility of war both in Europe and much closer to home in Ireland, was undoubtedly the hottest topic of conversation. In Dublin, the Bachelor's Walk incident, where a number of unarmed civilians had been shot dead by the military just days earlier, had taken Ireland to the very brink of civil war.

In addition to the breaking news at home and in Ireland, the bhoys sweating it out at Parkhead would also be recalling some of the military sights they had seen on their recent European tour. They had witnessed first-hand the massive German and Austro-Hungarian conscript armies during their exercise season. It would have come as no surprise had they known that the Germans alone could field almost five million trained men in uniform almost at the drop of a hat. There was enough military expertise among the players and staff at Parkhead to be able to discuss the chances of the small, professional, but entirely volunteer British army, should it be forced to confront the massive Continental conscript armies. The Celtic tourists had been very impressed by both German and Austro-Hungarian soldiers, particularly by their manners; they were obviously from good families, especially the ones they met at Mass. En route to Budapest, they experienced the much vaunted German railway system as it practised the rapid transportation of large numbers of troops. As the railway management prioritised troop trains, the Celtic tourist's found their own train held up on occasion. In Berlin and Potsdam they saw and marvelled at the new-fangled airships, the Zeppelins, and little did they imagine that the same airships would within a few short months become an object of aerial terror as they bombed British towns.

The prospect of war in Europe certainly concentrated the thoughts of some at Parkhead; in fact some had more of a personal interest than others. Several of the Celtic personalities had close family relations and friends who were members or former members of the Territorial Force (TF). They would have been all too aware that the part-timer battalions, only back home that weekend from their annual camp, were already buzzing about the situation in Europe. All officers and senior non-commissioned-officer (SNCOs) were ordered to leave contact addresses and the battalion's Special Service Sections were already deployed to guard key civilian and military locations. Willie Maley maintained very close links with the military, especially his father's old regiment, and counted many soldiers as his closest and oldest friends. Although his own two sons were still too young for military service, two of his nephews were members of reserve forces. The Celtic full-back Joe Dodds was himself a former TF reservist and his three brothers, James, William and Hugh, were all members of TF serving with D (Carluke) Company of the 8th Bn Highland Light Infantry (HLI). Joe Dodds initially thought that he may be recalled to service, having some outstanding reserve commitment but it was not the case. The oldest son, Thomas, of Celtic legend Tom Maley was a peacetime member of the Naval Reserve forces based at Govan, while his second son, Joseph (Josie), was a member of the 9th (Glasgow Highland) Bn Highland Light Infantry, a TF battalion based at Greendyke Street, Glasgow. Josie had been a member of the battalion, commonly known as the Glesga Highlanders, for a number of years. Educated at St Aloysius College, Glasgow, he was employed as a clerk with the Glasgow branch of Lloyds Insurance. Josie was a footballer of some talent being associated with the Queen's Park club. The Glasgow Highlanders attracted many of the sons of the Glasgow Irish middle class, including the Celtic directors McKillop and Kelly. John Shaughnessy, who joined the board in 1911, had considerable experience in military matters gained through his long association with the old Volunteer movement that predated the Territorial Force. On the eve of war, Colonel Shaughnessy was only recently retired and was still a member of the Officer Reserve. His younger brother, Alexander, was a member of the Legion of Frontiersmen. The Legion was a quasi-military organisation, recognised by the British War Office and composed of Victorian adventurers, Indiana Jones, great white hunter types. Already concerned about possible invasion and the strength of the British Army in comparison with their European counterparts, the Legion's first recruiting advertisement appeared in the Herald on 4 August. The Shaughnessy brothers allowed their legal practice offices in Hope Street to be used as the Frontiersmen's Glasgow recruiting base.

Despite its best efforts, Great Britain was being dragged into the European morass. At 2300 hrs (midnight 4/5 August by Central European time) with no German withdrawal from Belgium forthcoming, Great Britain declared war on Germany. The British Foreign office issued the following statement:

> Owing to the summary rejection by the German government of the request made by his Majesty's Government for assurances that the neutrality of Belgium would be respected, his Majesty's Ambassador in Berlin has received his passport, and his Majesty's Government has declared to the German Government that a state of war exits between Great Britain and Germany as from 11.00 pm on 4 August.

The Storm Breaks

On 5 August, the Glasgow Herald reported that in London, crowds of 100,000 gathered around Downing Street and Buckingham Palace to hear the news. In response to their wild cheering and patriotic singing, the King and Queen appeared on the balcony several times after midnight. Elsewhere around the country, the people's reaction to the news was mixed. In Glasgow, it was late and raining heavily, so for the most part the streets were deserted. The few who were out and about awaiting developments, received the news with barely a murmur and there was no demonstration of any kind. In the same edition of the Glasgow Herald, a single column inch announced that the Admiralty had seized two battleships ordered by the Turkish government and nearing completion in British yards. The move would enrage the Turks and push them further into the German camp. Winston Churchill's decision to commandeer the ships would have far-reaching consequences for many sons of Erin and of the Calton in the not too distant future.

That Great Britain would be at war was in itself nothing unusual. Since the formation of the Celtic club in 1887, the country had been involved in several localised engagements and two major wars in South Africa. This time, however, the conflict would be different for a number of reasons. For the first time since Waterloo and the defeat of Napoleon almost 100 years previously, Great Britain would be fighting in western Europe. Another novelty was that the enemy was not the French, but the English nation's ethnic cousins, the Germans. The war would be fought on an industrial scale never before experienced by mankind and every industrial and financial asset of the British Empire would by necessity be allocated to the war effort. Finally, for once, the war was not a British Imperial adventure, but was one that would quickly change from preventing German expansionism and European domination, to one of British national survival. Eventually, every man, woman and child would be required to put their shoulder to the wheel if the British nation was to survive.

With the British nation at war, the Glasgow Irish, particularly the Irish born, would soon be forced to address their dual nationality and confront their divided loyalties. How were they to respond to the British nation's bugle call having suffered decades of racism, bigotry, derision and marginalisation? The question for the Glasgow Irish was how much loyalty did they feel they owed to their new homeland? Just how Irish, Scottish or British did third- or sometimes even fourth-generation Glasgow Irish feel? On a personal level, just how much loyalty did they owe to their Protestant neighbours and workmates? What of the old maxim that "England's difficulty is Ireland's opportunity"? As the British nation rose to the challenge of total war, the Glasgow Irish were very quickly forced to decide whose side they were on. Military service in Great Britain would remain a voluntary act for the first eighteen months of the war and the decision whether or not to enlist remained a matter of principle, idealism and personal morale. It was therefore left to the individual Glasgow Irish male to decide for himself whether or not to take the "King's Shilling".

All the major players were now on the stage for one of the greatest of human tragedies. Most of the dominoes had toppled and much of the world was plunged into the abyss. The British declaration of war also committed her Empire and her great white dominions, Australia, New Zealand and Canada, to war. With four of the main protagonists, Britain, France, Germany and Russia, the possessors of overseas colonies, their participation in war would immediately involve around 40 per cent (700 million) of the world's population of 1.7 billion.

In Britain and Ireland, the Home Army mobilised and as previously agreed by Anglo-French military planners, Britain prepared to send the bulk of the Home Forces to the Continent to join the French Army in the field. The force to be known as the British Expeditionary Force (BEF) consisted initially of one cavalry and four infantry divisions comprising around 90,000 men. It was supposed to be six divisions, but two were held back after someone pointed out there would be literally no professional soldiers left to defend Britain. Telegrams flashed across the globe ordering the overseas battalions home from their policing duties throughout the Empire.

As for the British politicians, they turned their attention, most with a great degree of relief, from Ireland to Europe or as Winston Churchill had commented a few days earlier, "the parishes of Fermanagh and Tyrone faded into the mists and squalls of Ireland and a strange light began immediately, but by perceptible graduations, to fall and grow upon the map of Europe."

The Celtic,

Glasgow Irish

and the

Great War

The Storms Break

Season 1914– 1915

Planned publication August 2014

Abbreviations

General

AGM	Annual general meeting	IPP	Irish Parliamentary Party
AIF	Australian Imperial Force	IRA	Irish Republican Army
ANZAC	Australian and New Zealand Army Corps	IRB	Irish Republican Brotherhood
		ITGWU	Irish Transport General Workers' Union
AOH	Ancient Order of Hibernians		
ASC	Army service corps	LOL	Loyal Orange Lodge
BEF	British Expeditionary Force	LT	Lieutenant
Bn	Battalion	NCO	Non-commissioned officer
CAV	Cavalry	NUDL	National Union of Dock Labourers
CEF	Canadian Expeditionary Force		
CO	Commanding officer	NUWSS	National Union of Women's Suffrage Societies
C of E	Church of England		
C of I	Church of Ireland	OC	Officer commanding
COL	Colonel	ORs	Other ranks
C of S	Church of Scotland	OTC	Officer Training Corps
COY	Company	POW	Prisoner of war
CPL	Corporal	PTE	Private
CSGT	Colour sergeant	QM	Quartermaster
CSM	Company sergeant major	QMS	Quartermaster sergeant
CSS	Catholic Socialist Society	RC	Roman Catholic
CYS	Catholic Young Men's Society	RIC	Royal Irish Constabulary
DMP	Dublin Metropolitan Police	RSM	Regimental sergeant major
DORA	Defence of the Realm Act	SF	Sinn Fein
FA	Football Association	SFA	Scottish Football Association
FC	Football club	SGT	Sergeant
FP	Field punishment	SL	Scottish League
GHQ	General headquarters	SR	Special Reserve
GOC	General officer commanding	TF	Territorial Force
GSO	General staff officer	UIL	United Irish League
HLDRS	Highlanders	UILGB	United Irish League of Great Britain
HQ	Headquarters		
ILP	Independent Labour Party	UVF	Ulster Volunteer Force
INF	Irish National Foresters	YMCA	Young Men's Christian Association
INL	Irish National League		
INV	Irish National Volunteers		

Celtic Regiments (Regular Army)

A&SH	Argyll and Sutherland Highlanders
BW	Black Watch
Cams	Cameronians
Conn R	Connaught Rangers
GORDS	Gordon Highlanders
HLI	Highland Light Infantry
Inns Drags	Inniskilling Dragoons
IG	Irish Guards
KOSB	King's Own Scottish Borderers
KRIH	King's Royal Irish Hussars
LEINS	Leinster Regiment (Royal Canadians)
RDF	Royal Dublin Fusiliers
RIDG	Royal Irish Dragoon Guards
RInnsF	Royal Inniskilling Fusiliers
RIL	Royal Irish Lancers
RIRegt	Royal Irish Regiment
RIF	Royal Irish Fusiliers
RIRifs	Royal Irish Rifles
RMF	Royal Munster Fusiliers
RS	Royal Scots
RSF	Royal Scots Fusiliers
SCO RIF	Scottish Rifles
SG	Scots Guards
SGreys	Scots Greys

Index

Bibliography and Sources

Primary Sources

Appendix (G) to the Report on the State of Irish Poor in Great Britain (London 1836).
City of Glasgow Valuation Rolls (Mitchell Library, Glasgow).
Enumeration of the Inhabitants of Scotland (Statistical Tables Relative to the City of Glasgow and Other
    Matters) (James Lumsden and Sons, London, 1833).
Glasgow Corporation Minutes of Meetings 1914–1915 (Mitchell Library, Glasgow).
Glasgow (Barlinnie) Prison, Register of Criminal Prisoners (1882–85) (Scottish Records Office,
    Edinburgh, HH.21.70/1).
Register of Births, Deaths and Marriages (Registration House, Edinburgh).
Minutes of the City Parochial Board of Glasgow, 30 November 1847 (Mitchell Library, Glasgow).
National Census: 1841, 1851, 1861, 1871, 1881, 1891, 1901 and 1911 (General Register Office, Edinburgh).
National Census of Ireland 1901, 1911 (National Archives of Ireland, Dublin).
Birth, Marriage and Confirmation registers, St Mirin Parish, Paisley. (Scottish Catholic Archives,
    Edinburgh).
Soldiers Attestation, Discharge and Pension documents 1910–1919 (National Archives, Kew, London).

Newspapers/Periodicals

Belfast Evening Telegraph, Belfast News Letter, Daily Mail, Dundee Courier, Freeman's Journal,
Galway Express, Glasgow Catholic Observer, Glasgow Daily Record, Glasgow Evening Times, Glasgow
Examiner, Glasgow Herald, Glasgow News, Glasgow Star and Examiner, Golden Penny, Greenock
Telegraph, Hamilton Advertiser, Irish Independent, Irish News, Irish Times, Irish Worker, Kildare
Observer, Kilsyth Chronicle, Labour Leader, London Gazette, Motherwell Times, Paisley Gazette,
Scotsman, Scottish Referee, Scottish Sport, The Times, Weekly News, West Lothian Courier, HLI
Chronicle.

Books, Articles, Reports and Other Sources

Balantine, Ishbel. *The Singer Strike, Clydebank, 1911* (Glasgow Labour History Workshop, Clydebank
    District Library, 1989).
Beckett, Ian. *Home Front 1914–1918* (The National Archives, Kew, London, 2006).
Bedarida, Francois. *A Social History of England 1851–1975* (Cambridge University Press).
Best, Geoffrey. *Mid-Victorian Britain 1851¬–75* (Fontana Press, 1979).
Bowen, Jean and Desmond. *Heroic Option, The Irish in the British Army* (Barnsley, South Yorkshire,
    2005).
Bilsborough, Peter. *The Development of Sport in Glasgow 1850 – 1914*. Master of Letters, thesis,
    University of Stirling June 1983.
Bradley, Joseph M. *Ethnic and Religious Identity in Modern Scotland: Culture, Politics and Football*
    (Aldershot, Avebury, 1995).

Brown, Callum G. *Religion and Society in Scotland since 1707* (Edinburgh University Press, 1997).

Burows, John. Irish *The Remarkable Saga of a Nation and a City* (Mainstream Publishing Edinburgh and London, 2003).

Campbell, Tom and Woods, Pat. *The Glory and the Dream* (Edinburgh, 1986).

Chalmers, AK. *The Health of Glasgow 1818-1925* (Glasgow, 1930).

Clelland, James. *Statistical Tables Relative to the City of Glasgow* (James Lumsden & Sons, Glasgow, 1823).

Clelland, James. *The Rise and Progress of the City of Glasgow* (Smith and Sons, Glasgow, 1840).

Clyde, Robert. *From Rebel to Hero. The Image of the Highlander 1745–1830* (Tuckwell Press, 1998).

Cooney, John. *Scotland and the Papacy* (Paul Harris Publishers, Edinburgh, 1982).

Cousins, Geoffrey. *The Defenders A History of the British Volunteer* (Fredrick Muller, London, 1968).

Craig, Jim. *A Lion Look Back* (John Donald Publishing Ltd, Edinburgh, 1998).

Crampsey, Robert. *The Scottish Football League First 100 Years* (Glasgow, 1990).

Darragh, James. *The Catholic Hierarchy of Scotland* (John Burns & Sons, Glasgow).

Devine, TM. *Clanship to Crofters' War* (Manchester University Press, 1993).

Devine, TM and Mitchison R. *People and Society in Scotland: Vol. 1 1760–1830* (John Donald, Edinburgh, 1888).

Fraser, Hamish. *Scottish Popular Politics: From Radicalism to Labour* (Edinburgh University Press, 2000).

Fraser, Hamish and Maver, Irene, Eds. *Glasgow 1830–1912* (Manchester University Press, 1996).

Fraser, Hamish and Morris, RJ. *People and Society in Scotland Vol. II, 1830-1914* (John Donald Publishers Ltd, Edinburgh, 1995).

Gallagher, Tom. *The Uneasy Peace: Religious Tension in Modern Scotland 1819–1914* (Manchester University Press, 1987).

Gillion, Captain Stair. *The K.O.S.B. in the Great War* (Thomas Nelson & Sons, Ltd, Great Britain, 1930).

Greaves, Desmond C. *The Life and Times of James Connolly* (Lawrence & Wishart Ltd, London, 1986).

Grayson, Richard S. *The Belfast Boys* (Continuum UK, London, 2009).

Grierson, Maj Gen JM. *Records of the Scottish Volunteer Force 1859-1908.* (Wm. Blackwood and Sons, Edinburgh and London).

Gwynn, Stephen. *John Redmond's Last Years* (Edward Arnold, London, 1919).

Handley, James Edmund. *The Irish in Scotland* (Cork University Press, 1945).

Handley, JE. *The Celtic Story* (Stanley Paul, London, 1960).

Hannan, John. *The Life of John Wheatley* (Spokesman, Nottingham, 1988).

Harris, RG. *The Irish Regiments A Pictorial History 1683–1987* (Nutshell Publishing Co, Tunbridge Wells, 1989).

Haythornthwaite, Philip J. *The World War One Source Book* (BAC, London, 1992).

Henderson, Diana M. *Highland Soldier 1820–1920* (John Donald Publishers, Edinburgh, 1989).

James, Brigadier EA. *British Regiments 1914–1918* (Naval & Military Press, Heathfield, East Sussex, 1998).

James, Garry. *The Manchester City Years* (James Howard, 2012).

Jarvie, Grant. *Sport in the Making of Celtic Culture* (Leicester University Press, London, 1999).

Jeffery, Keith. *Ireland and the Great War* (Cambridge University Press, 2000).

Johnson, Christina. *Developments in the Roman Catholic Church in Scotland 1789–1829* (John Donald Publishers, Edinburgh, 1985).

Johnstone, Tom and Hagerty, James. *The Cross on the Sword, Catholic Chaplains in the Forces* (Geoffrey Chapman, London, 1996).

Karsten, Peter. *Irish Soldiers in the British Army, 1792¬–1922: Suborned or Subordinate?* Journal of Social History, Vol. 17, No.1 (Autumn, 1983). (Pub. Peter N. Sterns)

Kelly, Sir Robert. *Celtic* (Hay, Nisbet and Miller Ltd, Glasgow, 1971).

Kiberd, Declan. *1916 Rebellion Handbook* (The Mourne River Press, 1989).

Knox, William. An Industrial Nation: Work, Culture and Society in Scotland 1800–present (Edinburgh University Press, 1999).

Laffan, Michael. *The Partition of Ireland 1911–1925* (Dundalgan Press, 1983).

Lenman, Bruce P. *Integration and Enlightenment. Scotland 1746–1832* (Edinburgh University Press, 1992).

Levenson, Leah and Natterstad, Jerry H. *Hanna Sheehy-Skeffington: Irish Feminist* (Syracuse University Press, 1989).

Livingstone, Thomas. *Tommy's War. The Diaries of a Wartime Nobody* (Harper Press, 2008).

Lucy, John F. *There's a Devil in the Drum* (Naval & Military Press Ltd, 1998).

Luney, Derek. *Men That God Make Mad* (Vintage Books, London, 2007).

McConnel, James. *Recruiting Sergeants for John Bull? Irish Nationalist MPs and Enlistment during the Early Months of the Great War* (SAGE Publications, 2007).

McCorry, Helen. *The Thistle at War* (National Museums of Scotland Publishing, Edinburgh, 1997).

McCracken, Gordon A. *Bygone Days of Yore: The Story of Orangeism in Glasgow* (County Grand Orange Lodge of Glasgow, Glasgow, 1990).

MacDonald, Catriona MM and McFarlane, EW. *Scotland and the Great War* (Tuckwell Press, 1999).

McFarland 1990; Bradley 1995; 1881 *Census of Scotland.*

Marson, Dave. *The Children's Strikes 1911* (History Workshop, 1973).

Moloney, Alison and Jim. *Life After Victoria 1900–1909* (Pen and Sword Books Ltd, Barnsley, South Yorkshire, 2008).

Moncrieff, George Scott. *The Mirror and the Cross* (Catholic Book Club, London, 1960).

Mooney, Major Barnes. *The British Army of 1914* (Seeley, Service & Co, Ltd, London, 1968).

Nimmo, William P. *An Account of the Scottish Regiments 1808–1861* (Edinburgh, 1862).

O'Cathain, Mairtin. *Irish Republicanism in Scotland 1858–1916* (Irish Academic Press Ltd, 2007).

O'Drisceoil, Donal. *Peadar O'Donnell (Radical Irish Lives)* (Cork University Press, 2001).

Pinney, Thomas, Ed. *The Letters of Rudyard Kipling 1911–19, Vol. 4.* (University of Iowa Press, 1999).

Piper, Leonard. Dangerous Waters. *The Life and Death of Erskine Childers* (Hambledon and London, London and New York, 2003).

Potter, David. Willie Maley: *The Man Who Made Celtic* (Tempus Publishing Ltd, Stroud, Gloucestershire, 2003).

Ralston, Garry. *The Gallant Pioneers: Ranger 1872* (Derby Books Publishing Company Limited, Derby, ED21 4SZ).

Richardson, Neil. *A Coward if I Return, A Hero if I Fall* (Dublin, 2010).

Royle, Trevor. *The Flowers of the Forest* (Birlinn Limited, Edinburgh, 2006).

Ryan, AP. *Mutiny at the Curragh* (MacMillan & Co Ltd, London, 1956).

Ryan, Meda. Tom Barry: *IRA Freedom Fighter* (Mercier Press, Cork, 2005).

Sellwod, AV. *The Saturday Night Soldiers* (White Lion Publishers, London, 1966).

Sinclair, Sir John, *Analysis of the Statistical Account of Scotland* (John Murray, London, 1826).

Smout, TC. *A History of the Scottish People 1560–1830* (Fontana Press, Glasgow, 1972).

Smout, TC. *A Century of the Scottish People 1893–1950* (Fontana Press, Glasgow).

Smyth, JJ. *Labour in Glasgow 1896–1936* (Tuckwell Press, 2000).

Swift, Roger. *Irish Migrants in Britain: 1815-1914: A Documentary History* (Cork University Press, 2002).

Swift, Roger and Gilley, Sheridan, Eds. *The Irish in Britain 1815–1939.* (Rowman and Littlefield, 1989)

Various. *The Highland Light Infantry Chronicle, Vol. X, No. 2* (John Horn Ltd, Glasgow, April 1910).

Weir, Alec. *Come On Highlanders!* (Sutton Publishing, Stroud, Gloucestershire, 2005).

Westlake, Ray. *Kitchener's Army* (Spellmount Ltd, Staplehurst, Kent, 1998).

Wilson Brian. *Celtic A Century with Honour* (Glasgow, 1988).

Yeats, Padraig. *A City in War Time. Dublin 1914–18* (Gill & MacMillan, 2011).

Young, James D. *Socialism Since 1889: A Biographical History* (Pinter Publishers, London, 1988).